D1478172

DOUBLE PLAYS AND DOUBLE CROSSES

PRAISE FOR *DOUBLE PLAYS AND DOUBLE CROSSES*

"An eye-opening account of the Black Sox scandal that adds new and important infor- mation. A needed addition to any baseball library."—Mike Sowell, author of *The Pitch That Killed: Carl Mays, Ray Chapman, and the Pennant Race of 1920*

"The story of the 1919 Black Sox is also the story of the Clean Sox, and the 1920 season when the two camps butted heads in a manner not seen in the disputed World Series. Don Zminda sorts the 'laundry' of the Sox in this important extended view of the scandal that changed baseball forever."—Craig Wright, BaseballsPast.com

"A vital addition to the library of baseball history, Don Zminda tells the compelling story of how the 1919 Chicago Black Sox 'threw' the 1920 pennant before they were 'outed.' Countless words have been written about the infamous 1919 World Series, and here's the first look at the great 1920 team that likely gave away a number of games. As Chicago manager Kid Gleason said, 'I had the greatest ball club ever put together when those pinheads went wrong.' A 96-win club could have—should have—won well over 100. Here's how it happened."—Steve Steinberg, baseball historian and author of the award-winning *Urban Shocker: Silent Hero of Baseball's Golden Age*

"The story of the fixing of the 1919 World Series—and its substantial aftermath—has often been misleadingly written about and portrayed on the screen. Thankfully, White Sox historian Don Zminda gets it right, in the process shedding substantial and needed light on the aftermath. You want the facts about the Black Sox? Read this book."—Bill Felber, author of *Under Pallor, Under Shadow: The 1920 American League Pennant Race That Rattled and Reshaped Baseball*

"In order to fully understand the 1919 Black Sox Scandal, one must also closely exam- ine the play of the Chicago White Sox in 1920. Don Zminda tells us why in compelling fashion. It makes for a fascinating read."—Rick Huhn, author of *Eddie Collins: A Base- ball Biography*

"Zminda's *Double Plays and Double Crosses* is a fantastically researched, well-written, entertaining deep dive into the 1920 White Sox, American League pennant race, and 1919 World Series gambling scandal that finally came to light late in the 1920 season. It's an essential addition to the growing library of books about the Black Sox scandal."— Mike Lynch, five-time author and founder of Seamheads.com

"The 1920 baseball season—between the 1919 World Series and the expulsion of the Black Sox—was one of the most fascinating in history, as crookedness and rumors of crookedness cast a shadow over baseball and a wide assortment of its characters. With clarity and style, Don Zminda delightfully brings to life the season, its genesis, and its aftermath."—Daniel R. Levitt, author of *The Battle That Forged Modern Baseball: The Federal League Challenge and Its Legacy*

DOUBLE PLAYS AND DOUBLE CROSSES

The Black Sox and Baseball in 1920

Don Zminda

ROWMAN & LITTLEFIELD
Lanham • Boulder • New York • London

Published by Rowman & Littlefield
A wholly owned subsidiary of The Rowman & Littlefield Publishing Group, Inc.
4501 Forbes Boulevard, Suite 200, Lanham, Maryland 20706
www.rowman.com

6 Tinworth Street, London, SE11 5AL, United Kingdom

Copyright © 2021 by Don Zminda

All rights reserved. No part of this book may be reproduced in any form or by any
electronic or mechanical means, including information storage and retrieval systems,
without written permission from the publisher, except by a reviewer who may quote
passages in a review.

British Library Cataloguing in Publication Information Available

Library of Congress Cataloging-in-Publication Data

Names: Zminda, Don, author.
Title: Double plays and double crosses : the Black Sox and baseball in 1920 /
    Don Zminda.
Description: Lanham : Rowman & Littlefield, 2021. | Includes bibliographical
    references and index. | Summary: "This book is the exciting story of how one of
    the most infamous scandals in American history—the Black Sox scandal—continued
    for over a year following the 'fixed' World Series of 1919 until the truth began to
    emerge. It is a story of gamblers and crooks; a story of teammates betraying one
    another; a story of investigations and cover-ups"— Provided by publisher.
Identifiers: LCCN 2020036349 (print) | LCCN 2020036350 (ebook) | ISBN
    9781538142325 (cloth : acid-free paper) | ISBN 9781538142332 (ebook)
Subjects: LCSH: Chicago White Sox (Baseball team)—History. | World Series
    (Baseball) (1919) | Baseball—Corrupt practices—United States—History—
    20th century.
Classification: LCC GV875.C58 Z65 2021 (print) | LCC GV875.C58 (ebook) |
    DDC 796.357/640977311—dc23
LC record available at https://lccn.loc.gov/2020036349
LC ebook record available at https://lccn.loc.gov/2020036350

♾️™ The paper used in this publication meets the minimum requirements of
American National Standard for Information Sciences—Permanence of Paper
for Printed Library Materials, ANSI/NISO Z39.48-1992.

CONTENTS

CONTENTS

FOREWORD
Rob Neyer

This one is personal.

I've known Don Zminda for half my life. Which is saying something, since I've been alive for quite a while.

Early on, I got to know Don pretty well. I worked for him at a (then) little company called STATS, Inc., and although I've had better jobs since leaving STATS, I've never had a better boss. But I did leave STATS, while Don stayed. And stayed. And stayed, through all the ownership and management changes. He must have been as good an employee as he'd been a boss.

Throughout, Don and I kept in touch, mostly by way of the annual SABR convention every summer. Occasionally, I would miss one or Don would miss one, but most years we would (and still do) reconnect and talk about, *not* the old days at STATS, but about our families and especially our shared loves of baseball history and, of course, *books* about baseball history. Every year, we would troll the convention book room, then compare our new treasures.

Meanwhile, I just could not *wait* for Don to retire. Because I suspected that, once relieved of his 9-to-5 duties, Don would let his passions and his talents run wild, and people like me—and come to think of it, like you—would be delighted with whatever sprung from Don's fertile mind.

I have never been so right about anything in my life.

Don finally waved goodbye to STATS in 2016. Just three years later, Rowman & Littlefield published *The Legendary Harry Caray: Baseball's Greatest Salesman*, Don's masterful biography of the immortal broadcaster. 'Twas a perfect match of author and subject, as Don grew up listening to Harry call games for his beloved White Sox, and later Don must have heard Harry doing countless Cubs games in the 1980s and '90s (just as I did, a few hundred miles away in Kansas). Turns out we needed a real biography of Harry Caray, and now it's unlikely that we'll ever need another. (By the way—just being honest about this—I wasn't sure a broadcaster, *any* broadcaster, needed a full-bore biography. I've never been so happy to be so wrong about something.)

But as thrilled as I was to learn that Don was writing about Harry, I was doubly excited when he told me last summer that he was hard at work on a book about the Black Sox. Then I became *trebly* enthused when Don told me what the book would *really* be about: the Black Sox story most of us don't know, because it's been almost uniformly (at best) glossed over or (at worst) ignored.

In Amy Essington's 2018 book, *The Integration of the Pacific Coast League: Race and Baseball on the West Coast*, she writes about what's missed when the story of organized baseball's integration focuses almost completely on just two people. "Integration was a process that involved hundreds of players on dozens of teams in tens of leagues across the country and over decades," Essington writes. "If the story of integration ends with Jackie Robinson and Branch Rickey, we lose the story of what happened to everyone beyond those two men and the larger understanding of integration in sport as part of the social movement for civil rights that grew and developed during and after World War II."

I would never counsel anyone to not write more about Robinson and Rickey; you gotta follow your passions. I'm just not sure how much more I want or need to *read* about those two. When it comes to integration, there are still so many gaps in my knowledge, so I would rather learn more about the Pacific Coast League, or the Canadian-American League or the Sunset League. So, so many gaps.

Black Sox, same thing. While I realize there are still important unanswered questions about the crooked 1919 World Series and the courtroom dramas later on, I suspect I've crossed over into the land of diminishing returns. But there are still gaps in my knowledge. For years, I've wondered about the 1920 season, which has hardly been written about from the White Sox perspective. Think about it, though . . . in 1920, the owner and the manager and probably most of the players knew that some of the *other* players had conspired to lose a World Series, which enriched the conspiring players *and* cost their nonconspiring teammates a winner's share of the gate receipts. And yet somehow they all got along well enough to enter the season's final week with a fighting chance to repeat as American League champions! Even while some of them were almost certainly *still* throwing games!

Team chemistry, anyone? Herein, Don examines the myriad team dynamics in great detail, along with the ongoing stories about the widespread corruption that coursed throughout professional baseball in that era, including various game-fixing scandals in both the major and minor leagues. All of which gives us a far better picture of the Black Sox than we've ever had before.

Look, even after devouring *Double Plays and Double Crosses*, I'm not going to promise you I'll never read another book about the Black Sox.

It's a pretty safe bet, though.

Rob Neyer has written or co-written seven baseball books, including Power Ball: Anatomy of a Modern Baseball Game, *which won the Casey Award for 2018's best baseball book. He is currently the commissioner of the summer collegiate West Coast League.*

ACKNOWLEDGMENTS

During the 1970s—OK, most of the 1980s also—I was a classic underachiever: a graduate of Northwestern University's Medill School of Journalism with a job delivering mail on a beautiful lakefront route in Evanston, just north of the NU campus. I liked it, too: I wound up spending 21 years with the US Postal Service, and those were some of the best years of my adult life. I still had a dream to write, however, and I wanted to write about sports, particularly baseball. Somewhere along the way I landed a gig writing occasional articles for a little publication called the *APBA Journal*. The *Journal* was a monthly newsletter devoted to a baseball table game played with cards and dice, with the cards based on Major League seasons from past and present. When the APBA Game Company came out with a set of player cards for, say, the 1934 season, I would write an article for the *Journal* about the highlights of that season. My favorite historical season by far was 1920, and my favorite team was the 1920 White Sox. Joe Jackson! Eddie Collins! Eddie Cicotte! Buck Weaver! I loved the season, loved the team, loved the *story* of this amazing, but ill-fated, team. Sometime during the 1980s, when a writer for the *APBA Journal* asked me in an interview what my ultimate writing ambition was, I said: "I want to write a book about the 1920 White Sox."

This is that book. It took me 35 years or so to finally get around to writing it, but a few things—particularly a new full-time job working in sports for STATS, Inc.—delayed things a little. I am frankly glad I waited until now, because information about a subject like the 1920 White Sox is a whole lot easier to obtain than it was in 1985—both because of the wealth of information now available in digital form, and because so many talented people have done research about the Black Sox in the intervening years. And also because, since 1985, so many people have helped me become a better writer, and (hopefully) a better person. I would like to thank some of them here.

Let me begin with a deep bow in gratitude to the members of the Black Sox Scandal Committee of the Society for American Baseball Research. The work of the committee, which was started by the late, great Gene Carney in 2009, blazed the trail for works such as mine. On this book in particular, several members of the committee were an enormous help. Jacob Pomrenke, the committee chairman, shared files, helped direct me to things I needed, and provided much wisdom and advice. Bruce Allardice, an expert on many Black Sox subjects, was particularly helpful with investigating the potentially fixed White Sox games of the 1920 season. Bill Felber, whose book *Under Pallor, Under Shadow* is a definitive study of the 1920 American League season, went out of his way to help with questions about individual White Sox games during the season. And legal expert Bill Lamb, the 2019 winner of SABR's most prestigious honor, the Bob Davids Award, could not have been more generous in sharing his thoughts about legal questions concerning the Black Sox—and also with giving me permission to quote from his insightful email messages on these subjects.

Next, heartfelt thanks to Rob Neyer, who was gracious enough to write the foreword. Rob is an amazingly talented baseball writer, and a great person on top of that. As he notes in the foreword, Rob and I started working together long ago at STATS. At that time the company was new, and we were working our tails off to establish ourselves in the world of sports data and analysis. There were more than a few days when I wondered if I'd made the right choice in leaving that beautiful lakefront mail route. At first I was a one-person STATS Publications Department. One day John Dewan, the head of our company, told me that it was time to double the size of the unit by hiring someone to assist me. That person was Rob . . . and though I can't say the workload got much easier, I can definitely say that working beside such a trusted and hardworking colleague—as well as someone who became a lifelong friend—made that stressful time in my life, both work and personal, a whole lot more manageable.

I also want to thank the couple who gave me my start at STATS, which was the beginning of the journey that led to this book: John and Sue Dewan. And a big round of thanks to Bill James, the man who inspired me into thinking I could turn my love for sports (and sports data and writing) into a career. Bill was the first person to quote my work in a major publication, his fabulous *Baseball Abstracts*. More than anyone, Bill James put my name on the map in the business that became my livelihood.

Through Bill James and STATS I met Craig Wright, whose indispensable newsletter, *Pages from Baseball's Past,* has explored Black Sox issues on numerous occasions (along with hundreds of other historical baseball subjects). Thanks to Craig, a longtime friend, for permission to quote his research on Fred McMullin's role in the scandal. Additionally, Craig's deep insight into Black Sox matters, as expressed in many of his newsletters, have helped guide my own thinking.

Mike Lynch has written extensively about the Black Sox and their era, including a wonderful book called *It Ain't So: A Might-Have-Been History of the White Sox in 1919 and Beyond.* In the book, Mike used simulations to project how the Sox and their banished players might have fared had their Major League Baseball careers continued. Lefty Williams, 300 wins? Joe Jackson, 3,400 hits? It might well have happened. Mike also shared photos of the Black Sox with me, and his own works—including the fabulous Seamheads.com Negro Leagues database—were tremendously helpful.

I joined SABR in 1979, and my interactions with other SABR members over the years have been a constant delight, along with greatly increasing my knowledge of many baseball subjects. A number of SABR members are writers whose work has inspired me, and whose advice has helped guide my own work. I would like to salute a few of them who have particularly helped with my writing (with apologies to anyone I may have inadvertently left out): Jean Ardell, Mark Armour, Rob Fitts, Noel Hynd, Maxwell Kates, Dan Levitt, Andy McCue, Bill Nowlin, Ron Rapoport, Lyle Spatz, Steve Steinberg, Cecilia Tan, John Thorn, and Jerry Wood. Thanks also to Scott Bush and Deb Jayne for their gracious help when I visited the SABR office in Phoenix.

While I don't have individual names to thank, the staffs at the Chicago History Museum, the Harold Washington Library in Chicago, and the San Diego Public Library were a great help to me with manuscripts and microfilm necessary for my research. Thanks also to Cassidy Lent of the National Baseball Hall of Fame and Museum for his help with player files.

As a still-inexperienced 72-year-old author, I feel blessed to work with a helpful and supportive publisher. Thanks to Christen Karniski, Julie Kirsch, Erinn Slanina, Jessica McCleary, and the staff at Rowman & Littlefield for all you do to help my work make it into print. It is great to be working with you again.

On a personal level, I would like to thank some longtime friends and supporters, some of whom date back to my postal years and even earlier, when my path to success in sports and writing was a far-off dream: John and Sharon Chornish, Coleman and Nadine Colla, Mitchell and Donna Harrison, Brian

ACKNOWLEDGMENTS

Hayes and Deb Segal, John and Jan McCarron, Dave and Dena Mundo, Bob Zaborowski and Anita Koch, and Phil, Peg, Allison, and Philip Zminda, along with Matt Brown, Ethan Cooperson, Chris Dial, Paul Greenberg, Deb Klein, Ron Klemp, Skip Lawson, Jack March, Chuck Miller, Tony Nistler, John Ranos, Mike See, Meghan Sheehan, Stuart Shiffman, Jo Ann Shrawder, Aneel Trivedi, John Turnbull, and John Ungashick.

And most of all, thanks to the "home team": my stepsons Steve and Mike; Mike's wife Nancy; our grandsons Matt and Sean; and especially my wife, Sharon, who inspires my life—and my work—every day. We've come a long way since good old Route 83, honey!

INTRODUCTION

More than 100 years after it took place, the Black Sox scandal continues to fascinate. It's a story that has a little bit of everything. A group of talented and colorful baseball players, some of them men of Hall of Fame caliber. A handful of avaricious gamblers, including the most famous gambler of his era, Arnold Rothstein. A team owner (Charles Comiskey) accused, fairly or not, of exploiting and underpaying his players. Charges of a cover-up by men on the game's highest level. Courtroom drama that featured stolen documents and confessions, indicted figures evading trial, and a shockingly quick verdict. And finally, banishment for the players rendered by a shaggy-haired old man whose appearance, demeanor, and even name might have come from a Frank Capra movie: Judge Kenesaw Mountain Landis.

Then there are the twists and turns and things we still don't know that make the scandal one of America's greatest mystery stories. Which players were crooked, and who played it straight? Which games were fixed, and which were on the level? Who got the money, and how much did they get? Who double-crossed whom? As time has passed, we have gathered more and more information. But the honest answer to a lot of these questions is: we still don't know for certain, and probably never will. Which doesn't mean we won't keep trying.

Investigations of the Black Sox scandal began almost as soon as the 1919 World Series ended, but the "modern era" really began in 1963, with the publication of Eliot Asinof's *Eight Men Out*. Asinof was a fine writer and a wonderful storyteller, but his sources were limited—especially since many of the key figures involved in the scandal were either deceased or unwilling to discuss what happened. Some of the information he relied on—for example, the notion that

Comiskey seriously underpaid his players compared to other teams—turned out to be completely wrong. Given the resources he had to work with, he did an admirable job . . . but to fill out his story or make it more dramatic, he sometimes fabricated quotes or made up events. The end result is that—as Jacob Pomrenke, chairman of the Black Sox Scandal Committee of the Society for American Baseball Research, puts it—*Eight Men Out* is probably better viewed as a "nonfiction novel," like Truman Capote's *In Cold Blood*, than as the definitive work of research about the scandal.

We have come a long way since *Eight Men Out*—both the book and John Sayles's 1988 film, which is also entertaining and informative but full of fictionalized (and often incorrect) storytelling. The internet happened, and made archival information much easier to access and share. Important documents, like the grand jury testimonies of Joe Jackson and Lefty Williams, were uncovered and made publicly available. Researchers were able to access and share the new information, to the benefit of all. A landmark event came in 2009, when the late Gene Carney, one of the greatest of Black Sox researchers, started SABR's Black Sox Scandal Committee. The depth of information that this group has uncovered is astonishing.

In recent years, Black Sox research has expanded still more, with books and articles and newspapers and blog posts continually providing new information and opening more and more areas of research. However, one of the few areas that has *not* been extensively explored—especially in book form—has been the story of the Chicago White Sox of 1920, the season *after* the fixed World Series. Despite widespread suspicion that players on the 1919 team had sold out to gamblers, the fix wasn't definitively uncovered until September of 1920, when a Chicago grand jury began to investigate the scandal. In the meantime the White Sox had played nearly an entire season under a cloud of suspicion, with the players who had been involved in the fix working alongside their suspicious teammates. Yet the club was so talented that it almost made the World Series again. In the meantime at least some of the players who participated in the 1919 World Series fix were suspected of continuing to dump games in 1920, under pressure from some of the gamblers who had financed the 1919 fix.

The saga of the 1920 White Sox is the main focus of *Double Plays and Double Crosses*. It is not the only focus, however. Game-fixing and sellouts to gamblers had plagued baseball since its earliest days, with the fixes usually covered up by magnates fearful of allowing them to become public. In 1920, the dam finally broke. A Major League player, Lee Magee, who had been quietly released due to his crooked play, sued his team for lost salary . . . and the whole ugly story became public. In one of baseball's top minor leagues, the scandal-ridden Pacific Coast League, rumors of game-fixing during the 1919 season led to a months-long investigation resulting in page 1 stories and criminal indictments. And the suspected fix of an August 31 Cubs-Phillies game led to an investigation of crooked play by a Chicago grand jury, which soon turned its attention to the 1919 World Series. And quickly, the whole twisted story began to come out.

Double Plays and Double Crosses tells all of these stories, along with the story of the dramatic three-team American League pennant race between the White Sox, Cleveland Indians, and New York Yankees (featuring Babe Ruth's history-making first season in New York). But the primary focus is on the White Sox—from the day after the end of the 1919 World Series through December 31, 1920—with a chapter 1 prologue devoted to the White Sox of 1917 (the year the Black Sox shenanigans really started), and an epilogue summarizing post-1920 events. Who *were* these guys, and how did they manage to play together and keep winning? Much of the story is told through the eyes of the newspapermen who reported it: people like James Crusinberry and Oscar Reichow and Harry Neily and Larry Woltz. As I cover issues like Comiskey's decision to bring back seven of the eight players suspected of being involved in the fix, or games during the 1920 season that the Black Sox may have dumped, I am happy to share the insight of Black Sox historians like Jacob Pomrenke, Bill Lamb, and Bruce Allardice, members of SABR Black Sox Scandal committee and true experts in their field.

I have been a White Sox fan since I first began following baseball in the mid-1950s, and the saga of the 1920 White Sox has fascinated me since I first heard the story of this team that featured some of the greatest players in baseball history—as well as one of baseball's saddest stories. I hope you enjoy reading *Double Plays and Double Crosses: The Black Sox and Baseball in 1920* as much as I enjoyed writing it.

A quick note about the use of players' nicknames, a subject I am somewhat passionate about (I even wrote a slim little book on the subject a number of years ago). My research for this book included perusing several newspapers, either online or on microfilm, for every day of the narrative. Along the way I learned that George Weaver was Buck in every story, that Oscar Felsch was always called Happy, that Harry Leibold was always known as Nemo. And that's how they're known in the book. But "Shano" Collins was John Collins in 95 percent of the stories I encountered, and when they used the nickname it was more often Shauno or Shono than Shano. So in the book I almost always refer to him as John Collins, as reporters of the time did . . . anyway, John Collins suits him, as he was a tough, no-nonsense, dependable guy. Similarly, I learned that Claude

Williams was referred to as Claude more often than he was Lefty, so while I use both names, I have a bit of a bias toward Claude. As for Joe Jackson, when writers used a nickname for Jackson during this time, they usually called him "General." "Shoeless Joe" is a memorable nickname that I don't mind using now and then for variety. However, he's mostly just Joe Jackson here.

1

PRELUDE

1917

Saturday, June 16, 1917, was a wet, gloomy day in the city of Boston . . . and "gloomy" might be a good word to describe the way the Boston Red Sox and their fans were feeling as the home team took the field against the Chicago White Sox. World Series champions in both 1915 and 1916, the Red Sox entered Saturday's game trailing the first-place White Sox by two and a half games after a skid that included six losses in the team's last seven games. While Boston was sending its left-handed ace—22-year-old Babe Ruth—to face the White Sox and Eddie Cicotte on Saturday, Red Sox hitters were in a deep slump: the Bostonians hadn't scored a run since the first inning of their second game against the St. Louis Browns on Wednesday . . . a scoreless span of 26 consecutive innings.

The crowd of 9,405 that attended Saturday's game at Fenway Park included more than just the usual band of rabid Red Sox rooters (plus a contingent of French officers on leave from the Great War in Europe, the guests of Boston's management). Both Fenway Park and Braves Field, the home of the National League Boston Braves, were notorious for large contingents of gamblers who attended the games and openly bet on the action. Gambling had long been an issue for baseball, but over the last few years, lax security at Major League parks had made the situation even worse. "During the era of the National Commission [Major League Baseball's three-man governing body from 1903 to 1920]," wrote Harold Seymour and Dorothy Seymour Mills, "baseball's relationship to gambling was essentially a recapitulation of the early years but on a larger and therefore more dangerous scale. Open betting in the ball parks was rife, particularly in Pittsburgh and Boston."[1]

CHAPTER 1

At Fenway Park, the gamblers tended to congregate in the right field bleachers. And with the Red Sox in their mid-June tailspin, they were in a foul mood as the June 16 game began. "The truth is that during the last two weeks, the gamblers here have been stung, stung for a greater amount than in years," wrote James Crusinberry of the *Chicago Tribune* two days after the game.[2] The gamblers' anxiety increased when the White Sox quickly scored off Ruth in the top of the first—leadoff man John Collins (nicknamed Shano, sometimes spelled Shauno or Shono) singled, moved to second on Buck Weaver's sacrifice hit, and raced home on a two-out double by Joe Jackson. Meanwhile Boston's hitters continued their scoreless streak. As it began to rain in the top of the fourth, the White Sox scored again, with Chick Gandil driving in Happy Felsch, who had walked and moved to second on a passed ball. When rain started coming down more heavily, fans seated in the right field bleachers ran onto the field, seeking shelter in the covered stands along the first base line. This caused a delay of several minutes.

The Red Sox went out quietly in the bottom of the fourth, leaving the game one inning from becoming official. In addition, American League rules stated than once the White Sox batted and four and a half innings had been played, fans would lose "rain check" privileges entitling them to a ticket to another game if the contest was called. The legion of gamblers in the bleachers was well aware that if the game was called before becoming official, all bets would be canceled; shouts of "Call the game!" began ringing out from the stands. However, umpires Barry McCormick and Tommy Connolly let the game continue. With two out and John Collins at bat, the gamblers took direct action to bring the game to a halt. "When two men were out some fan in a long rain coat took command," wrote Crusinberry. "Waving to his comrades to follow, he boldly leaped out upon the field. In ten seconds he must have had 500 followers." With a mob of fans on the field of play, the umpires had no choice but to halt the game. "Later investigation made it practically certain that the trouble was started by the horde of gamblers that assembles each day in the right field pavilion and carries on operations with as much vigor and vim as one would see in the wheat pit of the Chicago board of trade," wrote Crusinberry.[3]

At first the crowd was fairly docile, simply standing in the field of play so that the game could not continue. Red Sox manager Jack Barry, fearful that the game would be forfeited to Chicago, implored the crowd to leave the field. This had some effect, and fans slowly began returning to the stands. "Just when play was about to begin again new leaders and recruits came from the gamblers' stand," wrote Crusinberry. "Some of them came from the left field pavilion, then the first crowd piled out of the boxes again. This time the mob was riotous. Officers, five all told, came forth. They were helpless, and didn't try very hard."[4]

With only the handful of police on hand to control a mob of several hundred, the White Sox implored McCormick to end the game and award the victory to Chicago by forfeit. His umpiring partner, Connolly, later said he felt that McCormick should have done so, but McCormick told the players to leave the field while the police attempted to restore order. This took about 35 minutes.

In the meantime, even more trouble ensued as the players of both teams, who had exited the field through the Red Sox dugout, congregated under the stands. "During the intermission there were a lot of interesting goings on under the stand, the Chicago players, it is alleged, figuring in several mixups," wrote Edward F. Martin in the *Boston Globe*. "Augustine J. McNally of Norwood alleged that he was assaulted by Buck Weaver and Fred McMullin of the Sox, who deny it, and Ray Schalk, in language not of the parlor, is said to have questioned the courage of a patrolman from the Boylston St. station, who was willing to show him, using Ray as the subject, that he was game enough." Two days later, Boston police would arrest McMullin and Weaver, who claimed he had been hit by a pop bottle during the melee, for assault. "McNally was one of the mob which attempted to break up the game Saturday," reported the *Tribune*, "and during the fussing is supposed to have bumped McMullin's fist with his eye. Also he is supposed to have had his fingers on the railing when Weaver let his bat fall."[5]

With the help of two mounted policemen, the field was finally cleared and, wisely or not, play resumed after sawdust was spread on the infield to make conditions more playable. "When play resumed the field was a quagmire," wrote John J. Hallahan in the *Boston Herald*. "It was not safe to play on. Manager Jack Barry argued with the umpires after the customary half-hour wait that playing on such a field was impossible. It did no good."[6] Mercifully, the remainder of the game was played without further disruption. The White Sox increased their lead to 3–0 with a RBI single in the top of the sixth; Boston finally ended its scoreless string, which had reached 33 innings, with two runs in the bottom of the eighth; and the White Sox put the game away with four more runs off Ruth, who pitched a complete game (as did Cicotte) despite allowing 10 hits, five walks, a home run (to Buck Weaver in the ninth), and a season-high seven runs. In his last year as a full-time pitcher, the Babe would go 23–12 with a league-leading 1.75 ERA, while batting .325 with two home runs.

But the story of the game was the riot on the field. The Boston press was merciless in its criticism of the hometown crowd, as well as slamming Red Sox owner Harry Frazee for his failure to provide adequate security. "Boston lost the game 7 to 2, but that was incidental to the weak handling of the bleacherites by the management," wrote John J. Hallahan in the *Herald*. "It was the most unsportsmanlike exhibition that has ever been given by a Boston audience. The management was entirely to blame because of the lack of police." Edward F. Martin in the *Globe* wrote, "The trouble might have been avoided had there been policemen stationed on the grounds. Those who were on duty were not on the playing field as they have been in former years and unquestionably the psychological effect of the presence of the men in blue about the field would have deterred the invaders from scaling the fence."[7]

The Chicago press was equally blistering. "Just why this betting ring is allowed in Boston and not tolerated in other cities has never been explained by the baseball magnates," wrote Crusinberry, "but it is supposed to carry a political angle which has the hands of the magnates tied. The attention of Major League presidents has been called to it in the past and even has brought forth statements from the baseball heads that there is no gambling. Any one present, however, can see the transactions and hear them plainly."[8]

In the next edition of the baseball weekly *Sporting News*, *Chicago Daily News* writer George S. Robbins wrote,

A riot of fans incensed at what are believed to be unfair decisions by umpires is one thing; throwing of pop bottles at offending players is another; even the use of fists to assert alleged rights or settle fancied grievances is another. These things only show that fans, players and managers are full of the spirit to win for the joy of winning.

But when a horde of gamblers, permitted to run riot in a major league ball park, seek to stop a ball game, and urge hoodlums to attack visiting players, to save their dirty coin—that is still another thing. All the rowdyism that could be crowded into a season, all the beating up of umpires, can not do the game half as much damage as the one incident that occurred in Boston last Saturday.[9]

Robbins called on American League President Ban Johnson, who had long campaigned against the presence of gamblers at MLB parks, to take action. A day after the Fenway Park riot, Johnson asserted that "gambling never has been tolerated by our league." He chalked up the problems at Fenway Park to the fact that Red Sox owner Harry Frazee "is new to baseball. There are many things with which he is not entirely familiar." Johnson himself hired the Pinkerton Detective Agency in an attempt to identify gamblers who were known to ply their trade at Boston's American and National League parks. The detectives produced a list of 60 well-known gamblers, which he shared with Frazee and Percy Haughton, the owner of the Boston Braves. But looking back at his investigation in a letter to the general superintendent of the Pinkerton Agency in 1921, Johnson wrote, "No benefit was derived from this course, for the reason we did not have the co-operation of Frazee and Haughton."[10]

In the meantime the influence of gambling—and the frequent occurrences of games featuring cash payoffs from gamblers to players or a payoff from one team to another to "lay down" against their opponent—remained largely unabated over the next few years. And no team would fall more heavily under that influence than the Chicago White Sox. In an extensive article written in 2012 about the Boston gamblers' riot and its aftermath, Jacob Pomrenke wrote, "It took the severity of the Black Sox scandal, plus Judge [Kenesaw Mountain] Landis' unilateral decision to permanently punish every player associated with it, to make it clear that gambling and baseball would not be allowed to mix so freely ever again."[11] But in the summer of 1917, all that was several years off, and the term "Black Sox" was yet to be coined. As the summer came to an end, the Chicago *White* Sox were headed toward an American League pennant and a World Series championship . . . by any means necessary, some would say.

The White Sox club that battled Boston for the American League pennant in 1917 had been steadily improving for several years. After Chicago had finished the 1914 season with a dismal 70–84 record, White Sox owner Charles A. Comiskey had shelled out $50,000 to purchase one of the best players in baseball, Philadelphia Athletics second baseman Eddie Collins. Then late in the 1915 campaign, he put together a package of players and cash worth an estimated $65,000 to acquire one of baseball's best hitters, Joe Jackson, from the Cleveland Indians. Collins and Jackson joined a White Sox roster that already included such talented players as catcher Ray Schalk; infielder Buck Weaver; outfielders Happy Felsch and John Collins; and pitchers Eddie Cicotte, Red Faber, and Reb Russell. In 1916 Comiskey added left-handed pitcher Claude (Lefty) Williams, who had won 33 games for the Salt Lake City Bees in the Pacific Coast League the previous year. As a result the Sox moved from sixth place (tied) in 1914 to third in 1915 and then second—only two games behind the pennant-winning Red Sox—in 1916.

Prior to the 1917 season, Comiskey added two new everyday players, purchasing veteran first baseman Chick Gandil from the Cleveland Indians and shortstop Charles (Swede) Risberg from the Vernon Tigers of the PCL. Gandil and Risberg added strength to the White Sox on the playing field, but it came at the expense of the club's already shaky team chemistry. Basically, the club split into two factions, one led by the college-educated, high-salaried Eddie Collins and the other by the tough, hard-bitten Gandil and his trusty sidekick,

Chick Gandil, who joined the White Sox in 1917, was one of the masterminds of the 1919 World Series fix. *Library of Congress Prints and Photographs Division*

Risberg. Collins and Gandil had an unpleasant history that dated back to June 1912, when Collins was still with the Athletics and Gandil was playing for the Washington Senators. On a play at second base, Collins leaped for a high throw, coming down just as Gandil was sliding in. According to the *Washington Times*, Eddie "bent his knee, letting Gandil strike one of them with full force as he slid for the bag." The result was a broken nose for Chick, who considered the incident anything but an accident. Neither did his teammates; the *Washington Post* noted two days after the incident that Senators players "are complaining that the Athletics have been roughing them up deliberately," citing the Collins-Gandil incident as "specific proof."[12] (Typifying his own brand of toughness, Gandil refused to come out of the lineup after suffering the broken nose, and in fact played a doubleheader that day.)

Then there was the relationship between Collins and Buck Weaver, one of the most popular players on the White Sox, both with teammates and fans. In 1914, the White Sox had named Weaver team captain, a major honor for players of that era; however, when the Sox purchased Collins after the season, they immediately stripped Weaver of the role and handed the team captaincy to Eddie. Weaver was also one of a number of White Sox players resentful of Collins's $15,000 annual salary; using the threat of jumping to the rival Federal League during its two-year (1914–1915) existence as a third Major League, Collins had wangled a five-year, $75,000 contract (including salary and bonus) from Comiskey. Shrewd work, to be sure, but it left Eddie making more than twice the salary of most of his Sox teammates. Weaver's feelings about Collins were best expressed in an "as told to" interview several decades later with broadcaster Hal Totten. Buck recalled that in the 1917 World Series against the New York Giants, the White Sox had "sharpened our spikes till they were like razors" in an effort to intimidate the Giants on the basepaths. Only one player, Weaver noted, refused to sharpen his spikes: Eddie Collins. "Why? Well, he was a different type of ballplayer. He never went in for that sorta stuff because he figured they might come back at him and he'd get hurt playin' there in the infield. He was a great guy to look out for himself. If there was a tough gent comin' down to second, he'd yell for the shortstop to take the play."[13] This doesn't quite jibe with the Collins-Gandil story, but maybe Gandil hadn't shared the incident with Buck.

By most accounts, Collins got along well with his superstar teammate, left fielder Shoeless Joe Jackson, but Collins came from a comfortable background and was a graduate of an Ivy League school while Jackson grew up dirt-poor and was well-known to be illiterate. There was not much commonality between the two, and Jackson fit in more comfortably with rougher types like Gandil and Risberg than with Collins or teammates such as pitcher Red Faber, the son of an affluent Iowa hotel owner, or catcher Ray Schalk, a man once described by *Baseball Magazine* as the brainiest catcher in baseball. The same was true of Sox center fielder Oscar (Happy) Felsch, who had only a sixth-grade education and was one of 10 children. Collins and Felsch would have their own issues; when Felsch jumped the team in 1918 to work for a Milwaukee gas company, it was rumored that a fistfight with team captain Collins was one of the reasons for Happy's alienation. Like Weaver and Jackson, "Felsch fraternized with the Risberg/Gandil group that was often in conflict with the higher-educated Ray Schalk/Eddie Collins faction," wrote James R. Nitz.[14]

On Sunday, September 2, the White Sox began a two-day, four-game series at Comiskey Park against the Detroit Tigers; Monday was Labor Day, and the teams would play a conventional doubleheader on Sunday followed by morning and afternoon games the next day. With an 83–47 (.638) record, Chicago led the second-place Red Sox (76–47, .618) by three and a half games . . . the same margin that the White Sox had held after that wild crazy June 16 game. The Tigers ranked fourth in the American League with a 65–61 (.516) record; at 16 games behind the White Sox, Detroit had little to play for apart from hoping to finish the season with a winning record.

If any dates could be said to have marked the start of the "Black Sox" era, September 2–3, 1917, would be the logical choice. Charges of game-fixing would later be made, and hotly denied, about this four-game set; at the very least, money changed hands between the teams in a manner that generated considerable suspicion. The story—or to be more precise, *stories*—would not come to light for several years, and a final ruling on the case wasn't made until baseball Commissioner Kenesaw Mountain Landis held a three-day hearing featuring more than 30 witnesses in January 1927. Even then people debated about what really happened, as they do to this day. The main accusations of suspicious play would come from the White Sox faction that would be accused of deliberately losing the 1919 World Series, led by Chick Gandil and Swede Risberg, and supported—at least some of the time—by Buck Weaver and Happy Felsch. Eddie Collins would lead the "deniers."

Overall the four games were reasonably competitive, but included enough unusual events to raise some eyebrows. On Sunday, the White Sox swept the doubleheader, winning the first game 7–2 and the 10-inning nightcap, 6–5. "The first was a gallop for the Sox, who had had a seven-run lead after the third inning was over," wrote *Detroit Free Press* reporter E. A. Batchelor. Press reports described "very amateurish fielding by the Tigers" (*Detroit Free Press*) and a White Sox run scoring when Tiger center fielder Ty Cobb lost a flyball in the sun (*Chicago Tribune*); the Sox stole three bases in the game, and Shoeless Joe Jackson had an inside-the-park home run. Eddie Cicotte allowed eight hits, all singles, in earning his 22nd win. In Sunday's second game, the White Sox blew a 3–1 lead in the top of the ninth, when Detroit scored four runs. However, the Sox tied the contest with two runs in the bottom of the inning; the tying run scored when Tiger shortstop Ben Dyer, on what the *Chicago Herald and Examiner* called the "prize bone play of the season . . . lapsed into unconsciousness" and held the ball while Eddie Murphy raced home. The Sox won the game in the bottom of the 10th when Eddie Collins walked, stole second and third, and then scored on Happy Felsch's sacrifice fly. Chicago stole six bases in the game, three by Collins, and Tiger pitcher George Cunningham yielded six walks. In addition, the *Tribune* noted that Tiger right fielder and future Hall of Famer

Harry Heilmann "quit running to first on a bounder to Risberg in the seventh of the second game. Manager [Hughie] Jennings instantly yanked him out of the game and sent [George] Harper to right field."[15]

In Monday's morning game, the Tigers led 5–2 after four and a half innings, but the White Sox scored two runs in the bottom of the fifth, two more in the sixth, and another in the eighth for a 7–5 victory. Once more Sox baserunners ran wild, stealing eight bases, and Tiger pitchers Howard Ehmke and Bill James allowed seven walks. The Monday afternoon game was a slugfest, with the White Sox once more coming from behind after trailing 7–5 to win 14–8. Red Faber, who had started the first game and allowed 11 hits and five runs in four and two-thirds inning, started the second game as well, lasted only an inning and a third in this one; Cicotte, who had pitched a complete game the day before, worked the final six innings in relief for the White Sox, allowing only four hits and one run for his 23rd victory. Bill James, who allowed seven hits and five runs (three of them unearned) in three relief innings for the Tigers, was the loser. The White Sox stole five more bases in this one, giving them 22 steals in the four-game set. For the series, Detroit pitchers permitted 20 walks and hit three Sox batters. In the *Detroit Free Press*, Batchelor wrote that the Tiger pitchers "either couldn't get the ball over or else grooved it and let the Sox slam it to the fences"; the *Detroit Times* mentioned that Bill James "worked a little while in each contest and managed to let the Sox down with five passes in five innings."[16]

Now, about that money changing hands: all sides agreed that sometime during the series Chick Gandil and the aforementioned Bill James met and discussed some sort of cash payment that would go from Sox players to Tiger pitchers . . . but to say the least, accounts differed about when the meeting took place, and about the reason for the payment. According to Gandil, the meeting took place prior to the first game on Sunday. Testifying before Judge Landis in 1927, Gandil recalled that he and James had talked about how things were going for the White Sox, and James told him, "Well, you fellows get out there and hustle. The boys won't bear down very hard on you." Seeing this as an offer by the Tigers to take it easy on the Sox in the series, "I told him that I would see that he got fixed up" if Detroit laid down against the White Sox. Swede Risberg, who had spoken to Landis a couple of days earlier, not only supported Gandil's account; he claimed that "I was informed by Mr. Clarence Rowland [the White Sox manager] before the series that everything was all fixed." "Pants" Rowland, who also testified at the 1927 hearings, hotly disputed Risberg's accusation, calling it "a damned lie." He pointed out to reporters that he had made extensive use of his best pitchers, including Cicotte, Williams, and Faber, in an effort to sweep the doubleheaders: "If the games were fixed and I had knowledge of it I could easily have bluffed my way through by working some of the second raters."[17] Another of the future Black Sox, Happy Felsch, said during the 1927 inquiry that he did not think that Rowland was involved, but supported the other details of Risberg's account.

Testifying at Landis's hearing immediately after Gandil, James called Gandil's account "an absolute lie." According to James, who had previously spoken to Landis about this series in 1921, the conversation took place between innings after the series had started, probably during the last game, and the subject discussed was not the Sox-Tigers series; it was Detroit's upcoming mid-September series against Chicago's main rival, the Red Sox. According to James, Gandil told him "there is $200 in it for every pitcher who beats Boston."[18] Whatever the reason for the payment, it would be made later in September, with virtually the entire White Sox team contributing to the pool.

Following their doubleheader sweeps of the Tigers, the White Sox traveled to St. Louis for a short two-game set against the struggling seventh-place Browns. The Sox took both games, 13–6 and 4–1 . . . and once again the subject of a team "laying down" against an opponent came up. However, this time the team that would come under scrutiny was not the White Sox, but the Browns. In an interview with a St. Louis reporter between the first and second games of the series, Browns owner Phil Ball was quoted as accusing his team of not playing with sufficient effort for manager Fielder Jones, who, interestingly enough, had managed the White Sox from 1904 to 1908 and had led the White Sox to their only previous World Series championship in 1906. Ball mentioned no specific games or incidents, and did not single out any particular players. But the article quoted him as threatening to cut his players' salaries by $100 for every $1,000 he lost on the season.

Pants Rowland was not pleased with the timing of Ball's statement. "What will the people in the East think when they read that the Browns have not been 'trying' against us?" he complained. "It will look as if a Western club is trying to help another Western club win the pennant. It isn't fair to the Chicago players."[19]

Ball's threats and blanket accusation infuriated the Browns, in particular three of the team's regular players: second baseman Del Pratt, shortstop John (Doc) Lavan, and outfielder Burt Shotton. All three refused to play for the Browns until Ball issued a retraction. Jones took the issue so seriously that he offered to resign as the team's manager if it would restore team harmony. Ball refused to accept the offer, and claimed that he had been misquoted. "I did not say you were laying down," he told his team. "When asked by a reporter if you were doing that I told him I did not know, but that I wasn't competent to be the

St. Louis Browns infielder Del Pratt took offense when team owner Phil Ball accused his team of "laying down," joining shortstop Doc Lavan in a slander lawsuit against the club. *Library of Congress Prints and Photographs Division*

judge of that." This placated the players enough to agree to end their walkout, but it didn't settle the issue. Two days later, Pratt and Lavan announced that they were suing Ball for $50,000 apiece, asking $25,000 for actual damages and $25,000 more for punitive damages.[20]

Though Ball kept trying to walk back on his statement—at one point he claimed that "laying down" didn't imply dishonesty, only that it meant the player was playing for himself and not for the team's interests—he soon learned the folly of making accusations without evidence to back them up. Lavan and Pratt refused to drop their lawsuits, even after Ball dealt Lavan and Shotton to the Washington Senators and Pratt to the New York Yankees . . . transactions that the three players were delighted to accept. Among the people who testified on their behalf was baseball immortal Ty Cobb, who said that a player's reputation would be damaged if he were accused by his manager of "laying down" and make it more difficult for him to find work. Ultimately Lavan and Pratt settled their lawsuit with Ball for a fraction of the amount they had sought. However, both felt that their reputations had been vindicated.

Del Pratt, Burt Shotton, and John Lavan would all do just fine after parting ways with Phil Ball. Pratt remained one of the American League's best second basemen through 1924, hitting over .300 in each of his last five seasons. He then continued his career in the minor leagues as a player and manager; along the way, Pratt "gained a reputation for developing young talent," according to baseball historian and author Steve Steinberg.[21] Within a few years Shotton and Lavan would return to St. Louis to play for the Cardinals. That reunited them with Branch Rickey, who had been their manager with the Browns before moving across town to begin transforming the Cardinals into the National League's most dominant team. Shotton remained a Rickey protégé for most of the rest of his life, including serving as Jackie Robinson's manager in Robinson's rookie season of 1947, after Rickey had moved to the Brooklyn Dodgers and broken baseball's twentieth-century color line. A lifetime .245 hitter, Dr. John Lavan had a much more distinguished career in medicine than in baseball. Lavan served as a lieutenant in the Army Medical Corps in World War I and was commander of the naval hospital in Brooklyn during World War II. He also served for a time as director of research of the National Foundation for Infantile Paralysis. He is buried in Arlington National Cemetery.

After their two wins in St. Louis, the White Sox came home and swept the Cleveland Indians in a brief two-game set; that gave Chicago eight straight victories and a 17–1 record in its last 18 games. The club now traveled to Detroit to play the Tigers again, and this is where the question of what Chick Gandil and Bill James had discussed in Chicago earlier in the month becomes even more confusing. In handing down his ruling about the case in January 1927, Judge Landis would point out that, just prior to this series in Detroit, Sox players had received their paychecks. If the Sox were going to pay off the Tigers for letting them sweep the September 2–3 doubleheaders, wouldn't this be the logical time to do so? But that didn't happen.

One possible explanation was offered by Buck Weaver in 1922; he claimed that *this* Sox-Tiger series was fixed as well. However, neither Gandil, Risberg, or anyone else ever mentioned the September 14–15 series being in the bag for the White Sox, and the Tigers did win one of the three games.

But the claim that the agreement was to reward the Tigers if they stepped up and beat the Red Sox in their September 19–20 series in Boston doesn't make much sense either. At the end of the last Sox-Tiger series in September, Chicago's lead over Boston was seven and a half games, with only thirteen games left on the White Sox schedule; by the time the Tigers–Red Sox series began on September 19, Chicago led by eight. Even after noting that the Red Sox had played fewer games than Chicago and trailed by only five games in the loss column, Boston would have needed a colossal White Sox collapse to have any chance to make up the deficit. Wouldn't it make sense for Gandil to tell James, "Thanks, but the race is over. Let's call off the reward stuff for some time when we really need help"? But that didn't happen either.

What happened—and this is one part of the story where everyone was in agreement—was this: on the last weekend of the season, when the White Sox had a day off prior to a season-ending series in New York and the Tigers were in Philadelphia to play the Athletics, Gandil asked his teammates to fork over $45 apiece for a fund to reward the Detroiters; with the blessing of Pants Rowland, Gandil and Risberg then took a train to Philadelphia and handed the money—accounts differ, but around $1,100 seems to be the most likely figure—to Bill James.

With one exception, every White Sox player except the scrubs and rookies, who weren't asked, agreed to contribute to the fund; this included icons like Eddie Collins, Ray Schalk, and Red Faber. The exception was Buck Weaver, but that wasn't due to any special sense of piety on Buck's part. According to Weaver, his Sox teammates knew that he was friendly with Tiger third baseman Ossie Vitt, and both spent their winters in California; "Weaver will take care of him," they agreed. "I never did give Vitt any money," Weaver told reporter James Kilgallen in the 1922 interview in which he made his bribe claims. "I waited until Christmas time and gave him a nice leather bag."[22] Whether or not this bag was worth $45 is probably a question best decided by the experts on *Antiques Roadshow*, but I think we can agree that it was the thought that counted.

In his 1927 hearings, which were open to the press and a page 1 story in much of the country, Landis invited a total of 38 people from the 1917 (and 1919) White Sox and Tigers to Chicago. Ultimately 33 of them testified; only Risberg and Gandil asserted that the payment to the Tigers was for laying down against the White Sox in the September 2–3 doubleheaders. (The judge's loosely-put-together list of invitees included Ed Walsh, who pointed out to Landis that he was no longer with the White Sox in 1917, and Jack Lapp, who could not appear because he had died in 1920.) Of the group later to be known as the Black Sox, Felsch, Cicotte, and Jackson elected not to attend the hearings, while Lefty Williams and Fred McMullin were not invited (likely due to the difficulty of traveling from the West Coast to Chicago on short notice). Buck Weaver, backing off completely from the charges he made in 1922, claimed he wasn't even in Chicago for the September 2–3 games in 1917. That wasn't true; he was out of the lineup due to injury, but present at Comiskey Park during the series.

At the hearings, Landis also looked into a claim by Gandil and Risberg that the White Sox had sloughed off in an end-of-season series versus Detroit in

1919 as a way of thanking the Tigers for their 1917 "cooperation." Once again Gandil and Risberg stood alone in their accusation. Landis exonerated the Sox-Tiger players with a warning that offering a team money to bear down against a particular opponent would no longer be tolerated.

At the same time that he was taking testimony on the Sox-Tigers shenanigans, Landis was looking into a charge made by former MLB pitcher Dutch Leonard that Leonard and his then teammate Ty Cobb had conspired with Tris Speaker and Joe Wood of the Indians to fix a game late in the 1919 season. At the very least, letters kept by Leonard and turned over to American League President Ban Johnson indicated that Leonard, Cobb, and Wood had tried to place some sizable wagers on the outcome. Interestingly, the game in question took place on September 25, one day before the start of that end-of-season Sox-Tiger series Landis was investigating along with the 1917 Sox-Tigers doubleheaders. Talk about busy times in the world of baseball scandals! Ultimately Landis exonerated Cobb, Wood, and Speaker of the game-fixing charge, while also ruling that going forward, players or team officials who bet on games involving their own team would be subject to lifetime suspension (a rule applied decades later to Pete Rose).

One more story of note before we end this review of an exceptionally busy September for the 1917 Chicago White Sox. On September 27, the day before Gandil and Risberg collected the money to reward the Tigers, Fenway Park was the site of an exhibition game between the Red Sox and a group of Major League All-Stars, with the proceeds going to the family of beloved Boston sportswriter (and former MLB player) Tim Murnane, who had passed away in February. Babe Ruth pitched the first five innings of the game, a 2–0 Red Sox victory before more than 17,000 fans. Buck Weaver started at third base for the All-Stars, which featured an outfield of Joe Jackson, Tris Speaker, and Ty Cobb. In a month full of suspicious behavior in baseball, it was easily one of the shining moments.

The White Sox finished the 1917 regular season with 100 victories—still a franchise record more than a century later—and faced the New York Giants, managed by John McGraw, in the World Series. The Sox won the first two games in Chicago, dropped Games 3 and 4 in New York, took the Series lead with an 8–5 victory at Comiskey Park, and then wrapped up the championship with a 4–2 win at New York's Polo Grounds. Red Faber was the winning pitcher in three of the four White Sox victories. The most memorable play of the Series came in the fourth inning of Game 6, with the score 0–0. On a grounder to third base, Eddie Collins, who was on third, raced home while Giants third sacker Heinie

White Sox players Joe Jackson, John Collins, Happy Felsch, Eddie Murphy, and Nemo Leibold at the 1917 World Series against the New York Giants. *Library of Congress Prints and Photographs Division*

Zimmerman chased after him in futile pursuit. Zimmerman was considered the goat of the Series as a result, but the Giants had left home plate unguarded and Zimmerman had no other recourse. "Who was I supposed to throw the ball to . . . [home plate umpire Bill] Klem?" he is said to have complained.

As was the case so many times during this dark period of baseball history, the 1917 World Series had its suspicious elements . . . and suspicious characters. Along with the eight members of the White Sox who would suffer lifetime banishment, Giants players Buck Herzog, Rube Benton, Benny Kauff, and Zimmerman would either be banished or find their names connected with scandals. Herzog's own manager had doubts about his performance in the 1917 World Series. In his book *Baseball As I Have Known It*, longtime baseball writer Fred Lieb wrote that "McGraw always felt that [Giants infielder Buck] Herzog deliberately played out of position against White Sox batters"[23] (a subtle way of helping the opposition that Joe Jackson and Happy Felsch would be accused of in the 1919 World Series, and a trick that Chick Gandil and Swede Risberg admitted using in a late-season 1919 game against the Tigers).

Those revelations would come later. For the White Sox and their fans, the 1917 season and World Series was a year full of joy. And no one seemed more joyful than Buck Weaver. In his story about Chicago's victory in Game 5, Crusinberry noted Weaver's delight as the Sox came from behind with a late-inning rally.

> All we can remember except the din of noise from the throng present was the capers of Buck Weaver in front of the White Sox bench. He danced around in a manner which indicated he had completely lost himself. He tossed his cap into the air and followed with his sweater and a dozen bats and three or four hats that belonged to spectators, and if there had been anything else within reach it, too, would have gone into the air. Everybody was in the air, figuratively speaking, because the Sox had come from behind and tied the score in a ball game that looked impossible to win.[24]

Two years later, Weaver and his teammates would drop a World Series that looked, to many, impossible to *lose*. In 1920, the truth about that Series would finally come to light . . . and the joy that Buck and his mates expressed in the 1917 World Series must have seemed a million years away.

2

A COLD (AND DRY) NEW YEAR

January 1, 1920, marked the start of a new decade, and the beginning of a new era in American life: one known as Prohibition. The Eighteenth Amendment to the U.S. Constitution, which prohibited the "manufacture, transportation and sales of intoxicating beverages," would take effect on January 17; enforcement would fall under the Volstead Act passed by Congress. The previous night's New Year's Eve celebration would be the last for the foreseeable future in which Americans could openly—and legally—enjoy a drink at a bar or restaurant. In Chicago, people had been partying hard well past the official start of the new year. The headline on page 1 of the January 1 *Chicago Tribune* was "1920 Arrives Wet: Cafes Become Booze Cafeterias." By morning the parties had ended, and the new year began with bitterly cold temperatures. The high in Chicago that day would only reach eight degrees, and drop well below zero overnight.

If Charles A. Comiskey, owner of the Chicago White Sox, had begun the new decade feeling bitter, cold, and tempted to find solace at a few booze cafeterias, it would have been understandable. Much had happened to Comiskey and his White Sox since the team had danced off the Polo Grounds diamond as 1917 World Series champions, and most of it had been bad. Even things that seemed to be causes for celebration—most notably, another American League pennant in 1919—would eventually get twisted and turned like a knife in Comiskey's back. And before this bitterly cold year had ended, a lot of people, many of them formerly trusted friends of the White Sox owner, would be lining up to help do the twisting.

In December 1917, *Baseball Magazine* had published an article titled "Charles Comiskey, the Prince of Magnates." It was written by American

Founder of the Chicago White Sox franchise, Charles
Comiskey never recovered from the Black Sox Scandal.
Library of Congress Prints and Photographs Division

League umpire Billy Evans and was full of praise for the White Sox owner. Evans wrote, "Comiskey is the most popular of baseball magnates. He has a following on the South Side in Chicago that supports the White Sox no matter what position the club happens to be occupying in the pennant race. In reality the fans follow Comiskey more than the team."[1]

The glow did not last very long, either for Comiskey or the White Sox. For one thing, there was a war going on, and its full effects were just beginning to be felt. Although the United States had entered World War I by declaring war on Germany in April 1917, the impact of the war did not begin to affect baseball until after the start of the 1918 season. On May 18, Provost Marshall General Enoch B. Crowder issued a "work or fight order" for what he termed "nonessential occupations," which included baseball. Any player between the ages of 21 and 35 who had not yet been drafted was ordered either to volunteer for service, perform some sort of war-related industrial work, or risk getting immediately drafted. Among the occupations providing immunity from military service were working for steel companies or shipyards. Some of these companies began inducing ballplayers to quit their teams and work for them, thereby providing immunity from the draft.

The first important MLB player who left his team to work in a shipyard was none other than Shoeless Joe Jackson of the White Sox. As a married man, Jackson had originally been granted a Class 4 deferment by his local draft board. But when the government began feeling the pressure to add more men to the military in early 1918, Jackson's draft board ruled that his wife was not dependent on him and reclassified him 1-A. In May, Jackson was ordered to take his physical and was notified that he would be inducted into the army between May 25 and June 1. But on May 13, Jackson notified the White Sox that he had taken a job at the Harlan and Hollingsworth Shipbuilding Company in Wilmington, Delaware. Jackson's draft board protested, but the shipyard registered Joe as a "necessary employee," which made him exempt from the draft. Within a few weeks, Jackson's teammates Lefty Williams and Byrd Lynn had agreed to join him at the shipyard. Other Major League players accepted similar offers from defense-related companies.

These moves generated a storm of criticism throughout the country, particularly after it was learned that players had been offered as much as $5,000 a year—a salary higher than most Major League players were earning—to work at the shipyards. It was also charged that most of their work consisted of performing for the company baseball teams, which were derisively referred to as "paint and putty leagues." The players themselves were labeled "shipyard slackers."

No one was given a tougher time than Joe Jackson. On June 6, the *Chicago Tribune* ran an editorial titled "The Case of Joe Jackson." Among other things it stated,

> Joe Jackson, until recently of the White Sox ball team, besides possessing extraordinary athletic talents, is a man of unusual physical development. Presumably he would make an excellent fighting man. But it appears that Mr. Jackson would prefer not to fight.
>
> The facts seem to be that Jackson was about to be drafted into the army, whereupon he obtained a position in an eastern shipyard. He is said to be doing his part to beat the Huns by painting ships. Whether or not this work is camouflage—we refer to the method of painting—has not been announced.

The editorial concluded with praise for "those ballplayers who have entered the military forces. They will undoubtedly make a good record, and it is these men in particular that we shall want to see on the diamond."[2]

When Williams and Lynn joined Jackson at the shipyards a few days later, Charles Comiskey weighed in. "I don't consider them fit to play on any ballclub," he said with anger. "I would gladly lose my whole team if the players wished to do their duty to their country, as hundreds of thousands of other young men are doing, by entering the army or the navy, but I hate to see any ballplayers, particularly my own, go to shipyards to escape military service."[3] His harsh words did not bring the players back, and in early July Comiskey received another jolt: Happy Felsch announced that he was quitting the team to take a $125 a month job for a Milwaukee gas company.

While the vilification of these players continued well after the war ended with an armistice on November 11, referring to them as "slackers" was probably unfair. Jackson, for example, was without much question the sole support for his wife and widowed mother. He also had three younger brothers who had already been inducted into the military. Sox catcher Byrd Lynn had been reclassified by his draft board despite the fact that he had a wife and two children; he had appealed the reclassification and expected to succeed, but figured he would eventually be drafted and took the shipyard job in the interim. Williams was in no danger of imminent induction, but probably took the job out of friendship to Jackson—the *Sporting News* referred to the two of them as "inseparable companions"—and Lynn, his former minor league teammate. Happy Felsch's motives are hard to completely decipher, as was often the case with Felsch. Earlier in the season, he had left the club to care for a brother who had been injured in an army accident. He had also been rumored to be involved in a fistfight with Eddie Collins, and he had grievances with Comiskey over a bonus he felt he deserved but said he had not received (Comiskey insisted that the bonus, for Felsch staying sober, had been paid).[4]

As for the shipyard work, it was anything but "slacking," not only for Jackson but for many other players who worked in the yards. According to an article by Geoff Gehman for the SABR Black Sox Scandal Committee newsletter, Jackson put in over 40 hours a week supervising a riveting gang at the shipyard; his group helped build a record 24 warships for the Emergency Fleet Corporation . . . essential work indeed. Gehman added that Shoeless Joe "also raised money for the Red Cross while moonlighting in Sunday games for the Reading Steel and Casting Company." As for his ballplaying at the shipyard, "[Jackson] and other Reading players were praised for stopping overworked munitions workers from boozing away their one free day."[5]

Jackson wound up playing only 17 games for the White Sox in 1918 (hitting .354), and the season was a disaster both for Comiskey and baseball in general. Due to the "work or fight" order, Major League Baseball agreed to end the season in early September, and Major League attendance was only a little over 3 million, a record low in the 16-team era and down over 2 million fans compared to 1917. While some of the difference was due to the war-shortened season, attendance was down by over 1,000 fans per game (4,186 per game in 1917, 3,031 in 1918). The defending World Series champion White Sox finished in sixth place in the American League with a 57–67 record; even worse, Sox attendance for the season was only 195,081, down nearly a half million from 1917 when the club led the Major Leagues with a home attendance of 684,521. White Sox per game attendance was down by over 5,000 (from 8,665 to 3,484).

Even one of the few bright spots for the 1918 White Sox, the signing of pitcher Jack Quinn, ended bitterly for Comiskey. A veteran spitballer who had pitched for several Major League clubs, Quinn was pitching for the Vernon team in the Pacific Coast League when the league suspended operations in midseason 1918. (The PCL was a number of minor leagues which had stopped play due to the war.) Baseball's National Commission ruled that players from these leagues were free agents who could be signed by any club, but that their contracts would revert to their former minor league team once league operations resumed. Comiskey signed Quinn to pitch for the White Sox, and he was one of the team's best pitchers for the rest of the season, posting a 5–1 record with a 2.29 ERA.

Comiskey was naturally interested in keeping Quinn for the 1919 season, only to learn that the New York Yankees had purchased Quinn's contract from Vernon at almost the same time the pitcher joined the White Sox. Both teams felt that they had a legitimate claim to Quinn's services, and asked the National Commission to make a ruling. The three-man commission, which consisted

of American League President Ban Johnson, National League President John
Heydler, and Cincinnati Reds President Garry Herrmann, ruled—probably
correctly—that Quinn belonged to the Yankees. Comiskey and the White Sox
were furious; they felt that they had followed the protocol established by the
National Commission and had never been given a chance to bid on Quinn's
services. The commission somewhat apologetically agreed, but stuck with its
decision. Quinn went on to have several good seasons with the Yankees and
remained in the Major Leagues until 1933, pitching until the age of 50.

Comiskey blamed Ban Johnson for the Quinn fiasco. The two had once been
close friends and had worked together in helping make the American League a
successful organization. But due to a series of disagreements, some professional
and others personal, they had become archenemies. After the Quinn decision it
became open warfare. A year later, the rift would become a huge impediment to
exposing the fixing of the 1919 World Series.

The story of Comiskey's 1919 White Sox—and particularly the World Series
that several members of the team conspired to deliberately lose—has been told
many times. Long before Eliot Asinof's seminal *Eight Men Out* was published
in 1963, a narrative had been widely accepted that described what transpired
in the following terms:

- The White Sox players were poorly paid and poorly treated by the miserly
  Comiskey.
- The underpaid, mistreated players were easy marks when gamblers
  approached them with an offer to throw the World Series for money.
- At least one of the players involved in the fix, Joe Jackson, took the gamblers' money but elected to play honestly. Other players also may have
  played to win.
- Comiskey and other baseball officials knew of the scandal, but chose to
  cover up what they knew.

Due in good part to the work of the Society for American Baseball Research's
Black Sox Scandal Committee, which was created by the late Gene Carney in
2009, we all know that at least some of this narrative can be questioned.

Take the White Sox salaries, for instance. Thanks to the work of researchers
Bob Hoie and Michael Haupert, we now know that Charles Comiskey's White
Sox were anything but poorly paid compared to other Major League teams of
the period. In fact, the 1919 White Sox had one of the highest team salaries in
Major League Baseball, if not *the* highest. Overall the Opening Day team payroll

for the 1919 White Sox was a little over $88,000, third highest in the American League behind the Boston Red Sox and the New York Yankees. Although detailed figures for individual National League clubs are not available, these were likely the three highest paying clubs in the Major Leagues. This is despite the fact that the White Sox were coming off a 1918 season in which they had finished in sixth place, with an enormous drop in attendance. Hoie found that by the end of the 1919 season, the White Sox had the highest payroll in Major League Baseball, including salary and bonus payments.

Thanks to a multiyear contract that he had signed under the threat of jumping to the rival Federal League in 1915, Eddie Collins earned $15,000 in 1919, second in the American League behind Ty Cobb of the Tigers ($20,000). The supposedly underpaid Eddie Cicotte had a salary of $8,000, making him the second-highest paid pitcher in the league behind the legendary Walter Johnson ($9,500). Buck Weaver's $7,250 salary was the second highest for a third baseman, behind Home Run Baker of the Yankees ($11,583). Chick Gandil's $3,500 salary was tied for fifth among American League first basemen, probably about where he should have ranked. The same was true for Swede Risberg, who ranked sixth among AL shortstops at $3,250. Happy Felsch's $3,750 salary was for the last year of the multiyear contract that Felsch had signed after the 1916 season; considering that he had jumped the club during the 1918 season, it would appear that Felsch had little to complain about. Perhaps the only truly underpaid player among the eight later known as the Black Sox was Lefty Williams ($2,625). However, Williams was one of the Sox players who left the team in 1918 to work in a shipyard; additionally, bonuses paid to Williams for his 1919 work increased his figure to a more reasonable $3,500.[6]

Considering his talents and accomplishments, Joe Jackson's $6,000 salary seems a pittance, but the simple truth is that throughout his career, Shoeless Joe did a very poor job of negotiating salaries; he routinely opted for the security of a multiyear contract for figures that were well below his true value. In 1914–1915, Jackson, who was then a member of the Cleveland Indians, was one of many star players who received substantial offers to join the rival Federal League. Shoeless Joe, who was loyal to the Indians, chose to spurn the offers. But unlike Cobb, Tris Speaker, or Walter Johnson, to name three, Jackson failed to use the leverage of the offer from the Feds to negotiate a better deal with the Indians. In fact, Jackson signed a multiyear contract with the Indians for only $6,000 a year, just as the Indians were about to trade him to the White Sox. According to noted baseball historian Lee Allen, Joe's wife Katie, who was dead-set against Joe joining the Federal League, was the driving force behind Jackson signing this contract. Allen wrote that Mrs. Jackson "led her husband to [Cleveland owner Charlie] Somers' office and made him sit down and sign an American League contract that tied him up for more than four years, through the season of 1919."[7]

In his biography of Comiskey, *"Commy"*—a book that, interestingly enough, was published in late 1919—Chicago sportswriter G. W. Axelson wrote,

> Comiskey has less trouble with his players than perhaps any other owner in the game. The reason is because he plays no favorites. He alone is the judge of the worth of the man he signs and after one contract there is seldom any grounds for complaints. The player depends on Comiskey for a square deal and if he delivers, he knows that he is going to get everything that is coming to him.[8]

But while Comiskey was no skinflint compared to other MLB owners, his players were well aware that "he alone is the judge of the worth of the man he signs"—and that (especially now that the Federal League was long gone) they had little leverage if they disagreed with his assessment. They also knew that game-fixing was not at all uncommon in those days, and that it generally went unpunished. "If a man can sin with impunity," wrote Eliot Asinof, "he will continue to sin—especially if he gets paid for it."[9]

If the players needed any reminder of this, they received a timely one in February 1919 when the National League acquitted Cincinnati Reds first baseman Hal Chase on a charge of game-fixing. In August of the previous year, Chase had been suspended for "indifferent playing" by his manager, Christy Mathewson, a baseball legend with a sterling reputation. It was soon learned that one of Chase's teammates, pitcher Jimmy Ring, had reported that Chase tried to bribe him to help lose a game Chase had bet on; a player on an opposing team, New York Giants pitcher Pol Perritt, had also lodged a bribe attempt against Prince Hal. When Chase denied the charges and sued the Reds for lost salary, the league scheduled a hearing to investigate the charges.

A player known both for his acrobatic defensive skills and the frequency of suspicious errors he committed, Chase had been involved in various controversies throughout his professional career, which had begun with Los Angeles of the Pacific Coast League in 1904. Several times he abandoned his team to join another club in a different league; on several other occasions he was accused of not giving his best effort, or of attempting to bribe other players to help him throw games. But things always seem to work out for Chase's benefit.

A perfect example came in 1910, when Chase was a member of the New York Yankees. Prince Hal was accused by his manager, George Stallings, of "laying down" in an effort to get Stallings fired, with Chase campaigning to

Hal Chase's acquittal by the National League on 1918 game-fixing charges may have emboldened other players—including the Black Sox—to cheat. *Library of Congress Prints and Photographs Division*

take Stallings's place. Ban Johnson himself investigated the charge and not only exonerated Chase; he laid into Stallings, writing that the manager "has utterly failed in his accusations against Chase. He has tried to besmirch the character of a sterling player."[10] Thereupon the Yankees fired Stallings and hired the sterling player to replace him as a player-manager . . . just as Chase had hoped. He was a failure as a manager, lasting one season after taking a team that had been in second place under Stallings and leading it to a sixth-place finish the next year. But Hal Chase always landed on his feet. In fact, his next stop would be the White Sox, with Comiskey trading for him in 1913. He lasted a year with the Sox before jumping the club to join the Federal League in midseason 1914. The White Sox filed suit to try to get him back, but failed. When the Federal League folded, Chase joined the Reds, winning the National League batting title in 1916 before lapsing into familiarly suspicious behavior.

In their charges against Chase for game-fixing in 1918, the Reds seemed to have Chase dead to rights. But they didn't . . . at least not in the opinion of National League President John Heydler, who was ruling on the evidence. Mathewson was now in the military, serving in Europe and unable to attend the hearing. He provided an affidavit describing various defensive lapses by Chase—miscues that Chase, who had brought three lawyers, a clerk, and a stenographer to help defend him at the hearing, could attribute to errors in judgment. Pol Perritt also provided an affidavit; however, he had no witnesses to support him, and the bribe attempt he reported did not involve any specific game or dollar figure. The key witness against Chase was Jimmy Ring, who was present at the hearing, and Ring's testimony was a mess; he was nervous and contradicted himself about several details under cross-examination by Chase's lawyers. He was no better when interviewed privately by Heydler later. Meanwhile Chase was confident and self-assured in his own testimony. He did not deny giving money to Ring, but told Heydler that his motives were pure. "If I want to slip a 20 or 50 to some kid down on his luck, so what?" said Chase. "All these rookies are underpaid anyway."[11]

In his public ruling acquitting Chase, Heydler was critical of Chase for acting "in a foolish and careless manner," and said that the Reds were justified in bringing the charges. "There was, however, no proof that he intentionally violated or attempted to violate the rules in relation to tampering with players or in any way endeavored to secure desired results in the outcome of games." He was more candid in a letter to Reds President Garry Herrmann. The only direct evidence against Chase, he told Herrmann, was that of Jimmy Ring, whose testimony before Heydler differed from what he had written in his affidavit. And that was a problem for Heydler. "To have found Chase guilty on this man's unsupported testimony would have been impossible," he told Herrmann. "The repetition of similar charges without direct and positive proof to substantiate the same will do the game irreparable harm."[12]

John Heydler served as National League president from 1918 to 1934, dying at age 86 in 1956. His ruling in the 1918–1919 Hal Chase case was probably the most controversial of his career, and many still cite it as a prime example of baseball ignoring evidence of crooked play and looking the other way. But Heydler was ruling on evidence placed before him, and it would not have been fair to find Chase guilty based on past reputation and rumors—especially given Ring's shaky testimony. In his SABR biography of Heydler, Stephen V. Rice wrote,

> Heydler had no choice but to exonerate Chase. An editorial in *Baseball Magazine* explained: Heydler "found a mass of rumors, half rumors and bare suspicions mixed in with a few suggestive facts and nothing more. Of evidence in any technical sense, there was none, and without evidence it would have been a criminal act to blast the reputation of any ball player.[13]

While his handling of the 1918 Chase case deserves some sympathy, Heydler would be much more culpable for his—and the National Commission's—failure to vigorously investigate the 1919 World Series.

Despite his acquittal by Heydler, there was plenty of circumstantial evidence against Hal Chase, which one would think would be enough to make any team hesitant to add Prince Hal to its roster. But that didn't happen, either. Two weeks after Heydler's ruling, the Reds traded Chase to John McGraw's New York Giants, a team that not only had Pol Perritt, one of Chase's main accusers, on its roster, but had added a new member to its coaching staff: Christy Mathewson. Strange bedfellows indeed. Prince Hal had landed on his feet again, and any player tempted to pick up some money by dumping games surely noticed.

In the case of the 1919 White Sox, the gamblers didn't need to go to the players. Eddie Cicotte later told a Chicago grand jury that the players began discussing a possible fix of the World Series during a train trip east (likely in August). They had heard that during the 1918 World Series, some unnamed players had been offered $10,000 to throw the Series (no evidence has ever been presented to support this claim). "We never held any secret meetings but we would meet one or two at a time and we all agreed that for a piece of money we would throw the World Series," Cicotte said. "I was supposed to get $10,000."[14]

Cicotte was smart; he insisted on getting his money in advance. Overall, however, the fixing of the 1919 World Series was done about as haphazardly as any criminal enterprise in American history. White Sox players told friends and players on other teams not to bet on Chicago; similarly, gamblers warned other gamblers. So much money was bet on the White Sox's opponents, the Cincinnati Reds, that the odds shifted in Cincinnati's favor even though the American League had won eight of the last nine World Series and the White Sox were considered one of the strongest teams in league annals. Everyone noticed, including writers who were covering the Series.

Prior to the Series the players held a couple of meetings to discuss the fix. By later accounts seven players attended the meetings: Felsch, Cicotte, Gandil, McMullin, Risberg, Weaver, and Williams; Joe Jackson did not attend, but both Williams and Jackson himself later testified that Williams kept Jackson apprised of what was being discussed. However, they never really discussed exactly *how* they would guarantee losing the series without arousing too much suspicion. Nor did they discuss how they would guarantee payment from the two groups of gamblers they were conspiring with. They left the details to Chick Gandil, who proved to be as untrustworthy as any of the gamblers.

But then, the sheer scope of the fix made it unlike anything that had ever happened before. Game-fixing had plagued baseball since professional ball had begun in the mid-nineteenth century. But this wasn't a small-scale fix involving one or two players and a few hundred dollars. This was the World Series, baseball's signature event, and a conspiracy involving over $100,000 in payoffs promised to at least half the regular position players on one of the teams, along with its two best pitchers. Little wonder that it was so difficult to keep things under control.

Yet as for how the players went about guaranteeing that they would lose the Series, and who did what to see that it happened, the truthful answer is: we'll never know for sure. "There are uncharacteristic plays and some suspicious moments," wrote Charles Fountain, "but over the course of nearly a century there has been no confirmation that any of the plays, however carefully dissected, were indeed deliberate errors."[15] Maybe they weren't trying to lose at all. For most of the rest of their lives, the players involved in the game-fixing discussions all insisted that while they may have taken money from gamblers, they played to win once the games began. (Buck Weaver by all accounts never received any money, though the testimony of others stated that he attended at least two of the planning meetings.)

We will never know for sure. But just as you can't prove that the players who would become known as the Black Sox played dishonestly in the 1919 World Series, you can't prove they played *honestly* in every game situation, either. We do know, without much if any doubt, that seven players accepted a substantial amount of money for promising to lose the Series—and then proceeded to do so. To me, giving them the benefit of the doubt about the honesty of their play seems like quite a stretch.

The actions of the White Sox players before, during, and after the 1919 World Series is still a subject of vigorous debate more than 100 years later. And so are the actions of Charles Comiskey, who was aware that something suspicious was going on almost as soon as the World Series began. According to the diary of Comiskey's secretary, Harry Grabiner, excerpts from which were published in Bill Veeck's 1965 book, *Hustler's Handbook*, a Chicago gambler named Mont Tennes had contacted the White Sox after Game 1 and alerted them that the odds had shifted suspiciously toward Cincinnati prior to the first game. After the White Sox also lost Game 2 in a somewhat suspicious fashion, Comiskey had Grabiner contact John Heydler, a member of the three-person National Commission. Heydler was the logical choice for Comiskey to contact, as he had no faith that he would be treated fairly by his archenemy Ban Johnson, and the third member of the Commission was Garry Herrmann, owner of the

Reds, Chicago's World Series opponents. "Heydler could not believe that there could be anything wrong, as he said rumors regarding World Series had always cropped up," Grabiner wrote, "but I insisted that as my duty to baseball that if anything did exist expedient action should be taken." When Grabiner persisted, Heydler relayed Comiskey's suspicions to Johnson, who had already been alerted about the fix rumors by both noted Chicago baseball writer Hughie Fullerton and *Sporting News* publisher J. G. Taylor Spink, a Johnson ally. But Johnson dismissed Comiskey's suspicions, supposedly telling Heydler, "That's the yelp of a beaten cur!"[16] When the rumors persisted, especially after the White Sox lost the World Series, the dysfunctional National Commission still made no investigation. With Johnson in a battle to hold on to his power against an insurrection led by the White Sox, Red Sox, and Yankees, and Garry Herrmann facing pressure to resign his spot, the commission was on its last legs.

With the National Commission seemingly uninterested, Comiskey took it upon himself to investigate his own team—something that could easily lead to a conflict of interest between getting the truth and the possible destruction of his own team. And that's what happened; for the rest of his life, Comiskey's investigation would be plagued by questions. Had he been thorough, or did he go just far enough to ensure he didn't find something overly incriminating? Was he looking for the truth, or just a way to hide what really happened so that he could re-sign his players? Was he trying to save baseball, or trying to preserve the value of his own franchise? It never stopped.

Comiskey's suspicions ran deep from the beginning. On October 10, the day after the World Series ended, Hugh Fullerton, a tireless reporter and an investigator of high moral standards, wrote a nationally syndicated column that included some provocative speculation. "Today's game in all probability is the last that ever will be played in any world's series," he wrote. "Today's game also means the disruption of the Chicago White Sox as a ballclub. There are seven men on the team who will not be there when the gong sounds next spring and some of them will not be in either major league."[17] Fullerton did not name the players, but he later revealed that Comiskey was the source of this information; in fact Commy had shared his misgivings about his team to Fullerton before the Series even started.

A day after the publication of Fullerton's explosive column, the *New York Times* reported that Comiskey was offering $20,000 (a figure reported, probably more accurately, as $10,000 by other sources) for evidence that the White Sox threw the World Series. He also withheld the World Series paychecks of the suspect players for a period of time. He indicated, at least for public consumption, that he did not expect much. "I believe my boys fought the battles of the recent World Series on the level, as they have always done," he said, "and I would be the first to want information to the contrary."[18]

He quickly got a nibble. Two White Sox fans who had lost money betting on the Sox in the World Series, Max Ascher and Sam Pass, contacted Sox manager Kid Gleason and advised him to get in touch with an East St. Louis, Illinois-based theater owner and gambler named Harry Redmon. Gleason and Sox executive Tip O'Neill traveled to East St. Louis the next day and met with Redmon. A year later, Comiskey summarized the meeting as follows: "Redmond's [sic] story to Gleason and O'Neill was of such vague and uncertain character that no one would have been justified in taking affirmative action as would destroy the character and reputation of men, even though they were ball players."[19]

We know from Harry Grabiner's diary that Redmon's tale was hardly "vague and uncertain." This is what he wrote about the meeting:

> The players were supposed to have received $15,000 per game from the gamblers. The go between for the players was supposed to be [St. Louis Browns second baseman Joe] Gedeon and [former major league pitcher] Bill Burns while [former boxing champion] Abe Attell was to handle the betting. The gamblers who paid for the fix were [Carl] Zork, Redmon, [Ben] Franklin, a St. Louis mule buyer, and 2 Levi brothers from Des Moines. The name of [Arnold] Rothstein was also mentioned. The players on the White Sox mentioned as being: Williams, Jackson, Felsch, McMullin, Risberg, Gandil, Cicotte and Weaver, the last two both being crooked in the first game and then turning.[20]

This proved to be mostly accurate information. Although Redmon denied being in the room with the players, he offered to put the White Sox in touch with Carl Zork, who he said had been present.

What Redmon told Gleason and O'Neill would have been enough to blow the scandal wide open if Redmon was willing to stand by his story in public . . . which frankly seems doubtful. After the scandal broke open in September 1920, Hugh Fullerton wrote that Gleason had cornered the man who was accused of bribing the players and "is said to have choked him and tried to force a confession from him"; he added that "one of Gleason's close friends" had told him, "The man told him he was afraid to squeal for fear he would meet the fate that another St. Louis gambler who had been killed, had met." When Redmon testified about his role in the scandal before a Chicago grand jury in October 1920, he claimed that he had no involvement in payment to the players ("The money was never raised, it was dropped right there as soon as I knew anything about it"). He also denied that he had wanted any reward for passing along information to the White Sox. Carl Zork, who Redmon testified "wanted to bring his lawyer along" when he met with Gleason and O'Neill in October 1919, filed an affidavit for the same grand jury that stated, "I never had any conference either in St. Louis or Chicago with baseball players or anyone else or aided, abetted, involved, suggested, inspired or advised that the World Series or any one game thereof should be fixed."[21]

But whether or not Redmon and/or Zork would publicly attest to what they knew about the scandal, Comiskey had to be disturbed by what Redmon told him. For the time being, at least, he kept the information under wraps.

In the meantime, the notion that there was something crooked about the 1919 World Series was being widely ridiculed in the nation's sporting press. Christy Mathewson, who had heard the fix rumors and had sat with Fullerton during the series as the two agreed to look out for suspicious plays, said in the last of a series of columns he had written about the World Series for the *New York Times*, "The rumors and mutterings about the honesty of the series are ridiculous to me." He then described how difficult it would be to fix a game and wrote, "I honestly think that if ball players on a world's series team found their fellows trying to toss one off they would kill the guilty ones."[22]

The nation's leading baseball paper, the *Sporting News*, published a number of stories asserting that the notion of crooked play was ridiculous. In a story about Comiskey's offer of a $10,000 reward for evidence of a fix, the paper scoffed, "He might as well have offered a million, for there will be no takers, because there is no such evidence except in the mucky minds of the slinkers who because they are crooked think all the rest of the world can't play straight." The same article contains a notorious anti-Semitic slur against the gamblers who lost money on the series, under the assumption that most of them were Jewish: "Because a lot of dirty, long-nosed, thick-lipped and strong-smelling gamblers butted into the World's Series—an American event, by the way—and some of said gamblers got crossed, stories were peddled that there was some-thing wrong with the way the games were played."[23]

There was still a brave few who took the fix talk seriously. One was a gambling-oriented publication called *Collyer's Eye*; its editor, Bert Collyer, was unafraid to print articles full of rumors and speculation, sometimes based on scant or nonexistent evidence (one example: a since debunked claim that the White Sox had promised Eddie Cicotte a $10,000 bonus if he won 30 games in 1919) but often containing material about the Series fix that would prove to be spot-on. In November 1919, *Collyer's Eye* became the first publication to publicly name the eight players under investigation. Also still on the case was Hugh Fullerton, who had moved his base of operations from the *Chicago Her-ald and Examiner* to the *New York World* shortly after his explosive October

11 column (amid talk that the *Herald and Examiner* wanted him to tone down his muckraking). Fullerton would soon use his new forum to resume calling on baseball to investigate the possibility that the 1919 World Series had been fixed.

In November, Charles Comiskey was back in action. First, he had Harry Redmon come to Chicago to meet directly with him, and claimed he learned nothing new. "He could not give us any names, circumstances or facts upon which we could base a charge of crookedness and substantiate the same against any ball players engaged in the World Series," Comiskey commented in his November 1920 statement.[24]

The same month, Comiskey hired Hunter's Secret Service, a detective agency, to investigate persons of interest potentially involved in the alleged fixing of the 1919 World Series. Their White Sox contact was Comiskey's attorney, Alfred S. Austrian. Hunter and his operatives were tasked with spying on White Sox players and the St. Louis–based gamblers Harry Redmon said were involved in the fix.

Their first reports came out of St. Louis. One of the gamblers, Joe Pesch, owned a billiard hall, and Hunter's operative "E. W. M." dutifully began hanging out and playing pool with the regulars. He learned that taking bets on baseball was a substantial part of the poolroom's business and got pretty close to an employee named Al Roseberger, who told him: "There is no doubt in my mind but that the games were tossed by Cicotte and Williams; but just who was in on the deal, I do not know. I believe it will never be found out. Kid Gleason of the White Sox was here in St. Louis for three or four days, making an investigation. I do not believe he got anything definite."[25]

E. W. M. did not find out much about Carl Zork, other than the fact that he was president of the Supreme Waist Company and that "I find him to be a man who does not hang out about the [hotel] lobby." There was no "Abe Attell" listed in the St. Louis City Directory. Ultimately Hunter concluded that his St. Louis operative "was unable to connect up any absolute transaction that would warrant charging any player with conspiracy."[26]

In a series of articles that began in mid-December and continued into the new year, Hugh Fullerton called on baseball, particularly the National Commission, to investigate the charge that the 1919 World Series was fixed. In one of these columns Fullerton mentioned that he had asked Kenesaw Mountain Landis, then still a federal judge, "whether he will accept the responsibility of conducting an investigation if the powers of baseball are willing to submit the entire matter to him and assist him in bringing witnesses before him. I have asked Comiskey to use all his influence to bring about this investigation as quickly as possible."[27]

It is fascinating to speculate how the investigation of the Black Sox scandal would have changed had Landis assumed a major role in baseball—most likely as the head of the National Commission—at the start of 1920, rather than at the end of the year, when he agreed to become baseball's first commissioner . . . with dictatorial powers. The truth might have been uncovered far earlier, and many reputations might have been saved major damage. That includes Charles A. Comiskey, assuming that Comiskey had been willing to share the results of his investigation with Landis (something he was decidedly unwilling to do with Ban Johnson).

But that didn't happen, for a variety of reasons. So rightly or wrongly, logically or not, the job of investigating the suspicious behavior of the Chicago White Sox fell, by default, to the owner of the team. On December 30 the *Chicago Tribune* reported that Comiskey had met again with Harry Redmon, along with fellow gambler Joe Pesch. Harry Grabiner and Comiskey's attorney, Alfred Austrian, were also at the meeting. "The St. Louis parties came here at the request of Mr. Comiskey," Grabiner told James Crusinberry. "There had not been any rumors that they could give information of value. It developed, however, that they could only tell what some one else had told them and that they knew nothing we hadn't heard before."[28]

Crusinberry's December 30 *Tribune* story noted that one of the reports from St. Louis was that three members of the White Sox had met with Redmon and Pesch and said they were willing to throw one game a week during the championship season in exchange for $200 a game. "It was said the St. Louis men were willing to testify to that effect, but so far as is known the rumor didn't hold up at yesterday's conference."[29]

The suggestion that Sox players were also dumping 1919 regular season games is fascinating. Hugh Fullerton later identified the three players in question as Risberg, Williams, and Felsch. In a 2012 article for the journal *Base Ball*, authors Timothy Newman and Bruce Stuckman noted that Williams and Felsch, who had left the White Sox for war-related industrial work during the 1918 season, were undoubtedly short of money; that both held grudges against Comiskey for various reasons; and that Williams had been a minor league teammate of St. Louis Browns second baseman Joe Gedeon, a player with ties to St. Louis–based gambler Carl Zork. They pointed out that in his first three home starts against the Browns in 1919, Williams had allowed 10 runs and 14 hits in only six and a third innings pitched. These games featured some very suspicious defensive work by Felsch, who was 1-for-9 at bat in the three games (in the same contest Risberg had 2 hits in 11 at-bats, but committed no errors).[30]

Interesting stuff to be sure, but based on only a handful of games with no direct evidence of crookedness. In the meantime, Comiskey had more reports from his detectives coming in—this time about White Sox players.

3

DETECTIVE STORIES

On January 2, Hugh Fullerton posted his first column of 1920. In "an open New Year's letter to major league officials and club owners," he referred to the "grave charges" that had been made regarding a fixed 1919 World Series:

> I am rather shocked to discover that some of your number have tried recently to raise the charge that certain writers, among them myself, started these stories. These stories were not started, nor were they circulated, by baseball writers. They started before the series was played, were circulated during the series, and were so widespread in the West that detectives were employed to watch players.
>
> The scandal became so insistent that C. A. Comiskey, owner of the White Sox, was compelled in self-defense to investigate and to offer a large sum for proof that his players did not try to win. I never have indicated by a written word what I thought. From the time Mr. Comiskey made the offer, I have insisted that it is the duty of organized baseball to go to the bottom of the entire case, and either find those boys guilty or innocent.
>
> Unfortunately the National Commission has made no move. . . . One member of the Commission at least knew about the stories that were going around the morning of the second game of the series. Had he done his duty he would have started the investigation and then and there. He did not.[1]

Fullerton was referring to National League President John Heydler, with whom Comiskey had shared his misgivings in the early stages of the series. And Heydler had passed those misgivings on to Comiskey's bitter enemy, American League President Ban Johnson. Yet even Johnson dismissed the idea that a World Series could be fixed. In his serialized memoirs, published by the *St. Louis Post-Dispatch* in 1929, Johnson wrote, "The failure of a St. Louis gambler to get anywhere with the framing of the series the year before indicated that it would be impossible for conspirators ever to handle enough money to make buying the players worthwhile. Thus our guard was down when the blow fell."[2]

That was a common sentiment in baseball circles. Sportswriter Fred Lieb told Johnson biographer Eugene Murdock, "I said to myself they might fix a player, but they could not fix a whole team. I could understand how they might get to a man like [Hal] Chase, but never in my wildest dreams did I see how they could get to eight men on a team." *Baseball Magazine*, one of the game's unofficial organs, thought the possibility of a fix so absurd that it began regularly attacking and ridiculing Hugh Fullerton. In one editorial the magazine huffed, "It has proved . . . impossible to prevent Mr. Fullerton from making a public nuisance of himself, but we hope the National Commission or the Society for the Prevention of Armenian Outrages will be able to do something for him. He needs it."[3]

In his serialized memoirs, Johnson wrote that he might have taken action after John Heydler passed on Charles Comiskey's misgivings, if not for an undelivered message. According to Johnson, a St. Louis–based betting commissioner named Thomas Kearney had told one of the St. Louis Browns' major stockholders to alert Johnson that he was certain Game 1 had been thrown, based on the large volume of bets on Cincinnati. The stockholder considered the possibility of a fix so impossible that he did not bother to relay the tip. "Had that tip not gone astray," wrote Johnson, "I would have at once called the commission together to discuss action with the probability that the series would have been halted or perhaps called off, until the atmosphere could be cleared."[4] This is a nice story, one designed to make Johnson appear vigilant about possible game-fixing, but it doesn't make a lot of sense. Pretty much everyone in Chicago for the World Series was aware of the huge amount of money being bet on the Reds; Johnson did not need to be alerted to the news by someone in St. Louis.

However, Johnson did learn of Kid Gleason's post–World Series trip to St. Louis, writing, "All that came of this, I believe, was a threat by Gleason to whip one of the parties." Johnson then made his own trip to St. Louis and "had conversations with several persons involved." According to Harry Grabiner's diary, one of the people Johnson spoke to was Harry Redmon. But Johnson did not learn anything that he felt he could use. "Much of the evidence we did assemble was hearsay and circumstantial," he wrote. "None connected with the affair had as yet volunteered to turn State's evidence. Players involved could not be named openly for lack of proof. They sat tight and with effrontery faced it out."[5] Johnson sat tight as well.

One outlet unafraid to openly name the players under investigation was the ever-provocative *Collyer's Eye*. In its December 13 issue, "Special Investigator for Collyer's News Bureau" Frank O. Klein (possibly a pseudonym for *CE* publisher Bert Collyer) wrote, "Scandal talk and attendant betting coups anent the recent world's series was revived to-day when it was stated that Ray Schalk, doughty catcher for the Pale Hose, gave it as his opinion that Pitchers Williams, First Baseman Gandill [*sic*], Infielders McMullen [*sic*] and Risberg, and Outfielders Felsch and Jackson would be missing from the line-up in 1920." The same story also mentioned that Schalk was "reported as having trounced both Williams and Cicotte following games in which it was claimed that both pitchers deliberately double-crossed Schalk's signals"; that Comiskey had reneged on his promise of a $10,000 bonus to Cicotte for winning 30 games (a feat that the magazine mistakenly thought Cicotte had accomplished); that Cicotte had "fallen off the 'wagon'" on Chicago's last Eastern road trip and then "fell IN with certain 'interests' who afterwards were accused of framing the world's series and who, is positively known, cleaned up a moderate fortune on the outcome." It concluded with a report that Gandil "had purchased a new home and intended on embarking in the fruit-growing industry."[6]

Per this story, we now know that no evidence has ever surfaced that Cicotte was promised a $10,000 bonus; given that Cicotte's *salary* was less than $10,000, and that he was already one of the highest paid pitchers in baseball, it stretches credulity. We also know that Schalk spent the rest of his life denying that he had accosted either Cicotte or Williams (though many believed he was covering for Comiskey). As for Klein's report that Schalk had said that the seven White Sox players would not return in 1920, the Sox catcher neither confirmed nor denied it for several weeks. When he finally spoke to Chicago writer Oscar Reichow in a story published in the January 8, 1920 issue of the *Sporting News*, he not only denied making the quote, but insisted that the Series had been on the level. "I played in that World's Series and played to the best of my ability. I feel that every man on our club did the same, and there was not a single moment of all the games in which we did not try," said Schalk. "What I have to say is that it is not true that I said seven numbers of the White Sox would be found missing when the 1920 season began." Reichow, a veteran reporter for the *Chicago Daily News*, also stood up for the integrity of the series. He wrote that Schalk had caught every game and "is too smart a catcher to let any crookedness escape him." If anything was amiss, Reichow felt, Schalk and Eddie Collins would have noticed it.[7]

What happened here? Did *Collyer's Eye* get this part of the story wrong as well? Ray Schalk was notoriously tight-lipped when talking about the 1919 World Series, then and later, especially with reporters. Schalk biographer Brian E. Cook speculated that Ray may well have expressed the sentiments quoted in the story, but perhaps not directly to Klein, who may have overheard the

White Sox catcher Ray Schalk disowned statements attributed to him that the 1919 World Series had been fixed—perhaps to protect Charles Comiskey. *Library of Congress Prints and Photographs Division*

comments or been told about them secondhand. Rather than get into a controversy about the Series, Schalk may have thought it prudent to deny everything and say, "I saw nothing that looked crooked." Given his stance when asked about the scandal over the rest of his life, that seems a lot like Ray. Black Sox historian Gene Carney, among others, saw something more nefarious: he felt that Comiskey had already decided to cover up the truth about the scandal and was preparing to re-sign the players for 1920. So he told Ray to toe the party line. Given Comiskey's subsequent actions, that is not an unreasonable conclusion.[8]

By the time Ray Schalk had repudiated the *Collyer's Eye* story, Comiskey's detectives had been spying on White Sox players for more than a month. They weren't looking into *all* of the players who would later be known as the Black Sox, however. J. R. Hunter, the owner of the firm, was in California, home (or winter base) of Chick Gandil, Buck Weaver, and Fred McMullin. Another operative was looking into the activities of Happy Felsch in Milwaukee, while one was in Chicago, attempting to get information on Swede Risberg by befriending two women known to be close to Risberg.

For reasons never made clear, during this time period the operatives apparently did not spy on Eddie Cicotte, Joe Jackson, or Lefty Williams—the three players who would later confess their involvement in the scandal to a Chicago grand jury. They also did not investigate Risberg directly; like Gandil, Weaver, and McMullin, the Swede was spending the winter in California, but he was in the San Francisco area while the other three were in Los Angeles. Hunter made plans to go to San Francisco to check on Risberg after his Los Angeles work was done, but the White Sox pulled the plug on this idea, focusing instead on Swede's female friends in Chicago.

Williams spent the off-season in Wilmington, Delaware, once again working in a shipyard; in addition to the cost of sending a detective to the East Coast, that likely would have been a difficult atmosphere for a spy to remain discreet. The same applied to Jackson, who spent the winter in Savannah, Georgia, a Deep South city where a stranger from the North asking questions would have certainly aroused suspicion.

In Jackson's case, some scandal analysts assert that the White Sox didn't need to spy on him because Joe had already come to them after the World Series ended, bringing his payoff money and ready to spill the beans . . . only to be shown the door. Hearing this story, the analysts say, would have given Comiskey the direct proof of the scandal that he claimed to want but really desired to cover up.

The claim that Jackson attempted to spill the beans immediately after the World Series is often treated as established fact, but there is much reason to doubt that it ever happened. Over the course of his life Jackson would make varying claims about his knowledge of, and involvement in, the fix. Often these claims were not made until several (and sometimes many) years after the 1919

World Series, and they frequently contradicted, and in some cases improved upon, previous Jackson statements. In this case Joe's story, as related in a deposition, was that "I knew nothing about the throwing of the 1919 World Series until two or three days after the Series was over," when he was shocked to receive a dirty envelope with $5,000 from Lefty Williams. Without Joe's knowledge or permission, "certain players had used my name in negotiating with gamblers . . . that I was to help throw the games against my own team." This was a lie, as he had "played my very best during this series."[9]

"The very next day," continued Jackson, "I went to Charles Comiskey's office with the envelope containing the $5,000 and attempted to interview the club president concerning the transaction with Williams." Harry Grabiner, however, "slammed the door in my face" and told Joe to "beat it." When Grabiner traveled to Savannah in February 1920 to sign Jackson to a new contract, he told Joe that the White Sox "knew all about the facts concerning the payment of $5,000 to me by Lefty Williams," and that Grabiner "told me that they had the absolute goods on Cicotte, Williams and Gandil."[10]

These explosive claims were first made by Jackson in April 1923, in a civil suit that Shoeless Joe had filed against the White Sox for unpaid salary. As we will later see, the timing of the payment from Williams was in direct contradiction to the grand jury testimony of both Williams and Jackson himself in the fall of 1920; both said during their testimony that the payment had taken place *during* the Series, after Game 4. (It is important to note here that while Jackson, Williams, and Cicotte tried to repudiate their grand jury testimony at their 1921 criminal trial, their attorneys "made no claim that the accused had not spoken the words attributed to them in the grand jury record," according to retired prosecutor and Black Sox legal expert Bill Lamb.[11] The repudiation was based on an alleged promise of immunity made to the players.)

By the time his civil suit against the White Sox went to trial in 1924, Jackson had changed the timeline of the payment from Williams and the aborted visit to Comiskey from "two or three days after the World Series"—by which time both he and Williams had left Chicago—to the night of and day after the final game of the Series. This is perhaps a minor discrepancy, but not so for the differing dates in which Joe said he received the money. If he received money during the Series but neglected to report it while the fix continued, he was obviously part of the conspiracy whether or not he was playing to win. Jackson's explanation for the 180-degree difference on the dates and reasons for the payments from Williams was to absurdly state, "I never said that" (in 1920) over 100 times when his grand jury testimony was read back to him . . . leading the judge to issue a citation for perjury. The excerpts from Harry Grabiner's diary quoted in Bill

Veeck's *Hustler's Handbook* made no mention of a post–World Series visit from Jackson. Grabiner was a witness at Jackson's 1924 civil trial, and testified under oath that when he visited Jackson to talk contract in February 1920, the 1919 World Series was not discussed. If he was challenged during the trial about this or about blowing off Jackson in that supposed post–World Series visit, I am unaware of it.

But while the more sensational aspects of Jackson's 1923 deposition seem to be of questionable veracity, it is fair to ask: Why didn't Grabiner and the White Sox, who had elected not to send a detective to look into Jackson's off-season behavior, use this opportunity to grill Joe directly? They had the chance. On October 27, less than three weeks after the World Series ended, Jackson—presumably with his wife Katie wielding the pen for the illiterate Shoeless Joe—wrote to Comiskey, complaining about the delay in receiving his check for the player's share of the 1919 World Series money. Comiskey responded on November 11: "In answer to your recent communication, wish to state that there has been a great deal of adverse talk in which your name has been mentioned, along with several others, referring to and reflecting on your integrity in the recent World's Series." Comiskey added that he had nothing to do with the distribution of the shares, and that the National Commission had turned over the money to Kid Gleason for distribution. The letter concluded, "Would gladly pay your expenses to Chicago and return if you wish to come on in reference to the matter emanating from the World's Series."[12]

Jackson responded on November 15, writing (the misspellings are Katie's), "I sure am surprised to hear that my name has been connected with any scandle in the recent World Saries, as I think that my playing proved that I did all I could to win." He offered "to come to Chicago or any place you may say and clear my name and whoever started this will have to prove his statements."[13] The letter made no mention of the $5,000 he was supposedly shocked to receive, or the "important news" he later said he had wanted to share with Comiskey after the Series. It sounds, frankly, like the story Joe would tell for most of the rest of his life: I played honestly. I had no involvement with the people who were in on the fix. I couldn't be involved: look at my batting and fielding record! And perhaps he would have spun the same tale if the team had accepted his offer to come to Chicago . . . but barely a month after the World Series was over, they did not give him the opportunity to directly discuss things with them. That has to cast some doubt on the thoroughness of their investigation.

The failure to have Hunter's detectives investigate Eddie Cicotte is another troubling aspect of Comiskey's post–World Series behavior. Cicotte lived in the Detroit area, not that far from Chicago, and assigning a detective to him would not have seemed a major expense. Comiskey told Hugh Fullerton that the day after the 1919 World Series ended, he had sent for Cicotte to give him his World Series money and final paycheck, saying, "Tell him I want to give him his checks and talk to him."[14] But Cicotte left without going to the office. If that's what happened, maybe the Sox figured Cicotte was stonewalling and that there was no point in sending an agent to Michigan. But they couldn't know that for sure.

In addition, there was a line of inquiry about Cicotte right in Chicago that the White Sox apparently failed to utilize. In his summary of Harry Grabiner's diary, Bill Veeck noted this item from right after the World Series ended: "Mrs. Kelley at whose apartments the Cicottes live said that she overheard Cicotte say to his brother while in the bathroom, 'The hell with them I got mine.'"[15] The woman in question was Henrietta Kelley, Sox fan and landlady to Eddie Cicotte and his brother Jack, along with Sox players John Collins and Roy Wilkinson; Eddie Collins and Ray Schalk were said to be personal friends. Some sources suggest that Mrs. Kelley was Eddie and Jack Cicotte's sister, but that does not appear to be the case; an Ancestry.com search indicates that she was born in Canada to parents who were natives of the British Isles.

If the White Sox followed up on Mrs. Kelley's claim during the 1919–1920 off-season, there is no record of it. However, when a Chicago grand jury began looking into the 1919 World Series in September 1920, the quote resurfaced; Mrs. Kelley was dubbed the "Mystery Woman" and expected to provide explosive testimony. Some thought she did just that. A syndicated piece by James Kilgallen on the "inside story of the scandal" published on October 31, 1920, claimed, "When Cicotte read her testimony the next morning he began to weaken" and finally agreed to confess. In actuality Mrs. Kelley did not testify before the grand jury until *after* Cicotte (who appeared immediately before her) had confessed, blunting most of its potential impact. Her actual testimony may not have been incriminating to Cicotte anyway. Though at least one Chicago paper reported that Mrs. Kelley repeated the "I got mine" quote during her testimony, she herself denied it. "I don't know anything," she told reporters. "I never overheard any conversations . . . that would in any way help this investigation."[16]

Would it have helped the White Sox to go to Cicotte with Mrs. Kelley's information during the 1919–1920 off-season to see if he'd crack? Or send an investigator to her boarding house to try to get more information? It wouldn't have hurt to try. This is another situation in which the Sox could have taken more decisive action, but didn't, that was bound create suspicion about the thoroughness of their investigation.

The first player on whom Hunter's detectives filed reports was Happy Felsch, beginning in November of 1919. At the time Felsch was away on a hunting trip, but he did not appear to be living in the lap of luxury. "Operative #11" wrote that Felsch lived in a "rather poor neighborhood" with his wife, mother-in-law, father-in-law, sister-in-law, and the sister-in-law's two children. The home consisted of eight rooms with no bath ("the family is also crowded for sleeping quarters"), for which they paid $22.00 per month. Talks with neighbors and visits to nearby saloons yielded no useful information. Operative #11 then asked his home office for help, and a second detective, "Operative A. B. G.," joined him on November 21, posing as an oil lease salesman who wanted to connect with someone in the family with money to invest. This went nowhere and the detectives continued to be unable to make contact with Felsch, who was often out of town.

Finally, on December 12, Operative #11 had some good news to report. He had observed that a lot near Felsch's home was filled with Christmas trees and had learned that these were being sold by Felsch; the man on duty was Happy's father-in-law. The operative purchased a large tree. Finally making direct contact with Felsch, he said he was interested in purchasing a large number of trees. During the conversation that followed, Felsch mentioned that he had recently purchased a five-passenger Hupmobile for $1,875. He told the detective that "while trying to crank the machine, the handle slipped from his hand and hit him in the lip, making a big gash and loosening several teeth, so on this account he has decided to let his machine alone until milder weather sets in." The next morning the operative purchased 25 trees from Felsch.[17]

After the trees had been delivered, the detective and Felsch went to a saloon, where they had drinks, smoked cigars, and played pool until noon with several of Happy's friends. "Leaving the saloon, we then proceeded to his home, where he entertained me by playing the player piano which he purchased a short time ago for $560. During all this time very little was said about baseball, and on account of our short acquaintance did not make it advisable to press the subject." The operative helped gain Felsch's confidence by purchasing another 190 trees, saying that he had secured an order from the "Independent Market Co." Over the next few days the two continued to meet, playing cards and going to saloons; the detective's wife even went on a shopping trip with the Felsches. The operative also went to watch Felsch bowl. When the subject of baseball came up, Felsch spoke only in general terms. He mentioned that he and Cicotte were "bed partners while on the road"; in a conversation about the various team owners and officials, he said, without mentioning anyone by name, that "many of the officials have a great graft, the same as officials of a regular business."[18]

Substitute infielder Fred McMullin played an important role in the 1919 World Series fix by providing misleading scouting reports on the Cincinnati Reds. *National Baseball Hall of Fame and Museum*

On December 19, Operative #11 accompanied Felsch and a few of Happy's friends on a fishing trip to Beaver Lake, Wisconsin, that lasted several days. During the trip they talked about sports, including baseball. In one conversation Felsch "admitted all sports could be faked, even baseball . . . 'F' stated that it would be an easy matter for certain officials for club owners to have an understanding regarding a team ahead—to let a lower team get ahead or near the top, either by having one of the players make a fumble or miss; or the catcher can more easily give a player a bum steer and have him put out. He explained at length there are ways that this could be done, but nothing was said particularly touching on the matter we are interested in. Regarding the Worlds Series, he claims that he and the team were over confident and out of luck, because they had a much stronger team than their opponents and expected to walk away with the series." The operative added that "I find he readily speaks on a ball players moves, but when the conversation leads to matter under investigation, he is inclined, either to drop or change the subject."[19]

Operative #11 wrote that while he was away on the trip with Felsch, "my wife and Mrs. F "got real chummy" and talked about their husbands and their business. "Mrs. F said that before the World Series she and F were confident of winning and very much disappointed, also disgusted with their pitching staff, whom they blame for losing the games. They feel that Williams, the pitcher, was in no condition to pitch so an important game after being cautioned by the manager the day before not to drink. It seems that Williams some way or other procured whiskey or it was given to him by an outsider. This resulted in his losing the game."[20]

Operative #11 filed his final report on January 8, after returning from another fishing trip with Felsch. During one conversation on this trip the operative "had an opportunity to mention about a $10,000 reward that was offered for information of any dishonesty on the part of the players in the World Series games. . . . He did not seem at all interested and only said he had heard of it. Claims that he cannot imagine that any player would stoop so low, and deserve the opinion that's some hard loser has probably caused such a rumor to be spread. . . . My observation to date: I believe that 'F' is innocent, but at the same time believe he knows more than he cares to tell."[21]

While J. R. Hunter's operatives were at work in St. Louis and Milwaukee, Hunter himself was in Los Angeles to get information on or from Chick Gandil, Buck Weaver, and Fred McMullin. Like Operative #11, he had brought along his wife with the thought that she might befriend the players' spouses, but none of his reports indicated that this happened.

On November 26, Hunter telegraphed Alfred Austrian: "I am making some headway. Connected with McMillen [*sic*] who is now assisting me in meeting other players and friends of theirs. Important meeting next Friday night. May get some inside information at that time. As soon as I get something definitely will write fully."[22]

The reasons for Fred McMullin's involvement in the 1919 World Series fix have been a subject for debate since his banishment. A reserve infielder, McMullin batted only twice in the series, with one hit. Some writers, including Eliot Asinof, have felt that he became part of the conspiracy purely by accident; supposedly he overheard conversations about the planning of the fix and the other players cut him in to make sure he kept quiet. Others see his role as much more substantial, and some have considered him one of the ringleaders. But one role that he played for the team may have proven to be crucial: White Sox manager Kid Gleason assigned McMullin to scout the White Sox's opponents, the Cincinnati Reds, prior to the Series and file a report for the other players to use.

There is evidence that McMullin filed a phony scouting report that deliberately hampered the nonconspirators—the so-called Clean Sox. In his online newsletter, *Pages from Baseball's Past*, baseball historian Craig R. Wright analyzed the World Series performance of the Clean Sox position players compared to their Black Sox teammates. During the Series the Clean Sox batted .209 with a .504 on-base-plus-slugging percentage (OPS) . . . the Black Sox, who supposedly were *trying* to play badly at least some of the time, batted .255 with a .655 OPS (during the regular season, the two groups had performed almost identically in terms of OPS). The Clean Sox also struck out almost 60 percent more in the Series than expected, based on their proportional strikeout rates during the regular season. However, the Clean Sox performed significantly better in their second starts against Reds pitchers Hod Eller, Dutch Ruether, and Slim Sallee than in their first games against this trio—consistent with the notion that they had learned to rely on their own experience rather than McMullin's dubious scouting report. "We have motive, opportunity, and anomalies in the Series that fit a falsified scouting report being part of the effort to throw the Series to Cincinnati," concluded Wright. "Understanding the 'McMullin Factor' is a key element in better understanding what happened in the World Series 100 years ago."[23]

In late November, Hunter was able to connect with McMullin, who was working in the blacksmith shop of the Southern Pacific Railroad. Hunter wrote Alfred Austrian that "without disclosing my motive in talking to him, I found that he was very frank and outspoken. I established a standing with him through an official of the Southern Pacific R.R. where he is employed, and without going

Trailed by Charles Comiskey's detectives in the 1919–1920 off-
season, Oscar (Happy) Felsch later confessed his guilt to a reporter.
Library of Congress Prints and Photographs Division

into details I connected up with him both at his house and at my hotel." He summarized what McMullin told him in six paragraphs. Here are the highlights:

I am exceedingly sorry that the White Sox lost the championship games this year, as it throws suspicion on their players who participated in the games, myself included, and I would do anything to develop the true facts, as Baseball would be a dead issue if anything of that kind could be put over. . . .

If there was any frame-up to throw the game to Cincinnati, I knew nothing about it, and I am satisfied that there was other players beside myself who are in ignorance of any arrangement of that kind. If you analyze the situation from a scientific standpoint, you will readily see that there are only two men who could actually throw the game, and they are the pitcher and the catcher. There are others, of course who could contribute toward that end but they could not make it absolute. You could take it from me that if the game was fixed these gamblers did not reach but a very few of the players, possibly two or three, as that was all that was necessary. . . . An infielder or an outfielder could not do much as they might not have an opportunity to catch or pass a ball during the game that would have much bearing on the result. But it is very different with the catcher and the pitcher; they can absolutely control the situation.

While I do not want to accuse anyone, I am perfectly frank to say there were two men particularly—one man whose playing was absolutely a disappointment; they are Cicotte and Williams—the former especially so.[24]

McMullin went on to say that for Cicotte "to make such a poor showing during the final games was, to say the least, disappointment, and subject to suspicion." He called Williams's pitching "also disappointing, but not so marked." And he added that Gandil "showed up very poorly, and I could hardly figure him out." (So much for honor among thieves.) McMullin concluded that "the whole thing looks bad, and is open to suspicion, and on a general summing up our team as a whole did not make a proper showing. That result would occur if anyone, who is entrusted to an important situation in the game, was dishonest. He could in turn throw the whole organization out of line."[25]

McMullin told Hunter that he would see Gandil and would "get down to brass tacks with him as a matter of self-preservation, and see what I can rope out of him"; he said he would also see Weaver "and I will then meet you and we will work along such lines as you suggest." He later telephoned Hunter and said he was unable to get in touch with either player, but that he had made an appointment to see Gandil the following Sunday. Hunter concluded his report by writing, "I am satisfied that McMellan [sic] is honest in his intentions and will do anything he can; but he is very much worried that anything should leak out which would uncover him. I assured him that there was no fear of any exposure."[26]

Hunter next moved on to Chick Gandil, believed both then and now to be the ringleader of the World Series fix. Gandil, his wife, and his wife's parents had recently purchased a bungalow "worth about $8,500" in a new subdivision then called Los Angeles Massa. His address, listed as "3514 Chestey St." in the report, was actually at 5314 Chesley Avenue according to the 1920 census; the house, built in 1915, was still standing in 2020, with a current estimated value of $650,000–$800,000 according to various Los Angeles–area Realtors (the neighborhood is now called Park Mesa Heights). As the area was then a new one with many real estate firms doing business, Hunter made connections with a Realtor he knew personally and posed as the firm's representative in Los Angeles Massa, "and my visits to that area attracted no attention." He became friendly with Gandil and summarized Chick's statements to him as follows:

> I have been with Mr. Comiskey for several years, and certainly feel keenly the stories that appeared in different papers and magazines regarding our team being bribed to throw the world series to Cincinnati, but you can take it from me that I neither got any money nor was approached by anyone to make it possible to have Cincinnati defeat our team. I tell you frankly that this whole story originated from those gamblers who bet on our team to win each game or at least three-fourths of them, and when we made such a poor showing as to lose the first two, they began to squeal, and this started rumors of bribery, for which there was absolutely no foundation. Right now I feel certain that no man on that team got a dollar to lend himself to any crooked deal. It is true that possibly the showing our team made in the finals was not creditable to us, as there is no mistake that we had the better team of the two. But baseball is like any other game where conditions figure in decisions. We made some bad plays that rather demoralized our team, and we simply could not recover ourselves. . . .
>
> I had got so provoked at the stories circulated that I wrote to Mr. Comiskey that I did not want to continue in the game, and asked that he release me. I intend to remain on the coast and play on one of the local teams. I have got to go to the hospital for an operation anyway, and really feel as if I would not be able to play. I just had an operation on my hand as a result of injury in catching the ball.
>
> I have a nice little home here and an automobile—any man of ordinary means could support both. I have a mortgage of $3,500 on the house. I tell everybody that as they may think it is clear of incumbrance, and consequently may think that I got some of the money claimed by reports to have been paid off the White Sox boys to allow themselves to be defeated by Cincinnati.[27]

Gandil was very vocal about his unhappiness with the White Sox and his insistence that the team give him his release. In a November 18 article by Harry A. Williams of the *Los Angeles Times*—one of the few mainstream reporters who took the fix rumors seriously—Gandil called Comiskey "a strange contradiction. At times he is the best fellow in the world, and at other times he is very difficult to please. I think he has been influenced by the talk of bettors who lost on the White Sox. I have given the Chicago club my best at all times." He attributed his poor World Series performance to an injured hand, and stated his desire to secure his release from the White Sox so that he could play for Seattle of the Pacific Coast League. "My prospects in Seattle looked good, until this thing came up," he complained. "I fear, however, these reports will injure my chances until the situation is cleared up, as it should be in justice to the players."[28]

Another story in the *San Francisco Examiner* on December 8 said that Gandil "has a peeve as big as Pikes Peak" and that "he will quit baseball forever before he will play again for the White Sox." The story mentioned that Gandil had been a candidate to manage the Seattle club and aired his complaint that the White Sox had done nothing "to clear up the scandal developing from the world series and free the players from suspicion of crookedness. Chick wants his name cleared and then he wants to play where conditions are congenial."[29] The issue heated up again later in the month when the Seattle managerial post was still open, but the White Sox held firm. This dance would continue into the spring.

Summarizing his interactions with Gandil, Hunter wrote Austrian that he had "tested this man Gandil out" by having other people connect with Chick to see if he remained consistent, and found this to be the case. However, his comments directed Hunter toward Buck Weaver: "In his different talks, which we prearranged before meeting Gandil, the latter did not differ in the statements made to me as outlined above, except that there was a guarded inclination that Weaver should know, if anyone whether or not any money was handed to players to shape results."[30]

Buck Weaver was spending the winter in the oceanside town of Venice, California. Buck had received an offer from some Japanese universities to spend January and February in Japan to teach baseball at the schools, for a stipend of $2,000. Thomas Tominago, who made the offer on behalf of the schools, stated that Weaver, in his opinion, "is the smartest of all major leaguers wintering in southern California."[31] Buck declined the offer, as he had other plans for the winter and was concerned that the trip might make him late in reporting to spring training.

In an attempt to get Weaver to speak candidly, Hunter again used his contacts in the real estate business, asking a Realtor friend to connect with Weaver. The friend reported that Weaver "knew nothing personally about any frame-up to throw the game, but that some of the plays which resulted in losing the game, might be construed as being suspicious that something was wrong with the playing." He did provide a potential lead: "if any crookedness took place, that it was pulled up in Chicago, also that if any outsiders knew anything about it, it would be two girls, who lived on the South Side, where some of the boys used to visit when they were playing in Chicago or vicinity."[32]

Hunter later called on Weaver personally and had a general talk with him. Weaver appeared to think that Hunter was a reporter (something Hunter neither confirmed nor denied) and basically repeated the same story that McMullin had told; he knew nothing about any fix, but if anything crooked had taken place it would have been limited to two or three players:

> I am very sorry that we lost the Worlds Series to Cincinnati, as we certainly should have defeated them on merit as we had the best team, but I tell you honestly I don't know anything about any frame-up to throw the game. You can take it from me, that if anything of that kind was pulled off, that it was done through one or two players, and that it was not a matter of bribing half the team, as anyone who is crooked enough to approach a player knows that it would be necessary to bribe only about two or three players, who held important stations—that made it possible for them to fumble a play, so as to favor the competitive team, and thus lose the play to them. In conclusion, I know nothing definite about any bribery, but at the same time our boys did not play up to standard, consequently the suspecting public thinks something was pulled off that shaped the final result of our team losing. I'm very sorry how things turned out, as I know these rumors will hurt the popularity of baseball, and this naturally will reflect on the price the player should command if things kept running along as they did for years. If we drift into the position that horse-racing did before it was discontinued [many racetracks were closed during the war], baseball will share the same fate.[33]

Regarding his own impressions of Weaver, Hunter wrote, "I found Mr. Weaver a rather frank outspoken fellow and from what I could gather around the places of Venice, where he and all baseball fans hang out, I am inclined to believe he is honest, and as he says, knows nothing about the matter of crookedness in the final games of the season." So Hunter's visits with McMullin, Gandil, and Weaver produced nothing useful about their own involvement in the fix; in fact, like Operative #11 with Happy Felsch, he erroneously believed that McMullin and Weaver had no direct knowledge of the scandal. However, the leads on the two South Side girls in Chicago, which Weaver had related to the Realtor but not to Hunter (the "reporter"), seemed to provide some interesting leads about Swede Risberg. The leads were promising enough that the White Sox had Hunter cancel his trip to San Francisco to spy on Risberg directly.[34]

The South Side girls that Hunter referred to were Marie Purcell (whom Hunter's operative usually referred to as "Subject") and Florence Brown; they lived at the Drexel Arms Hotel at Oakwood and Drexel Boulevards. Hunter learned that Miss Purcell was Swede Risberg's lover and that Risberg was believed to have put up $500 for her to open up a manicuring parlor. Hunter believed that Miss Brown, who had reddish-blond hair, was the "striking blonde" referred to in an October 25, 1919, *Collyer's Eye* story by Frank O. Klein (Hunter had both the name and date of the publication wrong, but quoted the article correctly). According to the story, the blonde, identifying herself as a friend of Claude (Lefty) Williams, had attempted to place a $2,000 bet on the Cincinnati Reds with a "well-known layer of odds" during the World Series, telling the gambler, "This is Claude's money, or at least a good part of it." Hunter also suggested installing a dictograph recording device in Purcell's room "should we find that Risberg or any other players were going to visit, and in that way get inside plans which would not be discussed in the presence of operative or possibly not in the presence of anyone only the two participants."[35] (There is no record that this step was ever taken.)

Hunter's operative E. W. M., who had completed his investigative work in St. Louis, rented a room a few doors away from Purcell's and on December 17, after making acquaintance with the women, was able to engage them in conversation while the three were on a streetcar ride downtown. He learned that the two women shared their room with Brown's mother, and that Purcell's father was renting a room on the first floor of the hotel. The two women had recently moved to Chicago from Detroit, and were about to move to a nearby apartment with their families.

Later that day E. W. M. visited the women at Purcell's beauty parlor; that night he was introduced to Purcell's father and Brown's mother and had dinner with the women and parents. Afterward the women invited the operative to their room, and he spent the rest of the night with them, going out for a walk with them and then drinking and dancing with the women at the Ellis Cafe at 39th and Cottage Grove (a place frequented by Gandil, Risberg, and McMullin, according to *Collyer's Eye*) until 12:45 a.m. While in the room he noticed a picture of Risberg in his baseball uniform; when he asked who it was, Purcell told him it was "Swede Risberg, shortstop of the White Sox," and described him as "a wonderful friend of mine." At the cafe she told him that Risberg and his friends came to her hotel every evening during the World Series games in Chicago. She said that she had passes for all the World Series games in Chicago and "was with Risberg every evening during his stay in Chicago."[36]

E. W. M.'s last report of 1919 came on December 29. By this time he had become very friendly with the women and the parents (Purcell's father and Brown's mother): "They have become very much attached to me and I have a standing invitation to come to their room at any time . . . I am in their room nearly every evening, and matters of utmost personal nature are discussed in my presence. They look to me to solve their domestic troubles."[37]

During this time Risberg's name came up several times. On one occasion E. W. M. and the women were accompanied by a friend of Brown named Roy Theilen, who worked for the Goodrich Tire Company, for a night of dining, dancing, and drinking that lasted until 2:30 a.m. E. W. M. brought up Risberg's name several times, kidding Purcell about him. At one point Theilen remarked, "No wonder the 'Swede' lost these games. I would have too if there was as much in it for me as there was for him then. Then another thing, if he was with Marie every night, he didn't have much 'pep' the next day." At this remark, the operative wrote, "Subject gave Miss Brown a suspicious glance—in fact Subject colored up." Nothing more was said about the remark.[38]

In a later conversation E. W. M. asked Miss Brown who had given Purcell the $500 to open her beauty parlor; she said the money came from Purcell's father, which the operative did not believe. "I am satisfied that a little later on I can get the truth from her," he wrote. Regarding the Swede, E. W. M. wrote that "we have discussed Risberg frequently, and outside of Subject saying he was the best friend she had in the world, nothing of interest was said." He finished the report by writing that Purcell had told him "confidentially" to remain in Chicago as long as he could, and that "she would see to it that I met not only Risberg, but a lot of other baseball players, when they came to Chicago—that we could have some fine times together." The adventures of E. W. M., Miss Brown, and "Subject" would continue well into the new year.[39]

INSURRECTIONISTS

By January 1920, Ban Johnson had a problem very likely to distract him from investigating the 1919 World Series: he was struggling to hold on to his power as president of the American League. Since 1915, a series of disputes involving players and owners had resulted in a loss of confidence in the National Commission and presented a challenge to Johnson's once-dictatorial rule over the American League.

The first case was a dispute between the St. Louis Browns and Pittsburgh Pirates over the contractual rights to a brilliant young player, George Sisler. Johnson and the commission awarded Sisler to the Browns; that infuriated Pirates owner Barney Dreyfuss, once a staunch Johnson ally. In 1918, the Commission ruled that pitcher Scott Perry, who had been purchased from the Atlanta Crackers of the minor league Southern Association by the Philadelphia Athletics and was pitching very well for the Athletics, actually belonged to the Boston Braves due to an earlier transaction between the Crackers and Braves. A's president and manager Connie Mack, with Johnson's support, got a court injunction allowing him to keep Perry. This angered the National League so much that it threatened to cancel the World Series; while a compromise was reached allowing the A's to keep Perry after reaching a cash settlement with the Braves, National League President John Tener resigned rather than continue to sit on the National Commission with Johnson. Then came the Jack Quinn affair (see chapter 2), one more ugly dispute between Johnson and Comiskey; but for Johnson, Comiskey complained in a January 1920 article by Al Spink, the White Sox would have had "a good righthander" in Quinn to replace the

The unquestioned ruler of the American League during his early years as league president, Ban Johnson found his authority challenged in 1919–1920. *Library of Congress Prints and Photographs Division*

injured Red Faber in the 1919 World Series, "and would have beaten Cincinnati in the series for world honors."[1]

The most serious challenge to Johnson's authority came during the 1919 season, when Boston Red Sox pitcher Carl Mays walked out on his team. Mays, who was having a subpar year, was despondent over personal matters, and the Red Sox chose not to suspend him as Johnson felt was appropriate. He ruled that Mays could not be dealt to another team until he had returned to the Red Sox in good standing. When Boston defied Johnson by trading Mays to the New York Yankees, Johnson ruled that Mays was under indefinite suspension and ineligible to pitch for New York. The Yankees responded by going to court, just as Connie Mack had done in the Scott Perry case; they got an injunction allowing Mays to pitch for them for the rest of the season. The dispute continued into the off-season, with Johnson attempting to deny third-place money to the Yankees; he argued that any New York victories in which Mays had pitched should not count.

In late October, the New York State Supreme Court ruled that Johnson had no right to interfere in a transaction between clubs and made the injunction allowing Mays to pitch for the Yankees permanent. Emboldened, the Yankees joined forces with the Red Sox and White Sox—a group that became known as the "Insurrectionists" (also called "Insurgents" or "Insurrectos")—in a bid to drive Johnson out of baseball, or at least to severely curtail his power; the pro-Johnson faction was dubbed the "Loyal Five." Outnumbered in league-wide votes, the Insurrectionists challenged Johnson's authority—and the validity of his contact—in court, and the Yankees instituted a $500,000 damage suit against him. The three clubs even talked about withdrawing their franchises from the American League and placing them in a new league that would include franchises to compete with the AL in Cleveland and Detroit (Milwaukee, Baltimore, and Toronto were the other proposed cities for the new league). That particular idea was for a moment only a threat, but the bitter feud carried into the new year, and the notion of the Insurrectionists abandoning the American League would return almost exactly one year later—much more seriously this time.

As if the executive level of baseball did not have enough turmoil with the power struggle at the top of the American League, Garry Herrmann resigned as chairman of the National Commission on January 8; the move would take effect no later than February 11, when the leagues would be meeting jointly. Once again Judge Kenesaw Mountain Landis's name was being put forward as a possible new chairman, along with "Big Bill" Edwards, a former Princeton football star now involved in New York politics, and several others. Hugh Fullerton doubted that either Landis or Edwards could be elected unanimously, and added,

"Neither would accept if acceptance means becoming embroiled in the petty strife of the owners, and neither would consent to be the instrument of either faction. Besides that there is serious doubt whether a majority of the owners want an executive free from all the entanglements of the game. There are indications that they would prefer one of their own ilk."[2]

Columnist Al Spink quoted "one of the best-posted baseball men in Chicago today" that "No one in favor of square dealing, honesty and decency should be opposed to the election of Judge Landis as chairman of the commission." The baseball man thought that if Ban Johnson himself were to nominate Landis, the judge would be elected. *Cleveland Plain Dealer* writer Henry P. Edwards wrote that Landis had the support of both the National League and the "Insurrectionist" trio.[3]

However, Johnson had his own candidate, Milwaukee attorney Henry Killilea, and the Landis-for-chairman campaign became part of the Comiskey-Johnson feud, as well as the battle between Johnson and the Insurrectionists. "Killilea won't do at all. He's too close to Johnson," said Yankee co-owner T. L. Huston. "Comiskey is going to try his hardest to have Judge Landis appointed. I believe that Landis would be a wonderful man for baseball." Johnson and the Loyal Five, of course, were unlikely to support any candidate who was enthusiastically backed by Comiskey.[4]

When the leagues met in February, their first move was a blockbuster: the joint rules committee elected to outlaw the "trick pitches" that had helped fuel the Deadball Era, including the spitball, shine ball, and emery ball. For 1920, each team could designate two spitball pitchers who could continue to use the pitch (it was later decided to allow these pitchers to use the spitball for the remainder of their MLB careers); the other freak pitches that involved defacing or doctoring the ball were banned forever. This change would have a major impact on two members of the White Sox: Red Faber, whose primary pitch was the spitter, and Eddie Cicotte, who used the shine ball (a pitch that involved the pitcher rubbing the baseball on his paraffin- or powder-coated pant leg or uniform shirt to produce more movement), as well as an occasional spitter, as part of his repertoire. Cicotte was also said to use the emery ball (with movement produced by roughening part of the baseball with an emery board) on occasion. Allowed to continue using the spitter, Faber would remain an effective pitcher into the 1930s, when he was well past 40 years old; without his favorite trick pitches, Cicotte was still a very effective pitcher in 1920, but he did not approach the heights he had reached in 1917 and 1919.[5]

When the American League owners met on February 10, it was a long and stormy session. "The club owners merrily assailed one another and one

Yankee co-owners Jacob Ruppert (left) and T. L. Huston (right) led a revolt against Ban Johnson while promoting Judge Kenesaw Mountain Landis as head of the National Commission. *Library of Congress Prints and Photographs Division*

another's ball club," wrote the *New York Times*. "There were many times when all were talking at once. If the tense atmosphere of the meeting had not been broken often with bits of humor, it would have developed into a Donnybrook affair. . . . At one time Colonel Ruppert of New York and Phil Ball of St. Louis arose and faced each other and seemed to be all set for a passage of fisticuffs."[6] Finally, at around 1:30 a.m., the owners reached a peace agreement at last. It was a major triumph for the Insurrectionists, whose lawsuits and threats to leave the league proved to be major bargaining chips. The league agreed to reinstate Carl Mays as a member of the Yankees, without penalty; the Yankees were awarded third-place money for 1919; and perhaps most importantly, a two-man board consisting of Yankee co-owner Jacob Ruppert and Washington Senators owner Clark Griffith would now have binding power to review penalties or fines over $100 and suspensions of more than 10 days. In case of a tie vote by the board, a federal judge in Chicago, most likely Landis, would decide the issue. In exchange, the Insurrectionists agreed to drop all lawsuits.

The *New York Times* described the end of the meeting as follows: "From the hotel elevator stepped a lone, dejected-looking man; his face was drawn and pale. It was President Ban Johnson. None of his five loyal club owners were with him. He walked out of the hotel and disappeared. No word, one way or another, did he say about the settlement." Larry Woltz of the *Chicago Herald and Examiner* wrote that while Johnson managed to thwart the Insurrectionists' goal of removing him from office, "Johnson's authority in adjusting the internal troubles of the league is not what it formerly was. In the future he will be regarded more as an employee of the league, rather than dictator, a high-salaried figurehead, in fact. He has been shorn of the autocratic powers he enjoyed." The *New York Times* predicted that Johnson would soon resign: "He has given no inkling that he intends to step down, but the stripping him of his powers leads those to know him to believe that he will not care to serve long under the new restricted conditions."[7]

Johnson ultimately elected to remain as president, but at a high price for Major League Baseball. Judge Landis removed his name from consideration as head of the National Commission on February 14, and the position remained vacant due to Johnson's intransigence. "Johnson, who had refused to meet with the selection committee as long as Ruppert was on it, continued to block the appointment of a new chairman," wrote Harold Seymour and Dorothy Seymour Mills. "With no progress, let alone agreement, in naming a neutral chairman, Organized Baseball drifted in disarray through 1920."[8] Once again the only person conducting an investigation into the 1919 World Series was Charles A. Comiskey . . . and Comiskey had an obvious conflict of interest.

There was another "Insurrectionist" in baseball at the start of 1920: Babe Ruth of the Boston Red Sox. Ruth would not turn 25 until February 5, but as a pitcher he had already won 89 career games, posted two 20-win seasons, won an ERA title, and set a World Series record for consecutive scoreless innings that would not be broken until the 1960s. Ruth had shown so much ability as a hitter of unprecedented power that his pitching days were basically over. In 1919, though he was still pitching part-time (9–5, 2.97 while starting 15 games), Ruth had broken the all-time single-season record by hitting 29 home runs. It was widely believed—correctly, as it turned out—that he had only begun to tap his full potential as a slugger. If he wasn't yet indisputably the most famous player in baseball—Ty Cobb and Walter Johnson were still going strong—he was on the brink of claiming that honor.

Ruth knew it . . . and he expected to be paid accordingly.

The Babe had spent the 1919–1920 off-season on a barnstorming tour that finished in Los Angeles, where he was supposed to film several short movies. The film deal fell through, so he relaxed and played golf at the Griffith Park course in the company of several ballplayers, including another player who was unhappy with his contract: Buck Weaver. On December 23, the *Los Angeles Evening Express* reported that "Ruth has been dethroned as the world's hardest club swinger. . . . Ruth made a 340-yard drive from the tee, which wasn't at all bad. Then Weaver unlimbered his golf club and walloped the little sphere 370 yards."[9] The paper did not report whether Weaver, a switch-hitter in baseball, was swinging from the right or left side.

Prior to the 1919 season, Ruth and Weaver, both coming off excellent 1918 performances, had signed three-year contracts: Ruth for $10,000 a year, Weaver for $7,250. Although Weaver, who at 28 when the 1919 season started was several years older than the Babe, Ruth biographer Robert Creamer's comment about the Babe's contract could apply to Weaver, who in 1918 had batted .300 for the first time. "In retrospect it seems foolish for a rising young player to have tied himself to such a long-term deal," wrote Creamer, "but it must be remembered that the major leagues had gone through three consecutive seasons of uncertainty and falling salaries, what with the death of the Federal League and the onslaught of war. Abrupt salary cuts were common practice."[10]

Ruth of course had more leverage, and he began demanding that Harry Frazee, the owner of the Red Sox, double his salary to $20,000 a year; if he didn't get it, Ruth said, he might not play in 1920. Frazee, however, had cashflow problems. Although the Red Sox owner was a successful Broadway producer with many hit shows, his 1919 spring production, "A Good Bad Place," had opened and closed in a month. More serious were the revenue declines in his baseball business due to World War I. In addition, he still owed $262,000 to Joseph Lannin, the former owner of the Red Sox, for the purchase of the team in 1916. A note for that amount was due in November 1919, and Frazee didn't have the money.

The New York Yankees were happy to come to his rescue.

The Yankees had been steadily improving under manager Miller Huggins, with a third-place finish in 1919. When co-owner Jacob Ruppert asked what he needed to win the team's first pennant, Huggins told him, "Get me Ruth." Ruppert and Frazee worked out the details, which were totally to the Yankees' advantage. The Red Sox received $100,000—not $125,000 as originally reported—payable in four annual installments. Frazee needed cash so badly that he sold the notes at a discount to Yankee co-owner T. L. Huston's bank. Ruppert also made a personal loan of $300,000 (at 7 percent interest) to Frazee, who put up Fenway Park as collateral. And the Yankees weren't done fleecing Frazee: figuring that they might need to increase Ruth's $10,000 salary, they got Frazee to agree to pay half of any increase over $5,000 a year. If Ruth demanded a cash bonus instead of a salary increase, the Yankees would pay the first $10,000, but the Red Sox would have to pay anything over that up to $15,000. Adding it all up, economist and baseball historian Michael Haupert wrote that the Red Sox wound up paying the Yankees to take Babe Ruth.[11]

The teams completed the terms of the sale on December 26, but held off formally announcing it until Huggins had gone to Los Angeles to talk to Ruth. He found him at the Griffith Park golf course. The Yankees had anticipated that they might have some difficulty getting the Babe to agree to come to New York; a clause in the agreement said that if Ruth did not report before July 1, the deal was off and Frazee would have to return the money. As expected, Ruth was a tough negotiator, asking not only that the Yankees double his salary to $20,000, but that he receive a piece of the sale price as well. Ultimately they agreed to a deal: they kept his salary at $10,000 a year; however, Ruth received an immediate bonus of $1,000, with $20,000 in additional bonus payments payable over the course of the next two years. Thus his total compensation for the 1920 and 1921 seasons would be $41,000.[12]

The sale was formally announced on January 5. "We believe that Ruth will give us a team of which New York may be proud," said Ruppert. In a prediction that seemed outrageous at the time but turned out to be completely accurate, he added, "Why, I don't see any reason why that fellow can't knock out 50 home runs playing on the Polo Grounds." Meanwhile, Harry Frazee was claiming that he would use the money from the Ruth sale to strengthen the Red Sox. "With this money the Boston club can now go into the market and buy other players and have a stronger and better team in all respects than we would have had if he had remained with us," said Frazee.[13] That never happened; in fact, Frazee continued to unload more of his high-salaried players.

In Boston, reaction to the Ruth sale was surprisingly mixed. "Many followers of baseball claim that there is no player in the game who is worth paying $100,000 for, and that if the Boston club obtained such a sum, it is the gainer," one fan wrote the *Boston Globe*. Former Boston National League star Hugh Duffy said, "Star ballplayers do not make a winning team, and men of ordinary ability working for the interests of the club are greater factors in a winning machine than one individual." But Johnny Keenan, leader of the Royal Rooters, the team's passionate fans' organization, said, "Ruth was 90% of the Red Sox team last summer. It will be impossible to replace the strength Ruth gave to the Boston

Desperate for cash with debt payments due, Red Sox owner Harry Frazee earned a place in baseball infamy by selling Babe Ruth to the Yankees. *Library of Congress Prints and Photographs Division*

club. Ruth is a wonderful player, loves the game and gave his all to win."[14]

In Chicago, the *Evening Post* ran an article titled, "Which Do You Prefer: Joe [Jackson] or Babe?" and quoted Frazee as saying, "I could not get Joe Jackson for him in trade, and I know about two other stars that Ruth could not have been traded for." The conclusion, author Malcolm MacLean wrote, is that "it means simply that the White Sox set a higher value on Joe Jackson than on Babe Ruth, for whom the New York Yankees are reported to have paid $125,000. . . . Jackson unquestionably did more for the White Sox in 1919, when they won the title, than Babe Ruth did for the Red Sox, who finished in the second division."[15]

But would Jackson be back with the White Sox in 1920 . . . or would any of the eight players suspected of throwing the 1919 World Series? Comiskey's detective reports had mostly been completed, but he still had an operative in the field: E. W. M., who was in Chicago spying on Swede Risberg's lover Marie Purcell (whom he referred to as "Subject"), and her friend and roommate

Florence Brown. In early January E. W. M. wrote that, since the date of his last report (December 29), "I have been in almost constant company, with Subject, Miss B. and their folks, every evening." He had learned that Brown was "very friendly" with Fred McMullin and that both women "are on very friendly terms with most of the players of the Sox and frequently held some lively parties when they were in town."[16]

On January 3, E. W. M. reported, he had dinner with the women in the hotel café. "Subject had the blues and was melancholy," he wrote. "She, not feeling well, remarked that she wished she were dead." Brown rebuked her, telling Purcell that "you should be one of the happiest girls in Chicago" and that "I never had a beauty shop handed to me like you have. Just because business is bad for a few days there is no reason why you should wish yourself dead." Two days later, he reported, he was in Purcell's room with Brown and Brown's mother when "Subject" picked up a picture of Swede Risberg from the mantel. Looking at the picture and swinging it, Purcell remarked, "Well old kid you may swing worse than that, if you are not careful—if they know what I know." E. W. M. noted that the women "exchanged glances and the remarks were passed off," and added, "From what I have seen of Miss B and Subject to date and the remarks they have made, I am satisfied that they know all the ins and outs of the matter under investigation."[17]

On January 9, a news flash from San Francisco appeared in the nation's sporting press: "Charles 'Swede' Risberg, shortstop of the Chicago White Sox, announced today [January 8] he had retired from baseball and would open a restaurant here. Risberg expressed himself dissatisfied with major league salaries." A *Chicago Daily News* story by Oscar Reichow several days later quoted a San Francisco boxer named Spider Roach, who had been in touch with the Swede: "I was with Risberg the day I left San Francisco, and he told me several days before that he did not expect to rejoin the White Sox. He does not plan to quit baseball, but wants to get his release from the Chicago club so as to play in one of the Pacific Coast League towns. Of course he prefers San Francisco, and I understand he plans to have the club negotiate with the White Sox for his release. He told me he would much rather play on the coast, because he can make almost as much money, and besides he plans to go into business in Presidio. I don't know what that business is." Reichow speculated that "Risberg may be stalling and he may not be. . . . It is possible the Southside infielder is merely playing for an increase in salary, it seems to be the custom among many ballplayers who are dissatisfied with their stipends."[18]

On the evening of January 9, E. W. M. had dinner with Brown, Purcell, and a beauty parlor employee of Miss Purcell, a "Miss Mann," about whom he commented, "This girl is well posted on nearly everything that transpires." After dinner they went up to Purcell's room, where Brown's mother was also present, and the news story about Risberg retiring to open up a San Francisco restaurant became a subject of conversation. According to E. W. M., Mrs. Brown commented: "Well, I suppose he is going to take his $10,000 which he is supposed to have gotten in the Series and open up a restaurant." Purcell commented that Risberg knew nothing about running a restaurant and that he was only stalling to get more money: "He told me last fall he was going to hold out this season for more money and further more he is trying to get with the Detroit team," she said. "I think that's what's on his mind. I know that he is not going to quit baseball."[19]

E. W. M. used these remarks to lead the conversation to the "matter under investigation," and asked Brown point-blank what she had received out of the $10,000. She replied: "Oh he—I got a shop out of it." When he later asked her how much money she had gotten out of the $10,000, she replied, "Say, what are you trying to do—get something on me or looking for information," and laughed. She then changed the subject, and E. W. M. said that he gave them "a satisfactory reason for my inquiries." He concluded: "From the above, there is no doubt in my mind, but what both Subject and Miss B know considerable—it is just a matter of letting them talk themselves. Whenever questions are put to them on the subject, they change the topic of conversation."[20]

E. W. M. would not file his next report until late February, about two weeks before the White Sox would begin spring training in Waco, Texas. By then Comiskey had made his decision about who would be on his team in 1920.

On January 14 and 18, the *Chicago Herald and Examiner* ran a two-part series written by former Chicago Cubs owner Charles W. Murphy addressing the rumors that the 1919 World Series had been fixed. "Such talk should be stopped, because no club ever worked harder to win than the Chicago White Sox," Murphy assured his readers. "Professional baseball—the game as it is played in the field—is absolutely clean and honest. . . . Repeatedly since the blue ribbon classic I have heard stories that sounded so silly that they must have been started by persons having the delirium tremors."[21]

Three days after part 2 of Murphy's series appeared, Harry Grabiner announced that contracts to the White Sox players would go out in the mail during the last week of the month. He did not anticipate any trouble from holdouts or players who annually announce their intention of "quitting the game to go into business." When asked if he expected any argument from Swede Risberg, Grabiner replied, "No, I don't think Risberg will give us any trouble. We have heard stories that he intended to quit the game to go into business, but I doubt such tales. I have heard nothing from Risberg personally and as far as I know he'll be back with the team." Kid Gleason parroted the same line on February 3, saying, "Gandil will be back at first base and Risberg will be at short and we will have an infield second to none in the American League." A story a day earlier suggested that Gleason might personally head to California to re-sign Gandil and Risberg.[22]

These stories make it clear that by this time, Comiskey had decided to bring back the players under suspicion. He later related that he did so on the advice of his attorney, Alfred S. Austrian. Comiskey explained his rationale during his testimony at Joe Jackson's 1924 civil suit: "He said a rule of the league required clubs to line up their team personnel before Feb. 1 following the close of a season in order to protect club rights. During the late fall and winter of 1919, he said the matter of a thrown World Series had not really passed the stage of rumors, on which the club had been unable to obtain concrete information. On the advice of his attorney, Mr. Comiskey then went ahead with the signing up of the suspected players."[23]

This was a fateful decision, one that would forever affect—and in the eyes of many, taint—Charles Comiskey's reputation. Once considered a man of unimpeachable integrity, he would be pilloried as a man who knew his players' guilt and had enough information to get them thrown out of baseball . . . but who instead covered up what he knew in order to protect his bottom line. Even his investigation would be considered a sham, carried on only to make it appear he was looking for the truth. In some tellings, Comiskey would be painted as the major villain of the Black Sox scandal.

One writer who has vigorously defended Comiskey is Tim Hornbaker, author of *Turning the Black Sox White: The Misunderstood Legacy of Charles A. Comiskey*. While Hornbaker is very frank about wanting to restore the Old Roman's reputation, his book is hardly a see-no-evil look at Comiskey's life and the decisions he made. Regarding Alfred Austrian's advice that Comiskey should move forward with re-signing the suspected players to 1920 contracts, Hornbaker wrote,

> Austrian counseled him at great length, presenting the various options and relayed his extensive knowledge of the legal system. He knew that slander laws explicitly prevented the White Sox from defaming the reputations of any of the alleged players, and Comiskey had a lot to lose if he stepped over the line. In fact, he would have been unmercifully targeted in lawsuits that might have crippled him, not only financially, but mentally and physically as well . . . Austrian, based on his terrific comprehension of the facts in the case, recommended to Comiskey

a composed and undeviating trajectory. The inadequate potency of information left no other option but to enter the 1920 baseball season like all previous years. That meant contracts were sent out to the entire White Sox roster, including the allegedly tainted players—incredibly, with salary raises.[24]

While I have great sympathy for Comiskey and the difficult choice he had to make, I think that the "I did this on advice from counsel" argument is letting him off way too easily. Bill Lamb, a retired New Jersey prosecutor who has written extensively about the Black Sox scandal (including the 2013 book *Black Sox in the Courtroom*, which is considered one of the definitive works on the subject), commented on Comiskey's decision to attempt to re-sign the suspected players—and Alfred Austrian's advice—in a 2020 email to the author:

> Regarding Comiskey and the state of his knowledge about the fix, it is my opinion that the in-house investigation discreetly overseen by Sox corporation counsel Alfred Austrian had produced information sufficient for Comiskey to conclude that Sox players had thrown the Series. But rather than take action against the players and break up a championship team, he opted for self-interest and hoped that the matter would blow over—a strategy that almost worked, by the way. I am not without sympathy for Comiskey, and do not share the weird opinion of Gene Carney and others that the coverup of the fix was worse than the Series corruption itself. That is akin to thinking that the guy who concealed the murder victim's body after the fact is a worse offender than the killer himself.
>
> The claim that Comiskey felt powerless to act upon his investigation as the proof was not conclusive is weak, in my opinion. That he felt hamstrung by inconclusive proofs is, of course, the spin that Comiskey and Austrian put on the situation when obliged to testify at the Jackson civil trial in 1924. But it is thin soup, in my opinion. And the notion that Comiskey and Austrian feared possible defamation lawsuits by discharged Sox players is strained, at best. Without boring you with a treatise on defamation law (and I have been sued often enough by New Jersey State Prison inmates to have some expertise on the subject), there was no real prospect of a defamation suit being actionable. Jackson, Risberg, and Happy Felsch included defamation-based claims in their post-scandal civil lawsuits against the Sox, and those claims went nowhere.
>
> It also bears remembering that Comiskey was an employer facing a personnel issue, not a prosecutor confined to evidence admissible in court to make his case. Comiskey was not obliged to offer new contracts to Jackson, Williams, Felsch, and Risberg in February 1920. He chose to do so (as was his prerogative) in the hope that the Series corruption talk would peter out over time. That decision was hardly courageous, but understandable. In any event, I do not view Charles Comiskey (or Alfred Austrian) as the major villains in the Black sox scandal. The bad guys remain the corrupt players and the fix gamblers, in my opinion.[25]

Ultimately Charles Comiskey chose to protect his business—an understandable decision, but hardly an admirable one, and not one that potential legal consequences forced him to take.

It wasn't as though Comiskey didn't have an alternative to either releasing or bringing back the Suspected Eight (or Seven); other teams seemed very interested in their services. On February 7, *Collyer's Eye* reported that "a big deal is impending": the White Sox were about to trade Happy Felsch to the Philadelphia Athletics for pitcher Scott Perry, and Shoeless Joe Jackson to the Yankees for infielder Frank (Home Run) Baker. The Yankees would then send Jackson on to the Red Sox as one of the terms of the Babe Ruth deal. "With [Erskine] Mayer already transferred to Columbus, Cicotte sulking over alleged unfair treatment and refusing to play for Comiskey, and Williams, who made such a miserable showing in the last world's series, through as a major leaguer," wrote Joe Le Blanc, "the Sox boss has but two dependable pitchers, [Dickey] Kerr and [Roy] Wilkinson."[26] Thus the interest in Scott Perry, who had posted a 4–17 record for a miserable A's team in 1919, but with a respectable 3.58 ERA. In 1918, Perry had won 20 games (with a 1.98 ERA) for a 52-win Philadelphia club. The paper anticipated that Comiskey would continue to clean house by sending Gandil and McMullin to Los Angeles of the Pacific Coast League for Jacques Fournier, an excellent hitter who had preceded Gandil as Chicago's regular first baseman, and that Risberg would be traded or sold to the minors. That would have cleared out all the suspected players except for Weaver, whose crime appeared to be failure to report his knowledge of the fix.

None of that transpired, of course, but another deal involving a suspected player came much closer to happening. On Valentine's Day, the *Chicago Tribune* reported that the Yankees were interested in trading for Felsch, and were offering their regular first baseman, Wally Pipp, in exchange. If the Sox had agreed to the deal, they would have immediately washed their hands of both Felsch and Chick Gandil, who would not be needed with Pipp in hand. The club even had a viable replacement for Felsch under contract in Chicago native Johnny Mostil, who would in fact take Happy's place in 1921 and perform solidly on both offense and defense for the next six years.[27]

Why would the Yankees—or the Athletics or Red Sox—who had to be fully aware of which White Sox players were suspected of dumping the World Series—be interested in trading for any of them . . . even if Comiskey had privately shared the results of his investigation? In all honesty, it would hardly have been surprising, given the state of baseball at this time. If you could play ball, being suspected of having dumped games in the past was no big barrier to finding continued employment. Even the Black Prince himself, Hal Chase—after another season of suspicious activity that included charges that he and teammate Heinie Zimmerman had attempted to bribe other players to help lose games—was offered a contract for the 1920 season by John McGraw's New York Giants. The White Sox, still planning on bringing back Chick Gandil to play first base in 1920, turned down the Pipp-for-Felsch offer, but not out of any sense of morality . . . they preferred getting a quality pitcher in exchange for Felsch, and the Yankees wouldn't bite. "It looks as though we will go along with the same outfit we had last year," Comiskey stated.[28]

Meanwhile the White Sox were haggling with Joe Jackson over the terms of a new contract. In late January Comiskey had written to Jackson, "I am formulating plans for the season of 1920 pertaining to the personnel of the White Sox, and would like to hear from you at your earliest convenience as to your playing terms for the coming season." Jackson, who mistakenly believed that Buck Weaver was earning $10,000 (the actual figure was $7,250), responded that he wanted "a three year ironclad contract for ten thousand a year." Comiskey responded on January 29, with an offer of a $1,000 increase to $7,000, describing it as "a very liberal increase over the past season." Jackson quickly rejected the offer, writing, "I can make more money in the Billiard Buisness [sic] then you offer me." He not only wanted $10,000 a year for three years; he wanted a contract without baseball's infamous "10-day clause," which permitted ownership to void the deal at any point with only 10 days' notice. When the impasse and Jackson's threat to go into business made press reports, Harry Grabiner commented, "If Jackson can make more money in a business other than baseball, that is entirely up to him."[29]

But the White Sox wanted Jackson back, so Comiskey sent Grabiner to Savannah to personally get Jackson to sign. What happened in Savannah would become a major part of the Joe Jackson saga, with diametrically opposed accounts as to what transpired. Not under dispute is the fact that Jackson signed a three-year contract for $8,000 a year *with* the 10-day clause included. According to Grabiner, the illiterate Jackson agreed to the contract in the presence of his wife Katie, and signed it inside the Jackson home with both Joe and Katie aware that the 10-day clause was included. According to Jackson, Katie was *not* present when Joe and Grabiner met, and Shoeless Joe signed the contract on the hood of his car—only after Grabiner had assured him that the 10-day clause was not included. As noted earlier, Grabiner testified in 1924 that he and Jackson did not discuss the play of the 1919 World Series at this meeting. It's fair to ask why not; if the White Sox were as interested in getting the truth as they claimed, this would have been a perfect opportunity to grill Joe about what he knew.

According to Joe in his 1923–1924 lawsuit, Grabiner didn't have to grill him, because he already knew the truth; he claimed that Grabiner told him at this meeting that the White Sox "knew all about the facts concerning the payment of $5,000 to me by Lefty Williams," and that Grabiner "told me that they had the absolute goods on Cicotte, Williams and Gandil."[30]

Those differing stories would not surface for several years, however. For now, all that mattered was that Jackson would be back in 1920.

Meanwhile, other White Sox players were returning signed contracts for the 1920 season. On February 8 the press reported that Eddie Collins and Ray Schalk were in the fold; although terms were not publicly disclosed, by custom, we now know that both players signed three-year pacts: Collins for the same $15,000 he had received on his expired five-year contract, while Schalk, whose 1919 salary had been $7,083, got a three-year deal for $10,000 a year—the same figure that Jackson had demanded without success. Others followed: Dickey Kerr, John Collins, and Nemo Leibold (all boosted to $4,500), Red Faber ($4,000), and Eddie Murphy ($3,000). Substantial raises were the norm.

Among the suspected players apart from Jackson, big salary increases were also standard. Happy Felsch saw his salary jump from $3,750 to $7,000; Fred McMullin from $2,625 to $3,600; and Claude Williams from $3,500 (including bonuses) to $6,000, with bonuses of $500 if he won 15 games and $1,000 if he won 20. Eddie Cicotte was taking his time about re-signing, but was expected to be in the fold with a generous raise by the time the Sox headed to spring training. Buck Weaver ($7,250) and Swede Risberg ($3,250) were on multiyear contracts, but Weaver was campaigning for an increase, and Risberg's retirement talk was largely seen as a ploy to get more money.

Some historians have noted the big raises that Comiskey awarded his suspected players in 1920 and labeled the increases as "hush money" to keep the players quiet instead of talking about the scandal. This argument does not really hold water, because Comiskey was generous to his players across the board in his 1920 contract dealings. Historian Bob Hoie calculated that the Sox team payroll increased by about 32 percent from 1919 to 1920, with no significant difference as to whether or not the players were suspected of being part of the World Series fix. This should not be surprising, as heading into 1919, the White Sox were coming off a sixth-place finish in a war-shortened season that had featured a disastrous drop in attendance at Comiskey Park. Things had improved remarkably for both the White Sox and baseball in 1919, and of course the team was also coming off a pennant-winning season.

Chick Gandil, however, continued to play games with the White Sox. On February 22, I. W. Smoot, president of the Snake River-Yellowstone League, announced that Gandil had signed a contract to manage the league's team in St. Anthony, Idaho. Comiskey did not take the news seriously. "Yes, I heard Chick had signed with these fellows," he told reporters. "Maybe he has, but I think he'll be on first base for the Sox when the season opens. In fact, since the supposed signing took place I have had a couple letters from him, the last one only a couple of days ago. . . . Judging from his letters I think he wants to come back to the Sox and will come back. It's true he hasn't signed with me yet, but we've been corresponding, and I think we'll get together on terms and he will be on hand to play."[31]

However, Gandil continued to be coy. On March 4, the Los Angeles native showed up at the Chicago Cubs' spring training camp in nearby Pasadena and spoke to reporters. He listed three reasons for not yet signing with the White Sox. First, there was a large difference in salary terms between what he wanted and what Comiskey was offering. Second, he claimed that he could make as much money managing in Idaho as he could playing in Chicago at the salary offered him. Third, Mrs. Gandil did not want to go back to Chicago and have to deal with the city's "rent profiteering."[32]

Apparently wearying of this game, Comiskey headed for California several days later. "While his presence in the almond country was never stated to be for the purpose of having conference with the first sacker," wrote Forrest B. Myers in the *Chicago Daily News*, "it is thought a meeting will result in Gandil's forgetting the independent team in Idaho, which offers a salary of big league proportions, and which Gandil, aided and abetted by the wishes of Mrs. Gandil, says will hold him in the mountain country this summer."[33]

On March 5, the Cubs' camp had another visitor from Chicago's South Side nine: Buck Weaver. "Weaver's contract still has two years to run," wrote I. E. Sanborn in the *Chicago Tribune*, "but it does not expect to leave California before the end of next week, so it is uncertain whether he is playing to pull a Babe Ruth stunt by demanding a new contract or to the Yankees or merely has a distaste for Waco as a training camp."[34]

Back in Chicago, Comiskey's indirect investigation into Swede Risberg continued. J. R. Hunter's operative E. W. M., now using the code name S-1, reported that he was a roomer in an apartment at 5335 Prairie Avenue rented by Risberg's lover Marie Purcell, her friend Florence Brown, and Miss Brown's mother. "I have been constantly in their company," he wrote. He reported that he attempted to lead the conversation around to Risberg and baseball "at every opportunity," at one point stating that "from what newspapers and magazines had said, evidently the series was thrown and it appeared on the surface as though 'R' was in the deal. We argued the question for over an hour or so at length." Purcell and Brown claimed that they did not believe the Series had been thrown, citing a personal friend of Risberg who had lost $800 betting on the White Sox. "I came back at them by saying it was only natural for anyone carrying through a deal of that character not to be telling all his friends about it," wrote the operative, a statement with which Mrs. Brown agreed. She added that "no matter how good a man's character is, he has a price."[35]

S-1 continued to probe the matter, even looking through the mail for checks and other papers, but found nothing of value, nor did the women reveal anything pertinent to the investigation. When he asked Purcell about Risberg's plans for the season, she said she felt he was not coming back to the White Sox. But when he asked if she had heard this from Risberg or through someone else, she laughed and said, "Oh, I got it from the spirits," a remark he called "similar to many I receive from Subject and Miss B when I question them closely."[36]

However, when S-1 intimated that he might be asked to take some out-of-town work for his supposed employer, "They did not take to this arrangement in the least and begged me to do everything within reason so I could remain in Chicago for a few months longer in order to meet 'R' and McMullen [sic], also others, with whom they promised we could have good times." So S-1 stuck around. He would not report again until the season was about to begin in April.[37]

5

WACO

On February 27, two weeks before the White Sox would head for spring training, a major baseball story was reported from New York. "Big Baseball Scandal Due to Break; Zim, Chase and Lee Magee Are Involved," was the headline in the *Chicago Herald and Examiner*. "The biggest scandal in modern baseball is due to break within the next few days," wrote W. S. Farnsworth. He continued,

> It is understood that Hal Chase, first baseman, and Heinie Zimmerman, third baseman of the Giants, have played their last big league games, and their retirement at a time when both are valuable assets to the game will cause nation-wide surprise.
>
> At the meeting of the National and American Leagues two weeks ago it was rumored that Lee Magee, former Yankee, who last year played with the Cubs, was to be thrown out of baseball by mutual consent of the club owners. Since then he has been waived out and not even one minor league magnate asked for his services.
>
> A writer spoke to Magee about the matter. His reply was: "I guarantee you that I will not get the goat alone; at least one player will go along with me."[1]

The Chase/Zimmerman/Magee saga actually involved separate cases of alleged crooked play, each of them—not surprisingly—involving Hal Chase. Chase and Zimmerman, who had both been considered star players in their time, were over-30 teammates with John McGraw's New York Giants in 1919 (Chase was 36 years old; Zimmerman, 32). Both had played regularly for most of the season but saw little action in September, even though the Giants were still trying to catch the Cincinnati Reds in the National League pennant race.

While Chase, a longtime friend of McGraw's, remained with the team (with an injury cited as the reason for his not being in the lineup), Zimmerman finished the year under suspension. According to McGraw at the time, Zimmerman had been suspended for "breaking curfew." It would take months and the probing of a Chicago grand jury before the real reason came out: Chase and Zimmerman were accused of attempting to bribe other players into helping them lose games they had bet on. Zimmerman had confessed his involvement to McGraw and Giants owner Charles Stoneham in mid-September 1919. Even then, the Giants let McGraw's buddy Chase stick around for the rest of the 1919 season; took him along on a postseason barnstorming tour (where he would be accused of trying to induce teammates into dumping an exhibition game); and even offered him a contract for 1920, albeit with a $1,000 pay cut. (They also offered Zimmerman a contract, though apparently for so low a figure, he would be certain to turn it down.) It wasn't until Lee Magee began talking that Chase would finally be finished with Major League Baseball—this time for good. When Magee said that "at least one player will go along with me," he was talking about Prince Hal.

Magee, who had been born with the name Leopold Hoernschemeyer in 1889, was an infielder/outfielder who had played for several MLB clubs beginning in 1911. In 1918 he had been a teammate of Chase's with the Cincinnati Reds; he was sold to the Brooklyn Robins (the current Los Angeles Dodgers) prior to the 1919 season, then traded to the Chicago Cubs in midseason. He played solidly for the Cubs, hitting .292 in 79 games, while seeing action at six different positions. So it was a little mysterious when the Cubs released Magee in January 1920 and used the 10-day clause to void the second year of his two-year contract, without publicly saying why. No other teams were interested in his services, either.

Magee would not stand for it. "I have in my possession evidence showing that without cause the owners of major league teams unlawfully have blacklisted me," he said on March 6. "My attorney now is at work gathering evidence, and his suit will be filed soon to test the right of the club to exercise its option for my services in December and a month later release me."[2]

Major League officials offered no comment on why Chase, Zimmerman, and Magee had been let go with no other clubs willing to add them to their rosters, or even that they were the three players rumored to be blacklisted. This struck some people as just plain wrong. In an article for the *San Francisco Examiner*, former heavyweight boxing champion James J. Corbett—a highly respected San Francisco native known as "Gentleman Jim" and the brother of former Major Leaguer Joe Corbett, who had been Hal Chase's baseball coach at Santa Clara

University—expressed outrage over what he called "the secretiveness concerning the names of the men who have been 'blacklisted' by the majors." While he
applauded efforts to purge baseball of gamblers, he noted that baseball officials
had offered no evidence that the three players had been involved with such men.
"In fairness to all," he wrote, "the leaders should publish the names of the three
blacklisted men and give a full explanation as to the specific wrongdoing of each."[3]

However, Major League Baseball officials had no desire to "give a full explanation as to the specific wrongdoing" of any players suspected of involvement
with gamblers or game fixing, unless forced to do so. That would eventually
happen in 1920, but not for months.

After four seasons in which they had used Mineral Wells, Texas, as their spring
training home base, the White Sox elected to set up camp in Waco, another
Texas city about 120 miles away, in 1920. The club had trained in Waco once
before, in 1912, and was satisfied with the baseball facilities, but found the city's
hotel accommodations lacking. Since that time a new hotel, the Raleigh, had
been erected, and was considered one of the best in the state. The club cited
Waco's central location—within easy reach of Dallas, Fort Worth, and Houston—as another factor in the decision. Overall the move was considered a major
upgrade over Mineral Wells.

Waco is well-known as the home of Baylor University and also as the birth-
place of the Dr Pepper soft drink, which was invented by a Waco pharmacist
in 1885. But in the years between 1912 and 1920, the city had earned national
attention for something else: an infamous incident that would become known as
the "Waco Horror." In 1916, a 17-year-old Black man named Jesse Washington
was accused of raping and murdering Lucy Fryer, the 53-year-old wife of his
white employer in Robinson, Texas, a small town about seven miles from Waco.
Washington was said to have confessed to the crime, and at his trial in Waco
on May 15, a jury of 12 white men deliberated for only four minutes before
returning a guilty verdict and assessing the death penalty. "I am sorry I done it,"
Washington was quoted as saying after the verdict was announced.

Immediately after hearing the verdict, spectators in the crowd began shouting,
"Get the n——." A mob surged forward, grabbing Washington and dragging
him outside. He was then hanged and burned alive on the public square before
a crowd that was estimated at over 15,000—half of Waco's population at the
time—and included women and children. According to an Associated Press
story the next day, "When the flames subsided somewhat a number of persons
in the big crowd that witnessed the burning cut off the negro's fingers and

A large crowd gathering to witness the lynching of 17-year-old Jesse Washington in Waco, Texas, in 1915. The incident became known as the "Waco Horror." *National Association for the Advancement of Colored People Records*

other parts of his body." The mob was not finished. "Two hours later several men placed the burned corpse in a cloth bag and pulled the bundle behind an automobile to Robinson, where they hung the sack from a pole in front of a blacksmith's shop for public viewing," wrote James M. SoRelle in an article for the Texas State Historical Association. Graphic photographs of the lynching and its aftermath were published and made into postcards.[4]

Details of the brutal lynching of Jesse Washington were published nationally in the days following his murder—including brief stories in the major Chicago newspapers. The crime was also widely condemned in numerous editorials . . . often only to a degree. While decrying the brutality of the mob in a May 17 editorial, the *New York Times* wrote that Washington "had committed and confessed the crime which of all others comes nearest to depriving the perpetrator of all right to treatment as a human being, or otherwise than as a beast equally dangerous and abhorrent."[5] No one was ever arrested or prosecuted for the lynching of Jesse Washington.

During this same period, Chicago had had its own ugly incidents of racial strife, the worst of which began with the killing of another 17-year-old Black male. On July 26, 1919, Eugene Williams was part of a group of five Black teenagers whose makeshift raft drifted over an unofficial line that separated what were considered "black" and "white" beaches on Chicago's South Side lakefront. A band of angry white people began throwing rocks at the group, and Williams drowned after being hit by one of the rocks and falling underwater. His death incited a week of rioting, much of it in the area surrounding Comiskey Park. The violence resulted in 38 deaths (23 Black, 15 white), along with over 500 injuries and much destruction of property.[6]

According to writer Tim Odzer, the 1919 Chicago riots demonstrated to Black baseball pioneer Rube Foster the need to take positive steps to help improve African American life. Foster's dream was to organize a Negro baseball league—one that would be free from the control of white booking agents, who often dictated when and where Black teams played, along with taking the lion's share of the revenue. At a Kansas City, Missouri, YMCA on February 13, 1920— one month before the White Sox would head for Waco—Foster and a group of Black baseball team owners announced the formation of the Negro National League, to begin play in May. Although the formation of the league was little noted in America's mainstream newspapers—the *Chicago Tribune* announced the news in a small, 14-line story—the NNL and other Negro leagues that followed would showcase some of the greatest players in baseball history in the years before the Major Leagues family broke baseball's color line in 1947. Foster himself would be inducted into the National Baseball Hall of Fame in 1981.[7]

On Friday, March 12, a White Sox party of 36 pulled out of Chicago's La Salle Street station to head for Waco, scheduled to arrive around noon on Sunday. The Sox, by design, were the last of the 16 Major League clubs to open their spring camp. "Owner Comiskey of the south siders is one magnate who thinks a ball player should get into shape in a couple or three weeks," wrote James Crusinberry. The Old Roman felt that when they'd had lengthier spring trainings in the past, the team often got off to a good start but then faded in midseason.

Unlike current times, when all Major League teams train in either Florida or Arizona, the MLB clubs of 1920 set up spring camps in seven different states. In Texas with the White Sox were the New York Giants (San Antonio) and St. Louis Cardinals (Brownsville). Four teams trained in Florida: the Brooklyn Robins and New York Yankees (Jacksonville), the Cincinnati Reds (Miami), and the Washington Senators (Tampa). Georgia was the spring home of the Boston Braves (Columbus) and Detroit Tigers (Macon). The Philadelphia Phillies (Birmingham) and St. Louis Browns (Taylor) trained in Alabama, the Cleveland Indians (New Orleans) and Philadelphia Athletics (Lake Charles) in Louisiana, and the Pittsburgh Pirates and Boston Red Sox in Arkansas (both in Hot Springs). The Chicago Cubs, in Pasadena, were the only team training in California. The Cubs, whose players had the earliest reporting date (February 28), opened their spring camp more than two weeks earlier than the White Sox.

Another difference between then and now was the lack of Major League opposition for many of the teams. Some clubs finished spring training by barnstorming their way home in conjunction with a designated opponent: Reds/ Senators, Giants/Red Sox, and Cardinals/Browns were the 1920 pairings. These teams would play their opponent in as many as 20 different cities along the way. On the other hand, the White Sox were one of a number of teams that played no spring games at all against other Major League clubs. Instead their opponents consisted of minor league teams, college teams, and even semi-pro clubs. The White Sox split their spring team into two groups, with the regulars forming one squad and a second group of rookies and substitutes known as the "Goofs" (traditionally managed by veteran outfielder John Collins) playing an even more obscure set of opponents.

The White Sox squad that left Chicago was missing several key players. Eddie Collins, wintering in Philadelphia, had received permission to report late. Joe Jackson (from Savannah) and Buck Weaver and Fred McMullin (from California) were traveling directly to Waco from their winter homes. Eddie Cicotte was still unsigned, but was expected to be on the train. (Cicotte did arrive in time to accompany the team to Waco and signed his contract on March 14, with a salary increase to $10,000.)

The mystery men continued to be Chick Gandil and Swede Risberg. On March 7, the *Chicago Tribune*'s widely read "In the Wake of the News" column, usually written by the paper's former sports editor, Harvey Woodruff, expressed indifference about their return: "Chick Gandil and Swede Risberg have threatened to forsake the White Sox. Well there is an old saying that after you're gone you will never be missed and the world will go on just the same." The White Sox top brass didn't seem to agree. Charles Comiskey himself had headed West; it was assumed that his first stop would be to meet with Gandil, with Risberg to follow. Optimism abounded that both would return. "A telegram to the effect that Gandil will report at Waco next week was halfway expected at White Sox headquarters this morning," wrote Forrest B. Myers on March 9.[8]

No such telegram arrived, and bringing back Gandil and Risberg proved to be much more difficult than anticipated. When the White Sox had their first workout in Waco on Monday, March 15, Buck Weaver was still in Los Angeles, indicating that he would be a problem as well. A spectator at the Cubs' exhibition game that day, Weaver announced that he planned to stop in Waco to talk to Kid Gleason, then head to Chicago to discuss renegotiating his three-year contract, which still had two years to run. "It is Weaver's idea that he ought not to be expected to fulfill the rest of his three-year contract because Comiskey is a friend of [Red Sox owner Harry] Frazee, and Frazee did not compel [Carl] Mays or [Babe] Ruth to live up to their scraps of paper," said the *Chicago Tribune*. "If Comiskey does not want to pay the money he is worth, Buck contends he ought to be traded to New York, where he can get it."[9] With Eddie Collins yet to report, the Sox faced the prospect of starting the exhibition season without any of their starting infielders from 1919.

In the meantime, workouts were beginning. The daily program for the White Sox was as follows, according to Harry Neily:

8 a.m.—Arise and dress
8:30 a.m.—Breakfast
9 a.m.—Take off street clothes and put on baseball uniforms
9:30 a.m. to Noon—Practice at ball park
Noon—Walk back to hotel, take off baseball uniforms, bathe, put on street clothes, and eat lunch
1 to 2 p.m.—Rest
2 p.m.—Take off street clothes, put on baseball uniforms, and walk to ball park
2:30 p.m. to 4 p.m.—Practice
4 p.m.—Walk back to hotel, take off baseball uniforms, and put on street clothes

"Joe Jackson's trunk had not arrived this morning," wrote Neily on March 17, "but the general was so anxious to play ball that he went out and purchased a new pair of shoes and other paraphernalia and got himself to work."[10] Apparently, going shoeless was not considered.

On the other hand, pitcher Grover Cleveland Lowdermilk had chosen to go toothless, at least to a degree. In 1919 Lowdermilk's availability had been limited due to a sore arm, and he eventually left the club suffering from both "a kink in his throwing apparatus" and aching teeth. During this time of much more limited medical knowledge, the two were considered connected. "Now[adays] the teeth are being charged with almost every variety of physical upset," wrote Neily, "and the athlete who owns a kink in his hurling arm is expected to have the molars yanked, which is calculated to fix him up on the diamond, even though it slows him down in the dining room." So after a winter at his Odin, Illinois, home in which "even the home-grown maple syrup and buckwheat flapjacks bothered the troublesome teeth," Lowdermilk—who had read that Cubs pitcher George Tyler experienced great relief "after a tooth doctor took the ivory out of his mouth"—went to see the dentist. After the work had been performed, reported Neily, "Mr. Lowdermilk cast the elusive apple without kinks nor pains."[11]

Warren Corbett, author of a biography of former Major League player, manager, and executive Paul Richards, wrote in an email that the notion of extracting teeth to fix sore arms "was a fairly common remedy up through the 1950s. I can no longer cite chapter and verse, but Paul Richards, among others, prescribed it for his pitchers. The theory was that an abscessed tooth meant there was 'poison in your system.'" While pitchers as noteworthy as Hall of Famer Lefty Grove underwent this treatment, there is no medical basis for such thinking. SABR member and physician Steve Boren wrote, "I read about pulling teeth as a cure for sore arms when I was much younger. There is no real medical way this can help."[12] Lowdermilk himself pitched in only three games for the 1920 White Sox before returning to the minor leagues.

On March 18, Eddie Cicotte pitched to his teammates for the first time without benefit of his banned shine ball, and looked impressive, twice striking out Happy Felsch. "The new rules will not bother him a bit," Kid Gleason claimed. "He has all the stuff he needs without the 'shine ball,' or anything like that. As a matter of fact, three fourths of the time batters were squawking about him rubbing the ball on his trousers he was fooling them by good, old fashioned pitching. The 'shine ball,' so far as he was concerned, was mostly a myth, but he fooled a lot of them by faking it." After the workout Cicotte proclaimed himself in "great physical condition" and said, "I could go in there tomorrow and pitch against any club in the American League."[13]

Still, Cicotte didn't seem too pleased that he would be entering a new season without one of his best pitches. He blamed Washington Senators owner Clark Griffith, who had fought for years to outlaw trick pitches before finally succeeding. At practice a few days after his successful intersquad outing, Cicotte cleverly fashioned a fungo stick out of a bat that had split up the middle. He related, "I designed one of those things once and Spaldings patented it. They call it the Eddie Cicotte model fungo stick, and it sells for a dollar. You get a nickel for every sale. I've made a dime out of it so far. Now I got something else good, and I suppose Griff will have that barred."[14]

As the White Sox held their final workout a day before their first exhibition game on March 20, Larry Woltz wrote, "There was plenty of pep in today's work, 'Buck' Weaver being responsible. Weaver just naturally loves to play baseball. He appeared on the field with a brand new glove, purchased a couple of weeks ago so it looks like 'Buck' decided sometime back to rejoin the White Sox." As it turned out, Woltz was being overly optimistic.[15]

With the start of the exhibition season, the White Sox divided their team in two. The regulars traveled to Dallas for a game against the Dallas Submarines of the Texas League. The "Goofs" or "Yannigans," managed by outfielder John Collins, headed for Belton to take on the Temple A. C. team. The regulars defeated Dallas, 9–4, in their spring opener, though not without a few hiccups. Buck Weaver—not quite in baseball shape after a winter of golf—committed two errors and suffered a stone bruise in his right heel. Meanwhile Lefty Williams, who had avoided combat in World War I by working in a shipyard, was touched for a triple by Arthur J. Forrest of Hannibal, Missouri, a decorated war hero. The most notable moment of the Goofs' 13–6 win over Belton presaged *The Natural*: while chasing a double by John Collins, one of the Belton outfielders ran squarely through the fence, carrying two boards with him. Unlike Bump Bailey in the Barry Levinson film, "outfielder Dockery" survived.

While there may have been a bit of goofiness in the games managed by John Collins, Shano took his work seriously. "John Collins, than whom there is no whomer, is taking his sixth annual workout as a prospective baseball manager," wrote Harry Neily:

John is piloting the White Sox goofs through the wilds of rural Texas, collecting the nimble nickels in a variety of villages which have seldom seen major leaguers in action. This has proved wonderful training. He has learned to assume

81

One of the leaders of the so-called Clean Sox, John (Shano) Collins managed the White Sox substitutes or "Goofs" during spring training. *Library of Congress Prints and Photographs Division*

responsibility, how to get the best out of men and all the little knocks which make or break a manager. He is ripe now for employment as a major league pilot and nobody would give three cheers any louder than the members of the Sox should John be hired to head a club.[16]

Collins would eventually get his chance to manage a Major League team, but not until 1931 with the Red Sox. He lasted a little over a year piloting a miserable Boston team.

On March 22, Buck Weaver let the White Sox know that it wasn't his tender heel that was making him sore: as he had vowed to do earlier, Weaver quit the team and prepared to head to Chicago to battle with Charles Comiskey and Harry Grabiner for a new contract. "[Kid] Gleason had another talk with him last night, but Buck still contends that he must have more money than his contract calls for or he will not play," wrote Neily. "He seems to think he will win an agreement from owner Comiskey as soon as he reaches Chicago."[17] Some people in the White Sox camp thought that Weaver had been influenced by his winter golfing buddy Babe Ruth, who had successfully fought for more money despite having two years to go on his own multiyear deal.

While Buck was threatening to return to Los Angeles and go into business if the White Sox didn't satisfy his demands, he had to know that he didn't quite have Babe Ruth's leverage. Upon hearing of Weaver's move, Grabiner said: "When ball players see fit to break their written agreements it is time to quit dealing with them. Weaver was well satisfied with the three-year contract given him last year. At that time he thought he had been treated most liberally. Baseball is in a pretty bad way when players publicly admit their disregard to live up to their written agreements."[18]

On March 23, Weaver watched from the stands in Waco as the White Sox defeated the Holt team, described as "a fast semi-pro nine," 10–3. Buck returned to the hotel early and missed the ninth inning, in which the Holts got their three runs after the Sox brought in their outfield so that a local comedian named "Sunshine" could get a base hit. As for Weaver, the *Chicago Tribune* reported, "It is noticeable that the players are not giving him very much sympathy in his refusal to live up to his contract." They did reserve some sympathy for Lefty Williams, who was struck on the left forearm during batting practice by a line drive off the bat of Happy Felsch. For a time it appeared that the forearm was broken, but Williams suffered only a bad bruise.[19]

Back east, Lee Magee was talking again. "On Saturday," said Magee from Cincinnati on March 23, "I shall make public the charges on which the National League bases its action in barring me from its circuit. I'll show the documents, both in my favor and against me, and let the public judge whether I've been fairly treated. I'll add to this: I'm going to burn my bridges and then jump off the ruins. If I'm barred I'll take quite a few noted people with me. I'll show up some people for tricks turned ever since 1906. And there will be merry music in the baseball world." Magee's attorney, Robert S. Alcorn, said that a National League magnate had asked League President John Heydler to investigate charges against Magee, and added: "If Mr. Heydler persists in ignoring the case charges against the magnates and refuses to hear them they will be made public by Magee."[20]

Four days later, Alcorn announced that he had sent Heydler "statements naming four National League players in baseball gambling stories of which so much has been rumored, and it is up to Mr. Heydler now." According to Heydler, however, Alcorn's communication "does not contain the name of any ball player who is or has been connected with baseball at any time." As for Magee, Heydler said, "he threatened last week to blow up himself and others by a bomb, which he stated would go off March 27. I have urged him to speed up the explosion. I have heard nothing yet."[21]

The White Sox, of course, had a whole set of "unexploded bombs" . . . and they were trying to keep things that way while they brought back the Suspected Eight for the coming season. However, the team's brass continued to wrangle with Weaver, Risberg, and Gandil. As Weaver prepared to head to Chicago for his showdown with Charles Comiskey, Swede Risberg wired Harry Grabiner on March 24 that he would join the team on Sunday (March 28) in Dallas. But was his holdout over, or was he coming in for more haggling over salary? It still wasn't clear.

With less than three weeks to go before the start of the regular season, Comiskey and Grabiner had had enough. "Early in March we hadn't heard much from Gandil," said Grabiner on March 26. "He had been offered a contract for this season at an advanced salary. At that time he declared he did not care to play ball, but later negotiated with us. If he reports to the White Sox anytime between the present and April 14 he will be offered less money than we were willing to pay him a month ago. In other words, our offer of early March is withdrawn and if he cares to join the club he must start negotiations all over again." Regarding Risberg, Grabiner said that if he "comes to Dallas and does not care to work on his contract which has this season to run, he won't have to quit the Sox. He will be invited to report. If these men do not want to play baseball we must go out and make other arrangements." Comiskey was equally firm about Weaver: "Weaver signed a three year contract at his own demand and without my consent last spring, and he will live up to it or stay out of organized baseball for the rest of his life."[22]

When all was said and done, Risberg and Weaver—who went to Chicago and, as predicted, got nowhere with Comiskey—backed down and agreed to abide by their contracts; Gandil continued to hold out, but the door didn't seem quite closed yet. At worst, all but one of the suspected players would be returning.

As for Gandil, Harvey Woodruff's *Chicago Tribune* "In the Wake of the News" column, which in early March had suggested that Chick would not be missed, had changed its tune by month's end. Woodruff, who had succeeded the legendary Ring Lardner as conductor of the "Wake," was a distinguished writer who worked for the *Tribune* for 29 years, 18 of them as the paper's sports editor. He had been considered a finalist to fill the vacancy as chairman of the National Commission when Garry Herrmann retired.

"With Chick gone the Sox are minus one of the cogs of their winning machine," wrote Woodruff on March 30. "No youngster will develop into a second Gandil. That is a certainty. Possibly a trade may bring an experienced guardian for the initial corner. Even then there are few Gandils in the big leagues today. Chick was a great ballplayer in recent years. You can't take it away from him." Woodruff then went on to suggest that the Sox had a morale problem as a result of not vigorously defending their players from the 1919 World Series fix rumors, writing,

> Then there is another thing. The club is disorganized to some extent. The fact that Gandil is gone, that Weaver, Risberg, and Cicotte had difficulties with Comiskey indicates as much. The nasty rumors that trailed the last world's series have left their marks. The athletes no doubt feel that Comiskey and the other higher ups in baseball made no sincere effort to prove the rumors baseless. The stories have damaged the morale of the team. Kid Gleason certainly has a tremendous job on his hands.[23]

Harry Neily thought that Comiskey's firmness in dealing with Buck Weaver had helped put things in order. "Since the Weaver episode was settled by Magnate Comiskey in such decided fashion," he wrote on March 31, "the Sox have ceased talking about money and the poor, downtrodden ball player, and are paying attention to the work at hand. Manager Gleason is much relieved in mind, for the uncertainty of the club a week ago had him considerably worried." Like Woodruff, Neily thought the Sox missed Chick Gandil: "The return of Chick Gandil is the only thing needed to make Pop Gleason's happiness complete. [Ted] Jourdan is a good first baseman, but Gandil last year played the best first base ever seen in the major leagues, when he committed only three errors in 115 games and hit around .290."[24]

Whether or not Sox players were having major issues with the team's executives, at this point there did not seem to be a lot of internal friction between the men who would become known as Black Sox and their teammates. "The Sox may be having their troubles but not all is seriousness among the junketeers," wrote Forrest B. Myers of the *Chicago Daily News* on March 27. "Combines like Happy Felsch and Eddie Collins have value revealed only behind the scenes." Myers described some hijinks in which Felsch proudly showed his teammates his new cigarette holder, which he insisted was "a valued present made of a peculiar variety of ivory."

"Celluloid," shouted a chorus of the players.

"So we'll see," returned Felsch, confident that it would not burn, as he applied a lighted match. A miniature flash similar to a powder explosion took place and Felsch, master of the occasion, turned the cigarette holder into a torch as he led a cheering parade through the lobby.[25]

A few days later Larry Woltz commented on the budding friendship between Felsch and rookie pitcher Spencer Heath, a Chicago native. "Give this pair a can of burnt cork and they will make McIntyre and Heath look like a pair of Friday nighters," he wrote.[26] McIntyre and Heath were blackface comedians who had enjoyed great popularity over a span of 50 years beginning in the 1870s.

In a spring training game in Jacksonville on March 25, New York Yankees infielder Chick Fewster was hit on the temple by a pitch from Brooklyn Robins right-hander Jeff Pfeffer. According to the *New York Times*, "The impact sounded like a coconut shell cracking, and Fewster went down like an ox felled by an axe." He suffered a fractured skull and was unable to form words for several days. "About a teaspoon full of clotted blood was removed from Fewster's brain and drainage tubes had been put in," the *Times* reported in April 2. "The pressure also was taken off the nerves that paralyzed his speech."[27] Fewster did not return to action until July 5 and batted only 21 times in 1920, but he was able to recover completely and resume a Major League career that lasted until 1927. His injury was among the most severe suffered by a player from a pitch that struck him in the head; in August 1920, another Major League player would not be so fortunate.

As March ended the White Sox left Waco and slowly began working their way home. On April 2 they defeated the Houston Buffaloes of the Texas League, 12–6, scoring nine runs in the first inning. Buck Weaver, who had rejoined the team the previous day, hit two doubles and scored two runs in the inning. "Weaver was the life of the game," wrote Larry Woltz. "He seemed to enjoy it. He kept talking all the time. His heart is back in the game and he's the same old Buck."[28]

After three games in Houston the White Sox traveled to Shreveport, Louisiana, where they took on the Texas League champion Shreveport Gassers. Although they lost to Shreveport, 8–7, on April 5, Kid Gleason was pleased with the way his team was shaping up. "My men came South this spring in much better shape than usual," Gleason said. "Most of them worked during the winter, and they required only a few days on the ball field to work up speed. I haven't seen a ballclub get ready so fast in many years. They could start this season today and we would be set."[29]

From Shreveport the White Sox stopped in Little Rock, Arkansas; Memphis, Tennessee; Louisville, Kentucky; and finally Milwaukee, Wisconsin, taking on local minor league clubs at each stop. There were a few adventures. The Sox had an unscheduled day off in Tennessee when they discovered that their expected opponents, the Memphis Chickasaws of the Southern Association, already had a game scheduled that day against the minor league St. Paul Saints. When the Sox did take on the Chickasaws the next day, the game was called due to rain after four and a half innings, tied 0–0. Joe Jackson was not in the lineup due to a sore neck; Jackson said he had caught cold, but according to the *Tribune*, "Manager Gleason declares that Joe and [teammate] Byrd Lynn had a wrestling match and the catcher put a strangle hold on Joe and dislocated his Adam's apple." In Milwaukee, where the Sox finished their spring schedule with two games against the Brewers of the American Association, Larry Woltz wrote that on the second day, "The game was played to satisfy the cravings of several thousand fans who braved pneumonia and other cold weather diseases just to see Kid Gleason's family in action. It was so cold the athletes had to run around in circles trying to keep their hides warm."[30]

The April 10 edition of the *Chicago Evening American* included a tribute to diminutive (five-foot, six-inch) outfielder Nemo Leibold, who had come to the White Sox from Cleveland, along with Joe Jackson, in 1915. "He was tossed in as extra baggage," wrote Harry Neily about Leibold. "Under-sized and a low-geared, he kept plugging away, until now he is one of the most valuable lead off men in the big leagues."[31] Yet a competing paper, the *Chicago Herald and Examiner*, consistently misspelled the "valuable lead off man's" last name as Liebold. Nemo was only in his sixth year with the team!

While the Sox were in Little Rock, the *Tribune* reported some important news: "Manager Gleason has heard from Owner Comiskey, who says he has heard that Chick Gandil has gone to the Idaho Independent league for sure and that he will not be a member of the Sox this year. Everybody thought that Gandil would finally sign." A few days later, Larry Woltz reported that "Comiskey is not taking things easy while the Sox are staging their final exhibition games. He's after a first baseman, maybe a good one. He may land him before the season opens next Wednesday." Rumors had it that the White Sox were trying to deal for veteran first sacker Stuffy McInnis of the Red Sox.[32]

As the April 14 opener approached, Harry Neily addressed the issue of White Sox team harmony, a subject that would be much discussed in the months and years to come. He wrote,

> The Sox came home last night after a very successful training trip. All hands are in good physical order and none is ailing mentally. The Sox have had many a hearty laugh at stories written by so-called experts, relative to an alleged lack of harmony in the club.
>
> These stories—at least three of which we have seen—were compiled by writers none of whom has been within 2,000 miles of the White Sox since the last world's series and two of whom have had no communication with any official or writer attached with the club. . . .
>
> You can mark down these "internal dissension" stories as being as wrong as the ancient who contended that the world was flat and set out to sail off the upmost edge eventually coming back where he started.
>
> It has been our fortune and misfortune to travel with ten major league managers and none ever fetched a ball club out of the South with the members in heartier accord or more filled with the desire to go forth and grasp another pennant by the tail.[33]

Yet Neily wasn't predicting a pennant for this harmonic bunch. "As to the winning of the American League pennant," he wrote, "that is something else again. Competition will be keen. Cleveland will be a hard club to beat." The *Chicago Evening Post* listed the Indians as the top choice for the pennant, followed by the Detroit Tigers; the *Post* rated the White Sox as "Dangerous," along with the Yankees and Senators. Harvey Woodruff's "In the Wake of the News" *Chicago Tribune* column went no farther than saying, "The Sox are given a good chance against Cleveland and Detroit." In the *Daily News*, Forrest B. Myers mentioned Kid Gleason's optimism, but also noted that prophets were rating the Sox to finish fourth or battle with the Yankees for third place, with Cleveland and Detroit ranking one-two.[34]

"The big day is at hand," Larry Woltz wrote on morning of April 14. "At 3 o'clock this afternoon, the White Sox and Detroit Tigers will pry the lid off the local baseball season. Both clubs are fit, the grounds are in shape and if the weather man behaves himself everything should happen according to schedule."[35]

One of the most unforgettable seasons in baseball history was about to begin.

6

A GOOD START

The White Sox began the 1920 season by hosting the Detroit Tigers, a matchup that was somehow appropriate. Both teams had been involved in past behavior that would be deemed suspicious, dating back to the September 1917 double-headers discussed in chapter 1. In 1919, both the Sox and Tigers had finished the year with games that would be looked on with a suspicious eye for the next century. First there was the "Cobb-Speaker Game" between the Tigers and Cleveland Indians on September 25 (also discussed in chapter 1). Immediately following that game, the 1919 regular season ended with a three-game White Sox-Tigers series that the Sox would be accused of dumping to help the Tigers finish in third place (and also to repay the Tigers for their generosity in 1917). None of the suspicious details about these events had come to light by April 1920 . . . but the players on these teams had a history of (at the very least) mor-ally questionable behavior.

The Tigers had been managed since 1907 by Hughie Jennings, a former teammate of John McGraw with the legendary Baltimore Orioles of the 1890s. Jennings had won American League pennants in each of his first three seasons as a manager (1907–1909), but the Tigers had lost all three World Series and had not won a pennant since then. However, Detroit had finished a strong fourth in 1919, and with an offense led by the great Ty Cobb, the team was expected to contend for the American League pennant in 1920. Cobb, who had celebrated his 33rd birthday in December 1919, had led the American League in batting average in 12 of the 13 seasons from 1907 to 1919 (all but 1916).

For the April 14 opener, Jennings's starting pitcher was George (Hooks) Dauss, a right-hander who had joined the Detroit club in 1912 and who would spend his entire 15-year career with the Tigers. Kid Gleason held off on naming his starter for as long as possible, but went as expected with Claude Williams, a former Tiger who had made his Major League debut with Detroit in 1913. Lefty entered the game with a career record of 10–2 against the Tigers. Eight of the nine players in the White Sox Opening Day lineup had started the club's last game prior to spring training—Game 8 of the 1919 World Series. The only missing player was Chick Gandil, who was still stating his yen for the wonders of baseball in Idaho. Taking Gandil's place at first base was 24-year-old Ted Jourdan, who entered the game with only 46 career Major League at-bats.

The White Sox would have their share of "suspicious games" in 1920, but the season opener wasn't one of them. Before a Comiskey Park crowd of 25,000, the Sox prevailed, 3–2, in 11 innings, in "a contest that couldn't have been equaled had it been rehearsed," according to James Crusinberry. Williams, who went all the way for the Sox, was an out away from a 2–1 victory when future Hall of Famer Harry Heilmann homered into the left field bleachers to tie the game with two out in the top of the ninth. But Williams held the Tigers scoreless for two more innings, and in the bottom of the 11th Buck Weaver singled (his fourth hit of the game), stole second, and raced home on Eddie Collins's second double of the contest. "He was holding out for more dough this spring," Crusinberry wrote of Weaver. "If he goes along like he did yesterday, he can get any amount he asks."[1]

After noting the packed house, Crusinberry touched on the 1919 World Series. "Among those thousands were the countless bugs who, after the deplorable world's series of last fall, had raised a right hand and sworn, 'Never again.' They simply forgot all about the nasty rumors, the unexpected defeats, the bum playing, and all the other things, and went back for more."[2]

Despite the fact that he had brought back seven of the eight suspected players, Charles Comiskey apparently hadn't quite forgotten "all about the nasty rumors, the unexpected defeats, the bum playing, and all the other things" . . . at least not when it came to Swede Risberg. Agent S-1 (formerly known as E. W. M.) was still hoping to get information from Risberg's lover, Marie Purcell ("Subject"), and her friend Florence Brown. In April S-1 filed his latest report, the first since late February (at least one report that is mentioned is not in the Chicago History Museum files).

On April 13, the day before the White Sox opener, Risberg spent the evening with Purcell, Brown, Brown's mother, and S-1, not leaving until around 1:30 a.m. on the morning of the 14th (game time was 3:00 p.m.). They played cards but "'R' did not have a lot to say, except repeating something about going

White Sox shortstop Swede Risberg was spied on by one of Charles Comiskey's detectives, who befriended two female friends of Risberg. *Library of Congress Prints and Photographs Division*

to ask for more money. He told how Kid Gleason caught him coming into his [spring training] hotel in Dallas, Texas at about 2 A.M. in the morning."[3]

Prior to the game on April 14, Risberg phoned Purcell at her office and expressed a desire to see her again that evening. She told him she had an engagement, but he got her to promise to telephone him once her guest had left. S-1 was present when Purcell phoned Risberg that night, and reported that "Subject" and "R" conversed for about 15 minutes. When S-1 asked Purcell what Risberg had to say, "she said that 'R' claimed to have had a talk with Gleason—that things were partly settled, but the latter had insisted that 'R' be in his hotel every evening by 11:30 P.M. 'R' had remarked to Subject that this did not make any difference with him—that he would see her at every opportunity just the same."[4]

S-1's final report would be filed on April 30.

While the White Sox and Tigers were battling on Opening Day, Lee Magee was back in the news. In Cincinnati, Magee filed a $9,500 damage suit against the Chicago Cubs in Common Pleas court. He was seeking damages based on his $4,500 salary "and a possible $5,000 that he might receive should the Cubs win the pennant." He also alleged that along with dropping him, the Cubs would not permit him to play for any other Major League team. Cubs President William Veeck, father of future baseball mogul Bill Veeck, said, "We will fight Lee Magee's suit to a finish, and we fail to see where he has a legal chance to collect a red cent." Reds President August Herrmann commented, "Magee's suit is a joke." But Magee was determined to keep fighting.[5]

The White Sox and Tigers were idle for two days following Wednesday's Opening Day thriller, as both Thursday and Friday's scheduled games were postponed due to rain; there was even a little sleet and snow on Friday. The weather finally cleared on Saturday, April 17, and Eddie Cicotte took the mound for the first regular season game in which he would have to work without the now-illegal shine ball and emery ball. No worries . . . Cicotte was brilliant in shutting out the Tigers on five hits, 4–0 as the Sox improved to 2–0. He faced only 31 batters. Crusinberry quoted what Charles Comiskey had said in February, when the trick pitches were declared illegal: "You can legislate against the things a pitcher can do with his hands his feet, but you can't legislate against using his brain." Only once did a Tiger ask to have the ball examined, and when plate umpire Ollie Chill tossed it out, "Eddie took the new one and made the Detroit batters look like suckers."[6]

On Sunday the White Sox were scheduled to start a four-game series against the St. Louis Browns, but for the third time in five days, the game was rained out.

"The weather bureau, which has been going democratic ever since a week before the season opened, continued to be blind, deaf, and dumb to the public welfare and provided conditions against it was useless to contend," wrote I. E. Sanborn.[7]

But there was news on other baseball fronts. "Ban Johnson is intent on stamping out gambling in the American league this season," proclaimed the *Chicago Evening Post* on Sunday. Fred Turbyville reported that "Clay Folger, for fourteen years chief of police and detectives at League park in Cleveland, will be in charge of the small army of detectives who will be present at every game and besides, will keep a watch on any players under suspicion." According to Folger, "We generally have five or six men in the stands every afternoon. If they hear bets being made, they quietly inform the gambler that he is requested to leave the park. His money is refunded at the gate."[8] Folger did not say whether he was keeping a watch on any White Sox players under suspicion.

On Monday the Sox were rained out yet again, giving them four postponements and only two games played in six days. But Al Spink liked what he had seen thus far from the team. "Looking at the White Sox today, they seem better and stronger than at any time in the last five years. They look better, even, than in 1917, when they took the American league flag and the world's championship from New York to boot," Spink wrote in the *Evening Post*. "Comiskey, the old 'boss president' of the White Sox, when the campaign started this year determined to wash his hands of trouble and anxiety and gave the complete rein to Gleason. The latter, despite all obstacles, has gone along like a whirlwind, brushing obstacles aside, and after many difficulties he now has his team in fine, steady playing form."[9]

A day later, the Sox continued to raise the question of whether a team could be awarded a pennant with two wins, no losses, and 152 postponements. This time the game against the Browns actually got started, but "in a fog so dense the big score board in center field resembled a mirage and one could not distinguish 'Gasoline Alley' from Wentworth Avenue," according to Sanborn. With the Sox leading, 1–0, in the bottom of the third and poised to break the game open— bases loaded with none out—plate umpire Brick Owens stopped the game. By that point, the fog was so thick that the outfielders could not be seen from home plate, and after waiting for 10 minutes to see if the fog would lift, Owens called the game on account of "darkness," even though it was only 3:35 p.m.[10]

Finally on Wednesday, the Sox got a game in, and improved to 3–0 with a 7–4 victory over the Browns. After a sloppy top of the first in which two Sox errors led to two Brownie runs, the White Sox came back with three in the bottom of the inning and scored in each of the first four frames to roll, 7–4, for Claude Williams's second complete-game win. Joe Jackson, apparently unfamiliar with blue skies after days of rain and fog, lost two balls in the sun according to I. E. Sanborn, but also had a key two-run triple in the bottom of the first.[11] Fielding (and baserunning) misadventures, counterbalanced by hitting heroics, would be a common theme for Jackson in 1920. This makes it more challenging to assess whether Jackson was playing crookedly at times in 1920, as some have charged. By 1920, Jackson had slowed down in the field and was prone to be overly adventuresome on the basepaths. He could be careless, and try to do more than his body would allow. That could make him look bad.

On the other hand, Swede Risberg was 0 for 12 in the first three games, with no walks and three errors in the field. Detective Clay Folger, please note.

Wednesday's victory over the Browns was the last game of the Sox's opening homestand. The team now traveled to Detroit for the Tigers' home opener. The Tigers had lost each of their first five games, and they fell to 0–6 as the Sox walloped them, 8–2, behind Red Faber. It was a reassuring performance for Faber, who had spent most of 1918 in the military and was set back by illness and injury in the Sox's pennant-winning season of 1919. "Red seemed to have all the stuff that made him a terror to foreign batters in 1917," wrote Irving Vaughan. "He eased over fast ones, curves and even spitters, the latter variety being especially effective."[12] Joe Jackson had four hits and drove in four runs for the White Sox; after four games he was hitting .500 (7 for 14) with seven RBI.

After yet another rainout on Friday—Chicago's sixth in the first 10 days of the season—the White Sox improved to 5–0, and dropped the Tigers to 0–7, with a 7–1 win on Saturday behind Eddie Cicotte. Jackson, still hitting .500, had two more hits along with three RBI. With 10 RBI in the first 5 games, he was on pace to drive in 308 runs for the year. But it wasn't all good news for the White Sox. In the eighth inning, the Tigers' Ralph Young hit a hard smash up the middle; Cicotte knocked it down, threw Young out, and finished the game, but an X-ray the next morning revealed a fracture in the first joint of the index finger on Eddie's left hand. He was expected to miss a week to 10 days. Sunday's game, before 22,000 fans at Navin Field—over 68,000 witnessed the three-game series, an impressive total for that era—was a pitchers' duel between Lefty Williams of the White Sox and Howard Ehmke of the Tigers. Through nine innings the game was scoreless, with Williams allowing only one hit, a single off the pitcher's glove by Donie Bush in the fourth inning. Finally, in the 10th, the White Sox loaded the bases and Eddie Murphy—in the lineup because Happy Felsch was back in Chicago being treated for a boil—doubled over short for two runs. The Tigers got two hits and scored a run in the bottom of the inning, but Williams got Ira Flagstead to hit into a 5-4-3 double play to end it.

The Tigers were now 0–8 on the season, with five of the losses coming at the hands of the White Sox. Expected to contend, Detroit would start the year 0–13, a record for consecutive losses to start the season that would not be broken until 1988. "All of the Tigers have had their hair cropped close within the last day or so," noted the *Detroit Times* after Sunday's game. "Their batting strength seems to have been shorn along with their locks."[13]

The White Sox, meanwhile, were 6–0. In the six games the Sox had outscored their opponents, 31–10, and Kid Gleason had yet to use a relief pitcher. "The White Sox are the sensation of the American League," said an analysis of the Major League races in the *Detroit Times*. "Gleason has copped six straight games with three pitchers . . . Weaver, [Eddie] Collins and Jackson are doing most of their clubbing." The *Chicago Evening Post* quoted a letter from Dick Jemison, a former Atlanta sports editor now working in Detroit. "Score one against the baseball dopesters who counted the Chicago White Sox out of the pennant scramble of 1920," wrote Jemison. "In my estimation, they're going to be in the swim with both feet right until the gong rings next October or my fifteen years of watching baseball clubs in action and doping them has been so much wasted time."[14]

Jemison went on to praise the White Sox for "using their brains as well as their arms, legs and eyes." He praised Swede Risberg, who had bounced back from his 0 for 12 with 5 hits in 12 at-bats in the Detroit series. "Personally, I never have been an admirer of Swede Risberg. I thought that he was the weak cog in the Sox machine, but he's almost converted me to an admirer: at least if he plays many more games like the two I saw him play here, I'm willing to doff my Kelly to him as being as good a shortstop as any in the business."[15]

The White Sox now headed to Cleveland to take on the Indians, the club considered their most serious rival in the American League pennant race.

Ever since the Black Sox scandal broke, there has been a general consensus that some or all of the suspected players continued to dump games during the 1920 regular season. There was evidence from the Black Sox themselves:

- In his book *Bleeding between the Lines*, Eliot Asinof wrote that Happy Felsch "confessed he had helped to throw games during the 1920 season as well, just as Red Faber had said."
- Harry Grabiner's diary notes that in October 1920, Buck Weaver told a Sox official that during the 1920 season, Fred McMullin had offered him $500 to help throw a game (Weaver said he refused the offer).
- In the extended audio interviews of Lawrence Ritter's *The Glory of Their Times*, Joe Wood said that Eddie Cicotte, his former teammate with the

Red Sox, told him that the White Sox had been under pressure *not* to win the pennant in 1920 ("We don't dare win."). While not quoting any source directly, Ban Johnson said the same thing about the Sox during the Chicago grand jury hearings in September.[16]

Additionally, numerous members of the team, along with writers and league officials, voiced their suspicions that regular season games were being thrown in 1920. Eddie Collins, the first to speak up, was reported to have aired his charge of crooked play directly to Charles Comiskey in September. Many others followed.

In a 2016 article for the SABR *Baseball Research Journal*, Bruce Allardice, a professor of history and political science at South Suburban College and a member of the SABR Black Sox Scandal Research Committee, wrote, "In sum, every 'Clean' Sox regular (Schalk, Shano Collins, Eddie Collins, Leibold, Murphy, Kerr, and Faber), at the time, or later, accused their teammates of laying down in 1920. Known fixer Happy Felsch admitted as much. Add to that list of accusers two 'Clean' Sox backups ([Byrd] Lynn and [Harvey] McClellan), the Sox's manager, umpires, sportswriters, and American League President Ban Johnson, throw in the McMullin bribe attempt and Cicotte's admission, and it becomes clear that once again the fix was in."[17]

But while there is good reason to believe that games were being fixed in 1920, there is little consensus about how many games were dumped, and—with a few exceptions—the specific games that were involved. The number of games involved may well have been small. Without something like evidence of a payoff, it is of course impossible to know for sure.

In *Eight Men Out*, Eliot Asinof asserted that the opening game of the White Sox-Indians series on April 27 was fixed to let the Indians win. After noting Chicago's 6-0 start, he wrote,

> At this point, the good gentlemen from St. Louis seized the moment and took control. Joe Pesch and Carl Zork, [Abe] Attel's partners of the year before, made contact. The contact man was Fred McMullin. The instructions were familiar enough: they were to lose the first game at Cleveland.
>
> Immediately, the odds shifted, just as they had before the opening game of the past World Series. And once again, the betting skyrocketed, the odds ending up at 6-5, with Cleveland favored.[18]

Asinof did not list sources for his work, but a story in the *Chicago Evening American* on October 1, 1920, quoting "a prominent man who is quite familiar in the gambling world," referred to the betting activity on this game: "The

White Sox started off last spring winning six straight games before they went to Cleveland for their first game in that city. Naturally the Sox were favorites in the betting, but the tip was out that morning that Cleveland was the 'good thing.' It came from Kansas City and I know there were several thousand dollars of Kansas City money spread around in other cities. There was so much of it that the odds went to 6 to 5, with Cleveland the favorite. Cleveland won the game."[19]

The game was a tight pitcher's duel between Red Faber and Cleveland's Stan Coveleski. The White Sox led, 2–1, with two out and nobody on in the bottom of the eighth. Larry Gardner was at bat for the Indians. Then, according to Asinof, "A fly ball was hit over Jackson's head in left field. Swede Risberg went out to receive Jackson's throw and make the relay throw in. Risberg threw so badly that neither Buck Weaver nor Red Faber, who was backing up, could get their hands on the ball. The run scored, tying up the game, which Cleveland went on to win in the ninth."[20]

There are several newspaper accounts of this game available. The following are descriptions of the key play in the eighth inning:

Irving Vaughan (*Chicago Tribune*): "Gardner walloped a fly over Jackson's dome. Risberg relayed the ball to third base, but the throw was so wide that neither Weaver nor Faber could capture the pill, so Gardner scored. Risberg never should have made the peg, as there was no chance to beat the runner to the bag."[21]

Harry Neily (*Chicago Evening American*): "There was another play that went wrong, but that was a matter of stupidity. In the eighth, two hands being out, Gardner crashed one to left field. Jackson shagged the ball and threw to Risberg, who had gone to short left field. By this time Gardner was going into third standing up and there was no play at all, but Risberg cut loose and heaved to the stands and Gardner finished the circuit with the tying run. There was no occasion to throw, because there was nobody to put out at third, Gardner already being there."[22]

Forrest B. Myers (*Chicago Daily News*): "Gardner tripled past Jackson and scored when Risberg threw the ball to the grand stand."[23]

Larry Woltz (*Chicago Herald and Examiner*): "Gardner smashed a triple to deep left. Risberg took Jackson's relay and pegged to third. It was a mile over Weaver's head, the ball rolling to the grandstand."[24]

Henry P. Edwards (*Cleveland Plain Dealer*): "Gardner tripled to center and scored when Risberg's relay of Jackson's throw went to the grand stand."[25]

So, unanimous agreement that Risberg made a terrible throw, probably one he should not have made. In Chicago's two-run sixth inning, Jackson probably prevented a bigger inning when he was tossed out trying to stretch a single into a double. On the other hand, he did hit the single, and also had a double in the fourth inning that put runners on second and third with one out; the Sox failed to score, but you can't blame Joe for that. Buck Weaver had two hits in the game, including a double in the two-run sixth; he also scored the first White Sox run. Happy Felsch had one hit, a single that drove in the second White Sox run in the sixth. So it's logical to take Jackson, Weaver, and Felsch off the hook; McMullin, Cicotte, and Williams did not play . . .so the gamblers' plan was . . . Swede Risberg against the world? And all he could do was make one bad play that led to one of the three Cleveland runs.

Consider me very doubtful that this game was fixed.

Bruce Allardice, who has written extensively about the Black Sox, believes that fixed games took place in 1920, but doubts that they would have happened until later in the season. In an email to the author, Allardice wrote,

> With the absence of proof, I turn to the gamblers and try and imagine what a savvy gambler (one with enough money and pull to win enough to pay the Sox off) would have wagered on.
>
> In my opinion the gamblers wouldn't bother with bets on early season games, as there wasn't enough interest in them to see large sums wagered (and won). Logically, the gamblers would concentrate on later season games, probably games involving Boston and New York (where large bets could be made without notice, and where Sullivan/Rothstein were headquartered).
>
> If the gamblers wagered on who would win the AL pennant, they'd delay to see how the race was shaping out before trying to get the Sox to throw games. After all, why have the Sox throw games before it can be seen if the Sox are even in the race? Again, this argues for concentrating on late season games.[26]

In general I agree with Bruce's analysis, but not completely; as we shall see, the White Sox had some head-scratching performances prior to the later stages of the race.

On Wednesday, April 28, Cleveland beat the White Sox again, 5–4; the victory dropped the Sox (6–2) in the standings behind the Indians and Red Sox (both 8–2). Dickey Kerr, making his first start of the season for the White Sox, lasted only a third of an inning, allowing three hits, a walk, and three runs. Even then, the White Sox might have won if not for a sensational catch by Indians player-manager Tris Speaker, who robbed Joe Jackson (now hitting .483) of a possible triple with two on and two out in the seventh. On Thursday the Sox salvaged the series finale, 6–1, thanks to another sensational performance by Claude Williams, who improved to 4–0 with a 1.38 ERA after holding the Indians to two hits (one of them an infield hit).

The White Sox received bad news during the series when doctors discovered that Eddie Cicotte had a second fracture on his injured finger; the club now thought it might be three weeks before he could pitch again. Even so, Harry Neily quoted Cleveland writer Ed Bang, who warned Indians fans to "Keep your eye on the White Sox, for they will bear watching."[27]

Bang also addressed the issue of White Sox team morale. In later years it would be accepted as a given that after the shenanigans of the 1919 World Series, fractionalization between the "Clean Sox" and their suspected brethren was worse than ever in 1920—beginning with spring training. Typical was a comment in an article written 36 years after the fact, in 1956, by former *Chicago Tribune* writer James Crusinberry: "When I joined the White Sox in spring training, I noticed at once that the other seven suspected players formed a separate faction on the club. On the road these seven were always by themselves in the hotel dining rooms and lobbies and on the trains." This sounds like, at the very least, a highly visible cold war, but like Harry Neily earlier, Bang saw things differently—at least early in the season. "Manager Kid Gleason appears to have straightened out all the troubles and tangles, real or fancied, that existed among some of the players," he wrote. "The White Sox, bubbling over with pep and spirit, have been playing heads-up baseball, and must be rated as a dangerous contender."[28]

But if the White Sox did not necessarily have a morale problem at this point in the season, they did appear to have a Swede Risberg problem. After nine games, Risberg was batting .176 with five errors. Even good players can go through bad stretches, but in Swede's case it appeared to be deliberate. On April 30, Operative S-1 filed his final report to J. R. Hunter and Alfred Austrian. "Since then [April 14]," he wrote, "I have had several talks with Subject [Risberg's lover Marie Purcell], and felt her out as to what 'R' had told her. It seems that he had remarked on nothing of importance. I said that I had noticed in the papers 'R' was making several errors in the last few days. Subject said, 'He will continue to make errors until they give him the money he asks for.' I asked how she knew to which she said, 'Swede told me.'"[29]

As usual, Charles Comiskey and Alfred Austrian did nothing with this information.

"Will this be Joe Jackson's year?" *Chicago Evening Post* columnist Malcolm MacLean wrote on May 1. "Mr. Joe, ever since he broke into the American League, has been striving to lead it in batting just once. Ty Cobb, another southerner, has usually been in his path. . . . During the two and a half weeks of this pennant chase, Jackson has been going like a whirlwind while Cobb is way down on the bottom of the list." That afternoon Jackson had three more hits, lifting his average to .486, as the White Sox defeated the Browns, 8–5, in St. Louis. "The Sox threatened in the sixth, but their chance was wrecked by Risberg's poor base running," wrote Larry Woltz. "The Swede led with a single, and stole second. Schalk's infield out advanced him to third. With Faber at bat and the infield playing in, Billings' snap throw to Austin trapped Risberg and he was out."[30] Swede Risberg, doing those little things that don't show up in the box scores.

The Sox continued to shine in St. Louis, winning 7–3 on Sunday, May 2 (behind Roy Wilkinson in his first start of the year), and 7–1 on Monday (as Lefty Williams improved to 5–0), before the Browns routed Dickey Kerr, still struggling to get going, in the finale of the White Sox road trip on Tuesday, 12–4. With a 10–3 record, the Sox were once more leading the league. Jackson was leading the American League in batting average (.469), on-base percentage (.544), slugging (.735), and RBI (18), while Buck Weaver (.404) and Eddie Collins (.385) ranked third and fourth in the AL in batting average. Even Risberg had come alive with the bat, lifting his season average to .261.

Jackson and Williams had an adventure in St. Louis. "Joe Jackson and Claude Williams were grabbed as suspicious characters last night," reported the *Chicago Tribune* on May 2. "They were returning from a show, and when near their hostelry two plain clothes men stepped up and planted gats against the ribs of the respective athletes. After an explanation the boys were allowed to proceed home."[31]

Also of note on May 2: at Washington Park in Indianapolis, C. I. Taylor's Indianapolis ABCs won a doubleheader over Joe Green's Chicago Giants, 4–2 and 11–4, in the first official games in Negro National League history. The *Indianapolis News* reported that there were "more than 6,000 fans shouting approval"; the *Chicago Defender* called it "one of the largest and most enthused gathering [*sic*] of baseball devotees who ever assembled into being what is purported to be the most important and far-reaching step ever negotiated by the baseball promoters of our Race since the birth of the game more than forty years ago." The ABCs lineup featured the great Oscar Charleston, who had been recently acquired from the Chicago American Giants (a different club than the Chicago Giants).[32]

On Wednesday, May 5, the White Sox returned home for a five-game rematch with the Indians before embarking on their first Eastern road trip of the season. In the opener, Cleveland spitballer Stan Coveleski improved to 6–0 on the year with a 3–2 win over another master of the spitter, Red Faber. Faber allowed only six hits, but his own error in the sixth led to one run, and a two-base error by Happy Felsch to another. However, Felsch also had two hits in the game, and scored the second White Sox run on a single by Swede Risberg.

On Thursday, with famed singer Al Jolson—a big Indians fan—in the house, Cleveland won again by a 3–2 score, with undefeated Jim Bagby (5–0) beating Sox hopeful Roy Wilkinson (1–2). Cleveland's first run came from three Sox errors—one by Wilkinson and two by Risberg, who booted a Tris Speaker grounder and then dropped Ray Schalk's throw to second when Speaker attempted to steal. However, it was a strong outing by Wilkinson, a six-foot, one-inch right-hander making only his third career Major League start. "This is cheerful," wrote Harry Neily about Wilkinson's outing, "because it sustains the opinion of Manager Gleason that Wilkinson, on his pitching ability, is fit to be one of the four regulars."[33] Wilkinson would be a regular part of the Sox rotation until mid-June, when Dickey Kerr was strong enough to resume his regular spot.

The White Sox were now 1–4 against the Indians, with all four losses coming by one run. "All four games which were lost might just as well have been won by the Sox," wrote Neily, "but some untoward event (alibi for bad play) intervened to decide the contest otherwise, a situation which no doubt Pop Gleason has called to the attention of the hired hands in language much more copious and fluid than is at our command."[34] The Sox played better on Friday, thumping the Indians 6–1, as Claude Williams raised his record to 6–0 with a 1.26 ERA (and six complete games). But they looked awful on Saturday, as four Sox pitchers surrendered 16 hits and allowed six walks in a 10–6 defeat.

Suspected of dumping games in the 1919 World Series, Claude (Lefty) Williams won his first six starts in 1920. In September, he confessed to his role in the fix. *Library of Congress Prints and Photographs Division*

In the last game of the brief homestand on Sunday, the Sox dropped yet another one-run game to the Indians, 4–3. This was one of the 1920 games that Eliot Asinof believed the Black Sox dumped, and it definitely had some suspicious elements. The first Indians run came home via an error by Risberg (on "an easy bounder," according to Irving Vaughan), giving him 10 miscues in 18 games. The Swede later left the game in the seventh inning when he was spiked on the right knee by Indians catcher Steve O'Neill on a play at the plate (Risberg was expected to miss four or five days). In the top of the seventh the Indians scored their second run after Ted Jourdan and Eddie Cicotte, who was making an early return from his finger injury, failed to execute a 3–1 putout at first base. And Cleveland's two-run ninth inning was helped by a wild throw from Cicotte; "without this [error] the inning might have produced nothing," wrote Vaughan. In summing up the game, Vaughan described the Sox as "careless in their fielding and not at all particular about making base hits mean something."[35] Even then, the Sox might have won the game; trailing 4–0 entering the bottom of the ninth, the team scored three times and might have pulled it out had not umpire Brick Owens called out pinch hitter Eddie Murphy on a close play at first; the Sox were certain that Murphy had beaten the throw.

The White Sox now began a long road trip that included visits to six of their seven American League rivals, with the team not returning to Comiskey Park until June 4. With an 11–7 record, the Sox had dropped to third place, but still only two games behind the Indians. The offense, led by Jackson (second in the league with a .386 batting average) and Weaver (third at .384), continued to be excellent; Jackson was leading the league in slugging (.586, with Felsch third at .529) and RBI (20), while Weaver was tied for the league lead in runs scored (18) and second in on-base percentage (.464, with Jackson third at .449). However, the club's mound work was shaky except for Williams, and defense had been a season-long problem. "Last season the White Sox predominated over all their opponents as able fielders," wrote Harry Neily. "They gathered in the hard chances easily and in the pinches were exceedingly steady. The same crew this year have sloughed off six hard battles through lack of proper grabbing."[36]

However, the Sox were very much in contention, and the club apparently still had its sense of humor. "Last winter Buck Weaver invested $1,000 in oil stock," reported Irving Vaughan in the *Tribune*'s team notes on May 7. "After the game he received a telegram offering him $30,000 for his holdings. Buck wasn't sure but that some of his mates had framed the wire."[37]

"Why Do Honest Ball Players Stand for Crooks in Ranks?" was the title of an article in the May 6 edition of *Sporting News* by Chicago-based writer Oscar Reichow. "What is an unfathomable puzzle to me since the alleged World Series scandal of last fall is why the ball players in the major leagues have not taken some action toward keeping the great American Game free of crookedness. . . . Why shouldn't the players take it upon themselves to eliminate the crooks?"[38]

A fair response might be to ask why it was up to the players to police their own game, when the people who were running the sport seemed so indifferent to the subject. But in one part of Organized Baseball, that was about to change. On May 7, the league-leading San Francisco Seals of the Pacific Coast League announced that they were releasing two of their best pitchers, Tom Seaton and Luther (Casey) Smith. Charlie Graham, owner and manager of the Seals, would not provide specific details about why the players were being released but stated, "I believe, and my associates believe with me, that baseball must be kept above suspicion. From time to time rumors of the most serious nature have reached me regarding both these players, their practices and their associates. At first I refused to listen to them, but their persistency and their growth have persuaded me that, whether true or untrue, for the best interests of the San Francisco club and for the best interests of baseball Seaton and Smith should be released."[39]

While Seaton and Smith vehemently denied they had done anything improper, the move was completely supported by PCL President William H. McCarthy, a vehement opponent of gambling who had been on the job for only four months. On May 9, McCarthy announced that "I have today notified the San Francisco club to hereafter refuse admission to three known gamblers." He said he would work to clean every city in the league of baseball gambling within three weeks, and that "I would rather close every park than permit gambling to continue." The gamblers would not go away quietly, however. One of the three men banned by McCarthy, Roy Hurlburt, assaulted McCarthy at Geary and Powell Streets in San Francisco on the evening of May 10, punching him and knocking him to the ground. Hurlburt was arrested for battery, while another of the gamblers, Martin Breslauer, was jailed for vagrancy. McCarthy refused to back down and neither did the league, which authorized a budget of $20,000 to fund McCarthy's war on gambling.[40]

A few days later, the *Salt Lake Telegram* provided specifics on Seaton's and Smith's transgressions, which did not specifically involve game-fixing. "The two pitchers are indirectly accused of working a code system with gamblers who bet on whether or not the batter will hit, fan or receive a pass to first," the paper reported. "It is reported that large sums have been won each day one of the pitchers was in the box." The *Telegram* was one of many newspapers, particularly in the West, to praise Charlie Graham for his actions in releasing the players, estimating that the move might cost the team "more than $100,000 and probably the league pennant."[41]

The Pacific Coast League that William McCarthy and Charlie Graham were working to clean up had been notorious for years for its tolerance of gamblers, with accusations of major game-fixing operations late in the 1919 season. It might not be a coincidence that Chick Gandil, Fred McMullin, Swede Risberg, Buck Weaver, and Lefty Williams had all spent time in the PCL before moving up to the Majors.

Revelations about crooked play in the Pacific Coast League—and the Major Leagues—were just beginning.

7

THE ABSENT BROTHER

On May 11, the White Sox opened their long road trip with a series against the Yankees at New York's Polo Grounds. That same day, J. R. Hunter of Hunter's Secret Service sent a summary of his operatives' work to Charles Comiskey and Harry Grabiner. Hunter wrote that his agency had been asked by Comiskey's law firm, Mayer, Meyer, Austrian and Platt, "to investigate the basis for certain newspaper and magazine articles appearing in different mediums thru-out the country setting forth that the White Sox Players had entered into a conspiracy with certain gamblers whereby the players were to make it possible for Cincinnati to win and in turn the winnings of the gamblers was to be divided—part of which was to go to such players who were willing to enter into the agreement."[1]

Hunter set down what his operatives had discovered:

- "We assigned an investigator to St. Louis who covered all angles of secret inquiry which would develop grounds for such reports, but he was unable to connect up any absolute transaction that would warrant charging any player with conspiracy."
- "We located three different players in and around Los Angeles. . . . However, nothing developed from this angle to throw any additional light on the matter under investigation. These same men were interviewed semi-openly and they gained the impression that if they [*sic*] inquiry had anything to do with the ball playing interests it was a newspaper connection, but there were no additional points developed that would lend credit to the rumors referred to."

- "In the different angles of the inquiry, it developed that some of the players while in Chicago were accustomed to visit a certain apartment that was conducted by two young ladies. . . . We were not able to connect any definite connection between these girls and the ball players, where the former placed any bets that the Cincinnati team was to win the World Series, neither were there any documentary proof of betting stubs, account books or letters found in the apartment that would throw any light on the matter in connection."
- "In a general summing up of the entire investigation, all that can be said is that we covered the different points to get at the facts, but there is still that unsettled question: 'What prompted those open insinuations in the newspapers associating the names of your players with gamblers in the World Series of 1919?'"
- "In conclusion, we wish to thank you for your forbearance in this matter . . . you gave us your cooperation in time and money to get at the facts— reserving judgment as to the merits of the rumors, until such time as we would sift down the different rumors which were wafted from the sporting column of newspapers thru-out the country reflecting on your players."[2]

Curiously, the summary made no mention of Operative #11's investigation of Happy Felsch . . . leading one to wonder whether Hunter's final bill of $3,830.71—about what Felsch made in 1919—included all those Christmas trees that the operator had purchased.

Hunter's carefully worded summary seemed to be written in a way that would justify Comiskey's decision to bring back the suspected players (except for Chick Gandil, whom they had made some effort to re-sign): "You gave us your . . . time and money—reserving judgment as to the merits of the rumors." It is probably true that the work of J. R. Hunter's operatives, by itself, yielded nothing that would convict the investigated players in a court of law, or maybe even in the court of public opinion. But at the same time, Comiskey had more than just detective reports to help him decide what to do about these players for 1920. There were provocative leads beginning with the information provided by Harry Redmon. There was Redmon's mention (in October 1919) of Bill Burns, a gambler with direct involvement in the fix and a man who eventually proved willing to talk, but whom the White Sox did not attempt to contact. There were stories about the players' suspect behavior, often quite detailed, in *Collyer's Eye*. There were the suspicions of Kid Gleason and other White Sox players, expressed even while the World Series was going on.

Maddeningly, Charles Comiskey—with his obvious conflicts of interest—was still the only baseball official doing any investigation of the 1919 World Series. "In 1919," Black Sox historian Gene Carney wrote, "the National Commission was a lame duck, and American League President Ban Johnson was under fire from several club owners, including Charles Comiskey. There is little doubt that the struggle for power within baseball prevented a coordinated, thorough investigation into the rumors of bribery connected with the 1919 Series. What Comiskey learned, through the detectives he hired, he kept to himself."[3] And there the matter stood, as the White Sox continued their season.

Nearly a month into the 1920 campaign, Babe Ruth was looking like a flop. Entering the May 11 game against the White Sox, Ruth was batting .210, with a .290 on-base percentage, in his first 18 games in a Yankee uniform. He had hit only two home runs. He had also struggled in the field. Forced to open the season in center field due to injuries to other players, Ruth had muffed a fly ball on Opening Day in Philadelphia, costing the Yankees the game. The next day Ruth was presented a gift at home plate from an Athletics fan who owned a hat shop: a brown derby, which in those days was considered a symbol of ineptitude.

The May 11 game against the White Sox began Ruth's turnaround. Facing Roy Wilkinson, he hit a two-run homer to deep right field in the first inning to give the Yankees a 2–0 lead. In the third, he drove in another run with a triple. In the fifth, he homered again, this time off Dickey Kerr, for the final run in the Yankees' 6–5 victory. In a syndicated column written after each game in which he hit a homer (his stipend in 1920, soon to go way up, was five dollars per homer), Ruth—most likely with the help of a ghostwriter—wrote, "Well, I guess I'll polish up that brown derby they gave me in Philly and pack it down to the Bowery for a quick sale. After those two homers, that three bagger and a free ride to first today, maybe someone on the White Sox will want to buy the ticket from me." Of the pitch from Wilkinson that resulted in his first home run, he wrote, "That fast one, smack over the middle of the plate, was made for my bat. I couldn't miss it." He described the pitch from Kerr that produced the second homer as "a slow ball on the outside. It took an hour to get there waiting for me to murder it."[4] Babe Ruth, pioneer trash-talker.

On Wednesday Ruth homered again, and hit a single as well, as the Yankees routed the White Sox, 14–8. Claude Williams, who entered the game with a 6–0 record and a 1.26 ERA, saw his ERA more than double to 2.61 as he surrendered 14 hits, 10 runs (all earned) and two home runs in five innings. "One might say 'Kid' Gleason's white-hosed gladiators were in world's series form," wrote W. J. Macbeth in the *New York Tribune*. "'Lefty' Williams might have felt

Babe Ruth got off to a slow start in 1920, his first season with the New York Yankees, but began to turn things around in a May series against the White Sox. *Library of Congress Prints and Photographs Division*

right at home before the 'Kid' gave him the hook. The Reds in the last lamented world's series never peppered Claude harder than did Murderer's Row." Larry Woltz compared the White Sox to clowns from the Ringling Bros. circus: "The greatest show on earth never had a funnier bunch of comedians than we lamped up there under Coogan's Bluff today." But if the Black Sox were dumping this game, Williams was doing it by himself: Risberg was still out while recovering from his spike wound, and Jackson, Felsch, Weaver [moved to shortstop in place of Risberg], and McMullin were a combined 8 for 17.[5]

As a team the White Sox were struggling, and Irving Vaughan thought he knew why. "In going over the records of the last eight games, in which the White Sox were defeated seven times," wrote Vaughan, "one comes face to face with the fact that Chick Gandil is sadly missed. The absent first sacker was a great man in the pinch, probably the best on the team, and would be doubly valuable right now because the Sox pitchers are not very effective." Vaughan added that Ted Jourdan, Gandil's primary replacement, was "fielding in great style, probably as well as Gandil could, but not getting hits when needed."[6] Jourdan's batting average had dropped to .239.

On Thursday and Friday the scheduled White Sox–Yankees games were rained out, which probably was a relief to Kid Gleason. Risberg's spike wound was still bothering him, and he did not accompany the team to Boston, the White Sox's next stop. Meanwhile Eddie Cicotte, still recovering from his broken finger, was diagnosed with tonsillitis, and an abscess had formed in his throat that needed to lanced by a surgeon. "Eddie was somewhat blue all day," wrote Larry Woltz, "but his room mate, Billy [sic] Felsch, refused to leave the sick chamber, and at 5 o'clock this afternoon, Cicotte had laughed himself to sleep. It was his first sleep in two days."

With no game story to file, Harry Neily wrote an article suggesting that the baseball used in 1920 was livelier than in previous years—a theory now widely accepted as true. "Probably it will be denied officially that the present ball is livelier, but there is more rubber in the shell around the cork than there was two years ago," Neily reported. He described the numerous "wicked smashes" hit by players from both teams in Tuesday's game, and wrote that "the infielders on both sides had a terrible time."[7]

On Saturday at Fenway Park, the Chicagoans faced the Boston Red Sox for the first time in the 1920 season. The Sox-Sox season series deserves special scrutiny because Boston was the home base of Joseph "Sport" Sullivan, a gambler who was instrumental in setting up the 1919 World Series fix. Chick Gandil and Sullivan had been friends for a number of years prior to 1919, and it is likely that Eddie Cicotte also knew Sullivan dating back to his years with the Red Sox (1908–1912). Other White Sox players also knew Sullivan, and even socialized with him when they visited Boston. While Gandil was no longer a member of the team in 1920, Cicotte and the others were still around—and susceptible to potential blackmail from Sullivan, or perhaps just the lure of what seemed to be easy money.

Expected to struggle without Babe Ruth, Boston had gotten off to a surprisingly good start, and entered the White Sox series in second place behind Cleveland with a 14–7 record (the White Sox were third with an 11–9 mark). In the series opener on Saturday, the White Sox won 2–1, with fine performances from everyone in the lineup who would later have the term "Black Sox" applied to them. Start with defense: "The plays aiding [Faber] in times of trouble were catches by Jackson and Felsch and a stop and throw by Weaver," wrote Irving Vaughan. At bat, Jackson, Weaver, Felsch, and McMullin were a combined 5 for 14; Weaver broke a scoreless tie with an RBI single in the eighth, and McMullin scored the winning run after singling with one out in the top of the ninth. On the other hand, Vaughan also noted that "The gamblers are still doing business at Fenway park. Several hundred of them were gathered at their customary hangout in the right field pavilion."[8]

There was no baseball on Sunday due to local ordinance, but famed sportswriter Grantland Rice devoted part of his syndicated column that day to praise for Buck Weaver, writing that "if we had to cast a vote for Hustlin' Kid in the Ancient Order of Sons of Swat it would likely go to Buck Weaver, of the White Sox. Weaver is and had been to the White Sox what Johnny Evers was to the old Cubs, an everlasting inspiration in the way of pep. He is not only a great ball player but a great fighter, one who seems to give 103 percent of everything he has to each contest. Whether it's an ordinary scrap or a world series the general idea is about the same to Buck—give 'em all you got."[9]

When the series resumed on Monday, the White Sox faced Boston righthander Sad Sam Jones, whose performance against the South Siders in 1920 would be one of the major curiosities of a very curious season. Jones would have a long, productive Major League career—22 seasons, 229 wins, four World Series—but he entered 1920 with a 32–36 career record, albeit with a respectable 3.29 ERA. He had never pitched particularly well against the White Sox (4–6, 4.91 through 1919); in fact. Larry Woltz devoted much of his story on Monday morning to how much Buck Weaver and Happy Felsch enjoyed facing Jones. "Happy and I may not get safe hits off Sam every time we go to bat," said Weaver, "but every time we are through hitting we are crying to go back. And when you hit one off Sam—wow, how they do travel."[10]

Red Sox pitcher Sam Jones struggled against most American League opponents in 1920, but he was nearly invincible against the White Sox. *Library of Congress Prints and Photographs Division*

It was completely different in 1920. Against non-Chicago opponents that year, Jones was most definitely Sad Sam, posting a 7–16 overall record and a 4.46 ERA; against the White Sox, he was Walter Johnson, with a 6–0 record (six starts, six wins, five complete games) and a 1.94 ERA. Retrosheet has play-by-plays available for five of Jones's six starts against the White Sox; in those games the self-described Jones killers, Weaver and Felsch, hit a combined .152 (3 for 20 by Buck, 2 for 13 by Hap) with no homers and no RBI.

In his May 17 start against the White Sox, Jones scattered eight hits and defeated Roy Wilkinson, 2–1. If there was a goat for the White Sox, the main culprit seemed to be Ray Schalk. In the Red Sox first, the catcher "was unusually slow on a double steal," according to Irving Vaughan; a run then scored on an error by Weaver. Schalk made amends by driving in the tying run with an eighth-inning single, but in the bottom of the eighth Boston's Mike Menosky reached second when Schalk hit him in the back on his throw to first after Menosky had dribbled a grounder in front of the plate. The next hitter, Tim Hendryx, then drove in Menosky with a single.[11]

At the same time, there were a few plays worth noting that involved players later known as Black Sox. Chicago almost tied the game with two out in the ninth, but Joe Jackson, trying to score from first on Felsch's double, was tagged out at the plate to end the game. Along with that tag-out, Jackson had been caught stealing on a strike-him-out, throw-him-out double play in the seventh, with Felsch doing the fanning. Buck Weaver's error brought home the first Boston run . . . and after singling to open the fourth, Buck was tagged out when he "foolishly tried to make second on it," according to Vaughan. So could this have been a game that the White Sox dumped? I have to say no. Weaver, Jackson, Felsch, and McMullin had four of the eight White Sox hits, including both extra-base hits (doubles by McMullin and Felsch). The game-ending play, which began with Felsch's double, missed by inches being a two-run homer that would have given the Sox a 3–2 lead, according to Larry Woltz. And the White Sox hotly disputed the out call on Jackson—with some justification, it would seem. "The Chicago players, naturally, thought him safe," wrote James O'Leary in the *Boston Globe*, "and about half the spectators were of the same opinion." Larry Woltz wrote about the game-ending play, "You should have seen the White Sox. Quiet fellows like Eddie Murphy and [Harvey] McClellan were willing to lick their weight in wild cats."[12]

Tuesday was better for the White Sox—a 4–3 victory behind Lefty Williams, who was now 7–1 on the year—but in the final game of the series on Wednesday, Boston defeated Cicotte, 3–2. The game probably shouldn't have been close, as Cicotte was constantly in trouble, surrendering 14 hits. One bright spot for the White Sox was that Happy Felsch homered for the second straight day; with five home runs, he was tied with Babe Ruth for the Major League lead. Several decades later, Felsch would lament to Eliot Asinof, "You know the biggest regret? I got kicked out of baseball the year they souped up the ball. Why, I could've hit forty homers with that lively ball! Like Ruth!"[13]

The loss dropped the White Sox's record to 13–11. Twelve of the team's 24 games (and six of the last seven) had been decided by one run; the Sox were 4–8 in those games.

As the White Sox traveled to the District of Columbia for the first time in 1920, Lee Magee was back in the news. In U.S. District Court in Cincinnati, the Cubs asked for a dismissal of the suit that Magee had filed against the club. More importantly, they revealed why they had released Magee. After acquiring Magee in good faith during the 1919 season, the club stated, they learned during the winter "from the plaintiff [Magee] that he had been guilty of dishonest ballplaying . . . plaintiff was guilty of betting against the team of which he was a member and seeking to win said betting by intentional bad playing to defeat said team." Magee, the club said, had "confessed said facts to the defendant [Cubs] on or about February 10, 1920." The betting in question took place for a Cincinnati Reds-Boston Braves game in 1918, when Magee was a member of the Reds.[14]

Magee, typically, refused to back down . . . on May 27 he filed a motion asking that the club state the details of the alleged dishonest playing it claimed he had made. Judge John Peck of U.S. District court agreed with Magee, ordering the club to make its charges "more definite and certain." Trial was set for June 7 in Cincinnati.[15]

Also in the news as the White Sox prepared to face Washington: Ban Johnson announced a plan of "drastic action to stamp out gambling at baseball games of the American and National leagues." After meeting with Reds President (and former National Commission chairman) Garry Herrmann, and President Charles Stoneham and manager John McGraw of the New York Giants, "it was decided to employ a big detective agency" with "the intention to use these agents in catching gamblers, and that strenuous efforts would be made to smother the evil. [Johnson] also announced it planned to bar all gamblers from the leagues' parks."[16]

These were noble sentiments, to be sure, but the involvement of Stoneham and McGraw in an effort to stamp out gambling was curious, to say the least. In his SABR biography of Stoneham, Bill Lamb described the Giants' president as a "compulsive gambler" and "a regular at racetracks, casinos, and other gaming haunts." Stoneham was also involved in—and would later be indicted for fraud in relation to—an illegal form of stock speculation known as "bucketeering"; he would be acquitted after a contentious trial that included charges of jury tampering.[17] McGraw was also well known as a big-time gambler and had once been a business partner of Arnold Rothstein, the man considered to be the major bankroller of the 1919 World Series fix. And of course the Stoneham/McGraw

Giants never seemed to have problems employing players with histories of charges involving gambling and game-fixing . . . most recently McGraw's old pal Hal Chase. The "fox/henhouse" analogy would seem to apply here.

In a preview of the White Sox–Senators series that began on Thursday, May 20, Denman Thompson of the *Washington Evening Star* wrote of the Sox: "It was anticipated there would be dissension in the ranks to wreak havoc with their morale, their pitching staff was tipped as shot to pieces and the loss of Weaver and Gandil was expected to complete the wreckage of the champions. But the scrappy Kid Gleason has them pulling together with as much harmony as ever. Weaver returned to the fold and Gandil's absence apparently has not been felt with Jourdan holding up his end at first in acceptable style."[18]

Thursday's opener was one for the record books. Through nine innings the game was tied, 3–3. At that point the great Walter Johnson entered the game as Washington's third pitcher of the day; starting pitcher Red Faber was still going strong for the White Sox. With Johnson working five scoreless innings, it was still 3–3 entering the 15th inning. The White Sox took the lead with two runs; Washington fought back with two off Faber to tie it up again. But in the 16th, Johnson and the Senators fell completely apart. "The Sox landed on Walter with everything but their spikes and the Nationals [the seldom-used official name for the Washington franchise] did everything but try to swallow the ball," wrote J. V. Fitz Gerald in the *Washington Post*. "The finish was so much on the brie order that it looked as if Johnson, once the White Sox got a couple of runs, was tossing the ball so the Westerners would keep hitting until darkness would prevent the Nationals from getting a turn at bat." That strategy, if effective, would have negated the Chicago runs and reverted the score to a 5–5 tie. After scoring eight runs—through 2019 still the most runs ever scored by a team in the 16th inning of a game—the Sox made three quick outs in what appeared to be deliberate fashion; Fred McMullin, the final Sox hitter, simply stood with the bat on his shoulder and let umpire Tommy Connolly call three strikes on him. Faber then closed out the Senators for a bizarre 13–5 win. In the 16 innings, Faber allowed 18 hits, but zero walks.[19]

Before Friday's game the White Sox sold pitcher Grover Cleveland Lowdermilk—he of the extracted teeth—to Minneapolis of the American Association. The Sox and Senators then played another wild one, compiling 29 hits, 16 walks, and 20 runs before Chicago prevailed in 10 innings, 11–9. On Saturday the Sox scored in double digits for the third day in a row, winning 10–6 for Lefty Williams's eighth win. The offense finally ran out of steam on Sunday, losing to the Senators' Eric Ericson in the series finale, 3–1.

The White Sox now headed to Philadelphia for four games with the last-place Athletics amid speculation that they were about to make a deal for A's first baseman George Burns. A .287 lifetime hitter (through 1919), Burns would have been a definite upgrade over Ted Jourdan. But the deal fell through and Philadelphia sold Burns to the first-place Indians a few days later for $10,000 ("Such a move was to be expected," wrote Irving Vaughan, "as there are five clubs in the league determined not to aid the three clubs that made the fight against Ban Johnson last winter").[20] The Sox could have used him; in the decade of the 1920s, Burns batted .321 and won the American League Most Valuable Player Award in 1926.

They didn't miss Burns on Monday, routing the A's, 10–2, behind Red Faber. Buck Weaver had four hits in the game to lift his season average to .378, second in the league behind Cleveland's Doc Johnston (Joe Jackson was third at .373). Happy Felsch, leading the league in slugging with a .646 mark, hit his sixth home run to once again tie Babe Ruth for the Major League lead. For the remainder of the season Ruth would outhomer Felsch, 48–8, but Happy would nonetheless finish the year with the fourth most home runs in the American League.

On Tuesday, May 25, the *Chicago Evening Post* featured a long story by James Henle on the perils of baseball gambling. It began, "Is another world series scandal to develop this year? Are cheap gamblers, the bolshevists of sportdom, to ruin baseball as they have destroyed the public's confidence in boxing and racing?" Henle related how he had recently sat in the "betting ring" at the Polo Grounds in New York, where "Odds were freely quoted on the event, almost under the noses of the special policemen hired to prevent gambling." Without naming Arnold Rothstein, he wrote,

> Behind practically all the gambling in New York City today there is the sinister figure of one man whose name is on the tongue of every denizen of the underworld. This man bets in the thousands. He is said often to have as much as $100,000 wagered on the outcome of a pennant race. He has mysterious influence, the source of which few people know, and possesses connections which lead up to the biggest circles in the country. . . .
>
> This is cold-blooded betting we are talking about. Professional gamblers are doing it. And in a short time they have done enough to involve sufficient baseball players in a snarl of scandal to make up a nine. Seaton and Smith on the coast; Zimmerman, Hal Chase are stars who have been named in the public prints. And there have been plenty of scandalous stories about other ball players who have not been barred from the game.[21]

CHAPTER 7

The "scandalous stories" were just beginning.

On Tuesday and Wednesday, anyone betting on the last-place A's to beat the White Sox would have cleaned up. On Tuesday, rookie Roy Moore defeated the Sox, 5–1, for his first Major League victory—and his only win in 1920; he would finish the year with a 1-13 record. Moore added to the insult by hitting a two-run homer off Sox starter Roy Wilkinson (who fell to 1–5 on the year). "When one pitcher lets his rival home run what shall a person write about him?" wrote Harry Neily. "Postal regulations forbid as full expression as the circumstances warrant." The next day, the A's pounded Claude Williams, who had entered the game with an 8–1 record, 10–2. According to Irving Vaughan, "Williams only stuck on the job for four innings, which was about four too many."[22]

The Sox managed to win the series finale on Thursday, 6–1, behind a strong outing from Eddie Cicotte. Now it was on to Cleveland for a four-game showdown against the first-place Indians.

When the White Sox made their first visit to Cleveland in late April, the Indians had taken two of three games. But the editors of the *Cleveland News* had a problem: the hometown fans were being too rough on the White Sox players. According to the *News*,

> To the shame of Cleveland fans, it must be said that they have taken up the practice of hooting opposing players without any provocation whatsoever. Truth be told, we doubt if there is ever an occasion that warrants the hooting of a rival player, and when the fans take it upon themselves to hoot and use cat calls at such high-class players and gentlemen as Eddie Collins, George Weaver and Joe Jackson, it is time to call a halt.
>
> Collins, Weaver and Jackson are paid to give their best service to the Chicago club, and they are to be commended for their efforts in this direction. Instead of hooting them local fans, at least the fair-minded ones, should give them the applause that their excellent work merits. This trio was hooted frequently Tuesday when there was absolutely no call for it.

Ed Bang, the paper's sports editor, echoed that sentiment a few days later: "Visiting players regard Cleveland as just a little more unfair to the opponents of the home team than any other city. And umpires voice the same opinion. Instead of looking forward to their visits to this city, the Indians rivals and even the umps dread coming here."[23]

If the 1920 White Sox dreaded coming to Cleveland, a simpler explanation might be that it was because they had to play the Indians, who had beaten the

Sox in six of eight meetings thus far in the season. The trend continued in Friday's series opener, as Cleveland pounded Red Faber and three Sox relievers, 13–6; Dickey Kerr, still struggling, gave up four runs and seven hits in an inning and two-thirds, raising his season ERA to a hideous 10.90. Joe Jackson avoided hooting Indians fans the hard way: he missed the entire series due to ptomaine poisoning from some bad crabmeat he had eaten in Philadelphia.

It looked like more of the same in the first game of Saturday's doubleheader when the White Sox entered the ninth inning trailing, 7–3. When the Sox led off the inning with four straight singles to produce a run, Indians manager Tris Speaker brought in ace starter Jim Bagby to put out the fire. But after retiring two hitters, with one run scoring on a sacrifice fly, Bagby walked four straight hitters, forcing in three runs. Making up for his bad outing on Friday, Red Faber set down the Indians in the bottom of the ninth for an 8–7 Sox win. But the second game was another rout for the Indians; Cleveland pounded Roy Wilkinson, now 1–6, for 14 hits in an 8–1 victory.

Then came Sunday's game, one of the most painful of the season for the White Sox, and one of the most joyful for the Indians. Although pitching somewhat shakily, Eddie Cicotte took a 6–1 lead into the bottom of the seventh inning. But then his luck ran out. "What those mauling, mad, boisterous Indians did to Cicotte in the home half of the seventh was cruel. Yes, men, it was scandalous," wrote Larry Woltz. "They did everything but knock the ball down Eddie's sore throat." With a rally that featured five hits and a walk, Cleveland scored five times in the inning to tie the game; then, in the eighth, the Indians put two men on, and player-manager Tris Speaker drove in what proved to be the winning runs with a two-run single to left field. "Twenty three thousand howling, sappy, joyful and jubilant Clevelanders left the local ball yard this afternoon as the sun was sinking," wrote Woltz, making no mention of hooting at Sox players. "They will tell you that none other than Tris Speaker's Cleveland Indians will win the American League pennant." The loss dropped the White Sox to fifth place with a 19–17 record.[24]

The Sox finished their 23-day road trip with a visit to St. Louis to play the sixth-place Browns (13–21), who entered the series with a six-game losing streak. The series began with a Decoration Day doubleheader that started with a duel between two spitballers named Urban. Chicago's Urban (Red) Faber was good, but the Browns' Urban Shocker was better, pitching a six-hit shutout for a 2–0 St. Louis win. In the second game White Sox starter Claude Williams gave up 16 hits, but stranded enough runners (11) to prevail in 10 innings, 5–3, after the Browns had tied the game with two runs in the bottom of the ninth. The

Sox won it in the 10th on RBI singles by Buck Weaver and Joe Jackson, who was still recovering from the food poisoning that he acquired in Philadelphia.

With their doubleheader split on the last day of May, the White Sox finished the month in fourth place in the American League with a 20–18 record, six and a half games behind the league-leading Indians. For the month, the club had a losing record (13–16), due primarily to a pitching staff that had posted a 4.62 ERA in May. With Dickey Kerr still under par and Eddie Cicotte hampered by the broken finger and tonsillitis, the Sox pitching staff could be described as "Williams and Faber and then we must labor." Claude Williams was tied for the league lead in games pitched (12) and wins (9), while leading in innings pitched (97.0), strikeouts (43), hits allowed (103), and earned runs allowed (41). The heavy workload seemed to be getting to him: after recording a 1.26 ERA in his first six games (all complete-game victories), Williams's ERA for the next six was an ugly 7.43. Faber, who was fourth in the league in innings pitched (83.2), had been much more consistent, with a 2.37 overall ERA. "The Sox are in a bad way for pitching," wrote Irving Vaughan on June 1. "Gleason can't even take a man out when he is being hit. That is to be expected when a team tries to get along with seven pitchers half of whom are of no value."[25]

The White Sox offense, while averaging 5.0 runs a game, third-best in the league, was also highly dependent on a few players. Joe Jackson (.355), Buck Weaver (.345), Happy Felsch (.341), and Eddie Collins (.331) all boasted excellent batting averages and fine peripheral stats, but none of the other regulars had been productive. That led Harry Neily to become the latest writer to bemoan the absence of Chick Gandil. Neily wrote,

> To be frank, the Sox miss Chick Gandil or a man of similar ability much more than the box scores would indicate.
>
> Jourdan is a willing worker, but he is not a Gandil in experience. Until the last Cleveland game he had hit safely in eleven consecutive contests, but he is not the pinch hitter [what we now call a "clutch hitter"] that Gandil was. In fact, few players, even those whose averages top the .300 mark, drove in more runs than the absent brother.

In a rainy-day story a day later, Irving Vaughan expressed similar sentiments. "Right now it is a pretty good bet the Sox will not win the pennant," Vaughan wrote. "There is no way in the world for them to offset the loss of Gandil, who was the best man on the team to hit in the pinches. [George] Burns could have remedied this deficiency considerably."[26]

As it turned out, help was on the way, but not from Burns, and definitely not from "the absent brother." Ted Jourdan had turned his ankle running to first base in Monday's second game and would need to miss several days. In the interim the White Sox put John Collins, who thus far had played very little (only 50 plate appearances through May 31), at first. Shano filled the bill so nicely that Jourdan never got his job back. From June 1 to the end of the season Collins batted .307 with a .731 on-base-plus-slugging percentage (OPS) . . . not a star performance in the good hitting environment of 1920, but numbers that would seem comparable with what Gandil might have accomplished. As for coming through "in the pinch," Collins batted .320, with an .855 OPS, with runners in scoring position in the 1920 games for which Retrosheet has play-by-plays available. So no worries there. And one more thing: anyone who knew John Collins would attest that he wasn't the sort of man who would do business with Sport Sullivan.

The White Sox and Browns were rained out on Tuesday, June 2, but resumed play on Wednesday with a 7–3 Sox victory in a game that took less than 90 minutes. The Sox scored three times in the top of the first, with St. Louis starter Carl Weilman lasting only a third of an inning. Chicago starter Eddie Cicotte was efficient after surrendering a homer to Browns' leadoff man Jack Tobin on his first pitch of the game. The White Sox finished the long road trip with a 6–4 win on Thursday behind Roy Wilkinson, who recorded his second win of the year after six straight losses.

On Friday the Sox began a long homestand with a series against the last-place Tigers (13–26). The club had gone 11–11 on the three-plus week road trip and was in fourth place, five games behind the league-leading Indians, with a 22–18 record. The South Siders did not have a happy homecoming; Red Faber lasted only a third of an inning against Detroit, retiring just one of the first six hitters, and the Sox did not get their first hit off the Tigers' George Dauss until one out in the bottom of the seventh. The crowd of about 8,000—including women who were admitted free for Ladies' Day—was disappointing as well.

Saturday was better, a 4–1 win behind Claude Williams, who improved his record to 10–2. In three complete-game wins over the Tigers thus far in 1920, Williams had allowed only 11 hits and four earned runs for a 1.20 earned run average. But this was a curious outing for Lefty; he allowed four hits and one walk while facing only 31 hitters, but with two strikeouts and just five ground-ball outs, two of those coming on a double play.

Sunday's game, before a rabid crowd estimated at 27,000, was full of thrills. The Sox trailed 6–3 entering the bottom of the eighth, but tied the game with a five-hit inning. Then in the 11th, Happy Felsch singled, stole second, took third on a wild throw by Detroit catcher Eddie Ainsmith, and raced home with the winning run on a John Collins single. Felsch had helped preserve the tie with a sensational catch in the 10th inning. With Ty Cobb at bat, Irving Vaughan wrote, "It looked like a homer when Hap sprinted toward the fence, and [Ralph] Young, who was on first base, went so far on his way to the plate that he couldn't get back, being doubled easily." In the bottom of the 10th the Tigers kept the score tied with their own circus catch, this one by right fielder Ira Flagstead off Swede Risberg. On the play, Flagstead and Cobb collided. "Down went the Georgia Peach in a heap," wrote Vaughan, "and Flagstead made a complete somersault but held the ball."[27] Cobb tore ligaments in his left knee on the play and did not return to action until July 8. He finished the year well off pace in the batting average race with a .334 mark, his worst season average since 1908.

The White Sox finished the series with a makeup game on Monday, pounding out 16 hits to wallop the Tigers, 10–3, for Red Faber's sixth victory. John Collins led the way with four hits and five RBI. In six games since taking over first base, five of them Sox victories, Shano had gone 14 for 26 (.538) with 10 RBI and lifted his season average from .233 to .348. ("A handy old person," Harry Neily called Collins.[28]) With three hits on Monday, Joe Jackson raised his average to .378, second in the league behind Cleveland's Tris Speaker (.388).

With six wins in their last seven games, the White Sox had moved up to third place in the American League pennant race with a 25–19 record, only three games behind the first-place Indians. But the troublesome Red Sox—and Sad Sam Jones—would be next on the schedule.

8

TRIALS AND TRIUMPHS

On June 7 in Cincinnati, Lee Magee's lawsuit against the Chicago Cubs went to trial in U.S. District Court. Magee was attempting to collect $9,500 in damages for the Cubs' breach of his contract for the 1920 season. The trial, with Judge John W. Peck presiding, took three days. In his opening statement, Robert Alcorn, Magee's attorney, said,

> Testimony will show there was betting right along between teams in the major leagues and between individual players. We will show that Hal Chase, former Captain of the Cincinnati Reds, asked Magee at Boston to join him in a bet on the first of the two games at Boston July 25, 1918. Both Chase and Magee placed bets of $500 each with a betting commissioner named Costello, and gave their checks for that amount. The bets were that Cincinnati would win. The record of that game show Chase made no errors but that Magee unavoidably made two errors. We will show that Magee, in the thirteenth inning of that game, got a hit, stole second and scored the winning run. We will show that Magee not only never made a bet against the Cincinnati team, but he never made one against Brooklyn, or Chicago [the teams he played for in 1919] at any time.[1]

Murray Seasongood, attorney for the Cubs, had a much different account of the events of July 1918. "We will show that Magee and Hal Chase, on the night of July 24, 1918, conspired together and committed an act of treason against the Cincinnati club, their fellow players, the National League and the national game," Seasongood said in his opening statement. He said that Magee and Chase had gone to Costello with a proposal to fix a game, and after learning that they could put up any amount of money against their own team, agreed to lose the first game of the July 25 doubleheader; Pete Schneider, who was struggling with a 5–12 record, would be the starting pitcher. The two players bet $500 apiece on Cincinnati to lose, paying by check, with each also to receive one-third of the amount won by gamblers if Cincinnati lost.[2]

The plan to dump the game became harder when Schneider, who had heard rumors that teammates were on the take for this game, went to Reds manager Christy Mathewson and asked to be relieved of the starting assignment. (Schneider, who was pitching in the Texas League in 1920, did not testify at the trial but denied to reporters that he had been part of the fix.) Mathewson deferred Schneider until the second game and substituted Hod Eller, his best starting pitcher. "Try as Magee would," Seasongood said, "he was unable to lose the game." He described how, with the Reds leading 2–1 with one out and a man on first in the bottom of the ninth, Magee fielded a grounder which should have been an easy out and "threw the ball over second into the left field stand. Sports writers all described the play as the wildest made in a decade, but at the time excused Magee on the ground they thought he was worrying over expecting an early call into the army." Magee's wild throw brought home the tying run. On the sequence in which the Reds had scored the winning runs in the 13th inning, he described Magee's hit as "an easy grounder to short, but the ball took an ugly bounce and, striking the Boston shortstop, broke his nose." Describing Magee's stolen base, Seasongood said "Magee sought to give this play away, and his action so surprised the Boston catcher that he threw wild and Magee went to third." Magee then scored on Edd Roush's home run, which Seasongood described as "retribution from on high against Magee for committing the highest offense known to baseball and the one which strikes at the foundation of the national game."[3]

When testimony began, Magee was the only witness for the prosecution. He reiterated that he had notified the Cubs he was ready to play, but had received no reply. He might have won the case if he hadn't made the same mistake that would later help seal the fate of the Black Sox: he had double-crossed a gambler. Jim Costello was the defense's star witness, and Costello had plenty to say. He described how Chase and Magee had come to him with their proposition; when he told them that gamblers wouldn't trust them unless they bet some of their own money, they wrote checks to Costello for $500 each. Costello and the gamblers were satisfied that Chase and Magee had tried their best to dump the game ("It was a tough break, Jim," Chase told him; "we tried awful hard"[4]), and that probably would have closed the matter . . . if Magee hadn't gotten greedy and stopped payment on his $500 check (Chase, an honest crook, let his check go through). Costello said Magee tried to settle things by offering to tip him off

A trial to resolve Lee Magee's 1920 lawsuit against the Chicago Cubs for lost salary helped reveal the game-fixing that had become commonplace in baseball. *Library of Congress Prints and Photographs Division*

on future games that he and Chase were planning to fix, but Costello wouldn't go for it. Chase made good on half of Magee's $500, but when Costello did not receive the other $250, he filed suit against Magee in Boston Municipal Court; he also appealed to Reds President Garry Herrmann. He had the checks from Chase and Magee for evidence.

Other witnesses were also damaging to Magee. Christy Mathewson—who admitted under cross-examination that some members of the Reds had bet on games, but only on Cincinnati to win as far as he knew—called the play that Magee had botched in the ninth "an easy grounder." Mathewson also said that Magee had made "a bad start" on his stolen-base attempt in the 13th inning. Magee made another error on a wild throw after what Mathewson again called "an easy chance" in the bottom of the 13th. Two sportswriters, Jack Ryder of Cincinnati and Bert Whitman of Boston, stated their opinion that the errors by Magee were "not of the ordinary manner."[5]

On Tuesday, National League President John Heydler, took the stand for the defense. He testified that on February 10, 1920, Magee had admitted to Heydler and Cubs President William Veeck that he had bet against the Reds on the July 25 game. "'It was Schneider's turn to pitch,' Heydler recalled Magee telling him, 'but Christy Mathewson crossed them and put in Eller.' Magee said he played a miserable game, making several wild throws, and that Chase played several low balls badly. Magee said he did everything he could to 'throw' the game. Cincinnati won, and Magee said he suspected Chase of double-crossing him, and stopped payment on the check."[6]

"Repeatedly Magee had told both Veeck and myself that he was guilty of a crime against baseball," said Heydler, "and that he would do anything so he could remain in the game. On being questioned he said he knew of no other players who were connected with the betting, but repeatedly told us that if he had to get out of baseball he would take others with him." Heydler also said that Magee told him that Chase had intentionally cut his hand on a bottle in Boston so that he could opt out of the lineup; Chase then went to New York and arranged for more games to be fixed in an effort to square things with Costello. "There is nothing more deplorable or more harmful to the great national game than that it should be considered dishonest," Heydler said in concluding his testimony. "Such a thing would be a calamity next to dissolution of the republic."[7] William Veeck also testified for the defense and supported Heydler's account.

Taking the stand in rebuttal after the defense had rested, Magee insisted that he had bet on the Reds to win, and that he had stopped payment on the $500 check when he learned otherwise. He said that his play in the game had aided materially to the Reds winning the game, and that he did not play in the Reds' subsequent series against the New York Giants because he had learned that those games were fixed. Under cross-examination from Seasongood, Magee said he had known for some time before his meeting with Heydler and Veeck that Chase played crooked, but had made no exposé because league and club officials had not asked him for any information. He admitted that he had told Cincinnati newspapermen if he had to "jump off the bridge, others might have to jump with him," but denied that he made a similar statement to Heydler and Veeck.[8]

On Wednesday the trial concluded, with attorneys for Magee and the Cubs making their final arguments. Judge Peck told the jury that "If the plaintiff, unknown to the defendant, had been guilty of gross and flagrant misconduct . . . then the defendant should have the right to discharge him immediately, regardless of the ten days' notice provided for in the contract." He said that the jury "must consider the necessity of maintaining strict rules of discipline among players for that purpose and the necessity of upholding the public confidence in baseball games."[9]

It took the jury only 44 minutes to decide the case in favor of the Cubs. A jubilant Heydler characterized the verdict as "the greatest victory in the history of the national game in favor of clean ball." He said that the outcome of the suit made it apparent that the National League was determined to keep the game honest, so that fans would be confident that the games they attended were being decided on their merits. "I'm sorry for Magee," he concluded. "I'm sorry he allowed himself to become mixed up in this scandal. But by his suit he gave us the opportunity to prove in court—and that's the only place we could properly prove it—that we mean to keep baseball clean. Magee and Chase never again can play in the National League."[10]

Lee Magee left the courtroom without comment after the verdict was announced. Contacted in his hometown of San Jose, California, Hal Chase denied that he had bet on baseball games. "There is absolutely no truth in this statement by Magee, who claims I induced him to bet against the Cincinnati team when we both were members of that organization," Chase said. "I was exonerated of all charges of betting by the National Commission after it made a complete investigation."[11] But after the revelations of the Magee trial, people were no longer willing to give Chase the benefit of the doubt. "It is difficult to see how Lee Magee thought he had a ghost of a chance in his suit against the Cubs," wrote baseball historian Lee Allen, "but it is a good thing that he did, because were it not for the testimony the trial produced, it would still be possible to have doubts about Hal Chase."[12]

An editorial called "Baseball's Housecleaning" in the *Cincinnati Post* on June 10 stated, "There were expressions of fear on the part of some that the game would suffer because of the unfavorable publicity it received. They are dead wrong. Every word uttered in that court which exposed gambling operations was a good thing for the sport. . . . Players with an inclination to bet on games will think a long time before taking the dangerous step." The editorial noted that while "there have been rumors of gambling among ballplayers for several years, it has been 33 years [actually 43 years, since 1877] since players were barred from the game on charges of dishonest playing."[13]

Of course, the major reason why it had been 43 years since a player had been barred for dishonest playing was that baseball officials found it better for business to just cover up the dishonesty . . . something that was still happening in 1920. The public would find out fairly soon that players were still "taking the dangerous step" of fixing baseball games—some of them members of the Chicago White Sox. But the Lee Magee case, like the Pacific Coast League scandal that was simultaneously unfolding, was a major event that began to open peoples' eyes about how crooked baseball had been (and still was). "Costello's testimony doomed Magee's case, and the jury needed just 45 minutes to find in favor of the Cubs," wrote Sean Deveney. "But to get that win, baseball allowed the first crack to show in the barrier that had shielded the public from the problem of players mingling with gamblers."[14] Things were beginning to change.

On Tuesday, June 8, the second day of the Magee trial, the White Sox opened their home series against the Red Sox by meekly bowing to Sad Sam Jones, 4–1. Although Swede Risberg's error—his 14th of the year—enabled Boston to score its first run, it wasn't really a suspicious loss. Risberg tripled and scored the first Chicago run, Buck Weaver had one of the Sox's four hits, and Happy Felsch threw out a runner at the plate. Harry Neily did note that, "If [Boston right fielder] Harry Hooper had not lost his footing chasing Risberg's triple it is doubtful if the Sox would have made as much as one run."[15]

On Wednesday Boston won again, 3–2, in a game featuring one of the curious lapses in control by Claude Williams that had aroused suspicions in the 1919 World Series . . . along with a couple of other moments that would lead someone checking for suspicious activity to at least say, "Hmmm . . ." In the Red Sox fifth Williams walked the first two Red Sox hitters, and the runners moved up on a sacrifice bunt by pitcher Joe Bush. Harry Hooper was the next hitter. "With Hooper up," wrote Irving Vaughan, "Felsch moved over into right center in anticipation of doing business there, but the Red Sox vet upset the scheme by hitting a bit to left center for three bases, two scoring. Hooper got home on [Wally] Schang's grounder that would have retired the side had it not taken a nasty hop just as Weaver was about to grab it." Charles Dryden's story in the *Chicago Herald and Examiner* didn't mention Felsch moving over when Hooper came to bat, but did say, "Hooper picked out a spot midway between Jackson and Felsch as a desirable spot for a triple and he busted one to that place." The *Boston Herald* game story noted Felsch's shift, but with differing detail: "Felsch had moved over to left centre and the ball sailed midway between him and [right fielder Nemo] Leibold."[16]

Whatever the exact details in the June 9 game, curious defensive positioning by White Sox outfielders—leading to extra-base hits by the opposing team—had been one of the suspicious elements of the 1919 World Series. It was noticed at the time. After Game 5 of the Series—a game also started by Lefty Williams—Philadelphia writer "Jim Nasium" (a pen name for veteran writer/artist Edgar Forrest Wolfe) wrote,

> The White Sox owed their defeat this afternoon to the same faulty playing of the Cincinnati hitters that they have persisted in all through this series. We don't know where Kid Gleason got his advance dope on the Cincinnati Ball Club [ed.: from Fred McMullin] or whether he bothered to secure any; but anyway, it is all wet. The White Sox outfield had been playing [Greasy] Neale for a right field hitter when he never in his life hit a ball into right field. The pitchers have been pitching "Greasy" on the outside when every National League pitcher knows that

Neale won't hit a lick off any pitcher who keeps the ball inside. They have been pulling in the centre fielder with a hitter like [Edd] Roush up and this afternoon the first two times "Hod" Eller came to bat Felsch moved away over toward right field and Eller is a rank left field hitter.[17]

The *New York Times* story for Game 5 made a similar observation: "When Eller came to bat at the beginning of the inning, Happy Felsch moved over toward right field. There was a hole between Felsch and Jackson wide enough to send a regiment through. It is difficult to understand why the White Sox thought that Eller was a right field hitter." *Cleveland Plain Dealer* writer Henry P. Edwards and Indians manager Tris Speaker, who were covering the 1919 series, also commented on the strange play of the White Sox outfielders, both at the time and later. Remembering the series in 1948, Edwards wrote that Speaker had said, "Can you imagine Joe Jackson playing practically on the left field foul line for a batter who hits to left center nine times out of 10?"[18]

Arguing against the notion that the June 9 game may have been fixed is the fact that the White Sox hit Boston starter Joe Bush pretty hard, with Jackson doubling and tripling and Felsch belting a triple. It could have been worse; Irving Vaughan wrote that "Much of Bush's success was due to the fielding of the visitors. The White Sox peeled off hits in so many innings that a bobble at almost any time might have proved disastrous to 'Bullet Joe.'"[19] Additionally, Swede Risberg, by most accounts a helpful guy to have around when you want to try to lose a game, had left the club prior to the game. At the time it wasn't certain why Risberg had left; officially it was announced that he was heading to San Francisco to take care of a sick child, but rumor had it that he might be joining Chick Gandil to play in an outlaw league. (He was in fact attending to his child.)

On Thursday it wasn't close; the Red Sox pounded Eddie Cicotte for 14 hits in six innings in an 8–1 Boston win. While one could never be sure about Cicotte, he was coming back from injury and illness and definitely in a slump: in his last four starts he had allowed 43 hits in 31.0 innings, with a 6.97 ERA. The White Sox won Friday's series finale, coming from behind with two runs in the eighth to win, 5–4. Buck Weaver was the hero, homering in the first inning and starting the eighth-inning rally with a double.

The biggest White Sox news on Friday came from off the field: they learned that, finally and officially, Chick Gandil was banned from coming back to the team until at least 1923. The National Commission had instituted a new rule that any players who had jumped to "outlaw leagues" needed to apply for reinstatement or return to their clubs within five days; if they didn't, they could not return to their Major League team for three years. Gandil's time had now expired.

If the news about Gandil bothered the White Sox, you sure couldn't see it on the field. In fact the win over Boston on June 11 marked the start of one the team's best stretches of the 1920 season. Facing the great Walter Johnson and the Washington Senators in the first game of a series that began the next day, the Sox came from behind three times before pulling it out with two runs in the bottom of the ninth for a 9–8 win. Buck Weaver, who had three hits and three RBI in the game, won it with a single to center off Johnson, who went all the way for the Nats. On Sunday Weaver had three more hits as the Sox rolled, 9–3, for Claude Willlams's 11th victory. After a rainout on Monday, the Sox closed out the Washington series by scoring nine runs for the third game in a row to win 9–5, behind Cicotte. Eddie wasn't great, allowing 10 hits and five earned runs, but he went all the way to even his record at 5–5.

On Wednesday, June 16, the Yankees and Babe Ruth made their first visit to Comiskey Park during the 1920 season. The Yankees entered the series in second place in the American League pennant race with a 34–20 record, two and a half games behind the league-leading Indians (35–17). The White Sox were third with a 29–22 record, five and a half games behind Cleveland. Even without the presence of Ruth, this would have been an important series for the White Sox.

Ruth had been on fire since the White Sox and Yankees had met in New York five weeks earlier. In the 30 games beginning with the start of the Sox-Yanks series at the Polo Grounds on May 11, Ruth had batted .414 with 15 homers, 42 RBI and a slugging percentage of 1.000. The Yankees had gone 23–7 in those games. Ruth now led the American League with 17 home runs; Happy Felsch, with seven, was tied for second with Tilly Walker of the Philadelphia Athletics. And the Babe was just getting started.

The excitement that Ruth was creating in his first year with the Yankees was something unprecedented in Major League history. Consider his effect on attendance (note that we're computing attendance on per-game, rather than per-date basis, so that a doubleheader drawing 22,000 fans would have an average attendance of 11,000 per game):

- With a home attendance of 1,289,422, an average of 16,746 per game, the 1920 Yankees became the first team in Major League history with a single-season home attendance over one million. No other club apart from the Yankees would have a home attendance over a million until 1924, and the 1920 Yankees' attendance would remain a Major League record until the Chicago Cubs broke it in 1929.

- With Ruth as the driving force, the American League drew a record total of 5,084,300 fans to their games in 1920. A postwar boom was beginning and the National League had record attendance as well in 1920, but the NL total of 4,036,575 was more than a million behind the AL total.
- We don't have complete game-by-game attendance totals for all Yankee road games in 1920, but we do have the attendance figures that were published in newspaper accounts for 55 of their 77 road games. For those 55 games, the Yankees drew an average crowd of 14,444 per game. For all their other home games, the seven non-Yankee teams had an average per-game attendance of only 6,187. So it's not an overstatement that the presence of Ruth in a 1920 Yankee road game meant that more than twice as many people would show up.

Overall, Ruth was a gold mine to baseball, the American League . . . and especially to the Yankees. Economist Michael Haupert and accountant Kenneth Winter, who were able to examine the Yankees' financial ledgers held at the National Baseball Hall of Fame and Museum, calculated the team's profits on a yearly basis. In 1919, the Yankees had a team profit before taxes of $106,971. In 1920, the profit was $666,353.[20]

Ruth was such a hot story in 1920 that in anticipation of his first visit to Chicago, the *Chicago Evening Post* ran a feature story on Babe's wife Helen, who was identified only as "Mrs. Babe" and "Mrs. George Ruth." According to the article, they called each other "Hon," and the Babe was a "homebody" who didn't care for hotels. "Babe's going on the road," said Mrs. Ruth, "and when he comes back, I'll have a little place all fixed up for him. He certainly is a homebody if there ever was one. . . . Of course I realize that Babe's interests are divided like any other man's must be. Half of his life is baseball and the other half is me." The article also stated, "Like all idols of the public, Ruth's mail has grown to be a regular feature service. Among the daily 'income' are many 'sweet notes' from admiring young girls. Babe and Mrs. Babe have lots of fun reading them."[21]

In Wednesday's opener Babe the "homebody" found life on the road just fine, hitting a triple and a two-run homer as the Yankees defeated Red Faber, 7-4, behind Jack Quinn—the man Charles Comiskey insisted should still be a member of the White Sox. While the home crowd was pulling for the White Sox, it also seemed thrilled when Ruth homered; in fact, when the game was delayed by rain shortly after the Babe's four-bagger, anxious fans swarmed the press box, asking if the home run would still count if play could not resume (it would not have).

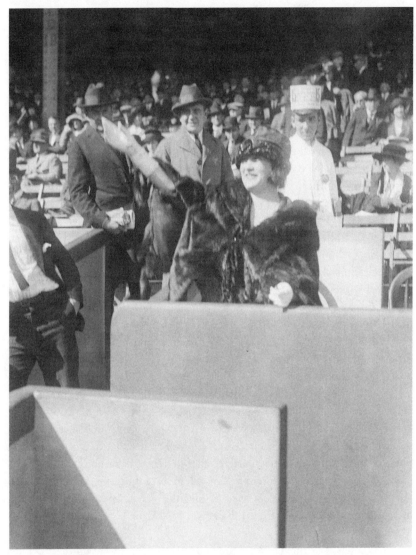

In a 1920 newspaper interview, Babe Ruth's wife Helen described
her husband as a "homebody." The truth was quite a bit different.
Library of Congress Prints and Photographs Division

On Thursday Ruth homered again, his 19th of the year, off Lefty Williams,
as the Yankees won again, 7–2. It was a three-run shot into the teeth of a stiff
wind. "Home run No. 19 was awe inspiring, to say the least," wrote Irving
Vaughan. "When Ruth came up to perpetrate it his ears tingled from the taunts

of the attending fans who had witnessed two strikeouts in previous appearances of the mighty one. Williams worked on him and got the count to two and two. Then came a beauty, waist high. Away went the pill, eastward bound, and the bugs in the right field bleacher craned their necks to watch it pass overhead. When it came down it was far outside the wall."[22] The ball landed in a public playground on the other side of the fence.

The White Sox held Ruth without a home run on Friday, but the Yankees made it 6–0 against the Sox thus far in 1920 with a 3–2 win. An encouraging sign for the White Sox was that Dickey Kerr went all the way in his best outing of the year. In Saturday's finale the Sox finally beat the Yanks, 6–5, before 28,000 fans. The winning runs came home on a two-run triple by Happy Felsch in the bottom of the 10th inning after the Yankees had taken a 5–4 lead with a run off Williams, who had relieved Eddie Cicotte, in the top of the frame. The victory was Williams's 12th of the year, tying him for the league lead with Cleveland's Jim Bagby. Ruth had been forced to leave the game early due to injury; coming in to second base on a force play in the second inning, Ruth was hit in the head by the throw to first from his California pal Buck Weaver, who was still filling in at shortstop for the absent Swede Risberg. The Babe attempted to continue playing, but after letting a fly ball soar over his head in right field, left due to dizziness.

The last-place Philadelphia Athletics were next on the schedule, and the White Sox were happy to see them: the South Siders swept a three-game series. In Sunday's opener Kid Gleason started Claude Williams, despite the fact that Lefty had worked an inning in relief the day before. Williams was less than sharp, giving up 14 hits, but went all the way for a 7–5 Sox win. After a rainout on Monday the Sox won the second game of the series, 2–1, on another strong outing by Dickey Kerr. The game was scoreless until the bottom of the eighth, when Eddie Collins singled with the bases loaded to bring in both Chicago runs. Eddie Cicotte completed the sweep with an eight-hit shutout in his strongest outing since Opening Day. The game featured a home run from Happy Felsch, his eighth of the year.

The White Sox finished their 24-day homestand with a three-game series against the first-place Indians. The sweep of the Athletics lifted third-place Chicago's record to 33–25, six games behind Cleveland. The Yankee series notwithstanding, the team was playing its best ball since the first week of the season. On the mound Cicotte and Kerr were coming around, joining Williams and Faber in what looked like a formidable starting rotation. Except for Ray Schalk (.221) and Nemo Leibold (.175), the Sox offense continued to be productive. Joe Jackson was hitting .387, third best in the league, with a .443 average for the month of June. Buck Weaver was batting .356, and .380 for the month. Happy Felsch was second in the league in slugging behind Babe Ruth, John Collins had filled the team's hole at first base, and Swede Risberg was finally back from his 17-day absence while caring for a sick child.

The Sox were 3–9 against the Indians thus far in the 1920 season, but all three wins had come in games started by Claude Williams. In Friday's opener Lefty's magic over Cleveland continued; he allowed eight hits, including four doubles, in a complete-game performance, but held the Indians to 1 in 10 at-bats with runners in scoring position as the Sox won, 6–3. The victory improved Williams's overall record to 14–4. "Williams reminds me more of Ed Plank than any pitcher I ever saw," said Eddie Collins. "He does not merely try to get the ball over the plate, but he pitches with a definite plan in view."[23] On Saturday the White Sox kayoed Cleveland's Ray Caldwell with a seven-run fourth inning, winning 12–7 behind Red Faber, who coasted (13 hits and four walks allowed) after getting a big lead. Joe Jackson had two hits to improve his batting average to .393.

With a chance to get within three games of first with a win, the Sox fell to Jim Bagby (14–2), 4–1, on Sunday before a crowd estimated at over 25,000. James Crusinberry described the Sox's play in this game as "rather messy doings," and the contest featured a few plays that could be considered suspicious—though it wasn't just the players later to be known as Black Sox who were involved in the messiness. With the Sox trailing 1–0 with one out and runners on second and third in the bottom of the fourth, Swede Risberg flew out to left field; Happy Felsch, the runner on third, trotted home without a play, only to be called by umpire Billy Evans when the Indians successfully appealed that he had left third base before the catch was made. "If that run had counted the whole complexion of the game would have changed," wrote Crusinberry. "The loss of it distressed the Sox players, both mentally and physically, and in the next inning they broke." Doc Johnston, the first Cleveland hitter in the fifth, hit "a drive past Risberg that should have been a single, but got past Felsch and Jackson for a two bagger." Johnston ultimately scored on a flyout, kicking the ball out of Ray Schalk's hands after a throw that had him beat (Schalk was charged with an error). In the top of the eighth, with Cleveland leading 2–0, two out, and runners on first and second, "Risberg cut loose with a high one on Speaker's smash. J. Collins couldn't hold the ball, though he leaped up and knocked it down." A run scored on the play, with an error charged to Risberg. Finally, in the Cleveland ninth, Bill Wambsganss scored the final Cleveland run after leading off with a double. "Either Eddie Collins or Risberg might have nabbed it," wrote Crusinberry, "but Felsch was the only one after it and couldn't get there in time." Describing the same play in the *Herald and Examiner*, Ed Reticker wrote, "Felsch played too deep."[24] In the game the White Sox were zero for six with runners in scoring position, with the outs made by Risberg (two), Felsch, Jackson, Weaver, and John Collins. Put me down as suspicious about the honesty of this game.

Despite the loss on Sunday, the Sox were full of optimism as they traveled to Detroit for a short three-game road jaunt. "The Cleveland club," said Kid Gleason, "has been hitting over its head. That outfield cannot bat .361 all season. They had no bad luck in the Spring. We did. I do not believe the Yankees can keep on hitting as they have to date. Why, our club is just beginning to go right. We have everybody back in the lineup. Cicotte has recovered his effectiveness and the infield is working as it used to."[25]

The Tigers had been an easy mark for the White Sox all season, and that trend continued in the three-game set in Detroit. On Monday the Sox pounded out 14 hits in a 13–5 victory for Eddie Cicotte's seventh win (and third over the Tigers). Happy Felsch's homer, his ninth of the year, was described as "the longest ever seen in the Detroit grounds." Tuesday's game was more competitive, with the Sox needing to come from behind to win, 8–7, with a three-run eighth. The victory went to Lefty Williams, his 15th of the year in only the team's 63rd game. Wednesday's finale was the laugher of the year for the White Sox, a 14–0 game that got so out of hand that 37-year-old Tigers coach Jack Coombs put himself in the game and pitched the final five innings (he only surrendered two runs). It was the 11th win in 12 games against the Tigers for Chicago.

With the victory, the White Sox finished the month of June with an 18–8 record. The team batted an even .300 for the month, while averaging 6.0 runs per game. The pitching staff was solid as well, with a 3.61 ERA. Joe Jackson was hitting .397, Buck Weaver .361, Happy Felsch .339, Eddie Collins .331. Felsch (.589) and Jackson (.565) were among the league leaders in slugging, and Jackson, Weaver, and Collins all had on-base percentages over .400. Even Swede Risberg had batted .314, with a .928 OPS, in June. On the mound Lefty Williams was either leading or tied for the league lead in wins (15), innings pitched (152), strikeouts (67), and complete games (13). Red Faber rank fourth in ERA (2.51).

"World's Series Scandal Re-Opened," *Collyer's Eye* headlined in its July 3 edition. "[Washington Senators owner] Clarke [*sic*] Griffith today announced that the American League was determined to probe the alleged scandal regarding the world series of 1919, between the White Sox of Chicago and the Cincinnati Reds to the very bottom," wrote J. Ashley-Stevens.

Griffith inquired if [Charles] Comiskey had made any overtures looking to the depositing of the $10,000 "reward" with his banking institution, and as requested by *Collyer's Eye*, investigators of which paper made an exhaustive investigation into the series. On being informed that he had not, Griffith stated very emphatically that he would "see it through."

"The investigations as published in *Collyer's Eye*," Griffith is quoted as saying, "reveal what we all along have contended, that everything was not 'on the up and up.' I am interested to KNOW whether Comiskey really had an investigation or whether his efforts were confined to suppression. President Ban Johnson in conversation with me today stated that if Comiskey did not come through with the reward the American league would then take it upon itself to do so, at the same time demanding all evidence in the possession of *Collyer's* investigators."[26]

Collyer's Eye had no follow-up in subsequent issues to this intriguing story. But it does raise an obvious question: If Charles Comiskey had truly been conducting a thorough investigation, why hadn't *he* been "demanding all evidence in the possession of *Collyer's* investigators" . . . dating back to October 1919?

Back home for a short but demanding homestand that featured eight games in six days, the Sox hosted the St. Louis Browns in a doubleheader on Thursday, July 1. It was Ray Schalk Day, and a crowd of over 20,000 fans was on hand to honor the durable receiver, who was about to play in his 1,000th career game for the White Sox (in this era of imprecise record-keeping, the club thought that he had already reached the milestone, which would actually occur on July 5). Between games of the doubleheader Schalk was presented with a silver chest and a tea set by Chicago mayor Bill Thompson. A squad of Marines hoisted the 1919 American League pennant, and the Ted Lewis band and a "shimmy champion" named Frisco entertained the crowd. Schalk's good friend Sam Pass, who had tipped off the team about Harry Redmon and the St. Louis gambling connection to the 1919 World Series, was one of the prime movers in the Schalk Day celebration.

As for the games, the teams split. The Sox won the first in 11 innings on a pinch single by Eddie Murphy; Eddie Cicotte went the distance in another fine performance. But game 2 went to the Browns, 4–1, with Dickey Kerr lasting only one inning. Roy Wilkinson, whose wife had given birth to a daughter that morning, pitched eight shutout innings in relief. On Friday the Sox fought back to tie the Browns after falling behind, 4–0, then tied the game again in the bottom of the ninth on a home run by Eddie Collins, but finally succumbed in 10 innings, 7–5, with Browns ace Urban Shocker topping Sox ace Lefty Williams. The winning runs came home on a scorching double by the Browns' "Baby Doll" Jacobson, with the ball caroming off Weaver's feet into short left field.

The Sox rebounded and finished the series with impressive wins on both Saturday and Sunday. Saturday's game was a 16-hit, 11–3 laugher behind Red Faber, who was now 10–6 with a 2.54 ERA. John Collins, who according to Crusinberry "seems to be solving the first base problem unassisted," led the offense with a single, a double, and a triple. "Folks are starting to learn that John, who joined the team in 1910, is a regular ball player," wrote Crusinberry.[27]

"The practice of grandstand fans of throwing the ball around playfully just to tease the coppers and ushers when a foul comes into the crowd seems to have a serious side to it," wrote Crusinberry in his "White Sox Notes" for Saturday's game. "On Friday and one day previous to that, women were hit by the ball. A woman wearing glasses was struck right over the right eye Saturday."[28]

On Sunday, July 4—the holiday would be officially celebrated the next day— the Sox finished the series with a 6–3 win behind Cicotte, who was making his second straight start on two days' rest. It didn't seem to be hurting him: Cicotte had gone 5–0 with a 1.91 ERA in five starts in the 16-day period since June 19. Joe Jackson went 4 for 4 in the game and was now up to .396, but a great play from Happy Felsch helped preserve the win. With the Sox leading 4–3 with a man on second and two out in the Browns' eighth, Earl Smith, "an aspiring youngster" according to Crusinberry (he was actually 29 years old and in his fifth season in the majors), "hammered a red hot single over second. Felsch galloped in like a race horse, scooped the ball perfectly, and fired to the plate, and Schalk touched [Ken] Williams on the tip of the right toe as he made a desperate slide for the plate."[29]

Throwing a ball around in the stands is dangerous, but apparently this is a tradition we need to bring back, according to James Crusinberry: "Can you remember away back when the fans at the Fourth of July games whipped out their revolvers and fired a cylinder full of shots when the first base hit of the game was made."[30]

Before heading out on another long road trip, the White Sox had three more games scheduled against the league-leading Indians: a morning-afternoon holiday doubleheader on Monday, July 5, followed by a single game on Tuesday. Despite their excellent play recently, the Sox hadn't been making much headway in cutting into Cleveland's lead. They entered the series still in third place with a 41–28 record, five and a half games behind the Indians (46–22). The Yankees (48–24), who had been even hotter than the White Sox, were now in a virtual tie with the Indians, though Cleveland led New York by nine percentage points (.676 to .667).

In a strange quirk of scheduling, the White Sox had already played the Indians 15 times, winning only five matches. After this three-day set the clubs had a single game at Cleveland on Sunday, July 25, but then wouldn't meet again until a final three-game series in late September. So this three-game set was a crucial showdown for the White Sox.

The Sox played it like they were determined to repeat as American League champions. For Monday morning's opener Kid Gleason selected Claude Williams, who was undefeated in four starts against Cleveland thus far in 1920 (three wins, plus one no-decision in a game the Sox won) as his starter, facing Ray Caldwell of the Indians before a crowd of 8,000. A two-run double by Joe Jackson gave the White Sox a 3–1 lead in the third, and Williams held it the rest of the way, winning, 5–3, for his 16th victory. In the afternoon game before a crowd of 25,000, Cleveland starter Stan Coveleski was coasting along with a 5–0 lead, having allowed only three hits, when the White Sox put together one of their most dramatic rallies of the year. The Sox sent 11 men to the plate in the frame and eight hit safely, bringing home six runs; John Collins drove in the go-ahead run with his second hit of the inning. Roy Wilkinson pitched a scoreless ninth to preserve the 6–5 win for starter Dickey Kerr.

Tuesday's series finale before 10,000 was a tight battle between Red Faber and Indians ace Jim Bagby, who entered the game with a 15–3 record. Through nine innings the game was tied, 3–3. Cleveland took the lead in the top of the 10th when Charlie Jamieson tripled with two out and Ray Chapman singled him home. But the Sox tied it in the bottom half on a pinch single by Eddie Murphy, who was batting for Faber. Then in the bottom of the 11th, with two out and the bases empty, Happy Felsch stepped to the plate. On a 2–0 count, "Hap stepped into it and clouted with all his might," wrote Crusinberry. "It wasn't a long high fly. It was a terrific drive that sailed out there and landed with a crash in the seats half way up to the top."[31]

The 5–4 win knocked the Indians (46–25) into second place, one game behind the Yankees (49–26); the third place White Sox (44–28) trailed New York by three and a half games. The Sox now headed east for a three-week road trip that included games against six of their seven American League rivals (all but the St. Louis Browns). The club was full of confidence. "We're just riding along easy now, while those fellows out in front are doing all the worrying," said one of the Sox veterans on the train ride east to Philadelphia, the first stop. Crusinberry noted that the Sox players were expressing greater respect for the Yankees than for the Indians. "We've got to lick New York to win the pennant," one the players remarked.[32]

They would get their chance on the upcoming trip.

9

ABE TELLS

As the White Sox were finishing their July 5–6 home series against Cleveland, the New York Yankees were in Washington, DC, finishing a series against the Senators. It was a happy day for the Yanks. They not only dismantled the Senators with a 17–0 rout that included a 14-run fifth inning; the victory put the Yanks in first place by themselves, one game in front of the Indians.

The Yankees had Wednesday off, so Babe Ruth elected to drive back to New York City, where the club was beginning a homestand on Thursday afternoon. Riding with Ruth in his brand-new touring car were his wife Helen; his Yankee teammates, Fred Hoffman and Frank Gleich; and Yankee coach Charley O'Leary, a longtime buddy of the Babe. Ruth was behind the wheel, with Helen next to him and the others in the back, as they rode down the Baltimore Turnpike. Some alcohol was consumed along the way.

At around 2:00 a.m. the group reached Wawa, Pennsylvania, a small town less than 20 miles west of Philadelphia. Ruth was driving fast and singing happily. There was a sharp turn in the road, and as they maneuvered the curve Ruth saw another vehicle heading toward them at great speed. As he hit the brakes and attempted to make room for the oncoming car, Ruth's vehicle went into a ditch and overturned; Helen and O'Leary were thrown from the car, with the Babe and the other occupants pinned beneath it. According to news reports, Ruth was able to raise himself on his haunches, lifting the vehicle up enough to enable the others to escape; they then held up the car so that Ruth himself could wriggle free. Remarkably no one was hurt except for a few bruises and scratches. Helen's stockings were almost torn off. Ruth himself had suffered a bruised knee. O'Leary, who was briefly knocked unconscious by the crash while a worried Ruth stood above him, thinking his friend was dead, is said to have uttered, "Where's my hat?" when he awoke.[1]

The group hobbled over to the nearby farmhouse of Coates Coleman, washed and dressed their wounds, and then telephoned for another car to drive them to Philadelphia, where they caught a train back to New York. (When the group arrived in New York City, they were startled to see a newspaper headline proclaiming, "RUTH REPORTED KILLED IN CAR CRASH.") Mrs. Coleman said that Ruth was badly hurt about the knee and limped painfully from the farmhouse to the car. When asked for instructions about what to do with his near-totally wrecked car, which was being towed to a nearby town, the Babe responded, "Sell it for whatever you can get. I'll do no more motoring during the baseball season."[2]

When the Yankees took the field against the Detroit Tigers on Thursday afternoon, Ruth was in his familiar spot in right field. In the seventh inning he legged out a triple, then ran home on a sacrifice fly by Bob Meusel. On Friday he hit his league-leading 25th home run. Eighteen years before the character of Superman debuted with an *Action Comics* cover showing the Man of Steel lifting a car over his head, the Yankees appeared to have a Superman in their outfield.

While Ruth and the Yankees were hosting Detroit, the White Sox began their road trip with a game in Philadelphia against the last-place Athletics. Facing rookie left-hander Roy Moore, who had lost eight straight decisions since defeating the White Sox in his first start on May 25, the South Siders broke open a scoreless game with three runs in the seventh, then addled five more in the ninth. Eddie Cicotte, who won his sixth consecutive decision for his 10th victory of the season, held the A's scoreless until the ninth inning when they made things interesting by scoring five times. John Collins was the Sox batting star with a pair of triples. "Jack Collins at first base is the principal reason why the White Sox, with heads up, are fighting for the lead in the American League pennant race instead of trailing in the second division as a disorganized team," wrote Harvey Woodruff.[3]

Facing the team for which he made his Major League debut in the series opener, Joe Jackson showed that his all-around skills were still formidable, with three hits, a stolen base, and a great play on defense. "In the second inning Joe Jackson skidded along the left field wall, brushing a blue coated copper aside and making a swell catch of [Jimmy] Dyke's [*sic*] long drive, which was ticketed for about three bases," commented James Crusinberry in the *Tribune*'s game notes. "The copper would have been justified in pinching Joe for robbery."[4]

Going for his 17th victory against the A's on Friday, Claude Williams was expected to have an easy time. But he gave up a three-run homer to Frank Welch in the first inning and a solo shot to Cy Perkins in the second, and the

White Sox never caught up. They did their best: trailing 5–1 entering the bottom of the ninth, the Sox scored three times and had men on second and third with no one out, but reliever Scott Perry retired Happy Felsch, John Collins, and Swede Risberg to preserve Philadelphia's 5–4 win.

On Saturday the Sox rebounded; the offense pounded out 16 hits and Red Faber pitched a five-hit shutout for a 6–0 win. The game was relatively uneventful, but on Monday, with no Sunday game to write about due to Pennsylvania's "blue laws," James Crusinberry devoted a column to an incident in the first inning of Saturday's contest. With Nemo Leibold on third base and Buck Weaver at bat, Philadelphia pitcher Rollie Naylor threw a pitch in the dirt. The ball appeared to hit Weaver in the foot, bounced up to nick A's catcher Cy Perkins in the throat, and then bounded off toward the grandstand. With that, Leibold ran home . . . but if the pitch had hit Weaver, "who lay on the ground smiling up at Umpire Tommy Connelly [sic]," it would be a dead ball and Leibold would need to return to first. Crusinberry continued,

> Weaver saw the situation. That's why he sat there smiling as if happy to see the Sox get a run. He wanted the decision made so that Leibold could score. Umpire Connolly stood with his eyes glued on Weaver. He thought the ball hit him in the foot, but knew if it did, it must have hurt like fury, and there was Buck, smiling and happy as if tickled to see the run scored.
> Nothing was said for a moment, and then the water began to come into Weaver's eyes and his forced smile departed. There was a twinkle in Tommy Connolly's eye as he said: "Go back to third base, Leibold, and you get up and go to first base, Weaver."
> Then Buck Weaver grabbed his injured foot and began rubbing it. "Say, it felt like the blood was running out of my toes and filling my shoes," said Weaver in telling about it afterward. "But I thought maybe I could get away with it."

Crusinberry, who in 1956 would write how he noticed from the start of spring training in 1920 that the seven suspected players had formed a separate faction in the club, wrote this about Weaver's July 10 ploy: "It characterizes the unusual spirit of Bill Gleason's men—a spirit that is almost sure to land the Sox on top if the pennant fight ever gets down to a close battle in the closing games of the season."[5]

The "spirit of Bill Gleason's men" would be much different when the closing games of the season rolled around.

When the White Sox–Athletics series resumed on Monday, the Sox had a new player: left-handed hitting outfielder/first baseman/pitcher Bibb Falk, who had recently earned a degree in civil engineering from the University of Texas. A 21-year-old Texas native and the son of Swedish immigrants, Falk had starred in football and baseball for the Longhorns, and came to the attention of the White Sox when they were training nearby; Charles Comiskey had signed him for delivery after his schooling was finished. He would have joined the club earlier, but was held back by a bout of bronchial trouble. Falk would play very little in 1920 but became a regular the next year as the successor to Joe Jackson in left field. He was no Shoeless Joe—who was?—but he went on to bat .312 with an OPS+ (on-base plus slugging percentage adjusted for park and offensive context) of 112 (signifying that he was 12 percent better than an average player) over a solid 12-year career. After retirement Falk became a successful manager and coach; returning to his alma mater in 1940, he led UT to 20 Southwest Conference championships and two College World Series titles.

Monday's series finale against the A's was a pitchers' duel between Chicago's Dickey Kerr and Philadelphia's Scott Perry. Kerr did not allow a hit through the first six innings, facing the minimum 18 batters (one batter walked but was caught stealing). He gave up three hits in the seventh, two of them infield hits, but escaped the jam. Perry was just as good, and the game was scoreless through eight innings, with each pitcher allowing only three hits. Eddie Collins led off the White Sox ninth with a home run that was barely fair, and Kerr set down the A's in order in the bottom of the inning for a 1–0 win.

From Philadelphia the Sox went to Washington for a four-game set. The Senators were in fourth place with a 37–35 record, well behind the White Sox, who were third with a 47–29 mark. The Sox were three and a half games behind the Yankees and Indians, who were in a virtual tie for first. Chicago won Tuesday's opener, 5–3, behind another strong outing from Eddie Cicotte, but it wasn't easy. The game was tied 3–3 through seven innings before the Sox scored single runs in each of the last two innings. The go-ahead run came home on a sacrifice fly from Buck Weaver.

On Wednesday it looked like another Sox victory when the team took a 4–0 lead with Claude Williams on the hill, but with some shaky White Sox defense playing a big part, Lefty couldn't hold it. This game deserves some study. With two Senators on base and two out in the fifth, Sam Rice hit a liner to right. Joe Jackson, playing right field because he preferred to avoid Washington's sun in left field, "attempted a shoe string catch when he should have taken the ball on the first hop," according to Crusinberry. "He missed connections and the ball skipped to the fence for a homer, three runs coming in." Crusinberry thought that Nemo Leibold, the usual Sox right fielder, might have caught Rice's drive. Aided by more questionable White Sox defense, the Senators scored three more times in the eighth. With one out, a man on second, and Braggo Roth at bat, Crusinberry wrote, "Roth boosted a fly ball out close to the right field foul line. Jackson had no chance to catch it, but ran in so far to take it on the bound that it hopped over his head and rolled away for a triple, letting [Clyde] Milan in with the tying run." With the lead run on third, "the Chicago outfielders came in close for the purpose of pegging to the plate should the next batter lift a fly ball. Young [Bucky] Harris was next, and he hit a fly ball all right, but it was a terrific drive to dead center. It never was twenty feet high, yet it sailed over Felsch's head for another triple, and only the liveliest kind of fielding by Happy and perfect relaying by Risberg prevented it being a homer." The run scored anyway on the third triple of the inning, a blast to right by Howie Shanks.[6]

For someone with an eye on potentially suspicious activity on the part of the 1920 White Sox, there are some items to consider here. Williams pitching well except for a couple of bad innings . . . three triples in one inning, plus an inside-the-park home run in another . . . questionable defensive plays . . . possibly questionable positioning. This sounds a lot like the 1919 World Series. I checked the game stories for the July 14 contest in three Washington papers; the only other Chicago paper I had access to, the *Daily News*, had a play-by-play account that ended with the fifth inning but described Rice's inside-the-park home run as follows: "Jackson tried to make a shoestring catch of Rice's liner, but missed the ball and it went to the right-field wall for a home run." The Washington papers all noted Jackson's attempt at a shoestring catch on Rice's home run, but saw nothing beyond an unsuccessful attempt to make a great play. On the three triples in the ninth, the one possibly discordant note was from the *Washington Herald* on Bucky Harris's drive: "Harris smacked a fast one to center on which Felsch made the mistake of running in. When he saw it was billed for extra bases he tried to reverse, but slipped."[7]

Given that Happy Felsch once famously told Eliot Asinof, "Playing rotten, it ain't that hard to do, once you get the hang of it," and gave Asinof a description of misplaying a flyball, this does create a little suspicion.[8] On the other hand, Felsch had a triple and an RBI in the game, and was robbed of an extra-base hit on a great catch by Sam Rice, according to the *Herald*. Jackson reached base three times in the game, and one of his two hits was a triple. Buck Weaver drove in two Sox runs, and Swede Risberg was 2 for 4. Even good players make misplays, and I am inclined to give the boys the benefit of the doubt here.

The scheduled White Sox-Senators game on Friday was rained out, so the teams finished the series with a Saturday doubleheader. It was a great day for the South Siders. Game 1, a pitching duel between Red Faber and Walter Johnson, entered the ninth inning tied, 1–1; the Sox broke it open by scoring three times, and Swede Risberg had the big hit—a two-run triple. In the second game the Sox, who entered the ninth trailing 5–4, loaded the bases for Joe Jackson. "Gen. Joe poled a tremendous drive to the flag pole in deep center for a home run, driving in three mates ahead of him and clinching victory by a score of 8 to 5," wrote James Crusinberry.[9]

The White Sox now headed to New York, where due to rainouts back in May, they were scheduled to play six games in four days. First place wasn't quite at stake—the Indians (54–27) had regained first place, a game and a half ahead of the Yankees (54–30) and three and a half in front of the Sox (50–30)—but it was obviously a "crooshal serius," as Harold Johnson of the *Chicago Evening American* put it. "Something is bound to occur within the next week to alter the aspect of the pennant campaign, according to the far-seeing Kid Gleason, who argues enthusiastically in behalf of the alabaster hose."[10]

As it turned out, something happened to the Kid in New York that would alter more than just the aspect of a pennant campaign.

On Thursday, July 15, a wet and gloomy day, Babe Ruth stepped to the plate at the Polo Grounds with two men on base in the 11th inning. It had been a wild, back-and-forth game between the St. Louis Browns and Ruth's Yankees, featuring six-run innings from each team. The score was tied, 10–10. Right-hander Bill Burwell, who 40 years later would be the pitching coach for the 1960 World Series Champion Pittsburgh Pirates, was on the mound for the Brownies. Charles Somerville of the *New York Evening World* set the scene, writing,

Betcher a new straw Kelly—mine's getting pretty well tanned now—against an ice cream cone that's been out in the sun that there wasn't half so much banging and shooting, whaling, walloping, attacks and counter attacks, ups and downs in the whole red and rowdy European war than waxed and waned on Coogan's Bluff yesterday afternoon. And the mud was just as bad as any Flanders Field. Twice the Polo Grounds was drenched. Players skidded on their ears or into one another and the hospital squad was carrying out pitchers every minute—or something like that.

But the finish. Ah—the finish!

Fine! Great!

The Browns, figuring as the heinies of the kick-up—scrapping, rampageous heinies nobody can deny.

But in the eleventh hour—I mean inning—the great Yankee fourteen inch gun, the Big Babe, crashed and boomed. Over the corner of the upper tier of the right grand stand sailed the winning shot.

The twenty-ninth homer for the King of 'Em ALL—equaling his record of last season, as well as lambasting forth the conquering crash in the fiercest old baseball scrap that ever was.[11]

In the Yankees' 83rd game, Ruth had tied the Major League single-season home run record that he had set one season earlier. The home run had one other distinction, noted by the *New York Times*: "It was the first hit in the American League under the rule passed last Winter which allows the batsman full credit for a home run even if a runner breaks the tie score before the big smash is cashed in at the plate."[12] Babe Ruth, constantly making history.

"Judging from the extraordinary interest being taken in Ruth, and the record crowds which are attending wherever the Yankees play, it looks as if New York would get the purchase price back the very first year," wrote Malcolm MacLean in the *Chicago Evening Post*. Red Sox owner Harry Frazee was insisting that, from his team's point of view, "the deal was the most successful ever put over in the American league." Frazee's argument was that "he can pay the salary of a high-class player just from the interest on the huge sum received." In addition, the Red Sox take from the 22 games his team would play against the Yankees "means much money in Frazee's pocket."[13]

Not many people were buying Harry's logic—particularly the owners of the Yankees. On Friday, July 16, the day after Ruth's record-tying home run, an estimated 20,000 came out to the Polo Grounds to watch the Babe try to break the record. He failed to go deep against the Browns' Bill Bayne in a 5–2 St. Louis victory. And there were over 30,000 on hand—the *Chicago Tribune* said 37,000—for the opener of the six-game series against the White Sox the next day.

Fans hoping for a Ruth homer on Saturday were disappointed, but Yankee fans had to be happy with the outcome: a 20–5 rout for Chicago's worst loss of the year. The White Sox looked totally unready for prime time, as they surrendered 22 hits and committed six errors, three of them by Buck Weaver. "They kicked and heaved the ball around in a manner that would have made a high school team ashamed of itself," wrote James Crusinberry.[14] Eddie Cicotte lasted five innings in taking his first loss since June 10, and relievers Spencer Heath and George Payne surrendered a combined 12 runs in three innings pitched. It got so farcical that Swede Risberg volunteered to pitch (Kid Gleason turned him down).

On Sunday, before 28,000, Ruth was homerless again—but the Yankees won again, 8–4, in a pouring rainstorm against Claude Williams, who surrendered all eight runs in five innings of work. Yankee outfielder Ping Bodie, referred to as "The Wonderful Wop" by *New York Tribune* writer W. O. McGeehan, was the hitting star with a single, a double, a grand slam home run, and six RBI.

Was this one of the games dumped by the Black Sox in 1920? It has several suspicious elements, including the fact that it was an important game played in the gambling center of New York City. Showing the kind of temporary lapse in control that he showed in the 1919 World Series, Williams walked three batters in the first inning, as well as allowing a double to Ruth and Bodie's grand slam. He also walked a batter in the third, helping lead to a New York run, and started the Yankees' two-run fifth by walking Wally Pipp. Jackson had two hits in the game, but Felsch, Risberg, and Weaver were a combined 0 for 13. Felsch had an error in the field (though he also had an outfield assist). Felsch and Weaver were each 0 for 3 with runners in scoring position. Even disregarding Jackson and Weaver, considered less likely to be helping dump games in 1920 (some Sox players would disagree), the performance of Williams, Felsch, and Risberg in this game is enough for me to put it in the suspicious category.

Adding to the general aura of intrigue about July 18 is that it appears to be the day that Abe Attell confessed his role in helping to fix the 1919 World Series to Kid Gleason. In a 1956 *Sports Illustrated* article, James Crusinberry wrote that this meeting took place in New York in late July; he said that the White Sox–Yankee game had been rained out that day, but the only White Sox rainouts in New York were much earlier in the season, and all the other details point to

In a meeting with White Sox manager Kid Gleason in July 1920, former boxing champion Abe Attell admitted his role in the 1919 World Series fix. *Library of Congress Prints and Photographs Division*

July 18—including the fact that this was the only White Sox eastern road trip covered by Crusinberry in 1920.

As Crusinberry described it, he was in his hotel room with Ring Lardner, the legendary writer who had previously worked with Crusinberry at the *Chicago Tribune*, when Gleason called the room. Kid said that Abe Attell was talking, and he wanted Lardner and Crusinberry to hear what he had to say. Attell was a former boxing champion and Arnold Rothstein colleague, and one of several gamblers who helped arrange the World Series fix. He did not know either Crusinberry or Lardner.

When they got to the bar, the writers stood close to Gleason and listened in while he talked with Attell. "So it was Arnold Rothstein who put up the dough for the fix," said Gleason.

"That was it," Attell replied. "You know, Kid, I hated to do that to you, but I thought I was going to make a lot of money and I needed it, and then the big guy double-crossed me, and I never got but a small part of what he promised."

Crusinberry wrote that for the rest of the season, "the seven suspected players acted as if they knew I was investigating them." However, he wrote nothing

White Sox manager Kid Gleason kept his team in the 1920 pennant race, despite suspicions that some of his players were dumping games. *Library of Congress Prints and Photographs Division*

about the meeting at the time, and if Gleason shared what Attell had told him with Charles Comiskey, the Sox owner did nothing about it before late September, when the scandal finally broke. Neither did Gleason.[15]

Entering Monday's doubleheader, the Yankees had beaten the White Sox seven times in eight meetings, and Babe Ruth was not impressed with the South Siders. In his ghost-written column that morning, Ruth wrote,

> I repeat what I already have said about the White Sox. They are not in this American league race at all. They are in third place because most of the other clubs have not played against them as they have against the Yankees and Cleveland. They do not match against the Cleveland club in the slightest sense as a contender with the Yankees. And certainly the Yankees have shown in the last few days that the Chicagoans cannot hope to battle us for a pennant.
>
> The Sox haven't the pitching. I said this before, but the evidence has been against me when other clubs were facing the rickety staff. It has required the Yanks to beat them down, and they have done it with small mercy.[16]

There was some truth in what Ruth was saying. Entering the July 19 doubleheaders the White Sox were 50–33 overall . . . but that record was largely a result of the Sox pummeling the Tigers (11–1) and Browns (10–4); against the other five clubs Chicago was only one game over .500 (29–28). Monday's first game went according to script, with the Yankees pounding Roy Wilkinson, 8–2. Game 2 looked like it was headed in the same direction; Ruth hit his record-breaking 30th home run off Dickey Kerr in the fourth inning, and the Yanks took a 3–1 lead into the seventh. But the Sox fought back, scoring three times in the seventh and four in the eighth for an 8–5 win. Ruth hit homer number 31 in the ninth. The record-setting home run came on a 2–2 curveball, according to the *New York Times*, describing the action:

> There was a resounding smack as bat met ball and the noise from the stand swelled in volume before the ball had started its descent. Every last fan knew this was the much awaited punch. . . .
> Ruth was just as happy over his success as was the crowd. While the fans howled in glee, tossed hats around the stand in reckless abandon and made the big stand a mass of waving arms, Ruth completed the journey to the plate and then beamed back with a smile that spurred the crowd on to greater exertion, if that were possible. Doffing his cap, the conventional response which usually stills a cheering crowd of fans, had no effect here. Several times on his way to the bench Ruth bowed his acknowledgments, but the din continued after he disappeared in the dugout. His march to left field at the close of the inning was the signal for

another outburst, and the applause was renewed when he came in after the White Sox had been retired in the fifth inning.[17]

According to the *New York Tribune*, Ruth's homer brought him a $100,000 contract to go into the movies. However, the White Sox won the game—and with four hits in the doubleheader, Shoeless Joe Jackson had improved his batting average to .401.

The Sox came from behind with a four-run ninth inning to win the first game of Tuesday's doubleheader for Red Faber, 7–5, despite allowing Ruth's 32nd homer. "When Ruth hit his homer fans upstairs and down sailed their straw hats or their neighbors' straws upon the field," wrote Crusinberry. "A couple of groundskeepers had to go out and gather up the remnants."[18] But the Yankees defeated Cicotte to win the second game, 6–3.

From New York the White Sox traveled to Boston for four games against the Red Sox, who had given them trouble all year. The series got off to a familiar start on Wednesday when the White Sox once again looked helpless against Sad Sam Jones, who defeated them for the third time in 1920, 2–1. But the rest of the series went Chicago's way. On Thursday Dickey Kerr allowed only four hits and no earned runs to beat the Red Sox 2–1, in one of his strongest outings all year. On Friday the White Sox trailed 5–0, but fought back with a pair of four-run innings to win again, 8–7. With three hits, including his 12th home run, and four RBI, Happy Felsch was the hero of Saturday's series finale, a 7–4 White Sox victory behind Eddie Cicotte, who was now 12–7 on the year.

With two hits in each of the three last three games against Boston, Buck Weaver was now hitting .352. Malcolm MacLean paid tribute to the switch-hitter's work effort. "Buck Weaver, when he joined the Sox, was woefully weak against the right-handed pitchers," he wrote. "Accordingly, he practiced for hours at a time hitting left-handed, until today he bats equally well from either side of the plate." While platoon splits are only available for part of Weaver's career (mostly 1918–1920), they mostly support MacLean's assertion. In fact, Weaver's numbers actually were better swinging from the left side: Buck's batting average hitting left-handed was .314 with a .731 OPS, versus .285/.712 hitting righty. "That he now can slam right-handers is shown by the fact that for years he had the highest batting average of any American leaguer hitting against Walter Johnson, the king of them all," continued MacLean. This assertion is also backed by the available data: among all players with at least 25 career at-bats against Johnson, Weaver's .481 batting average (13/27) was the best (though all 13 hits were singles). "Weaver has also studied placing the ball, and I doubt if there's a batter in the league who does it better than Buck," wrote MacLean.[19]

Sunday baseball was prohibited in Boston and much of the East, so after Saturday's game the Sox headed to Cleveland for a single game against the league-leading Indians. The Indians (59–31) were in a virtual tie for first with the Yankees (61–33), but led New York by seven percentage points (.656 to .649). The White Sox were four games back in third (55–35). In his fine book *Shoeless: The Life and Times of Joe Jackson*, author David Fleitz speculated that this game, a 7–2 Cleveland victory before a packed house, was one of the 1920 games dumped by the Black Sox. It definitely had its suspicious moments—particularly the pitching of Claude Williams and the defense and hitting of Swede Risberg.

Williams had started five games against Cleveland thus far in 1920, with four complete-game victories and a no-decision in a game won by the White Sox. In this one Lefty starting out by giving up a run in the first inning on a home run by Indians player-manager Tris Speaker—the *Chicago Tribune* game story said he "grooved one to Speaker," which suggests a fat pitch. Lefty issued walks in both the second and third innings, but no runs; he helped escape a second-inning jam on a great catch by Happy Felsch that the *Cleveland Plain Dealer* called a "sensational one-handed catch" and the *Tribune* called "the most remarkable piece of business done on the grounds all afternoon." Larry Gardner led off the Cleveland fourth with a double. Bill Wambsganss then "slashed to Risberg," according to the *Tribune*, "but with an easy play in front of him Weaver muffed the throw and Gardner was safe at third, from where he scored on Johnston's sacrifice fly to Felsch." Williams then gave up back-to-back doubles to Steve O'Neill and pitcher Stan Coveleski, who in fairness to Lefty was a decent hitter (.159 lifetime, but .225 in 1920).[20]

The White Sox got a run back in the fifth—Ray Schalk doubled, moved to third on a Williams groundout, and then scored on Nemo Leibold's sac fly—and another in the sixth that was all Black Sox: Weaver single, Jackson groundout, Felsch double. It was still 3–2 Cleveland in the seventh when Williams fell apart with some major help from Swede Risberg. With one out, Williams walked the opposing pitcher, Coveleski. He seemed out of the inning when pinch-hitter George Burns grounded to Risberg. "The latter, trying for a double play, pegged wildly past Eddie Collins and into the crowd in right field, Coveleskie [*sic*] halting at third," according to the *Tribune*. Ray Chapman doubled, scoring Coveleski and sending Burns to third; the *Plain Dealer*, in a summary that began, "Risberg did not look like a world's championship shortstop," wrote about this play that Swede "went to sleep with the ball in his hand and allowed Chapman to stretch a single into a double." Joe Wood then drove home Burns and sent Chapman to third; the *Plain Dealer*'s comment was that Risberg "let Wood's pop fly fall safely in front of him." Cleveland made it 6–2 on a single by Gardner to score Chapman, and scored a final run in the eighth after a leadoff double by Doc Johnston.[21]

Summing up, the suspicious elements in this game revolve mostly around the pitching of Williams (10 hits allowed, six for extra bases), and the wretched defense and hitting (0 for 4, including 0 for 2 with runners in scoring position) of Risberg. Weaver and Jackson were a combined 1 for 9 in this game, with a key error from Weaver, who was also 0 for 3 with runners in scoring position. Only Happy Felsch—2 for 4, an RBI, a great catch—seemed beyond suspicion. At the very least, it looks like Williams and Risberg weren't playing to win this game.

The White Sox finished their lengthy road trip with a two-game set against their favorite patsies, the Detroit Tigers. The Sox won both games, but not without some harrowing moments. On Monday Tiger starter George Dauss, who led the American League in hit batsmen three times in his career, hit Sox leadoff man Nemo Leibold in the ribs to start the game. Then he hit the next hitter, Eddie Collins, "squarely on the top of the head. He dropped like he was shot with a rifle. He came to after a few minutes and sauntered to first."[22] Both Leibold and Collins scored on a triple by Joe Jackson, but Collins had to come off the game after feeling dizzy. The Tigers refused to quit, erasing a 4–1 lead with three in the eighth, but the Sox finally put Detroit away with a two-run 10th inning. Dickey Kerr went all the way for his ninth victory, and fifth in succession. Tuesday was a little easier, though Collins was still out. The Sox scored twice in the first and led all the way for a 3–1 victory for Red Faber's 14th victory. Faber was even hotter than Kerr; he was 7–0 with a 2.57 ERA in nine starts since June 26, with the Sox winning all nine games.

Having posted a 13–8 record on their long road trip, the White Sox were back home on Wednesday, July 28. They finished the month with a five-game series against the last-place Philadelphia Athletics, a club they had beaten six times in seven previous games. In Wednesday's opener Eddie Cicotte had his best outing of the year, shutting out the A's on three hits for his 13th win in a 3–0 Sox victory that took just 81 minutes. Two days after his beaning in Detroit, Eddie Collins returned to the lineup and drove in two of the three Chicago runs with a third-inning single.

On Thursday, the clubs split a doubleheader. In the first game Lefty Williams, who had lost five straight starts, pitched a four-hitter for his 17th win as the Sox won, 4–2. Game 2 was tied 6–6 after nine innings, but the A's scored six runs in the top of the 10th to earn the split, 12–6. All six runs were unearned;

Spitballer Red Faber, who led the 1920 White Sox pitching staff with 23 wins, spent his entire 20-year MLB career (1914–1933) with the White Sox. *Library of Congress Prints and Photographs Division*

with the bases loaded and one out, Philly first baseman Ivy Griffin grounded to short, but with a chance for an inning-ending double play, Risberg threw wildly to the plate, letting two runs score and opening the floodgates. It was Risberg's 27th error of the season.

The clubs finished the series, and the month, by splitting the final two games. On Friday the Sox won 6–5 in 10 innings, for Faber's 15th win. The surprise hero was 31-year-old outfielder Amos Strunk, who had been acquired on waivers from the A's several days earlier. Filling in for Joe Jackson, who was out with a charley horse, Strunk had three hits, including the game-winning double. Strunk, a Philadelphia native who had debuted with the A's back in 1908, had been a fine player in his prime; he ranked in the top 10 in the American League in various categories several times in his career, had a career OPS+ of 112, and played in five World Series (four with the A's, one with the Red Sox). He ended up playing quite a bit for the White Sox over the remainder of the 1920 season, though not with the effectiveness he had shown in his best seasons.

The *Philadelphia Inquirer* summed up Saturday's game, a 5–4 A's victory, succinctly: "The White Sox could not hit Dave Keefe and ran the bases stupidly." The writer didn't mention a pop fly that Eddie Collins lost in the sun in the third inning, helping ignite a three-run inning for the Athletics. While this game is not high on any list of 1920 contests that may have been dumped by the Black Sox, it featured some head-scratching play from Happy Felsch and Swede Risberg. With the Sox trailing 5-1, Happy Felsch "led off with a double, but before anything more of the kind could happen he was picked off second by a yard on a toss from the pitcher," according to I. E. Sanborn. One out later, "Risberg dumped a Texas leaguer safely into short right a rod or two back of first and tried to make two bases on it without one cshance in a thousand." Sanborn also mentioned John Collins caught stealing that "might have been a phantom hit and run play," meaning that Collins was hung out to dry by the man at the plate. That would be Swede Risberg.[23]

The loss to the A's on July 31 finished an arduous month in which the White Sox had played 34 games in 31 days, with only three off-days. Playing 21 of the 34 games on the road, the club had posted a 22-12 record, with the offense hitting .305 and averaging 4.7 runs per game for the month. Eddie Collins led the offense with a .400 batting average and a .989 OPS. The pitching staff (3.82 ERA in July) had seven members, but in those very different times, the top five worked all but 11.1 innings for the month. Red Faber (6-0, 2.87), Eddie Cicotte (6-2, 3.09), and Dickey Kerr (5-2, 3.41) were good; Lefty Williams (2-6, 4.43) and Roy Wilkinson (3-2, 4.80), not so much.

Overall the White Sox finished the month with a 60-38 record, in third place and five and a half games behind the league-leading Indians (65-32). August would begin with a big home series against the second-place Yankees (64-37). Babe Ruth was coming to town, and Chicago was going slightly crazy in anticipation.

10

SCANDAL, TRAGEDY—
AND FIRST PLACE

"Fully 120,000 persons are expected to see the four games between the White Sox and Yankees, which start Sunday afternoon at three gongs," wrote Malcolm MacLean in anticipation of the August 1–4 series at Comiskey Park. "Requests for reservations have been received from places a thousand miles away. It's a complete sell-out of reserved seats, and the world series had little on this engagement."[1] White Sox team secretary Harry Grabiner announced that the gates would open at 10 a.m.—five hours before game time—for general admission seats in the grandstand, pavilions, and bleachers.

An estimated 45,000 fans—the biggest crowd to ever watch a baseball game in Chicago, according to the *Chicago Tribune*—were on hand for Sunday's opener, with Eddie Cicotte opposing the Yanks' Bob Shawkey. Some got in for free by climbing over a wall or breaking down a bleacher gate, despite efforts from the police to hold them back. People who could not fit into the seats were permitted to stand in the outfield, with a ball landing safely in that area ruled a ground-rule double. The rule came into play in Ruth's second plate appearance in the fourth inning (he had struck out swinging in the second). He lofted a flyball to left field; "it was so high in the air that Joe Jackson had plenty of time to back up into the packed throng behind him, which separated to admit him, and clutch the ball with his hands just before he toppled over somebody's feet and fell backward into the jam," wrote I. E. Sanborn.[2] Umpire Tommy Connolly ruled that Jackson had held the ball "momentarily," which was all the rules required, and called Ruth out. Yankee manager Miller Huggins argued that the play should have been ruled a double, to no avail.

To the disappointment of fans hoping to see the Babe clout a home run, Cicotte held Ruth and the Yankees at bay, shutting out the Yanks on five hits, 3–0. No Yankee got farther than second base, and Ruth was 0 for 3 with a strikeout and walk. When the count reached two strikes the Sox used an early version of a modern-day shift; on his final at-bat in the eighth inning, the Babe was thrown out by Swede Risberg, who was playing on the right side of second base. Interest in Ruth's performance was so intense that Monday's *Chicago Tribune* listed a pitch-by-pitch account of each Ruth plate appearance ("Cicotte began against Ruth with a ball that was wide. Then he curved over one strike, which was too low to suit Babe . . .").[3]

Cicotte had never allowed a home run to Ruth, and never would. In a piece for the *Tribune* on Wednesday, he explained that his philosophy was "to give him balls that can't very well be hit out of the park," and wrote that "a low spitter, which has downward break, is hard to hit for a long clout. . . . But a wise pitcher facing Ruth will never feed him spitters exclusively. I mix them up."[4] Of course, only a small number of pitchers were now permitted to use the spitball, and over his career Ruth would show the ability to take almost any pitcher deep (for instance, he had nine career homers against Cicotte's spitballing teammate, Red Faber).

On Monday, a crowd estimated at 30,000 by the *Tribune* got its wish: after drawing walks in each of his first two times up against Claude Williams, Ruth came up with a man on in the fourth and blasted a home run into the right field bleachers. The Yankees went on to a 7–0 victory behind former White Sox righty Jack Quinn. "I rather like Williams' pitching," Ruth wrote in his syndicated column. After describing the first two pitches of his fourth-inning at bat, he wrote, "Williams came back with a fast one over the corner of the plate about chest high. I stepped in and met the ball squarely just before it would have hopped. It went on a line over Leibold's head into the right field bleachers." The loss was the seventh in nine starts since July 2 for Williams.

On Tuesday, Red Faber drew boos from the crowd of 27,000 by walking Ruth three times—twice intentionally—in four trips to the plate; the Babe had an infield single in his only official trip to the plate. A few of the fans suggested that Faber change his nickname from "Red" to "Yellow." But the crowd had to be happy with the overall result: a 3–1 victory for Faber's 16th win. The Sox might have had another run, but Joe Jackson—in another of those plays when he seemed to overestimate his speed and baserunning acumen—was tagged out at the plate, without sliding, while trying for an inside-the-park home run. Ruth, who had crashed into the concrete wall trying to corral Jackson's drive, got an assist on the play with a nice relay throw to second baseman Del Pratt, who then fired home.

In Wednesday's series finale, before 25,000, Dickey Kerr faced Ruth five times and didn't walk him once: he held the Babe to a single in five trips to the plate as the Sox won, 10–3, for Kerr's 10th victory. Jackson led the offense with three hits and two RBI. "Dickie Kerr and I fought it out five times today. I wasn't walked once. I like that," Ruth wrote in his syndicated column. "The little White Sox southpaw is a smart pitcher and has a lot of nerve."[5]

While the White Sox were finishing their series with the Yankees on August 4, the Chicago Cubs were taking on the Philadelphia Phillies at Philadelphia's Baker Bowl. Claude Hendrix, the Cubs starter, was "hammered hard and freely when on the mound,"[6] according to James Crusinberry. In seven innings of work Hendrix allowed nine hits, including four doubles, and was in trouble in almost every inning; however, the Cubs only trailed 2–1 when Hendrix left for a pinch hitter in the top of the eighth. An error by Cubs second baseman Buck Herzog had helped the Phillies take the lead in the sixth.

Paul (Nick) Carter succeeded Hendrix on the mound in the bottom of the eighth and after retiring the first two hitters, walked the bases loaded. Speed Martin, who took over from Carter, forced home a run by hitting Casey Stengel with a pitch and then another by walking Cy Williams. The Cubs went out one-two-three to finish Philadelphia's 4–1 victory.

This contest would be little noticed at the time, but a Philadelphia gambler would later assert that the game had been tossed by the Cubs. The charge probably would have been given little credence except for the fact that on August 31, the Cubs would be accused of throwing another game to the Phillies—leading to the grand jury investigation that would finally snare the Black Sox. The Cubs players who would be accused of conspiring to dump the August 31 game would include veteran first baseman Fred Merkle, who did not play in August 4 game, and teammates Hendrix, Carter, and Herzog.

Game-fixing charges regarding the August 4 Cubs-Phillies game would not be revealed for several weeks, but on that day a major news story about crooked play broke on the West Coast: Pacific Coast League President William McCarthy announced that he had indefinitely suspended first baseman Baker "Babe" Borton of the Vernon Tigers and outfielder Harl Maggert of Salt Lake City Bees. The charge was that the two players had conspired to throw a game between their clubs the previous Wednesday. In addition, the league served notice to its clubs to refuse admission to Hal Chase, who was making his return to action, as it were, after the Magee trial. Reports stated that Chase was involved with a gambling ring and had suggested to players in the league that they could earn "easy money."

A key figure in the 1919–1920 Pacific Coast League scandal, former major leaguer Babe Borton claimed that he and some Vernon Tigers teammates had bribed players on other teams to help Vernon win the PCL pennant. *Library of Congress Prints and Photographs Division*

The suspensions were page 1 news across the league, as Borton and Maggert were major stars, while Chase was one of the most famous baseball figures on the West Coast. Borton, Vernon's captain and first baseman, had previously played for the White Sox and Yankees and had been part of the 1913 trade in which Chase had become a member of the White Sox. At the time he was hitting .326 and leading the Vernon Tigers in homers. Maggert, a 37-year-old career minor leaguer who was in his 11th season in the PCL, was hitting .370 for Salt Lake, which released him when the files were charged. According to reports, Borton had offered Salt Lake pitcher Ralph Stroud $300 to lose a game; Stroud had refused and notified his manager of the bribe attempt, but Maggert took up the offer. His method of helping Vernon was to get himself thrown out of a game in the first inning, squawk enough to get himself suspended, and then announce that he was "retiring." Chase, meanwhile, was accused of approaching Salt Lake pitcher Spider Baum with a bribe offer. Borton, Maggert, and Chase all denied the charges as the league continued to investigate. The story would soon get much deeper . . . and messier.

The Boston Red Sox followed the Yankees into Comiskey Park with a four-game series beginning on August 5. The Red Sox had been one of the big surprises of the early season, winning 21 of their first 30 games. While Boston had gone 22–45 since then to drop into sixth place, they had played the White Sox tough all year, splitting the 12 games between the teams.

Thursday's opener went to the Red Sox, 4–2, with Sad Sam Jones defeating Eddie Cicotte. The only questionable plays on the part of the Suspected Seven all involved Joe Jackson. Shoeless Joe was on first base after singling with one out in the third when Amos Strunk hit what should have been a bloop single to right field; reacting slowly when the ball dropped, Jackson was forced out at second. Then, leading off the bottom of the sixth with Chicago trailing 3–0, Jackson walloped a ball to left center that looked like a sure triple, "but as he rounded first base Mr. Joe was watching the flight of the ball and so was [Red Sox first baseman Stuffy] McInnis," according to I. E. Sanborn. "Moreover Stuffy was standing right in Jackson's natural runway. The subsequent collision knocked McInnis down and threw Jackson so far out of his stride that he could get only to second base."[7] Two flyouts followed, either of which could have scored Jackson from third. Sanborn also felt that a good throw from Jackson on Mike Menosky's two-run single in the Boston third would have retired the second runner at the plate. I personally would chalk all three of these miscues to poor baserunning and declining defense on the part of Jackson, and not to anything subversive. At bat Joe had three hits in the game, lifting him over the .400 mark again (.401).

On Friday the White Sox rebounded with a 4–3 win in 10 innings. Dickey Kerr, who got the win in relief of Claude Williams, drove in the winning run himself with a single. But on Saturday the Red Sox ended Red Faber's nine-game winning streak with a 4–2 victory, and Faber got no help from three of the Suspected Seven. Swede Risberg had three errors in the game, two of them directly leading to Boston runs, while going 0 for 4 at bat. On one of the plays, with Stuffy McInnis on third base with one out in the Boston second, "Swede grabbed [Gene] Bailey's bounder and pegged the ball 10 feet over Schalk's dome as McInnis waltzed homeward," according to the *Boston Herald*. Then with a man on third in the Boston ninth, "Risberg messed up an easy grounder from Foster and the big left-hander [Harry Harper] scored." In the last two innings, with Chicago trailing by one run in the eighth and two in the ninth, Happy Felsch—who was out of the starting lineup with an injury—and Fred McMullin came up as pinch hitters with men on base. Both struck out on three pitches. As for my suspicions about the honesty of this game, I will defer to Red Faber. "Why the hoodlums had some of the boys in their pocket all through the

1920 season, right up to the last week of the pennant," Faber told Eliot Asinof. I could feel it out there when I pitched."[8]

On Sunday, the White Sox bounced back to win the finale of the Red Sox series with a 2–0, six-hit shutout from Dickey Kerr; in 12 outings (9 starts) since July 5, Kerr had gone 11–1 with a 2.71 ERA. Happy Felsch returned to the White Sox lineup and hit his 13th home run.

The Washington Senators finished Chicago's homestand with a five-game series that began with a Monday doubleheader (one of the games was the makeup for a June rainout). The Senators had been struggling for over a month, with 10–24 record since July 6, and their struggles continued against the White Sox. On Monday the Sox won a pair of one-run games: 3–2 behind Eddie Cicotte (now 15–8) and 5–4 behind Claude Williams (18–11). With the sweep, the Sox (67–41, .620) moved into second place, two percentage points ahead of the Yankees (68–42, .618); Chicago still trailed the first-place Indians (69–36, .657) by three and a half games. On Tuesday the Sox won again, 4–3 in 10 innings, behind Red Faber (17–7, 2.55); Joe Jackson's single drove home Buck Weaver, who had doubled, for the game winner. The next day the Sox won their fourth straight one-run game, 2–1, on another strong outing from Dickey Kerr (13–5, 3.48); this time Weaver drove in both Sox runs with a seventh-inning single. In Thursday's series—and homestand—finale, the White Sox finished off a five-game sweep with a 7–2 victory behind Cicotte (16–8, 3.13), who won his second game of the series, while working on only two days' rest. Eddie Collins drove in five of the seven Chicago runs.

The victory over the Senators, the sixth straight win overall for the White Sox (70–41), moved them within a game of the first-place Indians (69–38), though Cleveland still had a three-game edge in the loss column. A long road trip to Detroit, Philadelphia, Washington, New York, and Boston now loomed, with the South Siders not due home until September 3. The White Sox were playing their best ball of the year, with a solid offense and all four members of the starting rotation seemingly in sync. "Everything is rosy on the South Side today and another American League pennant seems headed Chicagoward," wrote Larry Woltz.[9]

So it seemed at the time.

As the White Sox were finishing their homestand, the charges of crooked play in the Pacific Coast League grew much deeper. On August 10 Babe Borton, the suspended first baseman of the Vernon Tigers, claimed in an interview that during the 1919 season, a $2,000 slush fund had been created by 20 members of the Vernon team. The money was earmarked to bribe members of the league's Salt Lake, Portland, and Seattle teams to help Vernon win the league championship. He claimed that, just before the end of the season, his manager, Bill Essick, asked if Borton could get any Salt Lake players to lay down against Vernon, and Borton had said yes. He then agreed to pay Harl Maggert $500, Gene Dale $500, and Bill Rumler $250. Borton said that a teammate whose name he refused to divulge had agreed to pay Salt Lake infielder Eddie Mulligan $350, Portland catcher Del Baker $100, Portland pitcher Red Oldham $100, Portland catcher Art Koehler either $50 or $100, and Seattle pitcher Elmer Rieger $100.

Borton's claims were not outlandish. His Vernon Tigers club had narrowly edged the Los Angeles Angels for the 1919 PCL championship, and after the season the Angels had charged that the Salt Lake team had laid down to help Vernon. "Resentment smoldered during the winter and carried over into the 1920 season," wrote Larry Gerlach in a 2012 article about the scandal. But league President William McCarthy, who investigated the charges, called them "a mass of falsehoods, after several days of painstaking investigation, the interrogation of many witnesses and incessant inquiry and study." He did admit that, "Concealed beneath the mass of lies there may be some truth."[10] Following McCarthy's announcement, the Vernon club handed Borton his unconditional release.

But the story—and Borton—would not go away so easily. On August 12 the *San Francisco Examiner* reported that five days earlier, PCL player Rod Murphy had signed a statement that a notorious Seattle gambler named Nate Raymond had offered him money to throw games, and named Borton and Harl Maggert as players he had bribed. Raymond told Murphy that, with Borton as his agent, he had paid Maggert $1,000 to throw games in 1919. Raymond also told Murphy that he had earned $50,000 from his wagers during the 1919 season. McCarthy insisted that Murphy's statement confirmed his exoneration of the Vernon players and Salt Lake players apart from Borton and Maggert. "The pennant was not bought, and there was no 'slush fund' except that provided and furnished by Nate Raymond and his ilk," said McCarthy.[11]

For his part, Borton was able to produce documentation that in October 1919, he had sent a $500 check to Salt Lake pitcher Gene Dale and $200 to Dale's teammate, outfielder Bill Rumler, the 1919 PCL batting champion. According to Borton, Vernon pitchers had also helped Rumler win the batting crown by throwing him "straight fast ones." Borton also implicated several members of the Portland team whom he said had been paid off.[12]

Borton's repeated disclosures forced Harl Maggert, who was spurred by his wife to come clean, to finally confess his guilt to McCarthy. "I will admit that the Salt Lake player said some very startling things," McCarthy said after meeting with Maggert. "I hope that this is the beginning of the end of the scandal. If what

Maggert says is true I think that the Coast League directors will be in a position to clean up the mess in a short time."[13]

Despite McCarthy's optimism, the various threads of the scandal continued to unravel . . . and some were never looked into at all. As Larry Gerlach noted, McCarthy never seriously looked into Borton's charge that he had paid off multiple members of the Portland team. He also exonerated the Seattle franchise, focusing his attention on the Salt Lake team. On August 16, McCarthy indefinitely suspended Bill Rumler, an extremely popular player in Salt Lake City. (The suspension was later officially made a five-year ban.) A 29-year-old outfielder who had spent three seasons as a part-time outfielder with the St. Louis Browns, Rumler had followed his .362, 17-home run season for the Bees in 1919 by hitting .348 with 23 homers in 1920. He had played very well in a controversial series against Vernon late in 1919 before suffering an injury, and he even had an explanation for the $200 he received from Borton: Rumler said it was part of a "safety bet," a not-uncommon agreement between players on teams contending for a title, meant to ensure that the player on the team that lost out would get some postseason money. Given that the end result in this case was that a player on a championship team was sending money to a player on an also-ran, McCarthy's suspension of Rumler largely won praise . . . but not in Salt Lake City, where the Bees began to drop in the standings without Rumler and Maggert. Salt Lake officials also fumed that McCarthy hadn't seemed to make much of an effort to investigate the numerous Vernon players implicated by Borton. Bees President Bill Lane even considered filing a lawsuit against the league. The issue was far from settled.

While the Pacific Coast League scandal was obviously a bigger story in the West than in Major League cities, it was being watched in baseball circles across the country—and it had a particularly strong impact in Chicago. William Wrigley Jr., the principal owner of the Cubs, also owned the PCL Los Angeles Angels—the club that likely would have won the league championship in 1919 if not for the alleged game-fixing that benefited Vernon. Wrigley was outraged by the scandal revelations, and called on baseball to expel its bad actors. "The crooks and gamblers in baseball in baseball must go. Baseball is the greatest of American sports, and it must not be made less attractive with the public by the presence of dishonest players in its ranks," Wrigley said on August 12. "There is but one way to punish a gambling ball player, and that is to rid the game of him."[14] When the Cubs heard a report of game-fixing involving members of their own team at the end of August, they took swift—and public—action. The result was the formation of the grand jury that finally broke open the Black Sox scandal.

In the meantime, the National Commission, which logically should have been the organization looking into gambling and game-fixing, continued to flounder without a leader. On August 14, the *Chicago Herald and Examiner* reported that Ban Johnson was promoting Chicago judge Charles A. McDonald to fill the vacancy as chairman of the commission . . . but that National League President John Heydler preferred other candidates. McDonald would not become commissioner, but he would soon move into the limelight as leader of the grand jury that would be empowered in the aftermath of the August 31 Cubs game-fixing charge.

On Saturday, August 14, the White Sox began their lengthy road trip with a doubleheader at Detroit's Navin Field. The Sox won the opener, 5–2, on another strong outing from Dickey Kerr, who recorded his 14th win. Game 2 went to the Tigers, who defeated Red Faber, 6–1. The loss dropped the White Sox into third place in the tightly bunched American League race, with only a half game separating Cleveland (69–40, .633), New York (72–42, .632), and Chicago (71–42, .628).

On Sunday, the Sox completed their season series in Detroit with a 10–3 victory. The club's 12-hit attack featured the sixth—and final—home run of Swede Risberg's Major League career—though of course no one knew that at the time. Making his third start in seven days—all complete-game victories—Cicotte improved his record to 17–8, including a 4–0 mark against the Tigers.

As the White Sox traveled to Philadelphia on Monday, August 16, the first-place Cleveland Indians were beginning a crucial series at New York's Polo Grounds against the Yankees, who were in third but only a half game behind Cleveland. The starting pitchers were a pair of 18-game winners: spitballer Stan Coveleski for the Indians against Carl Mays, a hard-throwing pitcher with a tricky submarine delivery, for the Yanks. Mays would be shooting for his 100th career Major League victory in this game.

A 28-year-old right-hander who had pitched for three World Series championship teams with the Red Sox, Mays had been both a very successful and a highly controversial figure during his six-year MLB career. His decision to walk out on the Red Sox during the 1919 season—and his subsequent trade to the Yankees—had nearly torn the American League apart (see chapter 2). Even before that, Mays's pitching style had made him one of the league's most unpopular players. Though he had excellent control of his underhand delivery, Mays frequently hit opposing batters with his pitches, which often came in high and inside. "Mays is a low-ball pitcher," complained an opposing player. "How

Notorious for throwing at hitters, Carl Mays struck Indians shortstop Ray Chapman in the head with a pitched ball in August 1920, resulting in the only pitched-ball fatality in MLB history. *Library of Congress Prints and Photographs Division*

does it happen that when he puts a ball on the inside, it generally comes near the batter's head?" Mays shrugged off the comments, saying, "A twirler has a perfect right to put the ball on either side of the plate. But naturally no one has absolute control, and sometimes the pitcher who is trying to nick the corner of the plate will miss it altogether."[15]

On top of that, Mays's surly disposition made him unpopular even with his own teammates. "On the field, he was belligerent and argumentative, raging at anyone who stood in the way of his winning," wrote Mike Sowell. "He shouted at fielders who made errors behind him and belittled others for their shortcomings. Off the field, he was contemptuous of the lifestyles of players who liked to drink, smoke, or chase women, all vices that he shunned. He was intelligent and articulate, but he pulled no punches when pointing out the faults of others."[16]

Indians shortstop Ray Chapman, on the other hand, was as beloved a player as Mays was despised. A 29-year-old veteran in his ninth Major League season—all with Cleveland—Chapman was a skilled handler of the bat. He had led the American League in sacrifice hits three times and had become a well-above-average offensive player, particularly for a shortstop. Chapman also was smart and sophisticated; he was a talented singer and said to be "as much at home in the ball room as on the ball diamond."[17] He had recently married the daughter of a Cleveland millionaire, and was successful in his own right in the business world, working as secretary-treasurer of the Pioneer Alloys Company, a local firm. He had already decided to retire after the 1920 season to work full time for the company.

This was the background as Chapman stepped to the plate to open the fifth inning of the August 16 game, with the Indians leading Mays and the Yankees, 3–0. Chapman had already faced Mays twice in the game, both times in sacrifice bunt situations; he had sacrificed successfully the first time and popped into a double play the second. Mays's first pitch came in high and tight, and Chapman, seemingly transfixed, stood in his crouch as the ball crashed against his left temple with a loud crack that could be heard all over the park. Mays, assuming that his pitch had hit Chapman's bat, grabbed the ball and fired to first base. Meanwhile Chapman fell to the ground, with blood gushing from his left ear. Chapman was actually able to sit up and attempted to walk to the center field clubhouse, but he collapsed as he neared second base. After reviving briefly in the clubhouse, he fell unconscious and was taken to a hospital. That night surgery was performed on his fractured skull, but the injury was too severe. Ray Chapman died at 4:40 a.m. on Tuesday, August 17.

The death of Ray Chapman—to date still the only fatality in Major League history resulting from a hit by pitch—caused an uproar throughout baseball,

The victim of Mays's beaning, Ray Chapman was probably as beloved a player as Mays was despised. *Library of Congress Prints and Photographs Division*

and much anger directed toward Carl Mays. He received death threats, and the Detroit Tigers and Boston Red Sox demanded that American League President Ban Johnson banish Mays from organized baseball. Other teams, including the White Sox, considered making the same demand, but held back. Mays didn't help the situation by trying to shift the blame to plate umpire Tommy Connolly. "It was the umpire's fault," said Mays. "A roughened spot on the ball, sometimes even a scratch, will make a ball do queer things. Umpires are instructed to throw out balls that have been roughed."[18]

After wavering for a few days, Johnson decided on August 20 to take no action against Mays, pronouncing the case ended. He naively seemed to think that Mays was somehow too shaken to resume pitching. "I could not conscientiously attempt to make any trouble for Mr. Mays," Johnson said in his statement. "But it is my belief that Mr. Mays will never pitch again. From what I have learned he is greatly affected and may never be capable temperamentally of pitching again. Then I also know the feeling against him to be so bitter among the members of other teams that it would be inadvisable for him to attempt to pitch this year at any rate."[19]

Johnson badly misread both Carl Mays and the alleged strength of the boycott talk. Mays resumed pitching on August 23—one week after the fatal beaning—against the Detroit Tigers, one of the clubs most adamant about having him banished. The Tigers took the field quietly, and there were no incidents; in fact Mays breezed to a 10–0 victory for the 100th win of his career. As for Mays being shattered by the fatality, forget it. In his 13 appearances (10 starts) after the August 16 game, Mays was 10–3 with a 2.07 ERA.

But while Mays seemed to have moved on, the Chapman fatality appeared to hamper the performance of both the Indians and Yankees for a short period of time. For the first 10 days after Chapman's death (August 17–26), the Indians went 2–7 and the Yankees 2–5. While the Chicago White Sox were grieving for Ray Chapman along with the rest of baseball, on the field they were able to take advantage of the Cleveland and New York cold spells.

This was not apparent at first. Resuming their road trip in Philadelphia against the last-place Athletics on August 18, the Sox were shut out on five hits by rookie knuckleballer Eddie Rommel; Claude Williams (18–12) took the loss. The clubs were rained out on Thursday, necessitating a Friday doubleheader. In game 1 Red Faber got his 18th win, 7–4, thanks to the "Joe Jackson Show": the shoeless one drove in the first two runs of the game with a first-inning single and then broke the game open with a three-run homer in the seventh. The game was stopped at the end of the fourth inning, as the players on each team lined up along the foul lines and removed their caps in tribute to Ray Chapman, whose final at-bat had come in the fifth inning four days earlier. Jackson homered again in the second game, a two-run shot in the fifth that put the Sox ahead for good. Dickey Kerr was one out away from his 15th win when pinch hitter Lena Styles hit a grounder along the first-base line. It rolled foul just before Kerr picked up and tagged Styles. Thinking the game was over, fans poured onto the field, and when the umpires could not get the crowd to return to their seats, they awarded the game to the White Sox by forfeit. "We fooled 'em," cracked the colorfully named Philadelphia writer Jim Nasium. "They can't beat us the same old way all the time."[20] The doubleheader sweep moved the Sox (74–43) into a virtual tie for first place with the idle Indians (72–41), though Cleveland still held the lead by five percentage points (.637 to .632).

From Philadelphia the White Sox traveled to the nation's capital for a three-game series against the sixth-place Senators. Prior to Saturday's game several members of the team accepted an invitation from U.S. Secretary of Agriculture James T. Meredith to visit his department. "A moving picture man was on hand to 'shoot' the players and their host, who plans to use the films to boost the work of his department," wrote I. E. Sanborn.[21] Depending on which members of the team took part in the photo shoot, this film may have had a rather short shelf life.

The White Sox played Saturday's series opener without two regulars, Swede Risberg and Nemo Leibold, both out with hand injuries. Amos Strunk took over for Leibold in right field; as was usually the case when Risberg was out of the lineup, Buck Weaver moved over to shortstop while Fred McMullin played third. Strunk and McMullin were a combined 1 for 9 in the game, though Strunk led off the game with a single and scored the first run of the game. Weaver (three hits, three runs, two RBI) and Eddie Collins (two hits) were the offensive heroes as Eddie Cicotte got his 18th victory, 5–2. The victory was Cicotte's seventh in eight starts, with a 1.88 ERA, dating back to July 24. It would be a long time before Cicotte would have another quality outing.

While the White Sox were defeating the Senators, the Yankees were losing at home to the Tigers, 10–3; the Indians, still mourning the loss of Ray Chapman, were getting shut out twice in Boston, 12–0 and 4–0. Cleveland managed to record only three hits in each game. With that, the White Sox (75–43) were now in first place by themselves—and by a game and a half over the reeling Indians (72–43).

On Sunday the Sox took a firmer grip on first, increasing their lead to two full games by beating the Senators, 8–4, while the Indians were idle; the Yankees, who lost again to Detroit, 11–9, were now three and a half games back. The victory was the 19th of the year for Claude Williams, who wasn't great (10 hits allowed) but benefited from a 13-hit White Sox attack. Eddie Collins continued a long hot streak with three more hits. On the morning of June 10, Collins was hitting a season-low .298; in the 72 games since then, he had batted .396 with a .461 on-base percentage and .531 slugging.

Monday was an off day, and the White Sox got some bad news: Nemo Leibold, who had injured his right (throwing) hand on a slippery field in

Philadelphia, was X-rayed and diagnosed with a broken bone. Originally the injury had been thought to be only a sprain. Leibold was expected to miss about three weeks, but the injury was more severe than that, and he would not start another game until September 27. Though Leibold was batting only .226, he had been a productive player since late June, when his batting average had dropped to .175. In 54 games since June 28, Leibold had batted .270 with a solid .362 on-base percentage.

The hand injury forced Leibold to miss the most crucial part of the 1920 White Sox season, including the games which by most accounts were likely to have been dumped. Regarding what he observed while still with the team, Nemo's feelings are a bit of a mystery. In 1961, he told Ernie Harwell, "I roomed with Buck [Weaver] throughout the 1919 and 1920 seasons and never had an inkling anything was wrong." But in Donald Honig's 1977 book of interviews, *The Man in the Dugout*, Roger Peckinpaugh, who would be Nemo's teammate with the 1924–1925 Senators, said that during a Yankee visit to Chicago in 1920—most likely the games of June 16–19—Leibold told him, "Listen, something screwy is going on here. I don't know what it is, but it's something screwy all right. You guys bear down and you ought to take all four games." The Yankees did win the first three games of that series before dropping the finale in 10 innings. So who knows what Nemo Leibold really thought? It's another mystery about the ever-mysterious Chicago White Sox of 1917–1920.[22]

After their off day on Monday, August 23, the White Sox finished their series with the Senators on Tuesday. (Kid Gleason tried to talk Washington owner Clark Griffith to move the finale up to Monday so that the Sox would have two days off before their next series in New York, but Griffith wouldn't go for it.) With Red Faber on the mound, hopes for a series sweep were high. But Faber didn't have it, allowing four hits, a walk, and a hit batsmen in the fourth inning as Washington scored four times on their way to an 8–5 victory. Even so, the Sox (76–44) headed to New York after another off day on Wednesday with a two and a half game lead on the Indians (73–46), and with the Yankees (74–48) three games out.

The Chicago writers traveling with the White Sox were full of optimism. "Fickle Father Knickerbocker and his sportively inclined brothers have undergone a change of heart regarding Kid Gleason's earnest young White Sox," wrote Harold Johnson of the *Evening American*, teasing the New York writers who had joined the Sox bandwagon after earlier writing the team off. "This town [New York] is all agog over the White Sox's climb to leadership. Record breaking crowds are expected," wrote Oscar Reichow in the *Daily News*. Larry Woltz of the *Chicago Herald and Examiner* wrote, "The New York scribes are picking the White Sox to win the pennant, but they won't admit it in their papers." And in the *Tribune*, I. E. Sanborn wrote that the Sox were "Complacently looking down from the top of the American league ladder."[23]

Who could guess that, for the White Sox, the season was about to take a disastrous turn?

THE SUSPICIOUS SLUMP

On Thursday, August 26, the White Sox began their final visit of the 1920 regular season to New York's Polo Grounds. Babe Ruth continued to be the story for the Yankees. In the 35 games beginning with the second game of the July 19 Sox-Yankee doubleheader—the game in which Ruth had broken his single-season home-run record of 29—the Babe had hit 14 more home runs, giving him an otherworldly 43 homers for the season. However, the Yankees had a losing record (17–18) over the period, and Ruth himself was in a bit of a slump, with only one home run and a .231 batting average over his previous eight games.

"Of what importance are Babe Ruth's home runs?" wrote Malcolm MacLean a few days before the start of the White Sox-Yankees series. The following illustration may serve to show where they stand as a national institution:

> The Western Union has a wire running to all the ball parks in the east and central west. It goes into the National, American, International, Western and American association grounds—perhaps some others, too—and over this wire are flashed the batteries and the score by innings, the latter being posted on scoreboards.
>
> Nothing else is permitted over this wire, which perhaps is the largest circuit of any line in America, except Babe Ruth's homers. The latter are flashed the moment they are made.[1]

The wire was active in the first inning of Thursday's game; Ruth homered into the right field lower deck with a man on base off Dickey Kerr. It was part of a wild opening inning that saw the White Sox score four runs and the Yankees three. New York tied the game with a single run in the bottom of the third, but from then on it was all Chicago: the Sox scored three runs in the fourth inning, four in the seventh, and five in the eighth for a 16–4 victory—Chicago's highest scoring output of the season. John Collins had two doubles, a triple, and three RBI; Happy Felsch had a double, two singles, and four runs driven in; Swede Risberg had two hits and four RBI; and Eddie Collins had three singles and was robbed of a fourth hit on a sensational catch of a line drive by Yankee second baseman Del Pratt. The White Sox had 11 hits in 15 at-bats with runners in scoring position. They even rubbed salt in the Yankees' wounds: with the Sox leading 12–4 with the bases loaded in the eighth, the South Siders pulled off a triple steal, with Eddie Collins swiping home (Weaver and Jackson were the other base stealers).

With the combination of the Sox's victory over the Yanks and a 3–2 loss by the Indians to the last-place Athletics, Chicago (77–44) now led Cleveland (73–47) by three and a half games, with New York (74–49) four games back. On top of that, the White Sox learned before Friday's game that Ruth would not be in the Yankees' starting lineup; he had suffered an infection from an insect bite while working on a film, and would not return to action until September 3. The film, which was called "Headin' Home" with the Babe as the star, was being shot in Hackensack and Fort Lee, New Jersey; the Yankees permitted Ruth to work on the film even on Yankee game days when the club was at home. (Now *that's* a ballplayer with power!) "Ruth would drive up to location each morning, wrap up his movie work, then leave without removing his makeup for batting practice at the Polo Grounds, where his teammates would find a source of endless amusement in the heavy pancake adorning the Babe's countenance," wrote baseball film historian Hal Erickson.[2]

The White Sox were rolling, the Indians and Yankees were reeling, Ruth was out of action. Even the mosquitoes (or maybe it was the chiggers) were helping the White Sox cause. Another pennant seemed inevitable.

"You know, in 1920, when I was with the Yankees, we finished three games out of first place, and I'll never know whether we should have won it or not," Roger Peckinpaugh told Donald Honig. "The White Sox—they call that team the Black Sox today, don't they?—were monkeying around so much during the year you could never be sure. The scandal didn't come full bloom until near the end of the season. We'd play them one series and they would look terrible; we'd play them the next time and they'd look like the best club in the world. That's the way they set themselves up that year."[3]

On Friday the Sox selected Eddie Cicotte as their starting pitcher; the Yankees went with Carl Mays, making his second start since the fatal beaning of Ray Chapman. Talk of teams refusing to take the field against Mays was still in the air, but the White Sox met before the game and voted unanimously to play. "Boiled down to a few words," wrote I. E. Sanborn, "the attitude of the Gleason tribe in this controversy is just this: If Mays has the nerve to go along pitching, and if the owners of the New York American League club have the nerve to go on pitching him, and if the American league and the American public wants to see Mays pitch, what's the use of trying to tell them about their business?"[4]

The White Sox hit Mays freely, amassing 15 hits in his 10 innings of work, but the submariner was able to escape often enough to keep the Yankees in the game. The Sox left 14 runners on base, but it was a team effort, with players later known as both Black Sox and Clean Sox failing to come through. Felsch had three hits; Weaver had two, including a game-tying double in the ninth. Cicotte allowed two walks in the early innings that resulted in Yankee runs, but with seven hits and four runs allowed in eight innings, pitched better than Mays. Perhaps the only play that might have raised eyebrows came in the 12th, when Swede Risberg was tagged out at the plate on a close play while trying to score the lead run. I checked several papers and no one questioned Swede's baserunning, so there wasn't really anything that appeared to be amiss. The Yankees won it in the bottom of the inning on an RBI single by Peckinpaugh off Dickey Kerr.

However, Saturday's game—a 3-0 Yankee victory—is one that Black Sox historians have long considered suspicious. The White Sox managed only six hits: two by Joe Jackson, two by Eddie Collins, one each for Amos Strunk and Ray Schalk. On one of Jackson's hits, a two-out single that would have put men on first and third, he was retired after rounding too far past first base; after his other hit, he was doubled up on a lineout by the next hitter, Happy Felsch. Buck Weaver and Felsch each went 0 for 4; Felsch left three runners on base. Swede Risberg was 0 for 3, all three times via strikeout (including twice looking). And one of the Yankees' runs came after an infield hit that three Chicago writers thought should have been an error by Risberg. "Risberg and Weaver were the best players New York had," wrote I. E. Sanborn.[5] However one feels about Jackson and Weaver's participation in game-fixing during the 1920 season, this one looks pretty bad—particularly in light of the way the Sox performed in their subsequent series in Boston.

Even as it was being played, the White Sox's performance in their August 30–September 1 series against the Red Sox was looked on with suspicion. Given that three players involved in the 1919 World Series fix (Cicotte, Felsch, Weaver) would subsequently admit that games were being fixed in 1920, the timing and location of this series made it an obvious target for tomfoolery. It was being played in Boston, headquarters of Sport Sullivan, one of the masterminds of the

1919 World Series fix; with the White Sox in first place (even after losing the final two games in New York, the South Siders led the Yankees by one and a half games and the Indians by two and a half) while Boston was floundering in fifth, there would be good odds on the White Sox to win; and if the gamblers wanted to make sure the White Sox would not be in the 1920 World Series—which would totally make sense, since there would be too many suspicious eyes on the Sox to attempt another fix—the time to get them out of first place was now.

In Monday's opener, Sad Sam Jones continued his season-long dominance of the White Sox, beating the South Siders for the fifth time in 1920 with a five-hit, 4–0, shutout that increased the Sox's scoreless streak to 20 consecutive innings. Chicago had five hits in the game: three by Eddie Collins (one of them a double), one a slow-rolling infield single by Happy Felsch, and the other a double by Swede Risberg . . . after which Risberg was caught stealing third on a "strike-'em-out, throw-'em-out" double play that stopped a possible rally. Apart from Collins, wrote I. E. Sanborn, "The rest of the bunch were as soft as a two-minute egg most of the time." Sox starting pitcher Claude Williams (19–13) gave up three of the four Boston runs, all on rallies that began with two out. In the first inning he issued a two-out walk to Tim Hendryx, then an RBI double to Stuffy McInnis. In the seventh he gave up a two-out double to Everett Scott, followed by an RBI single by Cliff Brady and a run-scoring double by Jones, the opposing pitcher. "Williams was hit hard," wrote James O'Leary in the *Boston Globe.* Boston got its final run off Roy Wilkinson in the eighth when, according to Harold Johnson, "McInnis tripled over Felsch's head" with two out, scoring Mike Menosky.[6] (Felsch did make some good defensive plays in the game, according to several accounts.)

On Tuesday the Red Sox pounded Eddie Cicotte (18–9) for 11 hits—including three by the opposing pitcher, Joe Bush (13–13)—and seven runs (six earned) to win again, 7–3, in a game that was twice suspended by rain delays. Cicotte's poor work was the main story. The headline of the *Boston Globe* game story was "Cicotte Hammered Merrily by Red Sox." In the *Boston Herald*, Ed Cunningham wrote, "The heaver selected yesterday was Eddie Cicotte and he was pounded for three runs when he resumed operations in the third, and in every other inning except the fifth Red Sox clouts being administered at just the proper time and consequently runs were scored with comparative ease." The White Sox got 10 hits off Bush, but as Sanborn wrote, "although Eddie was not hit much harder than Joe, the home swats were grouped where they hurt most, while those by the White Hose were too widely scattered to be dangerous."[7]

As for the other members of the Suspected Seven, they were mostly productive at bat in this game. Risberg was 2 for 4 and drove in the first Chicago run;

One of the ringleaders of the 1919 World Series fix, Eddie
Cicotte was suspected of continuing to dump games in 1920.
Library of Congress Prints and Photographs Division

Felsch was 1 for 3 with an RBI; Jackson was 1 for 4, Weaver 0 for 4. But apart
from a brilliant catch by Felsch in the Boston first, the group, including Cicotte,
was not helpful defensively. With two out in the Red Sox third, Mike Menosky
walked. Tim Hendryx, the next hitter, doubled; according to the *Chicago Daily
News* play-by-play, "Menosky went to third on the hit and also scored when
Jackson made a bad throw to the infield. Weaver recovered and threw to the
plate, but was late, letting Hendryx go to third. McInnis beat out a hit to Risberg, Hendryx scoring." Then in Boston's three-run seventh, the second run
scored as follows, according to Sanborn: "McInnis dumped a bunt toward first
and beat it before Cicotte could slide to the ball. Menosky scored and Hendryx
went all the way to third, while Eddie was slipping around on the wet turf."
Hendryx then scored the final Boston run on a force play.[8]

Writing about this game several weeks later after the scandal had broken
open, James O'Leary of the *Boston Globe* wrote, "Strangely enough one Boston
newspaperman, absolutely not suspecting anything improper during Boston's
seventh inning at bat, said to Oscar Reichow, a Chicago writer traveling with the
White Sox: 'They are playing just like they did in the World's Series.' 'That's

so,' was the reply." O'Leary also wrote, "This Boston story in circulation yesterday was to the effect that gamblers who had something on Cicotte, had told him that they must lose the game in Boston or they would break with him and show him up."[9]

While the White Sox were losing to Boston on August 31, the Chicago Cubs were at home to face the Philadelphia Phillies. Claude Hendrix, who had been accused by a gambler of dumping his start against the Phillies on August 4, was scheduled to work the August 31 game . . . but when the Cubs received a tip that the odds for the game had suspiciously shifted in favor of Philadelphia, they substituted their ace, Grover Cleveland Alexander, and offered him a $500 bonus if the Cubs won. Unfortunately they lost the game anyway, 3–0. While the Cubs had removed Hendrix, two members of the team who had performed suspiciously on August 4 did so again on August 31. Second baseman Buck Herzog committed a key error in the Phillies' two-run second inning, booting a groundball that could have resulted in an inning-ending double play with no runs scoring. Pitcher Paul Carter, who relieved Alexander, gave up a home run for Philadelphia's final tally.

After their experiences over the past year with the rumored game-fixing to deprive the Cubs-owned Los Angeles Angels from winning the 1919 Pacific Coast League pennant, the Lee Magee case and the possible game fix on August 4, the Cubs weren't about to let this one go. They began an investigation.

On September 1, the day of the final game of the Sox-Sox series in Boston, Malcolm MacLean reported that September 11 would be "Shauno Collins day" at Comiskey Park, with fans and friends honoring the longtime veteran who had been with the White Sox since 1910. "Collins is a gentleman, a regular fellow and one of the most deserving ball players who has ever worn a major league uniform, bar none," wrote MacLean. "When Chick Gandil jumped, the club folks thought it spelled disaster. But John stepped into the gap, plugged the enormous chasm and has steadily improved." Eddie Collins was acting as treasurer of the fund to raise money for the event, and the luminaries wishing to take part included legendary Broadway performer George M. Cohan, who sent his regrets but wrote, "I'd give my left eye to be there for the celebration." John Collins was more than just a fine player, MacLean concluded. "He has been an example to the recruits, all of whom look on him almost as a guardian."[10]

The way some of the White Sox had been playing lately, it appeared that they were following the example of Chick Gandil—not John Collins. "Eddie Cicotte was guilty of weird pitching against Boston yesterday, and Gleason went on a

A reported change in betting odds in one of Cubs pitcher Claude Hendrix's scheduled starts led to the grand jury investigation that uncovered the Black Sox scandal. *Library of Congress Prints and Photographs Division*

rampage after the matinee ended in a 7 to 3 score in favor of the hostiles," wrote Harold Johnson about Friday's game.[11] Gleason shook up his lineup a little, moving Buck Weaver from third to second in the batting order and shifting hot-hitting Eddie Collins from second to third. It didn't help, as the Red Sox completed the series sweep with a 6–2 win. On the surface, this game doesn't look very suspicious. Dickey Kerr (16–7), who pitched a complete game for the White Sox, gave up 11 hits and four walks; while two of the runs he allowed were unearned, the three White Sox errors were all by "Clean Sox" (Eddie Collins, John Collins, and Kerr himself). On offense seven of the nine White Sox hits came from players under suspicion (one from Weaver, two apiece from Jackson, Felsch, and Risberg), and Risberg drove in both White Sox runs.

However, there are good reasons to put this game into the questionable camp. Risberg's two RBI came on a bad-hop single that bounced off Red Sox third baseman Ossie Vitt's knee, and Weaver's lone hit came on a blooper. While Jackson had two hits, one was an infield hit, and he also grounded into a rally-killing double play. In Felsch's most important at-bat with two on and two out in the sixth, he popped out to the catcher. Eddie Collins thought that the error charged to Kerr, leading to Boston's first run, should have gone to Weaver. And Tim Hendryx's crucial two-out, two-run single in the sixth was a blooper that fell between Risberg and Jackson. According to Eddie Collins in a 1949 remembrance in which he admittedly got several details wrong, "When the inning ended, Kerr scaled his glove across the diamond. He looks at Weaver and Risberg who are standing together and says, 'If you'd told me you wanted to lose this game, I could have done it a lot easier.' There is almost a riot on the bench. Kid Gleason breaks up two fights."[12] (I will note that some researchers assign the Kerr blowup to the September 11 game against Boston.)

Whatever the case, the South Siders had now lost five consecutive games, and Wednesday's defeat dropped the Sox (77–49) into a virtual tie for second place with the Yankees (78–50), half a game behind the reviving Indians (77–48). Clearly something was amiss, and if the later reports about season-long friction between the "Clean Sox" and their suspected teammates may have been some-what overblown, there is no doubt that the friction existed in full force after the Boston series. It would later be reported that after this series, Eddie Collins went to Charles Comiskey and told him that the team was dumping games. According to Rick Huhn's biography of Collins, Comiskey admitted during Joe Jackson's 1924 civil suit that Collins had approached him after the 1920 Boston series, but only to talk about Cicotte. Collins, Comiskey claimed, "was concerned that Eddie Cicotte 'wasn't trying' and suggested that if the owner talked to Cicotte, the team would win the pennant. According to Commy, Collins told him the pitcher was 'nervous and coming to a break,' never that Cicotte was a crook."[13] Not everyone thought Comiskey was telling the truth about this conversation.

Whatever Collins said to Comiskey, other players would begin speaking up about their concerns. The team was coming apart.

Having finished their latest road trip with a 7–8 record, the White Sox traveled home by train to begin a three-week homestand. They even had problems on the

Convinced that some of his teammates were playing dishonestly in 1920,
White Sox pitcher Dickey Kerr reportedly fought with two of them in
a September game. *National Baseball Hall of Fame and Museum*

train ride: the club had been sold berths 11 and 12 in a 10-section car, leaving them short of sleeping space. They were hungry as well. "Yesterday morning there were fifty people waiting in line for breakfast in the lone diner, at one time," wrote I. E. Sanborn after arriving in Chicago, "and some of the passengers did not get their cantaloupe and eggs until almost 12 o'clock railroad time."[14]

Still, the club was back home for a three-week homestand, and the Sox would be on the road for only six of their final 28 games. "Manager Gleason is not worried over the recent showing of his club," wrote Larry Woltz. "The boys are a bit peeved, claiming they got the short end of a number of decisions. Be that as it may, they did not play good baseball in Boston and New York."[15]

On Friday they did not play good baseball in Chicago, losing the opening game of the homestand to the fourth-place St. Louis Browns, 2–1. Both Browns runs off Red Faber (18–11) came in the fourth inning. Baby Doll Jacobson beat out an infield single to second base; then Ken Williams got a single "that was too hot for Risberg to handle," according to the *Daily News*. Sanborn of the *Tribune* wrote that both runs came home when Earl Smith "poked a safe one past Jackson into the corner of left field." Neither play appeared to be overly suspicious, and the Sox had a chance to tie or win with two on and two out in the ninth; Risberg grounded to short to end the game.[16] The loss, the sixth straight for the White Sox (77–50), dropped the club into third place, though still only a half game behind the Indians (77–49).

Whether or not Buck Weaver was involved in any game fixes, the Sox slump seemed to be taking its toll on Weaver more than any other White Sox regular. During the six-game losing streak, Weaver had batted just .115 (3 for 26); during the five games beginning with the 3–0 shutout loss in New York on August 28, he was 1 for 20 (.050), with zero runs scored, zero RBI, zero extra-base hits, and zero walks. That doesn't necessarily mean that he was participating in the fix; even if he wasn't, he had to be aware of what was going on with the faction of the team he was closest to, and how it was tearing the club apart. It couldn't be easy for Buck, a popular, hustling crowd-pleaser who was known for playing the game with unabashed joy. However, Weaver's performance in these crucial games—and the comments expressed by Dickey Kerr and Eddie Collins—have to arouse some suspicion.

As the White Sox were about to take on the Browns in a doubleheader on Saturday, September 4, there was news about the suspicious Cubs-Phillies game of August 31. Cubs officials publicly reported that prior to that game, the odds had shifted from 2 to 1 on the Cubs to 6 to 5 in favor of the Phillies. "Barrels of money suddenly appeared in Cincinnati, Detroit, Boston and other bettor centers, which was placed on the Phillies," reported the *Chicago Evening Post*.[17] The Cubs announced that they were investigating but offered no explanation as to why they had changed starting pitchers from Claude Hendrix to Grover Cleveland Alexander prior to the game.

Newspapers across the country reported the Cubs' probe the next morning, and it was a page 1 story in the *Chicago Tribune*, which began a report headlined "Start Quiz to Save Baseball from Gamblers" as follows:

> Is baseball in danger?
>
> Is America's national game threatened with destruction by rumors of crookedness and gambling scandals connected with the selling of thousands of baseball pools and alleged wagers on games that run into the thousands?
>
> Will the game be killed by this enemy, which destroyed the sport of horse racing in many places, or will the charges prove only petty annoyances not strong enough to reach the game itself?
>
> These questions were asked by America's fans yesterday following charges of attempted crookedness in an insignificant game played last Tuesday in the north side park between the Cubs and Philadelphia.

The paper reported that an inquiry into the August 31 Cubs-Phillies game had been started by Cubs President William Veeck, along with the text of Veeck's statement to the press regarding his probe. The story stated that "Detectives are on the case and have been since last Tuesday"; that the gambling fraternity had reported that four members of the Cubs (later to be revealed as Claude Hendrix, Buck Herzog, Paul Carter, and first baseman Fred Merkle, who was removed from the Chicago lineup before the August 31 game) were in on the "plot to throw the game"; and that a telegram from a gambler in Detroit named one of the Cubs players as "someone whose play on August 31 should be watched." It also included the texts of telegrams the Cubs had received from gamblers alerting them to the shift in odds and possible fix ("They're betting on Philadelphia in all large cities. They got your team. Pitch Alexander and you will beat them"). Additionally, the *Tribune* reported these little nuggets: "The fact developed that at one time within the last year twenty-six ball players in the big leagues were under suspicion of working crooked deals with gamblers. There is a rumor at the present time that three members of the White Sox are under suspicion, yet are playing the game regularly."[18]

Over on the South Side, the members of the White Sox who under suspicion (way more than three) and their teammates hosted the St. Louis Browns in a doubleheader. The crowd was estimated at over 25,000 . . . "and, judging by the rooting," wrote I. E. Sanborn, "a considerable minority of those present had wagered on the Browns to win both games."[19] The Sox snapped out of their hitting slump with 12 hits and five runs in the first game, and the Brownies helped the Chicago cause by committing four errors; five double plays turned by the St. Louis defense helped limit the damage. One of them saved the game in the bottom of the ninth. With Joe Jackson on first after singling with one out, Happy Felsch hit a scorching line drive that appeared to be headed for extra bases and a White Sox victory . . . but Browns second baseman Joe Gedeon—whose involvement in the 1919 World Series scandal would soon be revealed—grabbed the liner on the fly and fired to first to double up Jackson. The game went into extra innings and the Browns won it in the 10th on a home run by Earl Smith off Eddie Cicotte (18–10), who was simply awful: 14 hits allowed for 27 extra bases. The 6–5 loss was the sixth in a row for the White Sox.

The Sox finally broke the losing streak in the second game with a 5–2 victory behind Claude Williams (20–13). After posting his 15th win in the club's 63rd game of the season on June 29, Williams had needed 15 starts and over two months to get to 20. Happy Felsch was the hitting star with three hits and three RBI. He also nearly put a teammate out of action. After striking out with two men on base to end the first inning, Felsch "threw the bat viciously," according to Sanborn. "It struck John Collins, who was waiting to bat, and knocked him groggy. But after a few minutes to regain his wind Shauno continued in the game. Pretty soon it will be necessary to screen the dugout to protect the Sox from accidents."[20] (Not to mention something to protect the players who were under suspicion from their teammates.)

While the White Sox were splitting their doubleheader in Chicago, the Yankees were splitting a pair in Boston; the Indians, back in winning form, were defeating the Tigers in Cleveland, 12–3, to retake undisputed possession of first place. It was still an airtight race, with the Indians (78–49) a half game ahead of the Yankees (80–52) and a full game in front of the White Sox (78–51). Babe Ruth belted two more home runs in the Yankees' twin bill, giving him 46 on the year—a number with significance. Back in 1895, a player named Perry Werden had hit 45 home runs for the Minneapolis Millers of the Western League—a minor league with Ban Johnson as its president and his then friend Charles Comiskey as owner-manager of the league's St. Paul Apostles franchise. With number 46, Ruth was now the known record holder for most home runs in a single season by a player in Organized Baseball.

The game 2 win on Saturday seemed to knock the White Sox out of their doldrums. On Sunday, the last game of the series against St. Louis, Dickey Kerr defeated the Browns 4–1 for his 17th victory, in a game that took only 75 minutes.

Weaver (2 for 3, run scored), Jackson (1 for 3, double, run scored, RBI), and Felsch (1 for 2, run scored, walk), all played solidly, but Swede Risberg's performance in the White Sox seventh with the game tied 1–1 was curious, to say the least. Felsch led off with a walk. John Collins had an infield single that moved Felsch to second. Asked to sacrifice, Risberg bunted badly and Collins was forced out at second, with Felsch advancing to third. Ray Schalk then singled to break the tie, bringing home Felsch and moving Risberg to third. Dickey Kerr, the next hitter, "lined a fly to center," wrote Sanborn, "and Risberg lost a chance to score by not being on base when [Baby Doll] Jacobson caught the ball. The Swede tried to retouch the bag and then go home, but was doubled up."[21] Risberg was also 0 for 3 at bat during the game; on the other hand, Sanborn singled him out for two good defensive plays, one of which prevented a run from scoring.

On September 6, Labor Day, the Detroit Tigers came to Chicago for a morning-afternoon doubleheader—reprising the much-analyzed twin bill between the clubs on Labor Day 1917 (see chapter 1). This time there was no talk of "laying down" on the part of either team. In the morning game before a crowd of 10,000, the White Sox won 6–2 behind Red Faber, who got his 19th win. The offensive star was Joe Jackson, who had two doubles, a single, a run scored, two RBI, and a steal of home on the front end of a double steal with Happy Felsch.

With the doubleheaders piling up, Kid Gleason selected rookie Clarence "Shovel" Hodge to make his Major League debut in game 2 before 30,000 fans. Hodge, who was six-foot-four (reporters thought he was closer to seven feet tall) and also known as "Shorty," had posted a 17–18 record for Nashville in the Southern Association, and had a losing career record as a minor leaguer (53–62). He stunned the crowd by pitching hitless ball into the eighth inning. Sammy Hale broke up the no-no with a one-out single to right; Hodge, who entered the inning leading 2–0, allowed one more hit in the frame and wound up giving four runs due to errors by Risberg and John Collins. But the Sox came back. Joe Jackson, who was having a heroic day, tied the game with a two-run homer in the bottom of the inning, and the White Sox won it in the 10th on an RBI double by Eddie Collins. Hodge, who walked seven but gave up only the two eighth-inning hits, went all the way for the victory.

On Tuesday, the investigation into the August 31 Cubs-Phillies game became much more than an internal probe by baseball officials and writers (along with William Veeck and the Cubs, the Chicago chapter of the Baseball Writers of America was looking into the case). Judge Charles A. McDonald, who had taken charge of the grand jury in Chicago criminal court at the start of September, instructed the jury to turn its attention to baseball by investigating the alleged fixing of that game. The grand jury was also charged with looking into the illegal operation of "baseball pools," a form of gambling that was said to generate revenue of over $40,000 a day in Chicago alone. Customers of these pools would pay anywhere from 20 to 60 cents to purchase a ticket that contained the names of four to six Major League teams. Cash payouts would go to ticket holders whose group of teams scored the most (or sometimes fewest) runs over the course of a week or day. It was estimated that over 100,000 Chicagoans each day were buying tickets for the pools.

"Baseball is our national sport," McDonald told the jury. "Its purpose is to furnish wholesome recreation and entertainment to the public. It has become part of the everyday life of every lover of clean sports in the country." He said that the popular interest in the game was due to the fact that "organized baseball has always been conducted in such a manner as to inspire the confidence of the public in the honesty and integrity of the respective players." He added that it was the duty of the grand jury "to investigate everyone implicated in the infamous conspiracy to bring the national game of baseball into disrepute." Cook County State's Attorney Maclay Hoyne offered his full support to the grand jury's investigation.[22]

McDonald was a lifelong baseball fan who had recently been championed, unsuccessfully, by his good friend Ban Johnson to become chairman of the National Commission. From the beginning, Johnson's fingerprints were all over McDonald's grand jury probe. According to Johnson biographer Eugene Murdock, McDonald contacted Johnson and National League President John Heydler on September 4, the day that news reports about the August 31 Cubs-Phillies game surfaced, and asked them to meet with him at Chicago's Edgewater Golf Course. At the meeting he asked Johnson—rather than Heydler, the logical person to ask about potential crookedness in a game involving National League teams—"if the charge that the August 31 Cubs-Phillies game was sufficiently serious for the grand jury. 'Most decidedly it is,' Johnson said. 'Then,' McDonald announced, 'I will lay the matter before the Cook County Grand Jury.'"[23] Once the investigation began, Johnson began to use his own resources to assist the probe—and to help steer McDonald into expanding the investigation to include a probe into the 1919 World Series.

Eddie Cicotte was in the news for a couple of reasons on September 7—first, as an author. In a syndicated article about the American League pennant race under his byline, Cicotte (no doubt with considerable help from a ghostwriter) wrote, "If any one of the three leading American League clubs can 'step out' right now it will be their pennant." Naturally he favored the White Sox, writing, "The Sox are determined to win. They take every loss hard, from Gleason to the bat boy." He wrote he had been asked if he would start Game 1 of the World Series should the White Sox win the pennant; "I replied I guessed it would be Faber. I had quite a responsibility when I went in last year with everything up to me. I pitched 40 games in my sleep before that eventful day. But—" He insisted he was anxious to try again in 1920.[24]

That afternoon, Cicotte was expected to be the White Sox's starting pitcher as the South Siders finished their series with the Tigers. Although he would be working on only two days' rest after a 10-inning outing on September 4 in which he had likely thrown over 140 pitches, Cicotte had been very effective on short rest during the 1920 season (he was 6–2 with a 3.25 ERA in eight starts, all complete games, on two days' rest in 1920). The White Sox also had won all five of his previous starts against Detroit that year. Instead Kid Gleason started Dickey Kerr on only one day's rest—not, the White Sox said, because of Cicotte's recent ineffectiveness, but so that Kerr could leave to visit his sick mother in St. Louis after the game. Kerr pitched poorly, and the White Sox managed only five hits, all singles, in losing to Dutch Leonard, 5–0. Happy Felsch had three of the five Chicago hits, but helped heighten the suspicions about his commitment to honest play with a major baserunning gaffe in the seventh inning. The White Sox were trailing, 5–0, but had loaded the bases with none out. Felsch, on second base, "strolled so far off second that [Detroit catcher Oscar] Stanage picked him off the bag by about a yard, there being nothing close about the verdict," according to Sanborn. The Sox ended up failing to score in the inning. Sanborn suggested Felsch had "carved his name yesterday up close to that of Fred Merkle," whose baserunning mistake had helped cost the 1908 New York Giants a pennant.[25] It was a galling and embarrassing loss, but the White Sox rebounded on Thursday, defeating the Browns in a makeup game, 5–3. Apart from Risberg, who was 0 for 4, all of the players under suspicion contributed to the win. Claude Williams went all the way for his 21st victory; Jackson had three hits and three RBI; Felsch drove in the other two runs and had a double; Weaver had two hits, including a triple, and two runs scored. The Sox (82–52) were still in third, but only a game behind the league-leading Indians (81–49). They were still very much in the race as the Boston Red Sox came to town.

Also in the news on Thursday, September 9: the *Chicago Tribune* reported from Detroit that "Extended investigation concerning the huge sums alleged to have been bet on the 'fixed' game between the Chicago Cubs and Philadelphia last week Tuesday finally has established that not more than $3,000, the usual average wagered daily, was placed. . . . The telegrams sent from here to President Veeck of the Cubs, in the opinion of the larger operators, were from tinhorn bookies who could not round up their books and wired Chicago, expecting that the Cubs would switch from Hendrix to Alexander and save their money for them."[26]

This makes it appear that the August 31 "fixed game" story was nothing more than a hoax made by disgruntled gamblers. There is also a school of thought that the whole thing was cooked up by Ban Johnson to get a grand jury investigation started, so that he could then expand it into a probe of the 1919 World Series . . . which is indeed what happened. But there are a couple of counterarguments to the idea that the fix story was simply made up. One is that both the National League and Cubs President William Veeck, a man of unquestioned integrity, took the fix allegations very seriously; indeed, none of the four players suspected of being in on the fix—Claude Hendrix, Buck Herzog, Paul Carter, and Fred Merkle—ever played in the National League after 1920 (Merkle saw brief action in the American League with the 1925–1926 Yankees). Additionally, copies of Ban Johnson's correspondence, available at the National Baseball Hall of Fame Library and on microfilm at the San Diego Public Library, indicate that far from cooking up the fix scheme, Johnson was actively investigating the matter. He corresponded with National League President John Heydler, Detroit Tigers owner/manager Frank Navin, and allies in the press about the August 31 game, and those people took the matter very seriously as well. For example, in a letter to Johnson dated September 10—the day after the *Tribune* dismissed the idea that substantial amounts had been bet on the August 31 game—Heydler stated, "From what I have so far learned, it is evident that there was *an unusually large amount of betting on the August 31 Philadelphia-Chicago game* [emphasis mine], with very little of the money being placed east of Pittsburgh. I do not like the looks of it."[27]

There seemed to be few limits to what the gambling fraternity could cook up in an attempt to gain an edge. As the New York Yankees were heading to Cleveland for a showdown series with the Indians on September 9, reports coming out of Pittsburgh, Cincinnati, Cleveland, Chicago, and other Midwestern cities hit the news wires stating that several members of the Yankees, including Babe Ruth, had been seriously injured in an auto accident (some reports said it was a railroad crash). This one *was* a hoax concocted by gamblers. "It was thought that before the canard could be discovered, large amounts of money could be wagered on the New York club at big odds in every poolroom in the country," reported the *New York Times*. "The object was to make the Cleveland Club the favorite and then place large sums on the New York Club, which won four straight games on its last trip to Cleveland." The story was discounted before much damage could be done, though Ruth's reputation for flipping over touring cars probably did not help.[28]

For most of the afternoon of the September 9 Red Sox–White Sox game, it looked like another discouraging loss for the South Siders. Back on the mound with four days' rest, Eddie Cicotte gave another listless performance: nine hits, four walks, a hit batter and five runs, all earned, in eight innings of work. In a reprise of his 1919 World Series performance, Cicotte also looked bad in the field, committing a throwing error in the two-run Boston first. The White Sox entered the bottom of the eighth trailing Boston and Joe Bush, 5–0.

But then the club came alive, putting together a rally that featured three hits, three walks, and five runs scored to tie the game. After reliever Roy Wilkinson set down the Red Sox in the top of the ninth, the White Sox won it in the bottom half. The rally began with singles by Amos Strunk and Buck Weaver; after an intentional walk to Eddie Collins and a force-out at home on Joe Jackson's grounder, Happy Felsch belted a single to left center to bring home Weaver with the winning run. Felsch's hit, wrote I. E. Sanborn, "erased all memories of his Tuesday faux pas."[29]

Well, not *all* memories. The September 11 issue of *Collyer's Eye* featured a story titled "Ouster of 'Wrecking Crew' Demanded of White Sox." It began, "Internal dissension, which earlier in the season threatened to shatter the pennant chances of the White Sox, has again broken out." The piece featured several anonymous quotes from a disgruntled Sox player. "We went into New York and Boston looking like pennant winners, and came out of the series looking like amateurs," said the player. "We have a good ball club, but its [*sic*] a house divided. Just why players should toss aside four or five thousand dollars of world's series money, is quite beside me." The player singled out Risberg and Cicotte's recent poor performance, along with Felsch's "crowning piece of merkleism" against Detroit. "All of this may be 'the breaks of the game,'" concluded the player, "but then there is another name and like murder it 'will out'—sooner or later." Joe LeBlanc, who wrote the piece, added that Sox players were interested in the grand jury investigation, feeling that the list of crooked players "would not be confined to members of the Cubs' playing staff."[30]

White Sox players weren't the only ones who had concerns about Eddie Cicotte's recent performances. On Friday, prior to the second game of the series against Boston, the team had Cicotte begin a period of morning drills under the supervision of Kid Gleason, who had been a successful pitcher early in his Major League career before becoming a position player. "It is apparent Manager Gleason did not think Eddie in condition, for he ordered him to report to the White Sox park every morning for practice," wrote Oscar Reichow in the

Sporting News. In the parlance of the times, suggesting that a player was "not in condition" often meant that he was suspected of drunkenness. The September 10 workout seemed to go well; according to the *Chicago Tribune*, "judging from the words of one who saw it, Eddie is likely to regain his form within a week."[31] But despite the fact that every game was crucial, the White Sox would not send Cicotte to the mound again until September 18.

Cicotte's teammates looked to be in form in Friday's game, coming from behind in the late innings for the second day in a row to beat Boston, 5–3, as Red Faber (20–11, 2.82) became the second White Sox pitcher to record his 20th win. Trailing 2–0 entering the bottom of the seventh, Chicago tied it on back-to-back doubles by Happy Felsch and John Collins, followed one out later on an RBI single by Ray Schalk. The Red Sox scored in the top of the eighth to take the lead again, but the White Sox came back with three in the bottom of the inning for the winning runs. A throwing error with the bases loaded by Red Sox reliever Waite Hoyt was the key play. The win was the seventh in eight games for the White Sox (84–52), who moved into a virtual tie for first place with the Indians (82–50). In terms of win percentage, Cleveland still held the lead by three points (.621 to .618).

Saturday, September 11, was John Collins day, with the veteran outfielder/first baseman receiving a $2,500 cash prize donated by fans prior to the game—a figure that was more than half of "Shauno's" $4,500 salary. The game, a sloppy contest all around on the part of the White Sox, was anything but a tribute to the straight-shooting Sox veteran; on the contrary, it was one of the games during the 1920 season suspected of being dumped by the players who were under the influence of gamblers. One reason is that the Dickey Kerr blowup discussed in the September 1 game account is sometimes assigned to this game. Eddie Collins's 1949 recollections, which seem to be the source of the story—I could find nothing in the newspaper accounts of either game about a fight in the dugout—get several details wrong and don't specify the game he was talking about. He conceivably could have been talking about either game, though his descriptions of events fit September 1 a little better. That said, I will go through the September 11 game in some detail.

Facing their season-long nemesis, Sad Sam Jones, the White Sox put runners on first and third with one out in the bottom of the first inning, but both Jackson and Felsch popped out. Dickey Kerr, the White Sox starter, retired the first two Boston hitters in the second, but Weaver fumbled Everett Scott's grounder and then threw the ball to the grandstand, allowing Scott to take second. Swede Risberg then booted Cliff Brady's grounder, putting men on first and third. But Kerr was able to escape the jam by retiring Jones on a force play. After Boston had taken a 1–0 lead in the fourth on Scott's RBI triple, Jackson singled to open the Sox half. Felsch, the next hitter, hit into a force play but then was caught stealing.

The wheels came off for the White Sox in the Boston fifth. After the Red Sox loaded the bases on a single, a walk, and an error by Eddie Collins, Ben Paschal singled to left, bringing home two runs. Ossie Vitt, the runner on first, was trapped between second and third after Paschal's hit, but "Weaver threw over E. Collins' head," according to the *Chicago Daily News*; the *Boston Herald* concurred, saying "Weaver tossed the ball into right field." However, the *Chicago Herald and Examiner* description said, "Eddie Collins dropped a throw from Weaver," and the *Boston Globe* concurred ("Collins muffed a throw from Weaver"). The error was awarded to Collins, which would seem to settle things. With the miscue Boston now had two men on base, and both scored when Tim Hendryx tripled down the right field line. Hendryx scored on a sacrifice fly to make it 6–0, Red Sox.[32]

The White Sox fought back with five runs of their own in the bottom of the fifth; four of them scored on a grand-slam homer by Jackson, which would seem to remove any doubts about his commitment to win this game. In the sixth, however, Boston scored twice more, with a triple over Felsch's head the key blow. The White Sox closed to within one again with two in the bottom of the seventh. Weaver was instrumental, driving in a run with a triple and then scoring on a groundout by Jackson. An error by Risberg helped produce Boston's final run in the eighth, making it 9–7.

So was this a crooked game? It's a tough call. Weaver and Jackson may have had shaky moments in the field, but on offense they drove in six of the seven Chicago runs. Risberg, who was 0 for 4 with two errors, was more suspect. Felsch may have let up on Hooper's triple and didn't do much at bat (1 for 4, plus caught stealing). On the other hand, the chief goat of the game seemed to be the usually solid Eddie Collins, who committed three errors. Overall, I personally I don't see enough evidence that Kerr's crooked teammates were working to lose the game for him to put this one in the suspicious category.

"Professional gamblers in various parts of the country are betting thousands of dollars on the daily results of the major league baseball games," wrote syndicated columnist Joe Vila on September 11. "A syndicate of New York and Chicago's 'sure thing' operators, accused last October of 'fixing' the first two World's Series games between the Chicago White Sox and Cincinnati Reds, are still doing business." After touching on the attempted ruse by gamblers that Babe Ruth had been injured in a train crash; the news that Hal Chase had been barred from Pacific Coast League ballparks; an update on an earlier report that Ban Johnson was still investigating the 1919 World Series, with news that "a prominent detective agency" was claiming that New York gamblers had "framed up" the first two games of the Series; John Heydler's probe of a 1919 bribe attempt of a Cubs pitcher; and the continued presence of public betting in Major League parks, Vila wrote,

> Organized baseball must resort to drastic action. The magnates cannot overlook the fact that the national game is in grave danger. Players who are under suspicion should be suspended and tried. There should be an appeal to the courts for the suppression of pool selling, which is robbing thousands of persons each day. By turning on the light, instead of hiding the truth, the major leagues will gratify the great army of baseball fans, eager for an honest sport.
>
> Expose the "sure thing" gamblers, so that it will be hard for them to find willing victims! There should be a Nation-wide crusade against the parasites who now threaten the life of America's finest pastime![33]

Things were beginning to come to a head.

12

THE GRAND JURY

As play began on Sunday, September 12, the American League pennant race was closer than ever. Only four percentage points and one-half game separated the top three teams . . . and the Yankees, in second place based on win percentage, ranked first in terms of games ahead/games back.

American League Standings, Morning of September 12, 1920

	Won	Lost	Pct.	Games Back
Cleveland	82	51	.617	0.5
New York	85	53	.616	—
Chicago	84	53	.613	0.5

The three teams were matched against the clubs with the three worst records in the league. The Indians were at home against the last-place Athletics, the Yankees in Detroit against the seventh-place Tigers, and the White Sox were hosting the sixth-place Washington Senators (59–71).

Of the three contenders, only the White Sox lost on Sunday, and I consider Chicago's 5–0 loss to the Senators more suspicious than the club's 9–7 loss to Boston the previous day, The Senators would have actually won the game 7–0, except for a freakish play in the top of the fourth. With Frank Ellerbe on first, Senators catcher Patsy Gharrity homered into the left field seats . . . but Ellerbe, who thought the ball had been caught by Joe Jackson to end the inning, wandered back to his shortstop position after touching third base and was passed on the base paths by Gharrity; by rule, Gharrity was out, ending the inning with no runs scored.

CHAPTER 12

The baserunning gaffe did little to limit the damage against Claude Williams, who was simply awful for the White Sox. In the first inning Lefty was lucky to escape without a run scoring after loading the bases on walks. In the fourth, Ellerbe's gaffe kept the game scoreless, but in the fifth Washington broke through after Williams allowed a leadoff single to the opposing pitcher, Harry Courtney; two more hits produced a run. In the sixth, "Williams gave a pathetic exhibition of pitching," according to the *Washington Post*. He hit the leadoff hitter to open the frame, gave up a single and a walk to load the bases, and then surrendered another hit to his pitching opponent: "Courtney clinched the matinee by clubbing a double over Felsch's dome."[1] Another run scored on an infield out. Meanwhile the Sox offense was shut down completely by Courtney, who entered the game with a 5–10 record and a 5.51 ERA. The Washington lefty allowed only five hits, two of them—singles by Jackson and Felsch—coming with two outs in the ninth. The other Chicago hits were by Eddie Collins, John Collins, and Swede Risberg, who struck out in his other two at bats. Consider me suspicious about this one.

On Monday, the White Sox rebounded big-time, pounding out 17 hits in a 15–6 rout of the Senators behind Red Faber (21–11). Pretty much everyone contributed on offense, but the biggest star was Happy Felsch, who had three hits, including a double and a home run, along with five runs batted in to give him 102 on the season. The home run, his 14th, was the final four-bagger of Felsch's Major League career . . . though of course no one knew that at the time.

Tuesday's press reports featured a response from White Sox treasurer Louis Comiskey, Charles Comiskey's son, to Joe Vila's claim that "according to a prominent detective agency, Chicago and New York gamblers had 'framed up' the first two games [of the 1919 World Series] by 'stiffening' certain members of the White Sox" (see chapter 11). Comiskey had sent Vila a telegram saying that it was his duty to appear before Judge McDonald's grand jury and give his evidence so that "the guilty may be punished and the innocent absolved." Comiskey's telegram pointed out that the White Sox owner had spent thousands of dollars trying to obtain the kind of evidence Vila was claiming he possessed. Vila responded three days later: "Telegram received. Regret business engagements here prevent my complying with request for assistance indicated in your wire."[2]

In the meantime, Vila—and others—continued to write about the burgeoning problem of gambling in baseball. Tuesday's *Chicago Tribune* included a report on open gambling at Major League Parks. "While detectives discovered and arrested five men for gambling on the ball game in the bleachers yesterday during the Sox-Washington game," a *Tribune* investigator reported, "big gamblers were operating in the boxes behind the home players' bench." A wager of $380

190

to $300—"probably much more than in the bleacher affair"—was made openly, but as no cash was exchanged, the police could do nothing.[3]

Tuesday's newspapers also included an article by famed sportswriter Grantland Rice reviewing his annual "All-American" baseball team. Of the eight position players selected by Rice, four were White Sox: Ray Schalk, Eddie Collins, Buck Weaver, and Joe Jackson. But that afternoon the four Sox stalwarts and their teammates could manage only seven hits against Senators rookie right-hander Jose Acosta, and the South Siders were shut out for the second time in three days, 7–0. "The White Sox kicked themselves out of the congested pennant race scramble," wrote I. E. Sanborn about the game. "Once when an error made an opening for the home team to start something the chance was thrown away by dumb baserunning." The baserunning gaffe came from Buck Weaver, who had singled with one out in the eighth. Buck got picked off first by Acosta, but the Cuban hurler took him off the hook by throwing wildly . . . only Weaver, after advancing to second, attempted to scamper all the way to third and got tagged out. The game also featured suspicious-looking fielding miscues from Jackson, Weaver, and (possibly) Felsch. Washington's three-run second inning off Clarence Hodge was helped by errors from Weaver, who dropped a throw, and Jackson, who fumbled the pickup on a Senators base hit. (Jackson later made a good play in the field, backing up to the fence in the sixth to rob Patsy Gharrity of a potential home run, but the Sox were trailing 6–0 at that point.) Washington scored again in the third on a triple that went between Jackson and Felsch—a scenario that had happened several times in the 1919 World Series. Hap later threw out a runner at the plate, but the score was 7–0 by then.[4]

The White Sox, who had defeated the Senators 16 times in 19 meetings entering this series, were shut out twice in three games by rookie pitchers, while playing sloppily in those games . . . and that raised suspicions even among members of the Washington team. "Some Senators players privately came to the same conclusion that investigators would soon reach: their opponents were not playing on the level," wrote baseball historian Bill Felber. "They did not discuss it openly, but they did discuss it, including the Indians, their next stop on the road after Chicago. '[Senators first baseman] Joe Judge tipped me off that Washington smelled something,' [Cleveland outfielder] Cuckoo Jamieson acknowledged several decades later about the White Sox's play in those games. 'I didn't know how to pick it up,' he said."[5]

Still in third place, the White Sox (85–55) were now two and a half games out of first; the Yankees (88–53) had grabbed the lead, with the Indians (84–52) a game and a half back. As the Sox prepared to face the Yankees in a three-game set, one Cleveland newspaper seemed to think the Sox were finished. "The White Sox are cracking," asserted the *Cleveland Press*. "The pitching staff has suddenly become shot. The infield, especially Risberg, has been piling up so many errors lately that rumors of a shake-up in the line-up are constant." The article noted that Kid Gleason was asked who would start the opening game against New York. "'It looks like Kerr,' he said. The Kid's remark about not starting Cicotte is significant. The Series veteran has been far off form."[6]

Yet just at the point where the White Sox were expected to fade from the pennant race, they began to play their best ball of the year, winning seven straight games and 10 of their next 11. While the motives behind the performance of this fractured team are never easy to analyze, Chicago's late-season spurt coincided with the increased focus on gambling and game-fixing that was starting to gain momentum, beginning with the probe into the August 31 Cubs-Phillies game, the summoning of the grand jury, and the provocative Joe Vila column. If gamblers like Sport Sullivan had the suspected players under their thumbs, things were starting to get too hot to risk calling the players' performance into question even more—particularly after the large number of suspicious games played by the Sox between August 28 and September 14.

The suspected players also had to be aware of the increased restlessness on the part of their teammates. In the September 18 issue of *Collyer's Eye*, "staff investigator" Frank O. Klein wrote, "From the south side comes the story that certain members of the White Sox team smarting under what they claim [were] 'listless efforts' of teammates had decided to go before President Ban Johnson determined to tell ALL THEY KNOW, and with the additional request that they be allowed to go before Judge McDonald and the grand jury."[7]

The Sox turnaround began on Thursday, September 16, before a crowd of 25,000-plus that was likely hoping to see both a Chicago victory and Babe Ruth's 50th home run of the season. "[The Sox] were fighting mad when they took the field, Kid Gleason having told them in the clubhouse that certain folks were accusing them of being quitters," wrote Larry Woltz.[8] The South Siders kayoed former teammate Jack Quinn—who entered the game with a 3–1 record and a 1.00 ERA against Chicago thus far in 1920—with a four-run second inning on the way to an 8–3 victory. Dickey Kerr pitched fearlessly to Ruth, who had two singles in five at bats. According to I. E. Sanborn, Kerr had only two pitches that were called balls in the Babe's five trips to the plate.

On Friday, before 35,000 spectators, the White Sox won again, 6–4, as Red Faber won his 22nd game. The Sox jumped on Yankee starter Hank Thormahlen with three consecutive triples in the first inning, by Eddie Collins, Joe

Jackson, and Happy Felsch. Thormahlen lasted only two innings; once again Ruth—0 for 3, plus an intentional walk—was held without a homer.

In Saturday's series finale, Kid Gleason held his breath and sent Eddie Cicotte—who, in the words of I. E. Sanborn, "had been sentenced to a second edition of spring training to get himself in shape"—to the mound for the first time in nine days. Eddie's teammates would brook no nonsense. When a reporter asked one of the White Sox players who would pitch the third game of the series, he replied, "Cicotte, and if he doesn't win, we will mob him on the field."[9] The White Sox made it easy for him; they kayoed the Yankee starter early for the third straight day (Bob Shawkey lasted an inning and a third) with three runs in the first inning and five more in the second. Cicotte eased up after another five-run frame made it 13-2; he gave up seven runs in the last four innings but was never in danger as the Sox rolled, 15-9, with a 21-hit attack. "It was estimated that over 42,000 fans witnessed the game," wrote Larry Woltz. "It was Chicago's record ball crowd." The throng was disappointed to see Babe Ruth held without home run number 50 once more.[10]

As the White Sox were sweeping the Yankees, there was news from the West about the Pacific Coast League scandal. Salt Lake City Bees outfielder Bill Rumler, who had been suspended for five years by League President William McCarthy, announced that he intended to sue the league for damages in the amount of $50,000. "I have waited for the league to do something in my case, but nothing has been done," Rumler said in a statement. He continued,

> Baseball is my profession and my livelihood. I cannot sit idly by while my bread and butter are being taken away from me by such high-handed methods as have been used. I am not guilty of betting on ball games. I merely participated in what everybody in baseball and perhaps many other sports know as "stake saving." It is done every year in the big leagues and every other league, and I have yet to hear of any player laying down because of this kind of agreement. It can't be called betting by any stretch of the imagination, and every legal man I have talked with emphatically declares that it cannot be regarded as betting.[11]

"If Rumler can get $50,000 damages from the Coast league, the men who have their money invested in baseball out this way had just well close up their parks," said McCarthy in response. "If Rumler can get damages, every other player who has been barred will bring suit. So far as I am concerned, the Rumler case is closed."[12]

However, the case was anything but closed—in good part because people in Salt Lake City thought that McCarthy was punishing their franchise unfairly, while ignoring transgressions in other league cities. "Weeks have rolled by since McCarthy took up the cudgels for purity in baseball, yet the only effect of his 'vigorous campaign' has been to demolish a superior ball club," said the *Salt Lake Tribune*. "Vernon, the real offender, with from eighteen to twenty players accused of bribery, goes merrily on its way, and so far as McCarthy appears to be concerned, it can so proceed to the end. Trustworthy reports from every town in the league are that gambling, instead of being stopped by McCarthy's much heralded 'war,' is more widespread than ever. . . . Whatever McCarthy may do or leave undone, the people of Salt Lake are well convinced that, in this matter, McCarthy is either not 'on the square' or he is not competent for the place he assumes to fill."[13]

The fight would continue.

In Black Sox lore, September 19, 1920, will always be known as the day that the "Loomis letter" was published in the *Chicago Tribune*. Fred M. Loomis of 4840 South Michigan Avenue was described in the introduction to the letter as "one of Chicago's most enthusiastic baseball followers and a personal friend of several members of the Chicago White Sox club." The letter, appearing on the first page of the Sunday sports section under the heading "Fan Seeks Answer to Rumors," got right to the point:

> Widespread circulation has been given to reports from various sources that the world series of last fall between the Chicago White Sox and the Cincinnati Reds was deliberately and intentionally lost through an alleged conspiracy between certain unnamed members of the Chicago White Sox and certain gamblers.
>
> I have been startled by these rumors and was inclined in the first place to give no credence to these reports, but where there is so much smoke there must be some fire.
>
> It is generally accepted among the fans of the country that Hal Chase and Lee Magee are refused recognition as ball players because of the alleged betting which they did on games.
>
> Up to this time baseball has been accepted by the public as the one clean sport above reproach in every particular and engaged in by men, both owners and players, whose honesty and integrity have been beyond suspicion and reproach.
>
> At this time, therefore, it occurs to me, and it likewise appears to others in the same light, that the game must be cleaned up and it must be cleaned up at once. It is immaterial how this is done, whether by the newspaper men or by the owners of the ball clubs, or by a committee of citizens, but no matter who does it, it must be done if baseball is going to survive.

Continuing, Loomis suggested, "An investigation might disclose there is absolutely nothing to these reports," which he felt was all the more reason why action should be taken in justice to the honest players. The question should be settled; dishonest players should be eliminated, and the game should be surrounded with a "protective policy" so that gamblers could not influence the decisions of individual games. He then mentioned the suspicious performance by members of the White Sox in recent games, writing,

> Only recently a friend of mine of unquestionable veracity told of talking to a player of a visiting team in which that player stated that it was shameful the way certain White Sox members were playing ball in that particular series. The player who made that statement stands among the highest in his profession, both as a player and a man.

Loomis stated that he believed that the "great body of fans" felt as he did, that "it makes no difference who is hit in this investigation, from the president of either major league down to the clubhouse boy in the smallest league in the country. The game must be protected." Finally, he made a specific recommendation:

> There is a perfectly good grand jury located in this county. The citizens and taxpayers of Illinois are maintaining such an institution for the purpose of investigating any alleged infraction of the law.
> Those who have in their possession the evidence of gambling last fall in the world series should come forward with it and present it in a manner that may give assurance to the whole country that justice will be done in this case where the confidence of the people seems to have been flagrantly violated.[14]

Loomis's eloquent letter received broad attention, and was widely viewed as a spur for Judge McDonald's grand jury to begin looking into the 1919 World Series. And that was the point. Many years later, *Chicago Tribune* sportswriter James Crusinberry admitted that he, not Loomis, had written the letter; he considered the grand jury's initial focus on the August 31 Cubs-Phillies game "as a chance to get them to investigate the rumors about the 1919 World Series."[15] Since McDonald's initial statement to the grand jury on September 7, the grand jury had done little baseball-related investigation, and the work was further hampered when State's Attorney Maclay Hoyne, who had vowed to assist McDonald, was defeated in the Democratic primary on September 15, prompting him to turn the case over to his subordinates.

It was probably no coincidence that on September 20, the day after the publication of the Loomis letter, the grand jury sprang into action. It requested the testimony of a number of prominent baseball people—including league presidents Ban Johnson and John Heydler, White Sox owner Charles Comiskey and manager Kid Gleason, Cubs President William Veeck, plus a number of noted sportswriters. Assistant State's Attorney Hartley Replogle, who was taking charge of the investigation, announced that he intended also to call several players and ex-players, including Hal Chase, Lee Magee, and Heinie Zimmerman, as well as New York Giants pitcher Rube Benton, who was said to have been offered $750 to lose a game. "The inquiry will first center on the Chicago-Philadelphia game of Aug. 31, which was the cause of talk of a baseball gambling scandal, and then on the world series between the White Sox and Cincinnati Reds in 1919," reported the *Tribune*.[16]

Ban Johnson was swinging into action as well, using his own sources to support McDonald's inquiry. Unlike the winter of 1919–1920, when he was struggling to hold on to his power as American League president, Johnson could more easily work to dig up information that his archenemy Charles Comiskey had more knowledge of his players' complicity in the World Series scandal than he had revealed. The grand jury investigation could also burnish the reputation of his friend Judge McDonald, whom Johnson still hoped could become chairman of the National Commission.

For the next few weeks, the activities of the Chicago grand jury would be a major national news story.

On September 19, another notable baseball event took place in Chicago, though it was little noticed at the time: in their final home game of the 1920 Negro National League season, Rube Foster's Chicago American Giants defeated the Indianapolis ABCs, 8–2, at Schorling's Park on the South Side, about three blocks south of Comiskey Park. It was the final home game of the season for the American Giants (43–17–2), who easily won the championship in the league's inaugural season. Future Hall of Famer Cristobal Torriente was the American Giants' leading hitter with a .411 average. It was a successful first season for both the league and the American Giants, who drew an estimated 200,000 fans to their home games in 1920. The Negro National League continued to function until 1931, one year after Foster's death. The league's motto was, "We are the ship. All else is the sea."[17]

In his SABR biography of Rube Foster, Tim Odzer wrote, "Foster was a well-respected leader who turned black baseball into a successful enterprise; his devotion to the league was incredible, and he often helped teams in poor finances out by paying their payroll out of his own pocket. Teams such as the

The founder of the Negro National League, which began play
in 1920, Rube Foster spent his life in Black baseball as a player,
manager, executive. He was elected to the National Baseball Hall of
Fame in 1981. *National Baseball Hall of Fame and Museum*

Chicago American Giants and Kansas City Monarchs often were more profitable than white baseball teams, which helped spawn black baseball leagues in
the south and the east. Foster's tenure as president laid the groundwork for the
future success of the Negro Leagues."[18]

A short walk away from Schorling's Park, the White Sox were facing the
last-place Philadelphia Athletics at Comiskey Park on September 19. In the
opener of a three-game series, Claude Williams did not look like a pitcher who
was committed to victory; he gave up three runs in the third inning due to a

combination of Philadelphia hitting and errors by John Collins and Williams himself. According to the *Philadelphia Inquirer*, "The inning proved the one time classy southpaw was not worth while so Manager Gleason yanked him and sent Roy Wilkinson to the slab."[19] Wilkinson gave up a run in the fourth to put the White Sox down, 4–0, but he and Dickey Kerr (three scoreless innings) shut the A's down the rest of the way, and the Sox fought back with a run in the fourth and four more in the sixth for a 5–4 victory. Joe Jackson had two runs scored and three hits, including a double and a triple; Happy Felsch was 1 for 2 with a walk, a run scored, and two RBI; Swede Risberg was 1 for 4 and scored the winning run on the front end of a double steal.

The next two days were easier for the White Sox. On Monday Red Faber took a 13–0 lead into the ninth inning before easing up and allowing six runs (three unearned) as he earned his 23rd victory. Swede Risberg was the Sox batting hero with a 4 for 4 performance. In the series finale on Tuesday, Eddie Cicotte looked like his old self in earning his 20th victory, 9–2, for the White Sox's sixth straight win. For the second day in a row, Risberg went 4 for 4 to lead the offense; Buck Weaver added three hits, including a triple. Cicotte did have one tense moment, but one of the suspected players bailed him out. With the Sox leading 4–2 with two out and two Athletics on base in the bottom of the third, "[Joe] Dugan caught one on the end of his bat and pasted it on a line over center field," according to I. E. Sanborn's account. "It looked good for two or three more Athletic tallies, but Felsch tore back, took a look at the flying sphere as it shot over his head, and arrested it with a one handed pinch while going at top speed in the outfield."[20] Cicotte held the A's scoreless the rest of the way.

Despite the hot streak, the White Sox (91–55) had gained only one game on the Indians (91–52) in the standings; they still trailed Cleveland by a game and a half—and by three games in the important loss column. After a day off on Wednesday, the clubs would meet in a crucial three-game series in Cleveland. Kid Gleason had the club travel to Cleveland by train so that they arrived early on Wednesday; that gave them a day of rest in the city before the series started. "The Sox are confident. They came in this morning with a fighting spirit," wrote Larry Woltz. "The Gleason team has been known to win nine and ten games in a row. If they can do it again the new American League bunting will float over Comiskey Park. If they slump here they are through."[21]

It was probably just as well that the White Sox had gotten out of Chicago, because the grand jury hearings were all about gambling, game-fixing . . . and them.

The evidence-gathering phase of the hearings got underway on Wednesday, September 22, with few fireworks. Charles Comiskey was the first witness. Comiskey testified that he had had suspicions about the honesty of his team's play in the 1919 World Series, that he had withheld the Series checks of eight players for a time, that he had offered a $10,000 reward for information about the alleged bribing of his players, and that he had hired detectives to investigate. However, he said he had found nothing to substantiate the rumors of crooked play. When he concluded his testimony, the grand jury panel applauded him. The next witness, Sam Hall, a sportswriter for the *Chicago Herald and Examiner* who had led a probe into the Series conducted by the Baseball Writers Association of America, testified, "In my opinion the better team lost last year, but of course that does not prove the series was crooked. I have no positive knowledge of it."[22]

Testifying about the August 31 Cubs-Phillies game, Cubs team President William Veeck said that no tangible evidence had yet been found on which the prosecution of any players could be based. American League President Ban Johnson assured the grand jury that the powers of baseball would not attempt to whitewash any player, should incriminating evidence turn up, that he knew of attempts made to throw games in 1919, and hoped his investigation would clean everything up.

Easily the most substantial first-day witness was *Chicago Tribune* reporter James Crusinberry, the man who had anonymously penned the Loomis letter. "According to Crusinberry," wrote Bill Lamb, "Hal Chase had conceived the plot, partnering with Chick Gandil on the selection of the players to be corrupted. New York underworld financier Arnold Rothstein bankrolled the scheme." Crusinberry also testified about his July encounter with Kid Gleason and Abe Attell, in which Attell had admitted his involvement in the fix (see chapter 9). In addition, Crusinberry suggested that Sox fan and confidant Sam Pass, who had lost money betting on the White Sox, might be a useful grand jury witness.[23] Crusinberry's testimony would have been explosive, had it been made public. Fortunately for the White Sox, the grand jury hearings were conducted in private; while later testimony would often be leaked to the press, his was not (and neither was the testimony of any of the others who appeared on September 22).

But much more was coming, beginning with a banner headline on page 1 of the September 23 *Chicago Tribune*: BARE FIXED WORLD SERIES. The article, written by Crusinberry, quoted Assistant State's Attorney Harley Replogle as saying, "The last world's series between the Chicago White Sox and the Cincinnati Reds was not on the square. From five to seven players on the White Sox are involved"; Replogle would later deny making that statement, but a set of charges and countercharges involving National League players offered the first tangible evidence that the 1919 World Series had been fixed. New York

Giants pitcher Rube Benton, who was scheduled to appear before the grand jury that day, claimed that he had been offered an $800 bribe to throw a game in 1919 by his then Giants teammates Hal Chase and Buck Herzog; Herzog was one of the players suspected of involvement in attempting to fix the August 31, 1920, Cubs-Phillies game. Herzog not only flatly denied Benton's story in an interview with Crusinberry on the evening of September 22; he claimed that Benton had told Boston Braves players Art Wilson and Tony Boeckel that he had won $3,800 betting on the Reds in the 1919 World Series after receiving a tip from Hal Chase that the first two games were fixed for Cincinnati to win. Herzog provided Crusinberry with signed affidavits from Wilson and Boeckel supporting his story. The Wilson and Boeckel affidavits had actually been presented to National League President John Heydler in June, when Herzog had first been questioned about the alleged attempt to bribe Benton. Heydler had exonerated Herzog and told everyone to keep quiet. "Thus Herzog, Boeckel, Wilson and Heydler himself had evidence, by June 1920 at least, that the Series was tainted," wrote Harold Seymour and Dorothy Seymour Mills.[24] But Heydler had yet to do anything with the information.

Benton appeared before the grand jury on the afternoon of September 23. He repeated the story of the bribe offer from Chase and Herzog, which he claimed to have turned down (according to Benton, the later-blacklisted Heinie Zimmerman had called him "a poor fish" for turning down the bribe and instead winning the game). More substantially, Benton testified that Hal Chase had won $40,000 betting on the 1919 World Series based on a tip he had received from Bill Burns. He said that Giants teammate Jean Debuc had also received a tip from Burns to bet on Cincinnati, and that a gambling syndicate from Pittsburgh was said to be behind the fix.[25]

Two of the most provocative statements on September 23 did not come from the grand jury. State's Attorney Maclay Hoyne, who was in New York and not directly involved in the grand jury hearing after losing the Democratic primary, stated, "Judging from a preliminary investigation, I have no doubt the 1919 world's series was crooked and that at least one Chicago player was crooked." American League President Ban Johnson, meanwhile, addressed the 1920 American League pennant race, saying he had "heard statements that the White Sox would not dare win the 1920 pennant because the managers of a gambling syndicate, alleged to have certain players in their power, had forbidden it."[26]

Johnson's claim that "the White Sox would not dare win" echo what Indians star Joe Wood said that his former teammate Eddie Cicotte had told him: "I knew Cicotte very well, and he told me in the Winton Hotel that they didn't dare win in '20. 'We don't dare win.' He told me that before the season was over"

Cleveland Indians outfielder Joe Wood later reported that former teammate
Eddie Cicotte had told him that the White Sox "dare not win" the pennant
in 1920. *Library of Congress Prints and Photographs Division*

(see chapter 6).[27] It is entirely conceivable that Wood, talking to interviewer
Lawrence Ritter decades after the 1920 season, used Johnson's much-quoted
phrasing in quoting Cicotte. However, he seemed firm about the sentiment:

they won't let us win. Yet the White Sox, in Cleveland for a crucial three-game series, *had* been winning in recent days.

In the opener of the series before 26,000 fans at League Park on September 23, the Sox won again, in impressive fashion, 10–3. It was Chicago's seventh straight victory, and the win pulled the White Sox within a half-game of Cleveland. After falling behind in the Indians' first on Swede Risberg's 43rd error of the season, the Sox tied it in the fourth when Risberg stole home on the front end of a double steal. The Sox then scored three times in the sixth, with Risberg driving in a run; once more in the seventh, on an RBI double by Happy Felsch; and five times in the eighth, with Buck Weaver, Joe Jackson, and Felsch driving in runs. Dickey Kerr went all the way for his 19th victory.

Referring to Ban Johnson's "would not dare win" remark, the *Tribune* commented, "Certain Sox players who have heard the report are said to have been spurred on to make every effort to win as a vindication, regardless of athletic honors or monetary reward." Echoing that sentiment before Friday's game, Ray Schalk said, "I hope these stories continue to have the same effect on the players they had on yesterday's game. If they do we shall win the pennant." Kid Gleason defended his team from Johnson's charges: "There's nothing to it. It is all hearsay. That is what the entire mess has been. If Johnson has got anything concrete it is up to him to come up and give it cold turkey. They have not got a thing. If they had it would have been aired long before this." Despite the suspicions he was making in private, Eddie Collins agreed. "That sounds like a bad statement for President Johnson to make if he hasn't anything to back it," said Collins. "I am sure I know nothing about it. I am sorry to see Herzog's name mixed in this scandal, for I have always liked him and think him a great ball player."[28] Was Collins trying to protect Comiskey with this statement?

With a chance to grab the league lead with a victory on Friday, Gleason chose his ace, Red Faber, even though it was Claude Williams's spot in the rotation. Cleveland manager Tris Speaker selected late-season call-up Walter (Duster) Mails, who had been brilliant (5–0, 2.13) since joining the club on September 1. Mails, who had never won a major league game prior to 1920, was nothing if not confident. "This afternoon's game is won right now," he told a reporter before the game. "I'll be the most surprised man in Cleveland if I don't shut them out."[29]

It was a tense game throughout. The Indians scored in each of the first two innings. The run in the first came on a bloop single that dropped between Eddie Collins and Happy Felsch; the run in the second came after Ray Schalk, with a chance to catch Cleveland rookie Joe Sewell on a stolen base attempt, threw badly. Steve O'Neill, the next hitter, singled in Sewell, another late-season call-up and the man who had succeeded Ray Chapman as the Cleveland short-stop. Meanwhile Mails kept pitching out of trouble. In the first he struck out Felsch with two men on to end the inning. In the fourth the Sox had two men on with one out, but John Collins lined out to Sewell, who fired to second to double up Joe Jackson, who had broken for third.

Chicago's best chance came in the fifth. Mails struck out Swede Risberg to start the inning, then lost his control and walked three straight hitters. Finally Speaker ran in from center field and told Mails, "You are not getting your side arm ball over. Stick it in your pocket until the inning is over and use your overhand ball." Mails did as directed and struck out Buck Weaver; with that, wrote Cleveland writer Henry P. Edwards, "the immense crowd let out a roar that informed Clevelanders two miles away that something was doing at League Park." After hitting two hard liners that barely landed foul, Eddie Collins struck out as well. "Another tremendous roar arose from the throng," wrote Edwards about the Collins strikeout. "Women jumped up from their seats and screamed their delight. Men tossed their hats in the air, slapped each other on the back and acted like maniacs until the perspiration screamed down their faces." Mails allowed only one baserunner the rest of the way—a walk to Felsch—and closed out a 2–0 win that put Cleveland up by one and a half games again, ensuring that the White Sox would leave Cleveland in second place.[30]

Was this game on the level? Kid Gleason's switch of starting pitchers from Williams to Faber might suggest that he had been tipped off that Williams was planning to dump this game. On the other hand, this was the most crucial game of the season for the White Sox, and Faber was by far their most reliable starter . . . and Gleason sent Williams to the mound in another crucial game the very next day. As for the performance of the White Sox hitters against Mails in this game, an anonymous American League umpire later commented, "Mails pitched for Cleveland, and he didn't have a thing. But the Sox players didn't hit, and the Indians won the game."[31] This quote looks pretty damning . . . but it didn't come until after the eight Sox players had been indicted, and it doesn't stand up to scrutiny. There were two umpires for this game, Brick Owens behind the plate and Ollie Chill on the bases; Owens, the man most qualified to evaluate Mails's stuff, said afterward, "I never saw a ball take a sharper break than Mails' fast one today."[32] In addition, two of the three White Sox hits came from players who would be indicted the next week (Jackson and Felsch); the so-called Clean Sox were a combined 1 for 14 against Mails. And with all the stories about crooked play from the White Sox in the 1919 World Series that were coming from the grand jury while the Sox-Indians game was being played, it would be a mighty bold move to try to pull off another fix. I can't see it.

While the White Sox were losing to the Indians, testimony continued in the grand jury hearings. Rube Benton was on the stand again, insisting that the claim that he'd made $3,800 betting on the 1919 World Series was "a joke. [Giants teammate] Larry Doyle and I made a piker bet every day during the series. The limit was $20." Benton also tried to shift the attention toward the gamblers. "There has been a lot said about the players so far," said Benton, "but mighty little about the gamblers. I was told last fall that a deal to throw the world's series to Cincinnati had been engineered by a Pittsburgh gambling syndicate at a cost of $100,000. Five White Sox players were mentioned as in the confidence of the syndicate." Benton said that Cincinnati betting commissioner Philip Hahn told him that the five players were Cicotte, Felsch, Gandil, Williams, and a fifth player whose name he could not remember. But other witnesses refuted Benton, including Buck Herzog, John Heydler, and Hahn, who said he had no knowledge of a Series fix and had never said anything to Benton about it.[33]

At the end of Thursday's session, grand jury foreman Henry Brigham issued a statement: "The investigation is being conducted along orderly lines, and a great mass of real evidence is coming out. We have evidence to convince us that crooked work has been done, but we believe it has been confined to comparatively few players and is the result of the pollution of these players by an unscrupulous gang of professional gamblers, the same gang that have that have about killed the boxing game. . . . Enlightening testimony is coming from many men whose motives are sincere and purely sportsmanlike, with the intent of placing the game, and keeping it, upon the high level that it has occupied in the past."[34]

"I have at all times endeavored to be honest with the public, fair with my ball players, and, in turn, I believe my reward has been the confidence the people have shown in my integrity and honesty," wrote Charles A. Comiskey in an essay appearing in evening newspapers on September 24 and morning papers the next day. Comiskey wrote at some length about how he had sent for National League President John Heydler on the morning of the second game of the 1919 World Series after hearing rumors of crooked play; that he had approached Heydler and not Ban Johnson, "because I had no confidence in Johnson"; that he told Kid Gleason "to take out any ball player who did not appear to be doing his best"; and that when reports of a fix had continued after the World Series, he had sent Gleason and another man to see a gambler in East St. Louis who had been "crossed" by other gamblers during the Series, seeking information, to no avail. He wrote how he had spent hundreds of dollars bringing people to Chicago, that he had paid detectives over $4,000 looking for clues, that for several weeks he had withheld the checks of players mentioned in connection with the scandal; "it was only after I could get no evidence of crookedness that I cheerfully sent the checks in question to the players on my club." He continued,

> At no time since the playing of the world series did I have any co-operation from Johnson, or any member of the national commission, in ferreting out this charge of crookedness.
>
> Johnson now says that an official investigation was made. If so, it was made unbeknown to me, my manager or my ball players.
>
> The result of such an alleged investigation has never been communicated to me nor to the league.
>
> In line with the policy I have always pursued, I have offered to the state's attorney of Cook County and the judge of the Criminal Court who has charge of the present grand jury, every assistance by way of money or otherwise to turn up any evidence of crookedness that exists affecting the honesty or integrity of the great American pastime—baseball.
>
> I'll go further. If any of my players are not honest I'll fire them, no matter who they are, and if I can't get honest players to fill their places, I'LL CLOSE THE GATES OF THE PARK that I have spent a lifetime to build and in which in the declining years of my life I take the greatest measure of pride and pleasure.[35]

While Comiskey was attempting to get ahead of the story by assuming a statesmanlike stance, the morning newspapers of Saturday, September 25, were full of sensational charges about the fixing of the 1919 World Series. Some of them proved to be fairly accurate. For instance, the *New York Times* wrote about how "a professional boxer was approached at the Polo Grounds in New York by a player, since retired from organized baseball, and asked whether he could find a gambler who would pay $100,000 to fix the world's series." It related how Arnold Rothstein was approached, how the White Sox lost the first game with no money handed over, and how the boxer stiffed the players after the Sox had lost Game 2. (Colleagues of Rothstein insisted that he had not been involved in the fix, and Ban Johnson agreed.) The *Chicago Tribune* named the boxer—"Abe Attel" [*sic*]—and identified the retired player as Hal Chase; more significantly, a number of newspapers named the eight White Sox players "mentioned in connection with the charge that the world's championship was 'thrown' to Cincinnati": Buck Weaver, Happy Felsch, Claude Williams, Charles Risberg, Joe Jackson, Chick Gandil, Eddie Cicotte, and Fred McMullin.[36]

That afternoon, the White Sox took the field at League Park in Cleveland with Weaver, Jackson, Felsch, and Risberg in the starting lineup, and Lefty Williams set to take the mound. No one would have been surprised if the beleaguered Sox had fallen apart, but if anything it was the Indians who appeared nervous. With two out in the top of the first Eddie Collins singled off Stan Coveleski and Jackson doubled him to third; both scored on errors, Collins when Cleveland third baseman Larry Gardner threw wildly to first on Felsch's ground ball, and Jackson when first baseman Doc Johnston dropped the throw to first on John Collins's grounder. The White Sox scored twice more in the fourth, with hits by Felsch, Risberg, and Williams the key blows; Jackson homered deep to right for the final Sox run in the fifth. Meanwhile Williams was only in trouble in the fourth, when the Indians produced their only run and three of their five hits. "The Indians went down fighting, but all their efforts were wasted energy, for Claude Williams, Chicago left hander, puzzled them so completely they were almost as helpless as if they had gone to the plate without a bat in their hands," wrote *Cleveland Plain Dealer* writer Henry Edwards.[37] With the 5–1 victory, the White Sox (93–56) were again within a half-game of the first place Indians (92–54). Go figure.

While the Sox were looking good on the field, things were not looking so good for them in the grand jury room. Saturday's witnesses included former Chicago Cubs owner Charles Weeghman, who testified that in August of 1919, Chicago gambler Mont Tennes had told him that seven White Sox players had been "fixed" to throw the upcoming World Series by a New York gambler. He did not think that the gambler was Arnold Rothstein. "He has a lot of money and bets freely," Weeghman said about Rothstein, "but I doubt whether he would permit himself to be mixed up in an affair like this." Weeghman said he believed that he had shared the information he had received from Tennes with National League President John Heydler.[38]

In Cleveland, Ray Schalk told *Chicago Daily News* writer Oscar Reichow, "I intend to go in front of the grand jury and tell all I know, if they are going to drag me into this. The players who have been accused probably can tell a lot more about it than I can. It would not be right for me at this time to give the names of players I intend to submit to the grand jury. I think it is up to the players in the game themselves to protect the sport." Reichow mentioned that Schalk had reportedly fought with one or two Sox players during the 1919 World Series. "It is believed the White Sox catcher felt down in his own heart that there was something wrong with the playing of the first two games with the Reds," wrote Reichow. "Undoubtedly Schalk will submit this feeling to the grand jury to let it take it for what it is worth."[39]

From Cleveland, the White Sox traveled back to Chicago for a Sunday-Monday two-game series against the seventh-place Detroit Tigers (59–89); in an odd bid of scheduling, they would then have three days off before finishing the season with three games in St. Louis against the fourth-place Browns (74–72). Meanwhile the local papers continued to be full of news about the unfolding scandal. On Sunday the *Chicago Herald and Examiner* reported that a "new and important witness" had been found. Clyde Elliott, president of a local motion picture concern called the Greater Stars Production Company, said, "I know the 1919 series was crooked. I have plenty of knowledge to this effect, and am prepared to 'let everything go.'" Elliott said he had evidence that seven or eight White Sox players had been "bought" by a New York gambling clique. "What puzzles me is why the White Sox officials haven't taken any action before. I know that at least one of them has known all about the deal for a long time—months. But in the face of this the crooked players have been permitted to remain on the team, and probably have been 'collecting' from the gamblers this season, as well as last."[40] Elliott, who knew Harry Redmon through his theatrical connections, had served as a liaison between the White Sox and Redmon; he had accompanied Kid Gleason and Sox official Tip O'Neill to East St. Louis when they met with Redmon shortly after the end of the 1919 World Series. Elliott would later testify before the grand jury, but not until early October, after the scandal had broken wide open.

Sunday's *Chicago Tribune* included speculation about the delivery of a "mysterious package in the shape of currency" from Fred McMullin to Buck Weaver who, "when he came home and learned what had happened, stormed and refused to touch the thing, but later accepted it." Weaver's dentist was being sought as a witness. At Comiskey Park on Sunday, Comiskey admitted that he had been convinced after Game 1 of the 1919 Series that someone had "fixed" his players, and that he reported his concerns to John Heydler, who felt that "such a thing as crookedness in that game did not seem possible." Heydler said he had taken the matter up with Ban Johnson, who "replied with a rather curt remark that made me drop the matter." However, Johnson agreed to investigate. "I thought it was really his case and that he would handle it correctly," said Heydler.[41]

Comiskey's enmity toward Johnson was stronger than ever. "There's one man working on this investigation whom I did think was sincere in it, but I believe now he's using it for his personal gain," Comiskey said. "It was a terrible thing to see a story printed of crookedness on the White Sox recently, just before they went into a tough series against New York, but it was still worse to follow with a statement of blackmail of my players by gamblers just before they went into the series against Cleveland, a club to which this man is [financially] interested. I refer to Ban Johnson, president of our league."[42]

On the ballfield, the White Sox continued to win. On Sunday, before a crowd of 25,000, Eddie Cicotte gave up a run to Detroit in the first inning on his own throwing error, then didn't allow a run the rest of the way; the Sox scored three times in the bottom of the first and rolled to an 8–1 win, with their loyal fans sticking behind them. "When the White Sox made their appearance on the field they were cheered as though they were taking the field for a world's series game," wrote Larry Woltz. "Each man got an ovation as he sauntered to the bat. Hand it to the Comiskey followers: they are loyal."[43]

In the final game of the home season on Monday, Dickey Kerr shut out the Tigers in only 66 minutes, 2–0, for his 20th win of the season; that made the 1920 White Sox the first team in Major League history to have four 20-game winners (through 2020, only the 1971 Baltimore Orioles have matched the feat). The only runs of the game came after two were out in the sixth inning. After Buck Weaver was hit by a pitch, Eddie Collins singled to right field. Joe Jackson then singled to center, driving in Weaver, and Collins came home when Tiger shortstop Donie Bush fumbled the relay throw. With the win, the White Sox (95–56) remained a half-game behind the Indians (94–54). A pennant was still very possible.

But in the next 72 hours, the pennant . . . the team . . . and the franchise, all fell apart.

13

BUSTED

On September 26, as the White Sox were taking on the Tigers in the final home series of their season, a man who had direct involvement in the 1919 World Series fix was talking to a reporter . . . and what he had to say finally removed any doubt about what had taken place between gamblers and eight members of the White Sox—seven of them still on Chicago's active roster. The man was Billy Maharg, a Philadelphia native and former professional boxer who had briefly appeared in two Major League games in 1912 and 1916. Maharg knew all about the fix because he was one of the people who helped it take place. His story, as told to veteran sportswriter James Isaminger, appeared in the *Philadelphia North American* on September 27. It would almost immediately be syndicated across the country.

The major points of Maharg's story were as follows:

1. The eight players had agreed to throw the first, second, and final (eighth) game of the Series.
2. The offer to fix the Series had been made by Eddie Cicotte to Maharg and former Major League pitcher Bill Burns in a New York hotel room in September.
3. The players were promised $100,000 to throw the Series, but received only $10,000.
4. Abe Attell, who had made a fortune betting on the Series, double-crossed the players, as well as Burns and Maharg, by not coming through with the promised payoff.

5. After not getting their money (except for the $10,000, which went to Cicotte), the players in turn double-crossed Burns and Maharg by telling them that Game 3 was also fixed for the Sox to lose, but then winning the game. Burns and Maharg lost most of their money betting on the Reds in Game 3.

There was much about the fix that Maharg did not know; he was unaware of the separate deal that the players had made with Sport Sullivan, and he had only secondhand knowledge of the deal they made with St. Louis gamblers that revived the fix after Attell had stiffed the players. But his detailed, credible account would be hard for the players to refute.[1]

Eddie Cicotte, identified by Maharg as the man who proposed the fix to the gamblers, was the first to crack. On Tuesday morning he was summoned to Comiskey Park, where Charles Comiskey, Kid Gleason, Harry Grabiner, Comiskey's attorney Alfred Austrian, and Assistant State's Attorney Hartley Replogle were waiting. Confronted by Austrian and Replogle, Cicotte admitted his involvement in the fix and agreed to confess. He was driven to the Cook County courthouse, where he was interviewed in chambers by Judge McDonald, then taken to appear before the grand jury.

Unlike the grand jury testimony of Joe Jackson and Claude Williams, only a synopsis of Cicotte's testimony is available, based on notes compiled by an assistant state's attorney. Excerpts from his testimony were also read into the record during Joe Jackson's 1924 civil suit trial. The highlights:

- "As with any potential target of grand jury action, the Cicotte appearance commenced with recitation of the legal rights relinquished by the witness and Cicotte's voluntary waiver of those rights," according to former New Jersey prosecutor Bill Lamb. This is an important point, as Cicotte later claimed that Austrian and Replogle promised him that he would not be punished.
- Cicotte recounted a meeting with Williams, Jackson, Gandil, Weaver, Felsch, Risberg, and McMullin in the Ansonia Hotel in New York in September 1919 where the fix was first discussed. With only Gandil and McMullin present, one of the two "asked me what I could take to throw the series and I said I would not do anything like that for less than $10,000, and they said well we can get together and fix it up."
- About three days before the start of the World Series, in the Warner Hotel in Chicago, Cicotte met with Gandil, Felsch, McMullin, and Weaver—he

was unsure about the presence of Williams. Cicotte was concerned that "there was so much double crossing stuff" and wanted his $10,000 prior to the Series. When he returned to his room later, he found $10,000 under his pillow; he never asked Gandil or McMullin where the money had come from.

- Cicotte said "there were five of the players and himself in on the deal in the game," but "even with the money in his pocket he tried to win." He said he had had a change of heart after hitting the first Cincinnati batter in Game 1, Morrie Rath, with a pitched ball.
- After Game 1 was over he was "sick all night" and told Felsch, his roommate, "Happy, it will never be done again."
- He insisted that in his Game 4 loss, "I tried to make good but I made two errors . . . I didn't care whether I got shot out there the next minute. I was going to win the ball game and the series." However, he never offered to return the bribe money; "I couldn't very well do that." He used the money to pay off his mortgage and buy supplies.
- He offered no testimony about what the other players got, or what if anything they did to lose.[2]

When Cicotte had completed his testimony, courtroom officials met privately. Returning around 2:00 p.m., grand jury foreman Brigham summoned the press and announced that true bills indicting Cicotte, Gandil, Risberg, Jackson, Felsch, Williams, Weaver, and McMullin had been approved. The initial charge, which was stated to be made more specific later, was conspiracy to violate a state law.

Within a few minutes of the announcement of the indictments, Charles Comiskey issued a statement to the seven indicted players who were still active with the White Sox (all but Gandil). It stated,

You and each of you are hereby notified of your indefinite suspension as a member of the Chicago American League baseball club.

Your suspension is brought about by information which has just come to me directly involving you and each of you in the baseball scandal (now being investigated by the present grand jury of Cook county) resulting from the world's series of 1919.

If you are innocent of any wrongdoing you and each of you will be reinstated: if you are guilty you will be retired from organized baseball for the rest of your lives, if I can accomplish it.

Until there is a finality to this investigation it is due to the public that I take this action, even though it costs Chicago the pennant.[3]

After the announcement of the true bills, Replogle commented, "This is only the beginning. So far there has been too much talk and not enough action. From now on the grand jury is going to take things in its own hands and see that the truth is brought out."[4]

The session continued with the summoning of the "Mystery Woman," Cicotte's landlady Henrietta Kelley. As noted in chapter 3, Mrs. Kelley was expected to provide testimony that she had overheard Cicotte saying, "I got mine" to his brother in reference to the World Series bribe. However, she denied that she had overheard such a conversation.

The next witness would be much more substantial: Joe Jackson. After being told of Cicotte's admission of guilt by Alfred Austrian, Jackson had telephoned the chambers of Judge McDonald. Testifying at Jackson's 1924 civil trial against the White Sox, McDonald recalled the conversation. "He said that he had heard that Eddie Cicotte, White Sox pitcher, in testifying before the grand jury had implicated him but that he knew nothing about the plot," McDonald said. "I told him that I did not believe him and that he would be called to testify before either a grand or a petit jury. Fifteen minutes later Jackson called me again, saying that he had changed his mind and that he wanted to testify. Shortly afterward he and Mr. Austrian came to my chambers. Mr. Austrian said that Jackson had admitted being implicated, and then Mr. Austrian left us." Jackson then shared details of his involvement in the fix with McDonald prior to going before the grand jury. During this conversation, McDonald had a "distinct recollection" that Jackson told him "that he had made no misplays that could be noticed by an ordinary person but that he did not play his best."[5]

Jackson took the stand at around 3:00 p.m., questioned by Hartley Replogle. Fortunately for fans and researchers, Jackson's entire grand jury testimony has survived and is available at the Chicago History Museum and also online, at baseball-almanac.com and other venues. It began with Replogle telling Jackson "that any testimony you may give here can be used against you at any future trial," and reading the immunity waiver aloud to Jackson, including the phrase, "I hereby with said full knowledge waive all immunity that I might claim by reason of my appearing before the Grand Jury." Jackson signed the document.[6]

Replogle then began his questioning. Asked if anyone had paid him any money to throw the Series to Cincinnati, Jackson said, "They did. . . . They promised me $20,000, and paid me five." Chick Gandil had promised the $20,000; Jackson said he received the $5,000 from Williams after the fourth game . . . an important bit of timing, as it confirmed that he knew of the fix while it was happening. In his 1924 civil trial, Jackson would claim that he knew

In September 1920, Joe Jackson confessed his involvement in the 1919 World Series fix. Jackson would spend the rest of his adult life attempting to alter his story. *Library of Congress Prints and Photographs Division*

nothing of the fix until after the Series was over, when Williams surprised him by handing him the money.

Jackson said he did not attend the players' meeting at the Warner Hotel in Chicago, but that Williams had told him about it, and that Gandil had told him that the players had been double-crossed by Bill Burns. He testified that it was Gandil who had promised to pay Jackson the $20,000 ("Q. How much did he promise you? A. $20,000 if I would take part. Q. And you said you would? A. Yes, sir."). When Williams only gave him $5,000, "I asked him what the hell had come off here."

The questioning went into detail about how the money was to be paid to the players. Abe Attell was supposed to give Gandil money after each game to pay Jackson and the others, but that did not happen.

Q. At the end of the first game you didn't get any money, did you?

A. No, I did not, no, sir.

Q. What did you do then?

A. I asked Gandil what is the trouble? He says, "Everything is all right" he had it.

Q. Then you went ahead and threw the second game, thinking you would get it then, is that right?

A. We went ahead and threw the second game, we went after him again. I said to him, "What are you going to do?" "Everything is all right," he says, "What the hell is the matter?"

Q. After the third game what did you say to him?

A. After the third game I says, "Somebody is getting a nice little jazz, everybody is crooked." He said, "Well, Abe Attel [sic] and Bill Burns had crossed him," that is what he said to me.

The Joe Jackson of this testimony is not the Jackson who would claim that he didn't know about the fix until it was over (1924), or who claimed that—when he was propositioned before the Series in front of four people "who offered their testimony at my trial" (a complete falsehood)—he threatened to throw the man out of a window, then tried to get Comiskey to bench him when the fix talk continued (1949).[7] This Jackson knew all about the fix, agreed to take part in it for $20,000, then complained several times when he didn't get his money.

At one point, Jackson testified that he told Gandil, "I am not going to be in it. I am going to get out of that altogether." When he said he might tell Comiskey, Gandil threatened him with bodily harm. This makes Jackson appear to be a reluctant participant in the fix who only kept his mouth shut when threatened . . . but the conversation did not take place until after the fourth game, at the point when Jackson had become convinced that Gandil was trying to stiff him.

Q. Didn't you think it was the right thing for you to go and tell Comiskey about it?

A. I did tell them once, "I am not going to be in it." I will just get out of that altogether.

Q. Who did you tell that to?

A. Chick Gandil.

Q. What did he say?

A. He said I was into it already and I might as well stay in. I said, "I can go to the boss and have every damn one of you pulled out of the limelight." He said, "It wouldn't be well for me if I did that."

Q. Gandil said that to you?

A. Yes, sir.

Q. What did you say?

A. Well, I told him any time they wanted to have me knocked off, to have me knocked off.

Q. What did he say?

A. Just laughed.

Q. When did that conversation take place, that you said any time they wanted to have you knocked off?

A. That was the fourth game, the fifth night going back to Cincinnati.

Contradicting what he had told Judge McDonald in chambers, Jackson stated several times during his testimony that he had batted to win during the World Series, and did not make any intentional errors in the field. Asked if it had ever occurred to him to tell what he knew prior to this, he replied, "I offered to come here last fall in the investigation. I would have told it last fall if they would have brought me in." He also said he had played honestly in 1920, and knew nothing about other players fixing games. (He did admit there were "some funny looking games" in 1920.) Asked repeatedly about suspicious plays in the World Series, he could find only one, a botched double play by Swede Risberg. When he told Eddie Cicotte that he'd only received $5,000, Cicotte "said I was God damn fool for not getting it in my hand like he did." He was suspicious of the other players, not believing that Risberg and Williams (his longtime friend and roommate) had only received $5,000, as they had told him: "I think they cut it up to suit themselves, what little they did have." Regarding Buck Weaver being in on the deal, he said, "They [the other players] told me he was; he never told me it himself."

When Jackson proclaimed that he "wanted to win this year, above all times," Replogle responded, "You didn't want to do that so bad last year, did you?"

Jackson's reply was, "Well, down in my heart I did, yes."

Perhaps the saddest exchange was this:

Q. Weren't you very much peeved that you only got $5,000 when you expected to get twenty?

A. No, I was ashamed of myself.

Regarding the Cicotte and Jackson testimonies, much would be made later by defenders of both players that they testified that they were playing to win, and also that they later repudiated their confessions prior to their 1921 trial. But as noted in chapter 3, the repudiations were based on an alleged promise of immunity, not that the content of their testimony was inaccurate or unreliable. When Jackson did try to challenge his grand jury testimony at his 1924 civil trial, it was by repeatedly saying, "I did not say that" when the testimony was read to him . . . an absurd claim that was easily disproven by the grand jury transcripts, and one that led to a charge of perjury against Jackson.

I also do not give much credence to the argument that goes, "we took the money, but then we played to win." Every one of the Black Sox spent much of their lives trying to sell this version of the fix, which is of course impossible to either prove or disprove. In this case Jackson's own statement in Judge McDonald's chambers—"that he had made no misplays that could be noticed by an ordinary person but that he did not play his best"—gives some context to his gaudy .375 World Series batting average, which was mostly compiled either in games the Black Sox were clearly trying to win (Games 3, 6, and 7), or when the team was well behind in the score (Game 8). Shoeless Joe, the club's leading run producer, did not have an RBI in the 1919 World Series until Game 6. As for Cicotte, Black Sox historian and legal expert Bill Lamb wrote the author in an email, "Next to Joe Jackson, Cicotte is the most unreliable of the Sox players confessing involvement in the World Series fix. Like Jackson, Cicotte rarely said the same thing twice when it came to the fix, but always tried to minimize his own involvement, portraying himself as someone sucked into the Series corruption rather than being one of the primary instigators of it."[8]

After the Cicotte and Jackson confessions, Buck Weaver and Happy Felsch quickly denied involvement in the fix. "Any man who bats .333 [actually .324] is bound to make trouble for the other team in a ball game," said Weaver. "The best team cannot win a world's championship without getting the breaks." Felsch said, "It's all bunk as far as I'm concerned. I've always been on the square. All I want is a chance to face the grand jury." Abe Attell called the accusations of his involvement in the fix "bunk." He threatened to "shoot the lid sky high" and exclaimed, "You can say that the story placing any responsibility upon me for passing the $100,000 to the White Sox is a lie. It looks like Rothstein is behind these stories."[9]

That night White Sox players not implicated in the fix held a dinner celebration. "We've known something was wrong for a long time, but we felt we had to keep silent because we were fighting for the pennant," said team captain Eddie Collins. "Now it's all over and we're the happiest bunch in the world." Eddie Murphy, Amos Strunk, Nemo Leibold, and Ray Schalk were unable to attend, but telephoned to express their joy over the "clearing of the atmosphere."[10]

In something of a grandstanding move, Yankees owners Jacob Ruppert and T. L. Huston lauded Comiskey for "making a terrible sacrifice to preserve the integrity of the game" in suspending the eight players. . . . Therefore, in order that you may play out your scheduled and, if necessary, the world's series, our entire club is at your disposal." Not to be left out, Red Sox owner Harry Frazee said it was "the duty of each club in the league give one of its players to the Chicago White Sox to assist in its rehabilitation." Neither move could realistically be done under the baseball rules of the time.[11]

The Cicotte and Jackson confessions were a page 1 news story all across the country on the morning of September 29 . . . but with the press barred from the grand jury room, accounts of their testimony were wildly inaccurate. Cicotte, who was said to have wept on the stand, was quoted as saying, "I did it by giving the Cincinnati players easy balls and putting them right over the plate. A baby could have hit them. Then in one of the games—the second, I think—there was a man on first and the Reds' batter hit a slow grounder to me. I could have made a double play out of it without any trouble at all. But I was slow—slow enough to permit the batter to get to first and the man on first to get to second." Cicotte never made such an admission; on the contrary, he insisted that he had had a change of heart and was pitching to win. Nor did Jackson say, "When a Cincinnati player would bat a ball out in my territory I'd muff it if I could. But if it would look too much like crooked work to do that I'd be slow and would make a throw to the infield that would be too short. My work netted the Cincinnati team several runs that they never would have made if I had been playing on the square." There is also no evidence that Jackson, after leaving the courtroom, was confronted by an "urchin" who grabbed his coat sleeve and asked, "It ain't true, is it, Joe?" . . . to which Jackson replied, "Yes, kid, I'm afraid it is." (But it's a terrific story.) [12]

I am not sure what to think about the comments attributed to Jackson after his testimony, as quoted in the *Chicago Tribune* and other outlets. Some of them match Jackson's actual testimony pretty faithfully ("I got in there and I said: 'I got $5,000 and they promised me $20,000. . . . I told that to Judge McDonald. . . . He said he didn't care what I got. . . . I don't think the judge likes me"). It also contains Jackson saying, "Now Risberg threatens me if I squawk," with the much-quoted finish, "Swede's a hard guy." But the story also has Jackson saying, "A lot of these sporting writers that have been talking about the third game of the world's series being square. Let me tell you something. The eight of us did our best to stick it, and little Dick Kerr won the game by his pitching." [13] This is hard to believe, as the third game was widely thought to have been played honestly by the Black Sox in order to double-cross Attell, Burns, and Maharg. Most of the indicted players played well in this game, including Jackson (two hits) and Gandil (a key two-run single). It's puzzling.

Wednesday morning's grand jury hearing began with the testimony and confession of a third member of the White Sox: Claude Williams. Assistant State's Attorney Replogle began by telling Lefty that he had been indicted, "that anything he says can be used in evidence against him, but if he comes in and helps the State clean up this matter that might be taken into consideration and probably would be taken into consideration if [he] was found guilty and there was punishment meted out to him. This is an immunity waiver, Mr. Williams, you understand what Judge McDonald said to you?" Williams said "Yes, sir," read the immunity waiver aloud, said that he understood it, and then signed the waiver. [14]

After reciting his name, address, and giving a summary of his baseball background, Williams was asked about the throwing of the 1919 World Series. He testified that Chick Gandil had approached him in front of the Ansonia Hotel in New York and asked if he was willing to get in on a fix of the Series. Williams replied, "I will refuse to answer right now," but back in Chicago, agreed to join a meeting at the Warner Hotel. Present at this meeting were Gandil, Cicotte, Weaver, and Felsch, and two gamblers, "Sullivan and Brown . . . they were the fellows going to try and put over this deal." Boston gambler Sport Sullivan had made previous contact with Gandil and Cicotte. The identity of "Rachael Brown" has never been fully established, but many Black Sox historians think that he was actually Nat Evans, a business colleague of Arnold Rothstein. Sullivan and Brown were not directly connected with the Burns/Maharg/Attell

One of the gamblers who helped arrange the 1919 World Series fix, Joseph (Sport) Sullivan was indicted by a Chicago grand jury, but escaped extradition and never stood trial. *Library of Congress Prints and Photographs Division*

group with whom the players also negotiated. Payoffs to the players were discussed at this meeting and Williams said, "In my estimation I wouldn't consider nothing under $10,000. . . . I figured if I wouldn't get in on it, it would be done anyway, and I haven't got any money, and I might as well get what I can get. It was agreed upon and we all left." After the meeting Williams walked around outside with Weaver and Felsch; "They were just talking about it, how we would do it. . . . If it became necessary to strike errors or strike out in a pinch or anything, if a critical moment arrived, boot the ball, or do anything."

Prior to the start of the World Series in Cincinnati, Gandil told the players they would get $5,000 apiece after the second game and the remaining $5,000 after Game 4. At another meeting in Cincinnati—attending were Gandil, Williams, Weaver, Felsch, and Cicotte—Gandil told the group that Bill Burns and Abe Attell were getting up $100,000, to be paid in $20,000 segments after each game (loss). However, Williams received no money until after Game 4, when Gandil handed him two envelopes with $5,000 apiece; the second envelope was for Jackson. Gandil told him, "There is your dough, the gamblers has called it off." Williams was unsure whether the gamblers had backed out, or whether they were double-crossing the players.

Like Cicotte and Jackson, Williams insisted that he did not do anything intentionally to lose Games 2, 5, or 8. He admitted, "I might have pitched harder if I wanted to" in Game 2; as for Game 5, he said, "I pitched as hard in that game as I ever pitched a game in my life." He said he was nervous in Game 5 . . . "it made me sorry, I wished I was out of it and hadn't been mixed up in it at all." Prior to his loss in Game 8, Williams said he told Jackson, "If we have been double-crossed I am going to win this game if I can possibly win it." However he gave up four runs in the first inning and was taken out.

Missing from Williams's testimony was the claim—not made until many years later—that on the night prior to Game 8, he had been threatened with bodily harm, and bodily harm to his wife, unless he lost the game. Eliot Asinof later admitted that he had fabricated the character of the thug called "Harry F." who supposedly made the threat, so there is no evidence that it happened. But in a long article about the World Series fix that appeared in the *New York Evening World* on September 29, 1920—the day that Williams testified—Hugh Fullerton reported that just prior to start of Game 8, a gambler approached him and recommended that Fullerton get a bet down on the Reds. "You'll see the biggest first inning you ever saw in your life," the gambler told him. That is exactly what happened, and makes Williams's "I pitched to win" story less than convincing.[15]

Of note in Williams's testimony is that, like Cicotte, he placed Buck Weaver at two meetings where the fix was openly discussed . . . and testified that after the second meeting, Williams, Happy Felsch, and Weaver discussed how they would go about dumping a game. While no evidence has surfaced that Weaver ever received money for taking part in the fix, that doesn't necessarily mean that he was someone who just heard the proposition and turned it down, but refused to tell anyone about it (which to me seems bad enough). In Harry Grabiner's diary, a note about Kid Gleason's meeting with Harry Redmon in East St. Louis included a list of the players implicated in the fix, and ended, "Cicotte and Weaver, the last two both being crooked in the first game and then turning." While this appears incorrect about Cicotte given his suspicious performance in Game 4, it's not a crazy notion to think that Weaver originally agreed to take part, but dropped out when the players didn't receive a payoff promised after their Game 1 loss. Weaver had one hit in Game 1, a bloop single in the sixth inning when the White Sox were trailing 6–1. That's not incriminating on its own, but Eddie Collins found one play in the first inning involving Weaver to be highly suspicious. "I was on first base," Collins told Joe Williams in 1943. "I gave Weaver the hit-and-run sign. He ignored it and I was out a yard at second. Coming back to the bench I said to him, 'You took that sign and did nothing about it. Were you asleep?' Weaver snapped back: 'Quit trying to alibi and play ball.'"[16]

Finally, the October 1, 1920, issue of the *New York Daily News* includes this nugget: "Weaver's friends declare he will admit having been at the hotel meeting with the gamblers; that he refused to help lose the series for $5,000, contending that it was worth at least $20,000, and when he didn't get that declined to go into the deal."[17] Given that payoffs from two sets of gamblers could easily mean $20,000 for each player, that was not an unreasonable expectation. The Grabiner note and the Collins comment are both consistent with the notion that Weaver was in the fix for Game 1; it's possible that he backed out when the players didn't receive any money after the game. We will never know the answer.

Following Williams's testimony, the grand jury indicted Sullivan and "Brown" . . . although no one knew who Brown really was or how to find him. The rest of the day's session consisted of testimony from John Heydler and New York Giants manager John McGraw about the Magee, Chase, and Zimmerman affairs. "The case of Magee, who was thrown out of baseball, is a matter of court in Cincinnati. We have proof of Chase's guilt," said Heydler. He also sharply denied rumors that the upcoming 1920 World Series was fixed ("Any one who would suggest that the world's series has been 'fixed' ought to be shot") and said he had found no evidence that National League infielders Ivy Olson and Johnny Rawlings had won $2,000 betting on the 1919 World Series. McGraw testified that he had dropped Zimmerman after Giants outfielder Bennie Kauff had reported a $500 bribe offer from Zimmerman to throw games. Zimmerman angrily denied the story.[18]

As the work of the grand jury continued, State's Attorney Maclay Hoyne, who was still in New York, was calling for a halt in the inquiry until he returned to Chicago—and expressing doubt about the validity of indictments against the players. "I am not certain whether any crime has been committed," said Hoyne. He leaned toward the opinion that the only crime for which the players might be prosecuted and convicted was that of gambling or conspiracy to gamble—both considered misdemeanors according to Illinois law. As for the indictments, "They may have been voted, but an indictment is not an indictment until it has been returned in court." Judge McDonald brushed off the criticism and said the investigation would continue. According to Bill Lamb, "As the grand jury is an arm of the judicial, rather than executive branch, Judge McDonald had absolute and unfettered control of the proceedings and did not legally require the cooperation of the State's Attorney's office." Within two days, Hoyne backed down from his comments and endorsed the true bills submitted by the grand jury.[19]

The biggest scandal news of Thursday, September 30, came from outside the courtroom: Happy Felsch admitted to his involvement in the fix. Speaking to Harry Reutlinger of the *Chicago Evening American*, Felsch walked back from his denial of two days earlier, saying,

> Well, the beans are all spilled and I think I am through with baseball. I got my $5,000 and I suppose the others got theirs too. If you say anything about me don't make it appear that I'm trying to put up an alibi. I'm not. I'm as guilty as the rest of them. We all were in it alike.
>
> I don't know what I'm going to do now. I have been a baseball player during the best years of my life, and I never got into any other kind of business. I'm going to hell, I guess. . . .
>
> I didn't want to get in on the deal at first. I had always received square treatment from "Commy," and it didn't look quite right to throw him down. But when they let me in the idea too many men were involved. I didn't like to be a squealer and I knew that if I stayed out of the deal and said nothing about it they would go ahead without me and I'd be that much money out without accomplishing anything.
>
> I'm not saying this to pass the buck to the others, I suppose that if I had refused to enter the plot and had stood my ground I might have stopped the whole deal.
>
> We all share the blame equally.

Felsch called Cicotte's story "true in every detail" and said that he didn't blame Cicotte for coming clean; "I was ready to confess myself yesterday, but I didn't have the courage to be the first to tell." But he said he had "nothing to do with loss of the world's series. The breaks just came so that I was not given a chance to do anything toward throwing the game." He insisted that on his much-discussed misplay of a fly ball in Game 5, "I was trying to catch the ball." He also said that "the talk that we 'threw' games this year is bunk." (He would tell Eliot Asinof otherwise a few decades later.) And he said he was going to urge

Buck Weaver to talk to the state's attorney with him. But Felsch knew he'd been had. Reutlinger wrote,

> He smiled mechanically. "I got $5,000," he said. "I could have just about that much by being on the level if the Sox had won the series. And now I'm out of baseball—the only profession I know anything about, and a lot of gamblers have gotten rich. The joke seems to be on us."[20]

Despite the testimony and/or confessions of Cicotte, Jackson, Williams, and Felsch, at least one of the indicted players was holding firm. "It's the bunk— nothing to it," said Chick Gandil, speaking from a Lufkin, Texas, hospital, where he had been operated on for appendicitis. "The other players are trying to make a goat out of somebody, and I am telling the world that somebody won't be me."[21]

At Comiskey Park, where the White Sox were working out prior to heading to St. Louis for a season-ending three-game series against the Browns, Buck Weaver showed up in order "to seek an interview with the owner of the south side team in the hope on exonerating himself," according to I. E. Sanborn. "He was permitted to see Comiskey, but at the conclusion of his visit left the ball park with his head down and declined all requests for a statement as to the result of his conference."[22]

Meanwhile other voices were being heard—beginning with the teammates of the eight indicted players. "We are sorry, in a way, for the fellows who are caught in this jam, but we are glad everything is going to be shown up," said John Collins. "We suspected some of them in the world's series and we suspected them again because of the way they played on the last eastern trip. Some of them not only didn't try but really acted as though they didn't want to win. I have no idea what influenced their actions." Red Faber said, "It looks like we were double crossed in the world's series last year and in the pennant race this year, but we are not through yet." A player who referred to remain anonymous called out some of his indicted teammates by name, saying,

> When we started on our last eastern trip we had every reason to believe we would win the pennant. Suddenly Williams and Cicotte seemed to go bad without any reason. Some of us talked it over and agreed it looked like they were grooving the ball.
>
> Then Jackson, Felsch, and Risberg began dumping the ball to the infield every time they had a chance to get runs.
>
> We thought at first they might just be in a batting slump. But when some of us compared notes regarding the pitching and hitting we became more than suspicious.

It may as well be stated that some of us believe ever since the last world's series that we were sold by Cicotte and others.

Well, when the same men were suspected of crossing us at that time began to go bad on the last eastern trip we decided there must have been another sell-out. However, we have never been able to prove this.

Had we played anything like our regular game we would have come home with the pennant cinched. We all hope the grand jury will look into this end of the affair. If it fails to act we may take some action ourselves—if we can get hold of the players we feel sure did the cheating.[23]

Umpire Brick Owens charged that Cicotte had laid down in his August 31 start against the Red Sox. "Cicotte would put a lot of 'stuff' on the ball prior to the third strike," Owens said, "then he would send over a grooved fast ball without a thing on it. His work could scarcely be determined from the stands, but there was a lot of comment from the players."[24]

National League President John Heydler singled out Kid Gleason for some of the blame. "Gleason could have done much more to avoid all this," said Heydler. "From the information I gathered in the East from a baseball writer, Gleason openly accused some of his players while the series was being played. Ray Schalk was called into the conference and he supported Gleason in his contention. If this is true Gleason should have taken the players under suspicion out of the game."[25] (Heydler said nothing about his own failure to act on what Comiskey had told him.)

Syndicated columnist Alexander F. Jones referred to the indicted players as the "Benedict Arnolds of baseball" and interviewed several retired players and baseball figures. "Eight men on one team," said future Hall of Famer Roger Bresnahan. "I can't believe it. I can understand one crook anywhere, but eight on one ball club. Good Lord, there aren't that many crooks in one jail who would do a thing like this. Selling out for $5,000. Why, that is less than the loser's end on a world series [the loser's share of the 1919 World Series was actually $3,254]. I simply can't get it through my head."[26]

Legendary sportswriter Grantland Rice wrote that "Those mixed up in this crookedness are worse than thieves and burglars," but blamed the leaderless National Commission for not investigating much earlier. "In the Red-White Sox series of last October there was entirely too much smoke adrift for even a simple-minded person not to know that a big blaze of crookedness had been started somewhere," wrote Rice. "It was something more than gossip—but not quite a matter of direct certainty. Yet, if an aggressive, active National Commission had dived immediately into the task of developing all the facts by a thorough investigation, there would be no newly developed scandal starting through the game to-day. But the commission had no chairman—and outside of one or two useless, futile efforts carried out to only a minor extent, nothing whatever was done. So they attempted to cover up the fire. Or rather they attempted to put out the fire by covering it up. And now the blaze, that might have been choked off by a searching investigation and by full publicity, is going to do a lot of damage before the finish."[27]

The hostility toward allegedly crooked ballplayers was so intense that in Joliet, Illinois, where the Cubs were playing an exhibition game on September 30, a fan attacked infielder Buck Herzog, one of the players who had been accused of game-fixing. Shouting, "There goes the crooked Chicago ball players," a fan jumped upon the running board of Herzog's car as he was leaving the ballpark and slashed Herzog on the right arm, left arm and left leg with a knife. Fortunately the injuries were not serious.[28]

The grand jury hearings on Friday, October 1, featured the surprise return of State's Attorney Maclay Hoyne, who came back from New York with some potentially explosive news. After assuring the jurors that he had no doubts about their jurisdiction in securing indictments, he announced, "I have evidence that several of the 1920 games were 'fixed' and I have information that the forthcoming [world] series was to be 'fixed.' While in New York, I gathered together loose threads of a 1920 scandal in baseball which would far surpass that of last season. It appeared that the gamblers had met with such success that they were brazen in their plans to pollute the national sport. Rumors of their crookedness were floating from the housetops, as it were. . . . What will be the result? I will not say at this time, but I will venture the assertion that there is more and bigger scandal coming in the baseball world." He claimed that at least six 1920 games had been fixed.[29] Subsequent investigation found that no players had been approached about fixing the 1920 World Series, and Hoyne never produced any evidence about the fixing of 1920 regular season games.

Once again, the most significant news concerning the baseball scandals came from outside the jury room. Four of the indicted players—Buck Weaver, Fred McMullin, Swede Risberg, and Happy Felsch—announced that they had hired an attorney, Thomas D. Nash, to defend themselves in court against the charges. This was a major surprise, especially since Felsch had admitted his guilt to reporter Harry Reutlinger only two days earlier, and Weaver and McMullin had indicated that they would confess, according to the *Chicago Evening Post*. Asked if he was going to make a statement before the grand jury, Weaver grinned and said, "No, not as these other fools have done. I have been wrongfully accused and I intend to fight. I shall be in major league baseball next year . . . if not with the White Sox, then with some other club. They have nothing on me. I am going to hire the best lawyer in Chicago to defend me, and I'm going to be cleared." Regarding the rumors that he would confess, Weaver replied, "What can I confess? I fielded 1.000 and batted .333 [.324]. That doesn't look much as if I was 'fixed,' does it?"[30]

Risberg, responding to Jackson's claim that he had threatened him with bodily harm, said, "I made Jackson apologize for the stories he spread about me. I never threatened him. I'm no slugger, although I'm able to take care of myself." Asked why he was working with the other three players to defend themselves, Weaver said, "Their case is the same as mine. Jackson must have been affected mentally when he told that story he is said to have told—and here's another thing: I know that you'll have to put in the local color in this interview. But print what I say and don't describe me as being prematurely aged over this thing. Don't say that my shoulders are drooping, my head hanging and my back humped. I'm no condemned criminal and I don't like to be pictured as one."[31]

Two of the gamblers who had been linked to the World Series fix were also talking on October 1. "Within the next 48 hours I will be on my way to Chicago, and when I get there I will tell the Grand Jury or any other officials the whole inside story of the frame-up," said Sport Sullivan. "They have indicted me and made me a goat, and I'm not going to stand for it. I know the whole history of the deal from beginning to end. I know the big man whose money it was that paid off the Sox players—and I'm going to name him." Meanwhile the man Sullivan was thought to be talking about, Arnold Rothstein, announced that he was retiring permanently from the gambling profession. "From now on," Rothstein said, "I shall devote most of my time and attention to my racing stable and to the real estate business. It is not pleasant to be what some call 'a social outcast,' and for the sake of my family and friends I am glad the chapter is closed."[32]

It wasn't closed.

But the baseball story of October 1 that would prove to have the most lasting effect was the news that four Major League clubs—the Chicago Cubs, Chicago White Sox, New York Giants, and Pittsburgh Pirates—had announced their support of a Major League reorganization scheme known as the "Lasker Plan." Some months earlier Albert D. Lasker, a prominent Chicago businessman and the largest Cubs stockholder apart from William Wrigley, had outlined a plan to replace the National Commission. His feeling was that an executive council run by league and team officials could not be impartial when investigating matters that often involved their own self-interest (which was Charles Comiskey's situation, of course). Lasker proposed replacing the National Commission with an executive council composed of three distinguished people of the "highest caliber," all of whom had no connection to or financial interest in baseball. Some of the names considered were former President William Howard Taft, World War I Generals John J. Pershing and Leonard Wood, former Secretary of the Treasury William Gibbs McAdoo . . . and Federal Judge Kenesaw Mountain Landis. The power of this tribunal in ruling on baseball matters would be absolute.

The fact that it had taken nearly a year for Major League Baseball to uncover the Black Sox scandal gave new momentum to Lasker's plan, and the owners of the Boston Red Sox and Boston Braves quickly joined the White Sox, Cubs, Giants, and Pirates in endorsing the plan. Significantly, Ban Johnson, who had vetoed the choice of Landis as head of the National Commission prior to the start of the 1920 season, was not consulted by the owners who had signed on. They and other owners were prepared to proceed with or without the approval of the American League president.

On Friday in St. Louis, the White Sox took the field against the Browns minus the seven indicted players. Since Chicago's last game on Monday, the Indians (96–54) had beaten the Browns twice to increase their lead over the South Siders (95–56) to one and a half games. But the Sox were still mathematically alive, and the boys were putting on a brave front. "The spirit that surges through the ranks of the Pale Hose is the thing that impresses every one who associated with them on the train today and about the lobby of their hotel tonight," reported the *Chicago Tribune*. "To a man the loyalists of the old guard are overjoyed at their deliverance from the companionship of the fakers who not only double crossed the entire sporting world, but threw down their employer and their manager."[33]

Kid Gleason's makeshift lineup included rookie Bibb Falk, making the first start of his Major League career, in right field; little-used substitute Harvey McClellan, starting for the first time in 1920, at shortstop, and pinch hitter Eddie Murphy starting a game at third base for the first time since 1915. Things got off to a promising start when the White Sox scored three times in the top of the first, but Red Faber couldn't hold the lead; he gave up five straight hits and five runs in the third, and the Browns rolled to an 8–6 victory. Meanwhile the Indians were splitting a doubleheader with the seventh-place Tigers in Detroit; Cleveland's (97–55) second-game victory clinched a tie for first place. The White Sox (95–57) would need to win their final two games while the Indians were losing twice to force a best-of-three game playoff. It wasn't to be; the Sox did their part with a 10–7 win on Saturday behind Dickey Kerr (21–9), but by then the Indians had already polished off the Tigers, 10–1, to clinch the pennant.

On Sunday the White Sox lost a meaningless game to St. Louis, 16–7; the defeat left the club with a 96–58 record and a .623 win percentage. Through 2019, only the 1917 (.649) and 1919 (.629) American League champions have had a better winning percentage in Sox franchise history.

One could only imagine how much better that win percentage might have been had the 1920 White Sox played it straight all season.

14

A BITTER MONTH

The 1920 World Series began on Tuesday, October 5, at Brooklyn's Ebbets Field. While Wilbert Robinson's Brooklyn Robins had many fans, Tris Speaker's Cleveland Indians were the sentimental favorites after winning the American League pennant despite the tragic death of Ray Chapman. A cartoon on page 1 of the *Cleveland Plain Dealer* on October 5 showed a Cleveland ballplayer, cap off and staring into the distance, with a flag captioned "Pennant" behind him. Chapman's face appeared in a cloud behind the flag, saying, "Carry On!" The caption of the cartoon said, "It pays to play clean."

Famed writer Ring Lardner was attending the World Series, writing a humor column for the Bell Syndicate. During his years as a Chicago-based sports and fiction writer (1907–1919), Lardner had often incorporated real White Sox players into his stories about the fictional pitcher Jack Keefe. Notable among these players was Eddie Cicotte, who had become a close friend of Lardner. In fact, Cicotte was one of the players featured in the final story of Lardner's Jack Keefe "Busher" series, "The Busher Pulls a Mays." It was published in the October 18, 1919, edition of the *Saturday Evening Post*—shortly after the end of the fixed World Series. Lardner, who relocated to New York shortly afterward, never wrote an article about the World Series fix; according to biographer Jonathan Yardley, "after the integrity of the games was conclusively undermined by the Black Sox scandal of 1919, he turned, in disgust and sorrow, to other subjects."[1]

In his October 3 column previewing the 1920 World Series, Lardner slipped in a little commentary on the previous year's Series, writing,

Personally I don't like neither club's chances and won't recommend neither of them because even a man like myself don't know everything. Last yr. for example I told my friends that the White Sox was a cinch and go bet on them, but that was because I didn't have no idear how many good ball players was playing for the Reds that never had their names in a Cincinnati box score. I wish I had my money back.[2]

A few of Eddie Cicotte's teammates were making more direct comments about their indicted teammates. "We lost the [1920] pennant because certain players—they are among the eight indicted by the Cook County Grand Jury—didn't want us to win," charged reserve catcher Byrd Lynn, who was Lefty Williams's minor league roommate and who had left the White Sox to join Williams and Joe Jackson in shipyard work during the 1918 season (see chapter 2). "We soon noticed how carefully they studied the score board—more than even the average player does in a pennant race and that they always made errors which lost us the game when Cleveland and New York were losing. If Cleveland won—we won. If Cleveland lost—we lost. The idea was to keep up the betting odds, but not to let us win the pennant." Reserve infielder Harvey McClellan mentioned the same pattern. "Several of the players noticed how the scoreboard affected the others," said McClellan, "and we felt all along that these men were regulating their play according to the play of other teams." McClellan also charged that the August 30–September 1 series in Boston had been deliberately thrown.[3]

Byrd and McClellan weren't imagining things: during most of September, the White Sox and Indians either both won, or both lost, on the same day the vast majority of time. From September 3 to 27 were 17 days in which both teams were playing different opponents. On September 6, both clubs played Labor Day doubleheaders, so there were 18 sets of "matched games." As the Indians were playing in the Eastern time zone while the White Sox were playing in the Central on all but two dates during this period (September 26–27), the Sox almost always knew whether Cleveland had won or lost before their own game had concluded. During this period, there was only one date (September 10) in which the White Sox won on a day when the Indians lost, and one date (September 12) in which the Sox lost on a day when the Indians won. There were 13 instances of both teams winning (on September 6, both teams won doubleheaders), and three dates on which both teams lost. Two of those dates in which both teams lost, September 11 and 14, featured White Sox losses that many historians have put in the "suspicious game" category. So Byrd's and McClellan's observations don't seem totally crazy.

White Sox catcher Byrd Lynn claimed that late in the 1920 season,
his crooked teammates watched the scoreboard and played to win
or lose depending on the performance of the Cleveland Indians.
Library of Congress Prints and Photographs Division

CHAPTER 14

As the 1920 World Series was about to open, Charles Comiskey found a way to reward the "honest" players on his team while making himself look good in the process. On October 4, he sent a letter to the non-indicted members of the 1919 White Sox, writing,

> If it be possible, I regret more than you do the occurrences of the 1919 world's series. The honest ball player is stronger today than ever.
>
> As one of the honest ball players of the Chicago White Sox team of 1919, I feel that you were deprived of the winner's share in the world's series receipts, through no fault of yours. I do not intend that you, as an honest ball player, shall be penalized for your honesty or suffer by reason of the dishonesty of others. I therefore take pleasure in handing to you $1,500, this being the difference between the winning and losing players' share.

While the difference between the winner's and loser's share in the 1919 World Series was actually close to $2,000 ($1,952.71), the players were grateful. "We, the undersigned players of the Chicago White Sox, want the world to know the generosity of our employer, who, of his own free will, has reimbursed each and every member of our team the difference between the winning and the losing share of last year's world series, amounting to approximately $1,500," they wrote in response.[4]

Comiskey received much praise for his gesture, and was largely being portrayed during this period as the innocent victim of a group of greedy players—a portrayal that would undergo a thorough revision in the coming years, and one that not everyone shared even at the time. For now, even some of Comiskey's former critics had softened. "I was inclined to censure Comiskey for not cleaning house last fall," wrote John B. Sheridan in the *Sporting News*. "Commy had moral, if not legal proof of the iniquities since confessed by his players. The grand jury investigation told Commy little that he did not know a year ago. He probably did not know many of his players were involved in the faking. But he is too keen a baseball man not to know trying from not trying when he sees it." However, I. E. "Si" Sanborn of the *Chicago Tribune* had told Sheridan that Comiskey did not know absolutely who was guilty, and feared hurting innocent players. "I believe with the Bible it is better that 99 guilty men should escape punishment than that one innocent man should suffer," wrote Sheridan. He finished by raising a question that people have been asking for the last 100 years: "What puzzled me most is how did the White Sox, honest men and crooks, get through the 1920 season as they did."[5]

The same issue of *Sporting News* included a photo collage of the eight indicted players with a famous caption: "Fix These Faces in Your Memory."

The eight were described as "players who committed the astounding and contemptible crime of selling out the baseball world. . . . Four of them are guilty by their own confessions and the evidence against the other four is so conclusive that their denials only add to the contempt in which they are held. . . . Some of the eight have been great stars in their day, but they will be remembered from now on for the depths of depravity to which they could sink."[6]

But—like Weaver, Risberg, McMullin, and Felsch, who had recently hired attorneys—Joe Jackson and Claude Williams weren't of a mind to slink away and wallow in those depths of depravity. A news report from Greenville, South Carolina, Jackson's home town, stated that Shoeless Joe and Lefty had sought the advice of a lawyer. "No comment on the baseball situation from them was available, except the reported statement that if the investigators will probe thoroughly they may find men higher up in baseball involved in the scandal," the report stated.[7]

In Chicago, the grand jury resumed its investigation for a day of testimony on Tuesday, October 5. Assistant State's Attorney Replogle began with a public announcement that the 1920 World Series was free of taint. "Every man on the Brooklyn and Cleveland team is as innocent as a newborn babe and in no way implicated in any baseball scandal past or present," he told the press. Most of that day's testimony concerned National League matters, including the Hal Chase and Heinie Zimmerman affairs. "Chase and Zimmerman are the only men who ever played on my team who are guilty of any wrong doing," said New York Giants manager John McGraw. The grand jury then shifted its focus to the White Sox and the 1919 World Series. Former Giants pitcher Jean Dubuc gave the jury a telegram from Bill Burns telling him to bet on the Reds to win; he added that he had been informed prior to the Series that it had been fixed. Kid Gleason, who was also called as a witness, said that while he had no definite information that the White Sox were throwing games in 1920, some things on the team's last Eastern road trip looked suspicious. The grand jury then recessed until the end of the World Series, which was won by the Indians, five games to two.[8]

The World Series did include one minor scandal: prior to Game 4 in Cleveland, Robins pitcher Rube Marquard was arrested for trying to sell eight box-seat tickets with a book value of $52.80 to an undercover detective for $400. Marquard was ultimately fined $1 for the transgression, but in the atmosphere of the baseball scandals that were being uncovered, the incident was a major embarrassment to the Robins. "The scalping ordinance was gotten up for the benefit of people who have supported a baseball team all the year in order to protect them so they could get tickets at a reasonable price when a World Series or an important game comes up," said Cleveland Common Pleas Court Judge Samuel Silbert. "It is an unfortunate thing, because baseball is going through its test period. For fifty years baseball has been regarded as a clean sport, but now the effect of a sudden scandal has made people dubious."[9] The Robins immediately announced that they were through with Marquard, a popular veteran who had spent his entire 13-year Major League career pitching in New York for either the Giants or Dodgers. Brooklyn traded him to the Cincinnati Reds in December.

Tongue in cheek, Ring Lardner reported his own "scandal," involving Indians reserve catcher Les Nunamaker. "It comes to light today that they's been a attempt to frame this serious after all," Lardner wrote prior to Game 6. "When Leslie Nunamaker was about to retire, the last night in N.Y. City he noticed that his pillow kind of bulged like [portly Dodger] Mgr. Robinson and he looked under it and found $16.00. This was evidently a bribe of $1 apiece for the guys that Mgr. Speaker messes up the batting order with pretty near every day. Nunie hasn't never lived in one big league town long enough to buy property and contract a mortgage so he left the filthy money under the ditto pillow and came back to Cleveland as clean as he left it."[10] Lardner's friend Eddie Cicotte must have winced a little reading that.

The October 14 issue of the *Sporting News* contained a long analysis of the White Sox by *Chicago Daily News* writer Oscar Reichow, focusing first on Buck Weaver and then on Charles Comiskey. "Weaver was an idol on the South Side, not because of his personality, but because of the aggressiveness with which he played. Few more aggressive ball players have ever been in the American League," wrote Reichow. When rumors began to surface that the 1919 World Series had been framed, "Weaver's name was never mentioned. Fans thought it impossible that he would figure in any such rotten affair like that, knowing his disposition to fight for a ball game every second he was on the diamond." Yet if Weaver knew what was being done, as Reichow seemed to think, "he made the mistake of his life when he did not rush up to President Comiskey after the first game was played in Cincinnati and explain to him what was being pulled off." The only thing Reichow could think of, if indeed Weaver "knew what was on the fire, is that he did not possess the courage to go to the front and uncover the dishonest men on his team."[11]

Reichow was equally unsparing about Comiskey's failure to more aggressively pursue the rumors of crooked play by his team, writing,

I have talked to several baseball magnates and managers since and have asked them what they would have done had they been confronted with the same situation. They all replied they would have taken every man at whom the finger of suspicion was pointed and yanked him out of the game. In my opinion that is what should have been done. I am compelled to criticize Comiskey for not doing it and for letting the players stay on his team this season. They should not have been permitted to put on a uniform on any team, considering the clouds that hung over their heads. I am inclined to feel that Comiskey and Gleason knew enough after their investigation, which they said they made, to step out publicly and say these were the men accused, and although nothing tangible had been obtained, enough had been found to keep them out of baseball.

Had Comiskey done this, Reichow felt, it was "almost a cinch" that one of the eight players would have stepped forward and confessed. Yet Comiskey had not done this . . . nor had he asked the American League to take action, saying, "Gentlemen, these are the facts. Get busy. Let's have some action. Baseball is being wrecked by a lot of piker gamblers and something must be done whether it wrecks my ball team or not." Instead, he wrote, "Comiskey let the affair drag . . . and said he could obtain nothing that would permit him to take any action against his players." The only defense that Reichow could mount for Comiskey was this: "He might have been poorly advised on the crookedness of the last World's Series, which, I think, is probably the only reason he did not tear his ball club to shreds last winter then build up a new one for this year."[12] Now, a year later, the club had been torn to shreds anyway.

On October 13, the *Chicago Evening Post* announced that it was offering a prize of $100 for "the best 800-word letter produced by any American fan on how to put baseball above suspicion. . . . Give us your ideas on how to clean out the crooks and put the game above suspicion." The referendum was open until November 15.[13]

The same day, the Chicago grand jury resumed its own attempts to "clean out the crooks." Things got off to a slow start. Ban Johnson had been working behind the scenes to elicit the testimony of St. Louis gamblers Harry Redmon and Joe Pesch, along with bookmaker Thomas Kearney. They were expected to appear before the grand jury now that it was back in session. But all three asked to postpone their testimony for various reasons, and the jury accomplished little of note for the next week. When it swung back into action on October 22, the grand jury re-voted its indictments of the eight players, plus Sullivan and "Brown," in order to overcome technical difficulties. Three new indictments were added at the same time: Abe Attell, Bill Burns, and Hal Chase.

According to the *Boston Globe*, "Officials of the State Attorney's office today said testimony had been given information that Chase, who was expelled from the major leagues and barred from league parks in the West for alleged gambling, was one of the chief instigators of the plot." Testimony was said to show that Chase had approached Abe Attell prior to the 1919 World Series and asked if he could raise $100,000 to bribe the White Sox players. Chase was also alleged to have approached Sport Sullivan, telephoning him from the hotel room of former MLB pitcher Jean Dubuc.[14]

The extent of Hal Chase's role in the fixing of the 1919 World Series has never been fully known. While Chase appeared to have been involved in facilitating the fix, he was likely not one of the primary players. Ultimately both Chase and Attell were able to use legal maneuvering to avoid extradition and never stood trial for these charges. Testifying as a prosecution witness at the players' 1921 trial, Bill Burns stated that Chase had helped him get in touch with Attell and Dave Zelcer, another gambler, after Burns and Maharg had been rebuffed in a meeting with Arnold Rothstein. But Burns mentioned no other involvement by Chase, who undoubtedly benefited financially from his advanced knowledge of the fix.

Attell himself issued a statement about the fix in late October 1920. Attell said he was broke when talk of fixing the Series began. "When I went to New York City to borrow money I was given the information about the series by Hal Chase and Bill Burns," stated Attell. "I first met Burns in Philadelphia, where I was watching a double-header with Cincinnati. At this game he and a prize fighter named Mohawk had Chase throw four games to Philadelphia, and I lost $4000. At that time there was a boy on the field betting for Chase and Burns. The boy's father kept the hotel where Burns and Chase and all the players were staying." Finding out that Attell was a friend of Arnold Rothstein, Burns met privately with Attell and helped him make up for the $4,000 by telling him to bet on Cincinnati, as the Series "was all fixed." In this telling Attell and Chase were simply people who bet on the Series, not masterminded it. "In the Grand Jury room they indicted Hal Chase, who is broke, and has not got a dollar. They indicted me, and I'm in the same position," Attell stated. "They indicted Bill Burns, who had a little money, but who had not a big enough stake to put up."[15]

Attell's story was self-serving to the extreme, and full of holes; among other things, Chase was playing for the New York Giants in 1919, not the Reds (if, while playing for the Giants, he was bribing members of the 1919 Reds to lose games, that *really* would have been a story!). Burns's testimony at the 1921 trial, putting Attell—but not Chase—at the center of the fix, went largely unchallenged. Neither Burns nor Attell credited Chase with being anything more than a useful go-between. (In another self-serving article for *Cavalier* magazine in 1961, Attell again claimed he had no involvement in the fix other than hearing about it, and didn't mention Chase at all, except as a guy who could make an error in a fixed game look convincing.)

The last major day of grand jury testimony was October 26. The first witness, St. Louis Browns second baseman Joe Gedeon, testified that he had been tipped off about the fix by a White Sox player (believed to be either Fred McMullin or Swede Risberg), and had won about $600 betting on the Reds through St. Louis gamblers Carl Zork and Ben Franklin. More importantly, Gedeon testified that he had been present at a gambler's meeting at the Sherman Hotel in Chicago after the White Sox had double-crossed some of the gamblers by winning Game 3. Present at the meeting were Zork, Franklin, Attell, Burns, and the St. Louis gamblers Harry Redmon and Joe Pesch. To get the players back on board, the gamblers wanted to raise $25,000 to pay them.

Harry Redmon was the next witness. He said that he had first learned of the fix prior to Game 3 from Pesch; Des Moines gamblers Ben and Lou Levi had passed along the tip, telling Pesch that "it's all framed up." They knew the names of the eight players involved. Redmon largely corroborated Gedeon's account of the meeting after Game 3. He said that he and Pesch had not contributed to the proposed $25,000 fund; Redmon claimed that "This money was never raised, it was dropped right there as soon as I knew anything about it." However, many people speculate that Carl Zork and Ben Franklin, who had bet heavily on the Reds, were able to raise the cash. (Zork, in a deposition filed with the City of St. Louis on October 27, stated, "I am innocent of any wrong doing or any charge against me of participating directly or indirectly in any attempt to aid or abet in any conspiracy to fix the World's Series of 1919.") Redmon said that he had lost $6,500 betting on the White Sox. Redmon also testified about the meetings he and Pesch had had with White Sox officials in which he related what he knew about the fix. When he talked with Comiskey, Redmon said, the White Sox owner "didn't say much of anything." As he was getting ready to go, Redmon told Comiskey, "It is a pretty serious blow; you can about make a goat out of a couple of these players and whitewash the rest of them. I guess this is the first time they ever done anything like this and they are sorry for it and you can get it all straightened out." Comiskey replied, "Yes, Jackson cost me seventy eight thousand dollars." Redmon said he had no interest in Comiskey's reward money.[16]

The White Sox issued a response to Redmon's testimony the next day. "Redmond [sic] never gave any one connected with this club any evidence upon which the club could act," wrote Harry Grabiner. Grabiner recounted the October 1919 interview in St. Louis that Kid Gleason and team official Tip O'Neill had conducted with Redmon; according to Grabiner, "Redmond could not . . .

tell us anything definite. . . . His story seemed to be merely the hard luck yarn of a loser." The White Sox, Grabiner stated, had made every effort to "verify his hearsay reports," but came up with nothing until the grand jury hearings had started. "When real evidence of crookedness was obtained this club acted in a manner which is well known, and need not be further referred to."[17]

While Redmon's October 26 testimony was substantial, the star witness of the session was Arnold Rothstein. The legendary gambler, who had volunteered to testify on the advice of his attorney, William J. Fallon, portrayed himself as an innocent victim, eager to clear his name; instead, he said he had been harassed by the Chicago press upon his arrival in the city. "Gentlemen," he was reported to have said to the grand jury, "what kind of country is this? I came here voluntarily and what happens? A gang of thugs bars my path with cameras as though I was a notorious person—a criminal event! I'm entitled to an apology! I demand one! Such a thing couldn't happen in New York! I'm surprised at you!"[18]

Rothstein's story was that he had been approached prior to the World Series by Bill Burns, who told him "that certain players on the White Sox had been 'fixed' and all I had to do was to put up $100,000 to pay the ball players." Rothstein said he had coldly turned down the proposition, telling Burns that he (Rothstein) "was on the square when it came to gambling," and calling Burns "a few harsh names." Rothstein said he had also turned down Abe Attell a day or so later. Asked by a juror if he had bet on the Series, Rothstein said he had paid no attention to the fix rumors and "backed my judgement, which was very poor, because after the series was over I was out just $6,000." He also had no idea who supplied the money to bribe the White Sox players. Afterward, he told reporters,

> I came to Chicago to clear my good name. I am not a "sure thing" gambler. I have never welched on a bet in my life. I have bet thousands in my time on baseball games. I will never bet on another baseball game. I am off professional gambling for life. My sport is my racing stable. If I want a little fun, why a few good hours at the good old American game of "draw" will be plenty.

Rothstein's innocent-man-wrongly-accused strategy worked perfectly. White Sox attorney Alfred Austrian cleared him of any wrongdoing; in fact, Austrian said, Rothstein's connection with the World Series fix "develops into one of honesty and integrity, and it further appears that he not only took no part in 'fixing' the world's series but did everything in his power to prevent its being fixed." Ban Johnson agreed, stating, "I found the man Arnold Rothstein and

after a long talk with him, I felt convinced he wasn't in any plot to fix the Series."
The grand jury agreed and gave Rothstein a clean bill of health.[19]

The last bit of substantial grand jury testimony came from Ban Johnson on
October 29. Johnson said that *Kansas City Post* sports editor Otto Floto had
told him that, prior to the August 31 Cubs-Phillies game that had started the
whole investigation, Cubs pitcher Claude Hendrix had wired a Kansas City
gambler named "Frock" Thompson, stating, "Bet $5,000 on Opposition." It
was thought that this potentially explosive bit of information might delay the
conclusion of the grand jury's work, but both Hendrix and Thompson quickly
issued denials. "The report that I wired this fellow Thompson is a lie," said
Hendrix. "I don't know Thompson. Someone is going to get into trouble for
tacking my name to such a wild tale. The more they investigate this affair the
better satisfied I'll be, because I know they will find there is not a word of truth
to it." Thompson also dismissed the story, saying, "I am not even acquainted
with Claude Hendrix and wouldn't know the gentleman if I saw him on the
street." The grand jury left it that at that, not even attempting to see if Western
Union had a record of Hendrix's telegram. To this day, the charge that the
August 31 Phillies-Cubs game was fixed has never been definitively proven . . .
or disproven.

The grand jury ended its work on November 6, issuing a six-page report
while also issuing six indictments to operators of the prolific—and profitable—
baseball pools. Regarding the indictments of the eight White Sox players and
five gamblers, the report stated,

> Strong enough evidence has been submitted to prompt our indicting eight play-
> ers on the various teams and five other men who, according to the testimony,
> conspired to have games of baseball "thrown." While we deplore the facts, we
> are certain general demoralization does not exist in organized baseball, and the
> American public may have confidence in the honesty and integrity of a great
> majority of professional baseball players.
>
> We also feel certain the leaders of organized baseball may henceforth be relied
> upon to eliminate any players whom they strongly suspect. With few exceptions,
> this has previously been done, and we believe this inquiry will have a clarifying
> effect.

The grand jury finished by stating that it was "gratified to find players who
immediately report to their managers the suggestions of 'fixing' and likewise
managers, who immediately discontinued players who were implicated in any
way in attempts to corrupt the game."[20]

Sadly, that sentiment did not seem to apply to the team whose players the grand jury had just finished indicting. The October 30 issue of *Collyer's Eye* included an article by Frank O. Klein titled "Collins Charges 1920 Games 'Fixed.'" After noting that the grand jury was closing its work, Klein wrote, "Probably the one unbroken link that remains to be forged is to 'prove up' the fact that Owner Chas. A. Comiskey KNEW. If this be necessary, I might add that Eddie Collins, field captain of the White Sox told me that he KNEW the series was fixed or at least believed so after two men went to bat in the first game at Cincinnati."[21]

"I felt sure that something was wrong," Collins told Klein, "even before we went to Cincinnati. There was quite some carousing by some of the players. Then I did not quite relish the presence of Joe Gedeon who took my room or rather my bed after we reached Philadelphia. He was hooked up with Risberg and McMullen [*sic*] and came on to Chicago and remained until the end. From what I gleaned it was he who wagered the money of the two above named. I mean the three of them parlayed whatever they 'got.'"[22]

Collins told Klein about the missed hit-and-run play by Buck Weaver in the first inning of Game 1 (related in chapter 13). "When I returned to the bench I immediately accused Weaver of not even attempting to hit the ball. I told this all to Comiskey." Collins then charged that Weaver and Eddie Cicotte had thrown many games in 1920. "The last series," said Collins, "at Boston and New York was the rawest thing I ever saw. If the gamblers didn't have Weaver and Cicotte in their pocket then I don't know a thing about baseball. The fact of the matter is we should have won the pennant again this season and probably would have, but for the throwing of games, by at least ten games."[23]

While the Chicago grand jury was finishing its work, a grand jury in Los Angeles was beginning a probe into charges that members of Pacific Coast League teams had been bribed to help the Vernon team win the 1919 league championship. Deputy District Attorney William C. Doran announced on October 15 that he had "the fullest confidence in bringing to light complete proof of one of the greatest bunko conspiracies ever perpetrated on the Pacific coast." According to Doran, it was probable that no team had bought over by the gamblers, "but he believes that enough individuals in all, or nearly all the clubs, were secured to prevent the public from having any possible chance of a square deal." Babe Borton, the first witness, testified that he had paid money to three members of the Salt Lake team, and one member of the Portland team, to throw games. Former Salt Lake outfielder Harl Maggert supported Borton's testimony, stating that he

In October 1920, future Hall of Famer Eddie Collins told a reporter that games fixed by some of his teammates had cost the White Sox the 1920 American League championship. *Library of Congress Prints and Photographs Division*

was present when Borton made the deal with Salt Lake players Jean Dale, Bill Rumler, and Eddie Mulligan.[24]

"Baseball (the business) stands indicted," wrote Hugh Fullerton in the October 30 issue of the *New Republic*.

> Baseball (the sport) has received a blow from which it will be a long time recovering. Eight ball players, men who were honored above their station or deserts, by a thoughtless public, have been revealed as takers of bribes. The officials, to whose welfare the business and sport of "organized" baseball was entrusted, have been exposed as incompetent. The honest ball players, or the majority of them stand before the public as mildly guilty of being accessories to the fact, in that all save a few knew or suspected the crookedness that was going forward and failed to protect their own reputations, their business and the sport from the ones who were guilty.[25]

Fullerton wrote that the revelations before the grand jury had "shocked the entire nation and, worse, wrecked the faith of millions of boys." The most severe blow, he felt, was not that the players had sold out and accepted bribes from gamblers, but that this could be done without detection from outsiders. Club owners, umpires, and players had long alleged that "the game could not be played dishonestly without detection." But dishonest players and gamblers had "proved that the game can and has been successfully manipulated, provided the honest players on the team do not 'squeal.'"[26]

Fullerton related how he and Christy Mathewson, "one of the most honest of players and managers," had heard rumors of a World Series fix but had discounted them. Watching every play during the Series, they had marked just seven plays as suspicious, and those were plays that could be explained as honest mistakes. An outsider could not detect crooked play to a certainty. He continued,

> An honest player on any team, however, will know, within a short time, whether or not his fellows are "trying" to win. The hope of the future, therefore, lies in securing players of character to disregard the code of the underworld which has ruled the game. The ethics of criminals, especially gamblers, forbid informing upon the guilty and, so long as the ball players who are personally honest persist in adopting this code, it will not be difficult for those players who are willing to sell themselves to find buyers.

Gamblers who had been driven out of making book on horse races had turned to baseball, "a much better sure thing," Fullerton wrote. Pool selling and betting on baseball became rampant, and immediately thereafter the rumors of crookedness began, especially during the World Series. Hal Chase's crooked play brought things to a climax, but when he was charged with game-fixing, players who knew the truth evaded testimony; Chase was acquitted and "promoted from the Cincinnati to the New York team." By the 1919 season, gamblers were boasting that they controlled players on a number of clubs. "Through it all the officials in charge of baseball adhered to their policy of curing an evil by declaring it did not exist and by using their influence over consciously or unconsciously subsidized sporting writers to suppress the accusations and punish those who demanded an investigation."[27]

"There was one man," Fullerton continued, "who gave more thought to the sport than to the money. He was Charles A. Comiskey." When his players were accused of dishonesty, Fullerton wrote, Comiskey insisted on either proving or disproving the charges against them . . . "and when the proof was furnished he expelled players worth a quarter of a million dollars to him from this club, and forced their indictment for conspiracy. Baseball in the hands for men like Comiskey is safe and clean."[28]

Some people would respectfully disagree.

15

HERE COMES THE JUDGE

As the Chicago grand jury was wrapping up its work, Major League Baseball was going through a separate—though connected—crisis. Before the crisis ended, MLB teams endured a bitter conflict that nearly tore apart the structure of the game.

At the heart of the matter were both the Lasker Plan, which was briefly discussed in chapter 13, and the revelations of the Black Sox scandal. Much of the groundwork of the Lasker Plan was done in the offices of Alfred Austrian, who had legal ties to both the White Sox and Chicago Cubs. Along with Austrian serving as counsel for the White Sox (by early 1920 he was also listed as a club vice president), his law firm had represented both chewing-gum magnate William Wrigley and Albert Lasker himself. In 1917, when Lasker purchased a significant share of Cubs' franchise stock from Charles Weeghman, one of his conditions was that the club retain Austrian as the Cubs' corporate counsel. The following year, Austrian clients Wrigley and Lasker purchased control of the club from Weeghman.

When the Black Sox scandal broke, pressure to bring in a new structure to run baseball greatly increased. The Lasker Plan—which advocated that Major League Baseball, and the minors as well, be run by a three-man panel of distinguished people not connected with the game—seemed like the most promising avenue. Austrian's office, wrote Harold Seymour and Dorothy Seymour Mills, "was a convenient rendezvous, since many of the owners avid for the plan or whose backing was needed to effectuate it were either located in Chicago or due there for the [grand jury] hearings."[1] National League owners quickly signed on to the plan, as did the three "Insurrectionist" teams who had battled Ban

Businessman Albert Lasker's plan to have Organized Baseball run by a three-man commission of non-baseball people nearly resulted in a war between the leagues. *Library of Congress Prints and Photographs Division*

Johnson in the 1919–1920 off-season: the New York Yankees, the Boston Red Sox, and Charles Comiskey's Chicago White Sox.

Shortly after the conclusion of the 1920 World Series, National League owners met in League President John Heydler's office and voted unanimously to adopt the Lasker Plan. They recommended that the leagues meet jointly in Chicago on October 18 to work out the details for implementing the plan. However, Ban Johnson refused to participate in the meeting, and the so-called

Loyal Five pro-Johnson American League teams (Athletics, Browns, Indians, Senators, and Tigers) stood with him.

Johnson was not necessarily against having non-baseball people taking charge of its executive council. However, he had his own candidate for the top position: Judge Charles A. McDonald, the hero of the grand jury hearings. According to historian David Pietrusza, Johnson "planned to create a public image for McDonald as a tireless guardian of baseball virtue," with McDonald's work in leading the grand jury investigation as the centerpiece. "McDonald was perhaps Johnson's only chance to recover control of that body [the new commission]—and of baseball."[2] Most of the other owners, however, preferred Judge Kenesaw Mountain Landis for the top spot.

When the joint meeting took place on October 18, Johnson and the Loyal Five were not present. Johnson had sent a telegram to Heydler, saying he did not think it advisable to discuss reorganization at this time, due to "startling evidence he thought might come before the Cook County Grand Jury." Heydler dismissed the request to postpone, saying that he could not see "what effect any further evidence coming before the jury could have on the reorganization question."[3]

At the meeting, the 11 clubs ratified the Lasker Plan, and gave the Loyal Five until November 1 to join them. If not, the 11 teams would proceed with a reorganization creating a new 12-team structure. The Eastern teams would be the New York Giants, New York Yankees, Brooklyn Robins, Boston Red Sox, Boston Braves, and Philadelphia Phillies; the West would be comprised of the Chicago White Sox, Chicago Cubs, St. Louis Cardinals, Pittsburgh Pirates, Cincinnati Reds, and a team to be named. The three commissioners would be elected for terms ending on December 31 in 1925, 1926, and 1927; the chairman would have the longest term, with a salary not less than $25,000 per year. Regarding the failure of the Loyal Five to attend the meeting, Heydler said, "This action is taken as a direct snub. We will go along without these five club owners, and I believe the committed will make recommendations so strong that we can progress without them." For now, the Loyal Five were sticking with Johnson. "We are the American League," said Philadelphia Athletics co-owner and team manager Connie Mack, "and when the time comes the American League will meet at the call of its president and no doubt will take action that will help baseball; that will help raise its standard and prevent scandals in the future."[4]

When the American League Board of Directors met in Chicago on October 29, they rejected the Lasker Plan. "The Board of Directors is of the unanimous opinion that the so-called Lasker plan will prove wholly ineffectual to accomplish the results which its sponsors seek," the board said in a statement.

The directors came up with a counterproposal: a committee of nine members, consisting of three from the American League, three from the National League, and three from the minor leagues, would work out a plan of reorganization. The board thought its own plan superior for two reasons: first, it included the minors, which the Lasker Plan did not, and second, the ability of a commission of eminent citizens with no connection with the game to take over "the management of baseball properties in which large sums of money have been invested is gravely doubtful. . . . We have no confidence in such a commission being any more able to stamp out gambling than the National Commission has been."[5]

The 11 other Major League teams appeared willing to do a little to mollify Johnson and the Loyal Five . . . but only a little. In his diary entry from November 1, Harry Grabiner wrote, "Lasker stated that at least six in the National League were in favor of the following tribunal—Landis, Chairman, [Cleveland sportswriter Henry P.] Edwards, [Pacific Coast League President William] McCarthy. Lasker is of the opinion that the minors should have representation and he would be in favor of even going as far as allowing the Loyal five to name one of the members providing Landis is the Chairman. Whatever is done by the Loyal five, Lasker stated that he was in favor of a fight to the finish regardless of the consequences."[6]

The minor leagues had their own thoughts on how they should be represented. Meeting in Kansas City, minor league leaders proposed a five-man commission for running the game. It would consist of one member appointed by the American League, one by the National League, and two by the minor leagues, with the fifth member appointed by mutual agreement. "The personnel of this commission, of course, will be determined by the three units agreeing," wrote Ban Johnson ally Harry Neily. "The supreme court of baseball will not be picked by the National League and the three dissenting members of the American. To such a proposition, the majority club owners of the American League have pledged their opposition."[7]

But the Loyal Five soon found themselves outmaneuvered as well as outnumbered. On November 3, Heydler invited the Loyal Five to meet with the other 11 clubs; however, they stuck with Johnson, who was still scheming. Giants President Charles Stoneham told Lasker that Ban Johnson had approached him about securing the rights to lease the Polo Grounds in the name of the American League; he would then replace the Yankees' Ruppert-Huston combination, who would not have a place to play, with an owner satisfactory to Stoneman. He would even let Stoneham pick the new owner—and the third member of the National Commission as well. Stoneham not only wasn't interested . . . he planned to tell Ruppert about this scheme when the leagues met a few days later.

On November 8, the 11 owners who had endorsed the Lasker Plan met in Chicago; the Loyal Five met separately in the same hotel. Washington Senators owner Clark Griffith, one of the Loyal Five, approached the other group, which invited the Loyal Five to join their meeting. But they issued an ultimatum: unless the Loyal Five agreed to adopt the plan by 4:00 p.m., the other 11 owners would move forward, even at the risk of a baseball war.

When the deadline passed without a word from the Loyal Five, the 11 other owners voted unanimously to ask Judge Landis to become the head commissioner at a salary of $50,000 a year. In addition, the White Sox, Yankees, and Red Sox resigned from the American League to join the National. The league's 12th team would be the first among the Loyal Five to ask to join the NL. If none of the Loyal Five was willing to abandon Johnson, the NL would place a new franchise in either Cleveland or Detroit—a nightmare scenario for the owners of the Tigers or Indians. (A day later, the National League announced that Detroit would be the site of the league's 12th franchise.) The 12-team circuit would be known as the New National League, with John Heydler continuing as president, secretary, and treasurer.

The group of 11 then sent a committee of six owners to Judge Landis's chambers to offer him the position of chairman of the new commission. The second and third members of the commission would be selected later, with one of the positions chosen by the minor leagues. The offer to Landis was for a seven-year term at a salary of $50,000 a year; Landis's annual salary as a federal judge was $7,500. Landis said he would take it under advisement, but the group was confident he would accept the position.

In response to the moves by the other 11 clubs, Johnson's Loyal Five put into operation a plan to put new American League franchises in Chicago, New York, and Boston. "We are the majority of the American League and consequently are the American League," said Clark Griffith. "The American League will operate this year with or without the Chicago, New York, and Boston clubs." The Loyal Five also asserted that the White Sox, Yankees, and Red Sox would not be able to take their players into the new league, arguing that players on a club belonged to the league under their previous contracts. Even if that were the case, the *Chicago Herald and Examiner* estimated that putting new clubs in the three cities would cost the American League close to 5 million dollars for stadium erection or leases, salaries for officials, and travel expenses. By contrast, the paper estimated that, if necessary, the National League could put a 12th team in Pittsburgh or Cincinnati for only $550,000.[8]

On November 9, newspapers across the country contained page 1 stories about the impending "baseball war." Many predicted doom for the Major

Leagues if such a war took place. "One [faction] or the other has certainly blundered, and probably both have done so, and a baseball war of two or three years may result," wrote James O'Leary in the *Boston Globe*. "That is all that would be required to make the baseball public quite sick of both factions." O'Leary also questioned the $50,000 offer to Landis. "If Judge Landis is worth $50,000 a year and two other members of a National Commission draw down $35,000 or $40,000 each, a player like Babe Ruth ought to be worth about $150,000. Whether he is or not, Babe is likely to think so next Spring, when it comes time to get into line for Spring practice, regardless of what his present contract with the New York club calls for. There are other players who may also have exaggerated ideas for their value to the game, and if there is a war, be out to sell their services to the highest bidder." O'Leary expressed the fear that "the baseball fan, who is expected to foot the bills, and has been doing so," might finally say, "A plague on both your houses; we want no more of either of you. Go hence."[9] (More than 100 years later, sportswriters would be expressing the same fears about the battles between Major League players and owners.)

Ty Cobb of the Detroit Tigers, still one of baseball's biggest stars, was standing behind Ban Johnson. "I am for the American League and for Ban Johnson," said Cobb. "From the players' viewpoint it looks to me as though the whole rumpus is due to politics and personal animosities on the part of the minority owners who have withdrawn. Ban Johnson's administration is a constructive one." But in an editorial titled "War in Baseball," the *New York Times* blamed Johnson for the difficulties. "The obstacle to reorganization was and is Byron Bancroft Johnson, President of the American League, who was once a brilliant and successful executive, and now seems to think that baseball exists for his greater glory," said the editorial. "Lincoln's confident belief that you can't fool everybody all the time, even if justified, may be beside the point. It is possible that you can fool enough people all the time to get away with whatever you are trying to get away with, but that theory is not a very safe foundation for a business in which millions are invested."[10]

Looking for allies, both leagues attempted to woo the minor leagues, which were holding their annual meetings in Kansas City. Johnson traveled to Kansas City in person and gave a fiery speech in which he expressed his eagerness to go to war with the National League. "War, in my judgment, is the best cleanser. I am for it, as I believe it will clean up baseball like it cleans up everything else," said Johnson. "What the game really needs is to be cleansed of some of its undesirable club owners, who have been a detriment because they openly allowed gambling in their baseball parks. The National League never had any stomach for a fight. It is an impossible organization."[11]

But Johnson quickly learned that, even if he was correct about the National League, his supposedly Loyal Five did not have stomach for a fight, either. "For all his fighting speech and vituperation, Johnson's game was ended," wrote Seymour and Mills. "His loyal quintet crumpled in the face of what was almost certain to be a wasting and useless approach. Even as Johnson was speaking, [Clark] Griffith was approaching Mrs. Ebbets [wife of the Brooklyn Robins owner] to arrange a meeting with her husband. Intermittent conversations between different members of the discordant factions followed." On November 11—two years to the day after the Armistice that ended the Great War—the Loyal Five agreed to meet with the other 11 owners the following day, without the presence of the league presidents, lawyers, or even stenographers.[12]

When they met in Chicago on November 12, the owners unanimously agreed to the election of Landis as commissioner. Interleague matters would now be decided by a vote of the 16 clubs; if no majority resulted, each league would cast a single vote, and if a deadlock still remained, Landis would cast the deciding—and final—vote. Lasker's three-man commission idea was also scrapped; as a *New York Times* headline put it, "Baseball Peace Declared; Landis Named Dictator." All this would become part of a new national agreement to be drafted by a nine-man committee consisting of three representatives each from the American, National, and minor leagues.

With the agreement in place, 15 of the 16 owners—all except Phil Ball of the St. Louis Browns, to the end Johnson's most loyal supporter—rode over to the Federal Building to officially offer the commissionership to Judge Landis. The judge let them wait for an hour; when he finally met with the group in his chambers, he expressed his reluctance to give up his federal judgeship. After being assured that his power would be absolute, Landis accepted an agreement that would allow him to retain his judgeship and its $7,500 salary; his salary as commissioner was reduced to $42,500, but with a $7,500 expense account added. He would officially take office in January 1921. In his statement of acceptance, Landis wrote, "The opportunities for real service to baseball are limitless. It is a matter to which I have devoted nearly forty years on the question of policy. All I have to say is this: The only thing in anybody's mind now, is to make baseball what the millions of fans throughout the United States want it to be."[13]

At the time that he accepted the commissionership of baseball, Kenesaw Mountain Landis was already one of the most famous judges in the United States—and arguably one of the most famous people in the country. Born in Midgeville, Ohio, in 1866—his father, a surgeon, had served at the battle of Kennesaw Mountain during the Civil War—Landis gained admission to the Indiana bar in 1889, despite not having a high school diploma or passing a bar

In November of 1920, Judge Kenesaw Mountain Landis agreed
to become baseball's first commissioner—one with dictatorial
powers. *Library of Congress Prints and Photographs Division*

examination. He became a federal judge in 1905, and two years later issued the
ruling that made him famous: in a judgment against John D. Rockefeller's Standard Oil Company, he issued a fine for the staggering amount of $29,240,000.
Although the fine was overturned on appeal, Landis became something of a
trust-busting national hero.

He continued to preside over a number of high-profile cases, including one
involving Major League Baseball. In 1915, the upstart Federal League sued the
American and National Leagues for antitrust violations. The Feds had a strong
case, but after testimony was finished, Landis delayed making a ruling. The
Judge was an avid fan with a frequent presence at the Chicago ballparks, and his
sentiments were obvious. "Do you realize that a decision in this case may tear
down the very foundations of the game, so loved by thousands, and do you realize that a decision must also seriously affect both parties?" he asked the Federal
League attorneys. "Recognizing that if he ruled in favor of Organized Baseball
he would be reversed on appeal, Landis simply stalled," wrote David Pietrusza.
When the struggling Feds finally agreed to an out-of-court settlement, Landis
was credited for helping save baseball . . . and put himself on the path that led
to his becoming commissioner.[14]

A colorful figure with white hair and a stern presence, Landis was a popular choice for baseball's most powerful position. "Bankers, lawyers, leading merchants and other prominent Chicagoans, in fact all lovers of the national pastime, hailed the move as the biggest step forward ever made in organized baseball," wrote Larry Woltz. "Baseball needed a touch of class and distinction," quipped comedian and social commentator Will Rogers. "So somebody said: 'Get that old boy who sits behind first base all the time. He's out there every day anyway.' So they offered him a season's pass and he jumped at it. But don't kid yourself that that old bird isn't going to make those baseball birds walk the chalk-line."[15]

In his first in-depth interview on November 28, Landis said, "The keynote of the entire new outlined plan is to rid our great national game of the sinister and oppressive burden of gambling. Untiring effort will certainly effect this, and untiring effort is what I propose to bring to bear. . . . As for the gamblers, they will be attended to with a firm hand." He had a warning for the indicted White Sox players: "Concerning the players implicated, suffice it to say that there is absolutely no chance for any of them to creep back into organized baseball. They will be and will remain outlaws. While it may be that no further fitting punishment will be found possible in certain cases, it is sure that the guilt of some them at least will be proved."[16]

Even Ban Johnson announced support of Landis's appointment. "I am for Judge Landis and I think these club owners have acted wisely," said Johnson. "Baseball will be placed on the highest possible standard now, and there will be no more fights. I am satisfied with everything that took place today."[17] But it wasn't long before Johnson began stirring up trouble again. In December, when Johnson needed to select the three American League representatives to help draft the new national agreement, he chose three members of the Loyal Five: Jim Dunn of the Indians, Tom Shibe of the Athletics, and Frank Navin of the Tigers. Then, in selecting the four owners who would comprise the league's board of directors for 1921, Johnson ignored the league's long-standing tradition of rotating the spots on an annual basis; although all three Insurrectionists were due for spots on the board, Johnson selected only one of them, Jacob Ruppert of the Yankees, along with three members of the Loyal Five (Dunn, Clark Griffith of the Senators, and Phil Ball of the Browns). When Ruppert refused to join the board in protest, Johnson named Shibe to replace him.

Yankee co-owner T. L. Huston exploded when he learned of Johnson's move. "Johnson's action in breaking the precedent of eighteen years in not electing New York, Boston and Chicago members of the Board of Directors indicated clearly that he and his 'Willful Five' are dissenters from the new Landis regime in baseball, and shows how very deeply he resents the part which these three clubs had in bringing about the new order of things," said Huston. "During the past year Johnson has fought the appointment of Judge Landis as Chairman of the National Commission, and successfully resisted the Judge's entrance into baseball until compelled to consent at the recent Chicago meeting. His show of acquiescence is the veriest hypocrisy." Huston finished by saying, "The elimination of Johnson would automatically restore tranquility."[18]

Johnson responded by writing, "At our meeting, it was the sentiment that two members should not be brought into the directorate, as they had attempted to wreck the American League. Mr. Ruppert of the New York club was elected a member of the board, but declined to serve." He also accused Huston of removing a private letter Johnson had written to Ruppert regarding the gambling situation in Boston. Huston's response was that since he was half-owner of the Yankees, the letter was his personal property. He also mentioned another letter from Johnson to Huston, written in 1918 while Huston was serving in France, that claimed Hal Chase was guilty of throwing games. Huston had shown the letter to John Heydler. "Johnson faltered in his duty to baseball as a whole when he failed to act then on the information he possessed. It is due to his failure and cowardice that recent baseball scandals were not averted."[19]

Two days later, Boston Red Sox owner Harry Frazee wrote Johnson an open letter which accused Johnson of "gross stupidity and incompetence" and called on him to resign. "Regardless of the attitude of anybody else in the American League, I want you to know that from this time on there can be no peace as far as I am concerned while you and I remain in the American League," wrote Frazee. "If you have any sense of justice or realization of the harm you have caused baseball, or had one spark of manhood or any regard for the game, which has made you possible, you would tender your resignation as president of the American League before causing any further harm."[20]

Harry Neily, a Johnson loyalist who was secretly performing investigative work in preparation for the Black Sox trial at Johnson's request, stood behind his old friend. "If there is any vast internal dissension in the American League as a result of the recent 'open' letters of Capt. Huston and Harry Frazee to B. B. Johnson it is their own fault," wrote Neily. "The head of the league declines to make any reply to the recent outbursts of the eastern magnates, a stand in which he receives the commendation of thousands of baseball fans who have been sickened by the petty bickerings of the proprietors of the national pastime." Neily's *Chicago Evening American* also called Frazee's open letter "mythical," claiming that Johnson had never received it.[21]

But Johnson seemed to have more detractors than supporters. "Neither of the two gentlemen who addressed the above billets doux in reply to the Christmas greetings from Chicago are hopeful of immediate affirmative response to their suggestion that the best thing to do for baseball is to get out of it," wrote the *New York Times*. "Ban thinks it's wiser to stick around and wait for the skids to be applied, rather than hit the toboggan slide of his own volition. 'It may be for years, and it may be forever,' according to his theory of his tenure in office, and he is not sure he could ever get another job anywhere near as soft as his present one."[22]

Damon Runyon had his own take on the situation, writing,

> Everything was to be perfectly lovely in the land of baseball as soon as Judge Landis got on his $42,500 per year job!
>
> But now see what has happened!
>
> Old Ban Johnson and his cohorts promptly given Messrs. Ruppert, Huston, Comiskey and Frazee, the American League minority, "the work" the instant they get the opportunity.
>
> They elect a board of directors without reference to American League custom and tradition, which would have put the minority back on the board, but in strict accordance with their own balance of power.
>
> There is a loud report, a sudden swirl of wings, and the dove of peace goes fluttering out the window, its tail feathers slightly disarranged by the bird shot out of the minority's wrath.
>
> The war begins anew.
>
> If Judge Landis can spare enough time from his $7,500 judgeship to give a little attention to this matter he may save some people quite a bit of money in legal fees.
>
> Incidentally, he might put Ban Johnson in his place just for once and give everybody a well-earned rest!
>
> If the judge can silence Ban, if only for ever so little time, he will win the earnest gratitude of the long suffering baseball public.[23]

In Los Angeles, the grand jury investigation into charges of game-fixing in the Pacific Coast League was continuing. The investigation took nearly two months. More than 50 witnesses testified, including players, team and league officials, sportswriters, businessmen, and gamblers. Babe Borton, the former Vernon Tigers player and chief accuser against other players in the league, testified three times and provided documentary evidence that included drafts for $100 paid to unnamed members of the Salt Lake Bees. He also gave the grand jury several potentially incriminating letters, including three from former Bees star Harl Maggert. However, Borton denied any involvement with gamblers.

Numerous players reported bribe attempts from either Borton or Maggert, but insisted that they had refused the offers. While most of the players accused by Borton flatly denied his charges, deputy district attorney Frank W. Stafford commented that perjury was a common practice in grand jury hearings, and estimated that one of every three witnesses was guilty of perjury in some form.

On December 6, the grand jury returned indictments against Borton, Maggert, Bees player Bill Rumler, and gambler Nate Raymond, who would later be associated with Arnold Rothstein. The charge was criminal conspiracy, a crime punishable by imprisonment not to exceed two years or a maximum fine of $5,000. Specifically, the four were charged with conspiracy to throw games during a series between Vernon and Salt Lake in October 1919. The indictments cleared the Vernon club of Borton's charge that Vernon players had raised a slush fund to win the pennant. "Maggert and Rumler," the indictment said, "did purposely, willfully and corruptly make errors, misplays, fail to bat the ball and by other apparent or not lapses of real skill."[24]

On the surface, these charges seem like a mini-version of the Chicago grand jury indictments, only with a smaller number of players charged, along with a single gambler. But the Los Angeles indictments had a much shakier foundation. In an article about the PCL scandal for the journal *Base Ball*, Larry Gerlach wrote, "An analysis of the grand jury's decision indicates it was based primarily on expediency, unsubstantiated claims, speculation and political bias. Faced with conflicting testimonies and the absence of tangible evidence, the jurors decided to limit indictments to the individuals who had confessed to bribery, Borton and Maggert, or those against whom specific allegations were made, Raymond and Rumler." Clearing the Vernon team apart from Borton made little sense; as Gerlach wrote, "if Tiger players did not participate in the bribery scheme, why did Borton alone risk his career by hatching a conspiracy to provide bonus money for Vernon?" The grand jury also did not indict Salt Lake pitcher Jean Dale, who had received $500 from Borton and who "was the most suspect of crooked play" among the Salt Lake players, according to Gerlach. Nor did the grand jury look into charges of league-wide bribery.[25]

Ultimately none of the indicted figures stood trial. On December 24, Judge Frank R. Willis dismissed the indictments, ruling that conspiring to throw baseball games was not a criminal offense according to California law—an issue that would be a bone of contention in the 1921 trial of the eight Black Sox players. In his ruling, wrote the *Salt Lake Tribune*, "Judge Willis said the players, in signing contracts with their teams, had entered into an agreement to play baseball to the best of their ability. But, he continued, admitting for the sake of argument they had not done so, their act amounted only to a breach of a civil contract and, he held, was in no way 'actionable as a criminal cause.'"[26]

In another foreshadowing of the Black Sox indictments, the decisions in the courtroom proved to be of no benefit to the players in the eyes of league officials. After learning of Judge Willis's ruling, PCL President William H. McCarthy said of the three players, "If the law cannot punish them, it remains for baseball to do its share, anyway, and to at least keep them from participating in professional ranks."[27] In January 1921, the league expelled Borton, Maggert, and Rumler; the National Association of Minor Leagues also expelled the three players, along with Jean Dale. Borton, Maggert, and Dale never played professional baseball again; Rumler played outlaw ball until 1928, then was permitted to return to the Pacific Coast League in 1929 with the Hollywood Stars—the former Salt Lake Bees, who had relocated to California in 1926. At the age of 38, he batted .386, hit 26 homers, and led the Stars to the PCL pennant. He continued to play minor league ball until 1932.

"Baseball historians generally have praised PCL president William H. McCarthy [who announced his retirement as league president in December 1920] for his leadership during the scandal," wrote Larry Gerlach. "But, the forceful banishment of gamblers from ballparks and determined rhetoric aside, his primary concern was minimizing public concerns about the extent of crooked play by 'whitewashing' the Vernon team and avoiding a comprehensive investigation during the playing season." Nonetheless, Gerlach wrote, "The Pacific Coast League scandal, which preceded the Black Sox affair in exposing and exiling players, significantly increased national awareness of the pervasiveness of gambling in baseball and established the actions necessary to combat it."[28] Both scandals would force baseball to be vigilant about the threat of gambling; as problematic as some of McCarthy's actions—and inactions—were, that was a good thing.

Although indictments had been handed down, the last two months of 1920 were anything but uneventful for the members of the Chicago White Sox—both indicted and unindicted. On November 5, Buck Weaver, Swede Risberg, and Fred McMullin posted $10,000 bonds, while protesting their innocence. "They ask the public to withhold judgment against them until they have a chance in court to prove the charges untrue," said the *Chicago Tribune*. McMullin had more to say when he returned to his Los Angeles home a week later. "I confidently expect to be playing ball with the White Sox in the spring," he said after hopping off the train. "So does Risberg, 'Buck' Weaver and 'Happy' Felsch. I know nothing about the plot which led to the throwing of the series, and cannot speak for publication at this time. I was not on the inside of what transpired so, as a matter of fact, have little to tell. Felsch made no confession, as reported. He told me that the one credited to him was supposed to have been given to a newspaperman over the telephone, and that he did not utter one word published and attributed to him. . . . I am innocent of any wrongdoing. This will be proved at the trial."[29]

Weaver, who had spent the previous off-season in the Los Angeles area, spent the winter of 1920–1921 in Chicago, tending the soda fountain at a drug store operated by his brother-in-law at 69th and Halsted Streets. "I will prove myself innocent at the trial and I will be back in the uniform next year," he told reporter James Kilgallen. "If I knew for sure the series was 'fixed' and was 'in' on it, I could have bet a lot of money, couldn't I; I could have made a big pile. I didn't get a nickel on the series. The only bet I made was with Louis Comiskey—a pair of shoes that we'd beat the Reds. That was after we lost the first two games."[30]

Asked about Eddie Cicotte's testimony that he had attended the meeting in the Warner Hotel in Chicago where the fix was planned, Weaver said, "Suppose you are asked to come and hear a proposition. You go and hear it. Then you say 'no'—absolutely no—and then you go ahead about your business and play ball. Are you a crook?" He told Kilgallen, "I will tell everything about myself, but there is one thing I won't do, and that is to say anything against anyone else. I hate a squealer."[31]

Weaver contributed $25 to a Christmas fund organized by Sam Hall, the sports editor of the *Chicago Herald and Examiner*. He included a note, signed "George D. Weaver," which finished, "This is not going to be the merriest Christmas in the world for me because I will have to wait until after the holidays for my trial. Then I will show the public what every baseball fan who saw the world's series, either in Chicago or Cincinnati knows—that I was trying my hardest during every minute of every game of that world's series."[32]

Despite his confession, Joe Jackson was also proclaiming his innocence. "I never have confessed to throwing a ball game in my life and I never will," Shoeless Joe said from his hometown of Greenville, South Carolina. That produced a prompt reply from Judge McDonald: "Jackson's testimony was made under oath before the Grand Jury. If he denies that testimony when he is brought to trial, he will be guilty of perjury and could be prosecuted under that charge."[33]

Another indicted figure, Hal Chase, both insisted on his innocence and proclaimed his lack of cooperation with the trial. From Los Angeles, Chase stated that he would not be responding voluntarily to the indictment issued against him. "If they want me let 'em extradite me," said Chase. "I am planning to go into business. Contracts in connection with it are already coming. If it were not for private reasons I would be glad to go to Chicago to testify, if they wanted me. They haven't anything on me."[34] Ultimately Chase would be one of several gamblers who were able to successfully resist extradition and avoid standing trial.

In mid-November, the *Chicago Tribune* reported that Eddie Cicotte would turn state's evidence and testify against his former teammates at their trial. "While no official announcement was made by the state's attorney's office," said the paper, "an official let it become known that except for Cicotte's testimony the jury never would have had sufficient evidence to indict more than one or two persons, and there would be little chance for conviction without the pitcher as a state witness." But a day later Cicotte's attorney, D. P. Cassidy, denied the report.[35]

In an email to the author, Black Sox historian and former prosecutor Bill Lamb commented on the idea of Cicotte testifying for the prosecution, writing,

Regarding the three players who admitted their fix involvement to the Cook County grand jury (Eddie Cicotte, Joe Jackson, and Lefty Williams), prosecutors conducted pretrial negotiations with Cicotte's lawyer (Dan Cassidy) about Cicotte turning State's evidence and testifying against his codefendants, but those negotiations ultimately foundered. How valuable Cicotte might have been as a prosecution witness would have turned on two things: (1) his candor, and (2) juror receptivity to codefendant testimony. Regarding the former, it is my view that Cicotte was far from forthcoming before the grand jury, minimizing his own deep involvement in the fix conspiracy and claiming ignorance regarding the identity of those who financed the fix. And if unindicted fix financier Arnold Rothstein was the actual target of desired Cicotte testimony, same would have been unavailing anyway, as Rothstein always used intermediaries (like Sport Sullivan and Nat Evans, aka Brown) when dealing with the corrupted players. So Cicotte does not strike me as likely a great prosecution witness, particularly against the gambler defendants whom he had no direct interaction with.[36]

With or without Cicotte testifying for the proposition, the road to a trial for the eight accused players and five gamblers was getting rocky. The November elections had resulted in the installation of a new Cook County State's Attorney, Republican Robert E. Crowe, who would now have charge of the trial. This meant that Assistant State's Attorney Hartley Replogle, who had secured the indictments, would need to be replaced. Another former ASA, Henry Berger, announced that he was joining the defense team of Abe Attell. And George Kenney, secretary to outgoing State's Attorney Maclay Hoyne, stated that the Cook County criminal docket had over 2,000 cases ahead of the Black Sox trial. "I don't believe the trial will be held before next summer," said Kenney—a prediction that proved to be 100 percent accurate.[37]

The change in state's attorneys quickly resulted in a messy situation. Shortly after his boss Hoyne left office, Kenney ordered Replogle to surrender to Hoyne copies of all statements and telegrams related to the baseball case. "It is said Attorney Thomas Nash, who represented Weaver, McMullin, and Risberg, indicted members of the White Sox, was nearby," reported the *Chicago Tribune*. Replogle refused, and Nash denied seeking or desiring the records, but a concerned Judge McDonald ordered that the grand jury record be impounded. Despite this Kenney was able to obtain copies of the documents for Hoyne, who insisted, "There was no scandal and no wrongdoing." McDonald was nonetheless concerned, and so was Judge Landis, who threatened a federal investigation if any grand jury records had been "tampered with or were missing."[38]

Within a short time, the fears expressed by McDonald and Landis came true. "The worst fears of baseball and judicial officials were realized weeks later when managing editor Keats Speed of the *New York Herald* began shopping redacted copies of the grand jury transcripts to various newspapers for a $25,000 syndication fee," wrote Bill Lamb. Hoyne denied responsibility, and Ban Johnson accused Arnold Rothstein of arranging the theft of the files. Rothstein denied stealing the files, as did attorneys allied with the various defendants. While evidence uncovered over the years involves several potential culprits, Lamb notes that "Most, but not all, Black Sox sleuths accuse Rothstein of engineering the thefts."[39]

In late November, one of the most respected members of the 1919–1920 White Sox, John Collins, spoke out about the scandal. Collins—whose nickname was listed as "Shono"—spoke at length from his Pittsfield, Massachusetts, home to Paul H. Shannon of the *Boston Post*. Shannon noted a "magnificent grandfathers' clock" in the hallway with an inscription that read: "Presented to Honest John Collins by the Loyal Fans of Pittsfield, Mass."[40]

After writing his own thoughts about the scandal, Shannon let his subject talk. "It is an awful thing to talk about," said Collins, "and it comes especially hard when you have to criticize men with whom you have worked for years—men in whose honesty and integrity you placed the fullest confidence." He said that when Shannon had reported talk of crookedness prior to the Series, "I laughed at the yarn." When Eddie Cicotte was badly beaten in Game 1, "we were willing to make allowances," as Cicotte had been complaining of a sore arm for the last month of the regular season. However, curious lapses continued, and "our players really began to be convinced that something was really wrong. . . . You saw the way that some of our men played all through that series.

Felsch, one the best outfielders in baseball, acted queerly when he went after two or three long drives. Others made errors, too." In an obvious reference to Joe Jackson and Buck Weaver, Collins said, "Some of the men accused of crookedness say that they hit well up in the averages for this series, and their fielding was nigh faultless. I won't argue for them along this line. I will only state that very few of these hits were made at the proper time and that errors were made just when they cost the most."[41]

After the World Series, Collins said, "Some of us got into communication with each other during the winter, and by the time spring arrived we had practically decided who the traitors really were." Suspicion pervaded the atmosphere once all the suspected players were in camp, and "we were two different outfits in the same club." He noted that in batting practice during the 1920 season, "the loyal players stood at one side of the plate and the others were by themselves. We seldom spoke, excepting to discuss a play or something connected to the game." He mentioned the suspicious series in Boston: "Cicotte was batted out of the box. Our men were hopeless at the bat. The big stickers fell down miserably."[42]

Collins expressed sympathy for Charles Comiskey, saying, "Poor Comiskey is to be pitied. I don't blame him a bit for the retarded investigation." He pointed out that Comiskey had relayed his suspicions to John Heydler, who "pooh poohed the idea," though Collins felt that "Commy should have gone to Ban Johnson. The reason he didn't is that they were on the outs." While the grand jury was taking credit for uncovering the scandal, Collins said, "I want to give the lion's share of credit to Jimmie Crusinberry, a Chicago newspaper man. Had it not been for his activity the game might not have been purged for a long long time." When talking about his indicted teammates, Collins said, "The only one of the crooks that I could make the slightest excuse for is Joe Jackson. His ignorance and illiteracy let him out to a great extent. I think he is easily influenced. But for the others I have no sympathy."[43]

Collins did not say he thought that Jackson played honestly; nor did he put in a good word for Buck Weaver. He held them as accountable as he did the other six players.

In late December, when American League magnates were in New York, working on the new national agreement—and a few owners were continuing their feud with Ban Johnson—Kid Gleason talked to syndicated columnist Joe Vila. He commented about his eight indicted players:

> I don't care to have any of those indicted players remain under my management. They must not be allowed to wear White Sox uniforms or play with any other

club in Organized Baseball. The baseball public demands the removal of every player charged with betting on ball games or associating with evil companions.

The indicted Chicago players were fools, pure and simple. They fell for a bunch of sure thing gamblers and barred themselves from the game that made them prosperous and would have maintained them handsomely for some time to come.

I had the greatest ball club ever put together when those pinheads went wrong because they couldn't withstand tempting offers to play dishonestly. Yet it was a hard task to obtain proof of their guilt until Cicotte squealed to the Grand Jury. Then the whole story was substantiated.

I haven't an idea how the White Sox will be reconstructed, except that Eddie Collins will play second base, Schalk will catch and the outfield will be covered by Jack Collins, Leibold and Murphy.

[Earl] Sheely and [Ernie] Johnson, new infielders, just purchased from the Salt Lake club, may help us a lot. Sheely is a heavy hitting first baseman, who is ready for major league ball, and Johnson has done excellent work at short and second.

It may be possible to arrange one or two trades before the winter ends. I need pitchers to replace Cicotte and Williams, but don't forget that Kerr and Faber still are with us. The White Sox next year will be above suspicion.[44]

EPILOGUE

Trials, Tribulations, and Thoughts

By design, the focus of this book primarily has been on the period from the day after the end of the 1919 World Series to the finish of the 1920 calendar year. Much occurred afterward, of course, and the lives and fates of the various characters in the story continue to be a topic of discussion over 100 years later. The story of what happened to these people after 1920 will be the focus of a subsequent work. In the meantime here is a brief summary of some post-1920 highlights involving the main characters, along with a few of my own thoughts.

Kid Gleason's 1921 White Sox may have been "above suspicion," but they weren't very good at playing baseball. The Sox won only 62 games in 1921, 34 fewer than the previous year, and finished in seventh place. The team's .403 win percentage was the worst in franchise history up to that point. John Collins wasn't part of that team; he was traded in March to the Boston Red Sox, along with Nemo Leibold, for future Hall of Famer Harry Hooper. Eddie Collins was still around, hitting .337; Ray Schalk (.252) was solid as ever behind the plate; and the duo of Red Faber (25–15) and Dickey Kerr (19–17) accounted for 71 percent of the club's 62 wins.

Their eight former teammates stood trial in July. The period from the time of the indictments until the start of the trial was basically one fiasco after another for the prosecution. Evidence was missing, including the transcripts of Cicotte, Jackson, and Williams's grand jury testimony; all three sought to have their confessions suppressed on legal grounds. Unprepared for a spring trial date, State's Attorney Robert E. Crowe dismissed the previous charges against the people indicted, then had new indictments filed, with several more gamblers now charged with the others. When the trial finally started, Sport Sullivan, Abe Attell, Hal Chase, and "Rachael Brown," who was probably Nat Evans using an alias, had escaped extradition. Arnold Rothstein, the main driver of the fix by most accounts, was never indicted.

With the probably fanciful notion that Cicotte, Jackson, and/or Williams would turn state's evidence no longer a possibility, the state's case relied heavily on Bill Burns, who had been retrieved from the Mexican border by Ban Johnson. Burns proved to be a witty and effective witness, but he only knew part of the story. The state won an important battle when Judge Hugo Friend admitted the grand jury testimony of Cicotte, Jackson, and Williams (re-created from stenographers' notes) after a challenge from the defense that the three had been promised immunity. Judge Friend determined that the defendants had confessed freely, and admitted their use as evidence, but only in redacted form . . . reference in the testimony to anyone other than the speaker was not permitted. That limited their effectiveness.

After Billy Maharg had testified in support of Burns's account, the state rested, with Judge Friend ruling that so little evidence had been presented against Buck Weaver, Happy Felsch, and gambler Carl Zork that he would overturn any guilty verdict against them. None of the accused players testified in their own defense, but the defense scored points in calling Harry Grabiner, whose testimony about the White Sox's profitability in 1920 undercut the argument that the fix had damaged the club. As the charge was conspiracy to defraud the public and there was no Illinois law against the corruption of sporting events, Judge Friend told the jury, "The State must prove that it was the intent of the ballplayers and the gamblers charged with conspiracy through the throwing of the World Series to defraud the public and others, *and not merely to throw games* [emphasis mine]."[1]

The jury needed less than three hours to come back with its verdict: not guilty for all defendants on all charges. This set off a wild celebration that ended with the jury and ballplayers adjourning to a nearby Italian restaurant. "There," wrote Bill Lamb, "the revelry continued into the wee hours of the morning, closing with the jurors and the Black Sox singing, 'Hail, Hail, the Gang's All Here.'"[2]

The celebration was premature. After learning of the verdict, Commissioner Kenesaw Mountain Landis issued a famous edict: "Regardless of the verdict of juries, no player that throws a game, no player that entertains proposals or promises to throw a game, no player that sits in a conference with a bunch of crooked gamblers, where the ways and means of throwing games are discussed, and does not promptly tell his club about it, will ever play professional baseball."[3]

He was true to his word: none of the eight players would ever again play in Organized Baseball.

They did play baseball, sometimes with several of the eight playing together, in exhibition games and "outlaw leagues" . . . anyone still in Organized Baseball who played against them also risked permanent ineligibility. Joe Jackson played into his late 40s. Chick Gandil, Buck Weaver, and Lefty Williams played in the Copper League, a circuit that also featured Hal Chase. Swede Risberg played in Manitoba and Minnesota and Montana and the Dakotas, playing shortstop and also pitching. He played against Booker's Flying Clouds. He played against the Joliet Prison All-Stars. He played against the House of David and the Colored House of David. He played against Negro League greats like Satchel Paige and John Donaldson, which is more than you could say about any league run by Judge Landis.

Some of them hoped for reinstatement, especially Buck Weaver, who petitioned Landis several times. When the Judge died, Weaver petitioned Landis's successors, always to no avail. He probably didn't help his case by trying to claim that he didn't know enough about the scandal to report it to anyone. Even in the days before his death in Chicago in 1956, Buck was telling James T. Farrell, "Landis wanted me to tell him something that I didn't know . . . I didn't have any evidence."[4] In truth, he had plenty of evidence of the fix well in advance of the Series.

Buck Weaver's failure to report the 1919 World Series fix led to his lifetime ban. He unsuccessfully fought for reinstatement for the rest of his life. *Library of Congress Prints and Photographs Division*

In 1933, when Joe Jackson was 45 years old, a group of businessmen from Greenville, South Carolina, his hometown, applied for a franchise in a new Class D league—the lowest level of the minor leagues. They petitioned Landis to let them hire Joe as a player-manager. Landis, as always, said no. Decades after his death in 1951, Jackson's advocates continue to petition for his reinstatement, in hopes that he can be elected to the Hall of Fame. Thus far the answer continues to be no.

Weaver and Jackson, along with Happy Felsch and Swede Risberg, sued the White Sox for unpaid salary. All of them collected a little money in settlements—for the most part very little. Of the four, only Felsch, late in life, admitted to playing crookedly. In the 1960s, Eddie Cicotte said, "I admit I did wrong." But most of them continued to insist on their innocence to their dying day. In 1969, 82-year-old Chick Gandil, the leader of the fix on the players' side and a man who almost certainly double-crossed his teammates by keeping most of the payoff money, told Dwight Chapin,

> Nothing. I never got anything. I'll tell you this, some the damndest liars there ever were got up on that witness stand in Chicago, especially that gambler, Sleepy Bill Burns. What was said at the trial made me want to start a suit right away but my mother talked me out of it. She didn't want the publicity and I went along with her.
>
> But now, from now on, I'm gonna sue the hell out of all of them. I'm tired of just taking it after all these years.[5]

He died a year later, still defiant to the end.

Charles Comiskey spent the 1920s trying to rebuild his franchise. He spent $100,000, then a record sum, for minor league third baseman Willie Kamm, who proved to be a fine player, but couldn't hit like Buck Weaver. Similarly, Bibb Falk was no Joe Jackson. Commy did do well with Ted Lyons, who pitched for the White Sox for 21 seasons, but most of the pitchers he brought in reminded no one of Eddie Cicotte or Claude Williams. When a worn-out Kid Gleason left as manager after the 1923 season, Comiskey hired Frank Chance, who died without managing a game for the White Sox. Then came Johnny Evers and Eddie Collins (as player-manager) and Ray Schalk (ditto) and Lena Blackburne, whose main claim to fame would be the cans of "rubbing mud" he supplied to umpires to take the gloss off new baseballs. Unfortunately, Blackburne rubbed his players the wrong way.

A mostly sympathetic figure after the Black Sox scandal broke, Comiskey found people turning against him during the 1920s. In 1924, syndicated columnist Frank Menke wrote a series of pieces about Comiskey and the Black Sox scandal with titles like "Comiskey Knew Series Crooked, Asserts Menke," and "Comiskey Concealed Truth of 1919 Games from Own Probers." Some of it was true; some of it peddled the shaky stories that Joe Jackson was trying to spin while battling Comiskey in court. The Comiskey-as-cheapskate tales, which were never accurate, began, and would get worse over the years. When Commy died at age 72 in 1931, many considered him a broken man. Comiskey was one of the first executives voted to the National Baseball Hall of Fame (in 1939), but such was the backlash against him that the great baseball labor leader Marvin Miller wrote, "[We do] not know to what degree the tightfistedness, mean-spirited and questionable tactics of the Chicago owner, Charles Comiskey, contributed to the conditions that made the players susceptible to gamblers but I've always maintained that the question 'Why isn't Joe Jackson in the Hall of Fame?' should be supplemented with 'Why isn't Charles Comiskey out?'"[6]

Judge Kenesaw Mountain Landis remained commissioner of baseball until his death at age 78 in 1944. His decisions could be arbitrary and inconsistent, but his importance in restoring confidence in the integrity of the game after the scandals of 1919–1920 is unquestioned. Landis's other legacy—his role in keeping Black players out of Organized Baseball—remains the greatest stain on his record. However, when it came to keeping baseball segregated, it should be noted that Landis received little, if any, pushback from the owners who hired him. "When Landis was gone and baseball was integrated, Landis served as a convenient scapegoat for the actions and attitudes of most of baseball," wrote historian Larry Moffi. "After Landis died, nobody rushed to sign black players with his supposed ban gone."[7]

Ban Johnson had lost most of his authority over the other American League owners by the time Landis had taken office, but he continued to make unsuccessful attempts to assert himself. His final challenge to Landis in the Cobb-Speaker case ended with his resignation in 1927. Johnson died four years later. National League President John Heydler, who was smart enough to defer to Landis, remained in office until he retired after the 1934 season. Heydler died at age 86 in 1956.

The success of Rube Foster's Negro National League helped spawn the creation of other Black baseball leagues and teams that continued to shine a light on Black baseball talent throughout the long period of segregation. "The Negro Leagues played an important role in stabilizing black baseball prior to the integration of Organized Baseball in 1946," wrote Merl F. Kleinknecht. "It insured that when the racial ban was finally lifted there would be an instant pool of talent to take advantage of this. The Negro Leagues were also a source of income to the black community, and in their heyday, they were the second largest black business interest per capita next to insurance companies."[8]

Arnold Rothstein was shot and killed in November, 1928, purportedly due to an unpaid $300,000 gambling debt. Barred from ballparks in Organized Baseball after the Black Sox scandal broke, Joseph "Sport" Sullivan continued to gamble on a smaller level before dying at age 78 in 1949. Bill Burns, who lived quietly and held several jobs after the Black Sox trial, died at 73 in 1953. Billy Maharg also faded into obscurity, working as a mechanic for the Ford Motor Company. He died at age 72 in 1953, about five months after Burns's passing. Abe Attell, who continued to deny his involvement in the fix while insisting that Rothstein had framed him, eventually went straight and opened up a restaurant, Abe Attell's Steak and Chop House, in Manhattan. A member of the Boxing Hall of Fame, the International Boxing Hall of Fame, the San Francisco Boxing Hall of Fame, and the Jewish Sports Hall of Fame, he died at age 86 in 1970.

A number of the writers who covered and wrote about the Black Sox scandal have been awarded the J. G. Taylor Spink Award, presented annually since 1962 by the National Baseball Hall of Fame to a baseball writer (or writers) "for meritorious contributions to baseball writing." Five of the first six winners—Spink himself (1962), Ring Lardner (1963), Hugh Fullerton (1964), Grantland Rice (1966), and Damon Runyon (1967)—covered the scandal, as did Fred Lieb (1972) and James Isaminger (1974). Unaccountably missing is James Crusinberry, who along with Hugh Fullerton did more than anyone in the mainstream press to maintain focus on uncovering the scandal. And while he worked for a small, gambling-oriented publication, Bert Collyer of *Collyer's Eye* broke more scandal-related stories than anyone.

After the 1920 season the White Sox wouldn't finish higher than fifth place until 1936, and would not return to the World Series until 1959—40 years after the fixed 1919 Series. Some people considered that a sort of karmic punishment for the Black Sox scandal. As a lifelong (and ever-hopeful) White Sox fan born in 1948, I was more prone to think, "That's baseball; we'll get 'em next year." In 2005, next year finally arrived: the Sox won their first World Series championship in 88 years, in glorious fashion (a 11–1 post-season that finished with four straight World Series wins over the Houston Astros). Watching on television from the STATS office in Los Angeles where I was working, I jumped as high as a 57-year-old man with a bad back possibly could when Paul Konerko caught the throw from Juan Uribe for the final out. Then I went home and watched the post-game celebration, finishing off a bottle of champagne in about 15 minutes.

If there was ever a Black Sox curse, surely the 2005 World Series championship ended it.

I will finish with a few thoughts about the scandal, the 1920 season, and the people involved.

LEVELS OF GUILT

Eight players were permanently banned for their involvement in the scandal. The evidence clearly shows that all eight knew about the scandal; that all but Joe Jackson (who was kept in the loop by Lefty Williams and Chick Gandil) sat in on meetings where the scandal was discussed; and that none of them did anything to stop it by reporting what they knew to their manager or White Sox executives (I am totally discounting Joe Jackson's late-arriving tales that he reported the scandal to team officials either before or right after the World Series).

This is not to say that all eight were equally guilty. Clearly the most active in planning and carrying out the fix were Chick Gandil, Swede Risberg, Fred McMullin, and Eddie Cicotte; Cicotte may have had second thoughts at some point, but not enough to return the $10,000 he was paid to lose games.

Next come Claude Williams and Happy Felsch. Williams, more than any of the eight, was woefully underpaid, likely conflicted from the start, and possibly coerced by physical threats into dumping Game 8. Felsch, who rightly or wrongly held some grudges with Charles Comiskey, seems to have gone along with things without giving it much serious thought . . . but that's an explanation, not an excuse.

Joe Jackson and Buck Weaver are the most sympathetic figures; both had excellent batting averages in the World Series, and there's no evidence that Weaver accepted any money. Jackson made himself look less guilty—and in his later tellings, totally innocent—with changes he made to his story over the years. Many people believe those stories; I personally put more weight on Jackson's testimony under oath during the grand jury hearings, where he mentioned asking Chick Gandil several times for the $20,000 he expected for his part in the fix. It's fair to ask that, if Shoeless Joe wasn't doing something to help lose games, why did he think he deserved $20,000? I am also mindful that Judge McDonald testified that Jackson had told him in chambers: "he had made no misplays that could be noticed by an ordinary person but that he did not play his best."[9]

The fact that Buck Weaver took no money makes him a more sympathetic figure than Jackson. If you've read this far, you cannot have missed the many contemporary stories full of admiration for Weaver and the all-out, hustling style of play he embodied. There was certainly a lot to admire about Buck. At the same time, it is undeniable that, from the planning of the 1919 World Series fix through the final stages of the 1920 season, Weaver aligned himself with, and stayed loyal to, the worst element of the Chicago White Sox team. According to the sworn testimony of several others who were in on the fix, Weaver sat in on meetings where the fix was discussed; Lefty Williams testified that after one of the meetings, Williams, Felsch, and Weaver walked around and discussed how they would go about fixing a game. The guy who hated to lose stood alongside the guys who, at the very least, had agreed to lose for money . . . until he was caught along with the rest of them.

Once the scandal broke, there weren't a lot of teammates rushing to Buck Weaver's defense . . . and not just because he kept quiet about what he knew for certain to be true. Not everyone thought that Buck Weaver always *played* honestly; Eddie Collins and Dickey Kerr certainly did not (Kerr had doubts about Jackson as well). Weaver's loyalty to his crooked teammates—and his performance in the games during the 1920 season that seemed most likely to have been fixed—don't exactly put him beyond suspicion. If his teammates were being blackmailed by gamblers into dumping games at points during the year, particularly late in the season, might not he (and Jackson) feel compelled to go along? Whether he always played honestly or not, Buck kept quiet, stood with the fixers—and paid a terrible price for it. It did not have to be that way. I subscribe to what Dickey Kerr said to reporter Ray Robinson in 1984: "If I had been approached," said Kerr, "I would have gone straight to Mr. Comiskey, the owner of the White Sox. Not getting any response there, I would have gone to Ban Johnson. Then, maybe, it would never have happened."[10]

1920 FIXED GAMES

It is pretty certain that the White Sox were fixing games in 1920. Three of the Black Sox (Cicotte, Weaver, and Felsch) admitted it at one point or another; their teammates universally thought so; so did players on opposing teams. As to why they were still fixing games, the chance to make a little easy money is a possibility, but I think it more likely that they were being blackmailed: go along with this or harm will come your way (including possibly by leaking the story). That is why I think it possible that both Jackson and Weaver could have been coerced into helping fix a few games during the 1920 season.

I mostly agree with Bruce Allardice that the number of fixed games in 1920 was likely fairly small, and concentrated toward the end of the season, when gamblers wanted to keep the White Sox out of the World Series. On pretty much everyone's list are the game in New York on August 28 and the three-game series in Boston from August 30 to September 1. I would add the two games in Washington on September 12 and 14, the July 18 game against the Yankees, the August 7 game against Boston, and three earlier games against the Indians that would have drawn a lot of betting interest (May 9, June 27, and July 25). No one will ever know for sure, of course. But without much question, fixed games cost the White Sox the 1920 American League pennant.

COMISKEY'S COMPLICITY

Thanks to the work of researchers like Bob Hoie and Michael Haupert, we now know that the notion of Charles Comiskey as a skinflint who invited the scandal by abusing and underpaying his players has been seriously in error; on the contrary, Comiskey was one of the more generous owners by the standards of his time . . . with the caveat that those standards gave the owners all the leverage.

A more difficult charge for Comiskey to escape is that by January or February of 1920, he had enough evidence of his players' guilt to banish them. Instead, he covered up what he knew and brought everyone back except Chick Gandil (and that wasn't for lack of trying). Two things are relevant here. One is that he clearly had a conflict of interest, as banishing the players would seriously damage the value of his franchise. The other is that there is a difference between not having enough information to convict his players in a court of law—which seemed to be Alfred Austrian's argument for re-signing the players—and having enough information to say, "I don't want these guys on my team any more."

Of course, an investigation into the crookedness of the 1919 World Series should not have been Charles Comiskey's responsibility; that should have been the job of the National Commission. And Comiskey did relay his suspicions to one of the members of the Commission, John Heydler, as early as Game 2 of the Series. Heydler passed on the tip to Ban Johnson, who dismissed it. I think any onus for a "cover-up" falls much more heavily on those two than Comiskey.

But that doesn't take Commy off the hook. I began this project as a Comiskey sympathizer, thinking that he sincerely felt that he did not have enough evidence to banish the eight players. I have changed my opinion in good part through the work of, and my own personal interactions with, historian and former prosecutor Bill Lamb, who ranks among the greatest of Black Sox researchers. As Bill put it in one of his emails, "It is my opinion that the in-house investigation discreetly overseen by Sox corporation counsel Alfred Austrian had produced information sufficient for Comiskey to conclude that Sox players had thrown the Series. But rather than take action against the players and break up a championship team, he opted for self-interest and hoped that the matter would blow over—a strategy that almost worked, by the way." In Comiskey's own time, in October 1920, Oscar Reichow made the same argument: "I am compelled to criticize Comiskey for not doing it and for letting the players stay on his team this season. They should not have been permitted to put on a uniform on any team, considering the clouds that hung over their heads. I am inclined to feel that Comiskey and Gleason knew enough after their investigation, which they said they made, to step out publicly and say these were the men accused, and although nothing tangible had been obtained, enough had been found to keep them out of baseball."[11]

I feel great sympathy for Charles Comiskey, as I do for most of the eight banished players (well, not so much for Gandil, Risberg, and McMullin). But I am compelled to say that bringing those seven players back in 1920 was a great failing on Comiskey's part . . . a great *moral* failing.

PERMANENT INELIGIBILITY FOR ALL EIGHT PLAYERS

The fact that the eight White Sox players were found not guilty by a Chicago jury has little relevance as to whether they should have been allowed to continue to play Major League Baseball. Merely throwing games, as noted earlier, was not a crime by Illinois law . . . but Organized Baseball would certainly be justified in banishing the players for doing so. Cicotte, Jackson, and Williams had confessed to taking money to lose the Series; their grand jury testimony, and the testimony of Burns and Maharg at the trial, implicated the others. The players' assertion that "we were playing to win in the World Series" can neither be proven nor disproven . . . even by a .375 batting average. The players agreed to take money for losing the Series; then they went out and lost it. That ought to be enough.

"Judge Landis suspended the eight players, despite the fact that they were acquitted in court, because he held the reasonable position that team sports must be held to a higher standard of conduct than what the law allows," wrote Joe Jackson biographer David Fleitz.

Failure to do so would eventually destroy baseball, because baseball survives only as long as the public has confidence in its honesty. That confidence was severely shaken in 1920; it took four years for the major leagues to match the attendance record set in 1920, and the Chicago White Sox did not surpass their 1920 attendance record until 1946. Judge Landis used harsh medicine in banning the eight Black Sox, but merciless as it was, it restored the public's faith in the game.[12]

The toughest case is Buck Weaver's, as there is no evidence that he took any money. His only really provable crime was guilty knowledge of crooked play that he failed to report. While players may have gotten away with this in the past, Judge Landis had good reason to draw the line with Weaver. Landis biographer David Pietrusza wrote,

> Before 1920 if one player approached another to throw a contest, there was a very good chance he would not be informed upon. Now, there was an excellent chance he *would* be turned in. No honest player wanted to meet the same fate as Buck Weaver. The Weaver decision had a great chilling effect on dishonest play—and *talk* of dishonest play. After Landis took control of baseball, only two new attempts at game-fixing took place at the major league level: the Shufflin' Phil Douglas case of 1922 and the O'Connell-Dolan affair of 1924. In both cases players approached to throw games almost instantly turned in their would-be seducers.
>
> When Cardinals outfielder Les Mann informed on the pathetic drunk Douglas and the Phils' Heinie Sand did the same to naïve Jimmy O'Connell, the shadow of Buck Weaver was not only in evidence, it was lengthening to cover—and protect—all of baseball. Without the forbidding example of Buck Weaver to haunt them, it is unlikely Mann and Sand would have snitched on their fellow players. After Landis' unforgiving treatment of the popular and basically honest Weaver they dared not to. And once prospectively crooked players knew that honest players would no longer shield them, *the scandals stopped.*[13]

Yet might not Landis have shown some mercy? Weaver petitioned for reinstatement for decades, long after he could have played Major League Baseball. Given that Weaver's crime was likely not as great as the others, Landis—with his point about the need to report solicitation of crooked play having been made loud and clear—could have reinstated Weaver somewhere along the way . . . only, however, if Weaver had admitted the truth about sitting in on the meetings where the fix was planned.

Similarly, when friends of Joe Jackson petitioned Landis to let the aged Shoeless Joe come back as the player-manager of his hometown team in the lower minor leagues, that might have been a good time for forgiveness . . . but again, only on the condition that Jackson fully own up to his participation in the fix. It never happened, however.

In this long, sad story, forgiveness has been hard to come by.

NOTES

Chapter 1   Prelude: 1917

1. Harold Seymour and Dorothy Seymour Mills, *Baseball: The Golden Age* (New York: Oxford University Press, 1971), 278.

2. James Crusinberry, "Riot at Sox Game Started by Gamblers of Boston," *Chicago Tribune*, June 18, 1917, 13.

3. James Crusinberry, "Fans in Boston Riot on Field As Sox Win, 7–2," *Chicago Tribune*, June 17, 1917, 17; Crusinberry, "Riot at Sox Game."

4. Crusinberry, "Fans in Boston Riot."

5. Edward F. Martin, "Fans Crowd on Fenway Diamond," *Boston Globe*, June 17, 1917, 1; "Two Sox Served with Warrants," *Chicago Tribune*, June 19, 1917, 11.

6. John J. Hallahan, "Attempt to Halt Game Fails; Red Sox Lost 7–2," *Boston Herald*, June 17, 1917, 12.

7. Hallahan; "Attempt to Halt Game Fails"; Martin, "Fans Crowd on Fenway Diamond."

8. Crusinberry, "Riot at Sox Game."

9. John S. Robbins, "Can't Hold Off Any Longer in This Case," *Sporting News*, June 21, 1917, 1.

10. John Alcock, "Sox Riot Brings Vow of War on Gamblers by Prexy Johnson," *Chicago Tribune*, June 18, 1917, 13; Letter from Ban Johnson to D. T. Green, BA MSS 16, Black Sox Scandal (American League Records) 1914–1969, National Baseball Hall of Fame Library, Cooperstown, New York, Johnson HOF Files, box 1, folder 7, May 6, 1921.

11. Jacob Pomrenke, "'Call the Game!' The 1972 Fenway Park Gamblers Riot," in *Base Ball: A Journal of the Early Game, Vol. 6*, ed. William Lamb (Jefferson, NC: McFarland & Co., Spring 2012), 3–15.

12. "Gandil Receives Broken Nose in Yesterday's Game," *Washington Times*, June 21, 1912, 14; Joe S. Jackson, "Sporting Facts and Fancies," *Washington Post*, June 22, 1912, 8.

13. Buck Weaver as told to Hal Totten, "1917: Chicago White Sox 8, New York Giants 5," in *The Third Fireside Book of Baseball*, ed. Charles Einstein (New York: Simon and Schuster, 1968), 490.

14. James R. Nitz, "Happy Felsch," in *Scandal on the South Side: The 1919 Chicago White Sox*, ed. Jacob Pomrenke (Phoenix: Society of American Baseball Research, 2015), 53.

15. E. A. Batchelor, "Tigers Drop Both Games to Chicago," *Detroit Free Press*, September 3, 1917, 11; G. A. Axelson, "35,000 Fans Go Wild As Sox Win Two," *Chicago Herald and Examiner*, September 3, 1917, 8; "Notes," *Chicago Tribune*, May 3, 1917, 11.

16. E. A. Batchelor, "White Sox Beat Tigers Twice More," *Detroit Free Press*, September 4, 1917, 9; "White Hose Profit by Wildness of Tige Hurlers and Cop 2 Games," *Detroit Times*, September 4, 1917, 4.

17. Irving Vaughan, "Rowland Will Use Box Scores As His Defense," *Chicago Tribune*, January 5, 1927, 19.

18. Don Maxwell, "26 Deny Charges of 'Thrown' Games," *Chicago Tribune*, January 6, 1927, 15–16; "What Chick Gandil and Bill James Told Landis," *Chicago Tribune*, January 8, 1927, 20.

19. "Rowland Provides Laugh in His Views on Sisler," *St. Louis Star-Times*, September 7, 1917, 13.

20. Clarence F. Lloyd, "Jones Ready to Quit to Restore Harmony in Ranks of Browns," *St. Louis Star-Times*, September 6, 1917, 13; John E. Wray, "Brownies' Revolt Ends; Owner Says He Was Misquoted," *St. Louis Post-Dispatch*, September 6, 1917, 24; "50,000 Damages Asked by Pratt and John Lavan," *St. Louis Post-Dispatch*, September 8, 1917, 10.

21. Steve Steinberg, "Del Pratt," Society for American Baseball Research, accessed April 6, 2020, https://sabr.org/bioproj/person/32b3be5d.

22. James Kilgallen, "Weaver Tells of 'Fixing,'" *Pittsburgh Press*, May 12, 1922, 30.

23. Fred Lieb, *Baseball As I Have Known It: From Honus Wagner to Johnny Bench* (New York: Coward, McCann & Geoghegan, 1977), 105.

24. James Crusinberry, "Sox 'Big Push' Brings Bedlam," *Chicago Tribune*, October 14, 1917, 17.

Chapter 2   A Cold (and Dry) New Year

1. William Evans, "Charles Comiskey, the Prince of Magnates," *Baseball Magazine*, December 1917, 209–11, 241–43.

2. "The Case of Joe Jackson," *Chicago Tribune*, June 6, 1918, 6.

3. "Comiskey Wipes 2 Shipbuilders Off Sox Roster," *Chicago Tribune*, June 12, 1918, 11.

4. George S. Robbins, "Desertions Rouse Old Roman's Anger," *Sporting News*, June 20, 1918, 1; David L. Fleitz, *Shoeless: The Life and Times of Joe Jackson* (Jefferson, NC: McFarland & Company, 2001), 148–53; Tim Hornbaker, *Turning the Black Sox White: The Misunderstood Legacy of Charles A. Comiskey* (New York: Sports Publishing, 2019), 257.

5. Geoff Gehman, "Shoeless Joe, the Babe and Bethlehem Steel," SABR Black Sox Committee Newsletter, December 2018, 9.

6. Bob Hoie, "1919 Baseball Salaries and the Mythically Underpaid Chicago White Sox," in *Base Ball: A Journal of the Early Game, Vol. 6*, ed. William Lamb (Jefferson, NC: McFarland & Co., Spring 2012), 17–34.

7. Lee Allen, *The American League Story* (New York, Hill & Wang, 1962), 82.

8. G. W. Axelson, *"Commy": The Life Story of Charles A. Comiskey* (Chicago: The Reilly & Lee Co., 1919), 309.

9. Eliot Asinof, *Eight Men Out: The Black Sox and the 1919 World Series* (New York: Holt, Rinehart and Winston, 1963), 15.

10. "Ban Johnson Decides Against George Stallings," *Buffalo Courier*, September 24, 1910, 9.

11. Donald Dewey and Nicholas Acocella, *The Black Prince of Baseball: Hal Chase and the Mythology of the Game* (Lincoln and London: University of Nebraska Press, 2004), 278.

12. Ibid., 279–80.

13. Stephen V. Rice, "John Heydler," Society for American Baseball Research, accessed April 5, 2020, https://sabr.org/bioproj/person/8d5071ae.

14. Edward Cicotte grand jury testimony, Chicago White Sox and 1919 World Series baseball scandal collection, Chicago History Museum, series 1, box 1, FF2.

15. Charles Fountain, *The Betrayal: The 1919 World Series and the Birth of Modern Baseball* (New York: Oxford University Press, 2016), 5.

16. Bill Veeck with Ed Linn, *Hustler's Handbook* (New York, G. P. Putnam's Sons, 1965), 258–59; Allen, *The American League Story*, 93.

17. Hugh S. Fullerton, "Fullerton Says Series Should Be Called Off," *Atlanta Constitution*, October 10, 1919, 8.

18. "Rumors Arouse Comiskey," *New York Times*, October 11, 1919, 10.

19. "Comiskey Denies Johnson Unearthed Crookedness," *New York Herald*, November 5, 1920, 13.

20. Veeck and Linn, *Hustler's Handbook*, 261.

21. Harry Redmon and Carl Zork grand jury testimony, Chicago White Sox and 1919 World Series baseball scandal collection, Chicago History Museum, series 1, box 1, FF2; Hugh S. Fullerton, "Expert for Evening World Tells How Championship Ball Games Were Thrown," *New York Evening World*, September 29, 1920, 19.

22. "Baseball Is Not Crooked in Spite of Big Bets on Games, Declares Christy Mathewson," *New York Times*, October 16, 1919, 26.

23. "Beware of Commy When He's 'Roused,'" *Sporting News*, October 16, 1919, 4.

24. "Comiskey Denies Johnson Unearthed Crookedness."

25. St. Louis detective reports, Chicago White Sox and 1919 World Series baseball scandal collection, Chicago History Museum, series 1, box 1, FF1.

26. Ibid.

27. Hugh S. Fullerton, "Judge Landis Asked to Take Charge of Investigation," *New York Evening World*, December 20, 1919, 8.

28. James Crusinberry, "Comiskey in Session with Gamblers on Series Scandal," *Chicago Tribune*, December 30, 1919, 11.

29. Ibid.

30. Timothy Newman and Bruce Stuckman, "They Were Black Sox Long Before the 1919 World Series," in *Base Ball: A Journal of the Early Game, Vol. 6*, ed. William Lamb (Jefferson, NC: McFarland & Co., Spring 2012), 75–85.

Chapter 3 Detective Stories

1. Hugh S. Fullerton, "Wishes Baseball Magnates a Scandal-Less New Year," *New York Evening World*, January 2, 1920, 22.

2. John E. Wray and J. Roy Stockton, "Ban Johnson's Own Story," *St. Louis Post-Dispatch*, February 15–16, 1929, 34, 7.

3. Eugene C. Murdock, *Ban Johnson: Czar of Baseball* (Westport, CT and London, 1982), 188.

4. Wray and Stockton, "Ban Johnson's Own Story."

5. "Editorial," *Baseball Magazine*, February 1920, 3.

6. Frank O. Klein, "Schalk Says 7 Sox Will Be Missing," *Collyer's Eye*, December 13, 1919, 1.

7. Oscar C. Reichow, "Ray Schalk Never Hinted at Anything Wrong in Series," *Sporting News*, January 8, 1920, 1.

8. Brian E. Cooper, *Ray Schalk: A Baseball Biography* (Jefferson, NC: McFarland & Company, 2009), 156–59; Gene Carney, *Burying the Black Sox: How Baseball's Cover-Up of the 1919 World Series Fix Almost Succeeded* (Washington, DC: Potomac Books, 2006), 259.

9. Frank G. Menke, "Joe Jackson Has Chance to Be Cleared in Scandal Case," *Nashville Banner*, April 23, 1923, 8.

10. Ibid.

11. William F. Lamb, *Black Sox in the Courtroom: The Grand Jury, Criminal Trial and Civil Litigation* (Jefferson, NC: McFarland & Co., 2013), 118.

12. David L. Fleitz, *Shoeless: The Life and Times of Joe Jackson* (Jefferson, NC: McFarland & Company, 2001), 195–97.

13. Ibid., 197.

14. Hugh S. Fullerton, "Expert for Evening World Tells How Championship Ball Games Were Thrown," *New York Evening World*, September 29, 1920, 19.

15. Bill Veeck with Ed Lynn, *The Hustler's Handbook* (New York: G. P. Putnam's Sons, 1965), 260.

16. Lamb, *Black Sox in the Courtroom*, 52, 62; "Grand Jury to Hear 'Mystery' Woman's Story," *Chicago Tribune*, September 28, 1920, 2; James Kilgallen, "Here's the Inside Story of the Baseball Scandal," syndicated in *Atlanta Constitution*, October 31, 1920, 2; Fullerton, "Expert for Evening World Tells," 19.

17. Happy Felsch detective reports, Chicago White Sox and 1919 World Series baseball scandal collection, Chicago History Museum, series 1, box 1, FF1.

18. Ibid.

19. Ibid.

20. Ibid.

21. Ibid.

22. Fred McMullin detective report, Chicago White Sox and 1919 World Series baseball scandal collection, Chicago History Museum, series 1, box 1, FF1.

23. Craig R. Wright, "The McMullin Factor," *Pages from Baseball's Past* (paid subscription newsletter), accessed June 17, BaseballsPast.com.

24. Fred McMullin detective report.

25. Ibid.

26. Ibid.

27. Chick Gandil detective report, Chicago White Sox and 1919 World Series baseball scandal collection, Chicago History Museum, series 1, box 1, FF1.

28. Harry A. Williams, "Gandil Statement Adds New Interest in White Sox Snarl," *Los Angeles Times*, November 18, 1919, 8.

29. "Gandil Says He Will Quit White Sox," *San Francisco Examiner*, December 8, 1919, 12.

30. Chick Gandil detective report; "Harry Neily, "Sox Refuse to Give Gandil Release," *Chicago Evening American*, December 23, 1919, 6.

31. "Weaver Spurns Offer to Coach Jap Squads," *Chicago Tribune*, January 2, 1920, 15.

32. Buck Weaver detective report, Chicago White Sox and 1919 World Series baseball scandal collection, Chicago History Museum, series 1, box 1, FF1.

33. Ibid.

34. Ibid.

35. Frank O. Klein, "Involve White Sox Pitcher in Attempted Wager on Reds," *Collyer's Eye*, October 25, 1919, 1; Swede Risberg detective reports, Chicago White Sox and 1919 World Series baseball scandal collection, Chicago History Museum, series 1, box 1, FF1.

36. Swede Risberg detective reports.

37. Ibid.

38. Ibid.

39. Ibid.

Chapter 4 Insurrectionists

1. Al Spink, "Commy Blames Pennant Loss on Quinn Decision," *Chicago Evening Post*, January 28, 1920, 24.

2. Hugh Fullerton, "Herrmann's Retirement Causes Odd Situation in Organized Baseball," *New York Evening World*, January 10, 1920, 10.

3. Al Spink, "Johnson Elected As Chairman Is Way to End War," *Chicago Evening Post*, January 7, 1920, 2; Henry P. Edwards, "Landis Will Probably Succeed Herrmann As Head of National Commission," *Cleveland Plain Dealer*, January 10, 1920, 16.

4. W. S. Farnsworth, "A.L. Insurgents Want Landis or Root for Commission Chair, But Not Killilea," *Chicago Herald and Examiner*, February 2, 1920, 12.

5. "Sweeping Changes in Baseball Code," *New York Times*, February 10, 1920, 19.

6. "Ban Johnson's Retirement Predicted by Baseball Men as a Result of New Peace Terms," *New York Times*, February 12, 1920, 13.

7. Larry Woltz, "Ban Johnson Shorn of Autocratic Powers," *Chicago Herald and Examiner*, February 12, 1920, 14; "Ban Johnson's Retirement,"13.

8. Harold Seymour and Dorothy Seymour Mills, *Baseball: The Golden Age* (New York: Oxford University Press, 1971), 271–73.

9. "Weaver Outhits Ruth," *Los Angeles Evening Express*, December 23, 1919, 24.

10. Robert W. Creamer, *Babe: The Legend Comes to Life* (New York: Simon and Schuster, 1974), 188, 205–13.

11. Jane Leavy, "Why on Earth Did Boston Sell Babe Ruth to the Yankees?" *New York Times*, December 30, 2019, https://www.nytimes.com/2019/12/30/opinion/babe -ruth-yankees-baseball.html?searchResultPosition=1.

12. Creamer, *Babe*, 210.

13. Frederick G. Lieb, "Ruth Brings Joy to Yankee Fandom," *New York Herald*, January 6, 1920, 22; James O'Leary, "Red Sox Ruth for $100,000 Cash," *Boston Globe*, January 6, 1920, 1.

14. John J. Hallahan, "Fans Differ in Regard to Sale of 'Babe' Ruth," *Boston Globe*, January 6, 1920, 1.

15. "Which Do You Prefer: Joe or Babe?" *Chicago Evening Post*, January 9, 1920, 10.

16. Swede Risberg detective reports, Chicago White Sox and 1919 World Series baseball scandal collection, Chicago History Museum, series 1, box 1, FF1.

17. Ibid.

18. "Risberg Quits Game," *Chicago Tribune*, January 9, 1920, 10; Oscar C. Reichow, "White Sox May Lose Services of Risberg," *Chicago Daily News*, January 13, 1920, 2.

19. Risberg detective reports.

20. Ibid.

21. Charles W. Murphy, "'Scandal Charges Prove Rumor Mongers' Ignorance of Baseball," *Chicago Herald and Examiner*, January 14, 1920, part 3, 4; Charles W.

Murphy, "Series Scandal Talk Sure Sign of Big Interest," *Chicago Herald and Examiner*, January 18, 1920, part 3, 5.

22. Fred A. Marquardt, "Sox to Give Exhibit Games in Milwaukee," *Chicago Daily News*, January 21, 1920, 19; Larry Woltz, "Kid Gleason Insists He's Not Worrying about Those White Sox Holdouts," *Chicago Herald and Examiner*, February 2, 1920, 11; Oscar C. Reichow, "Kid Gleason on the Lookout for Hurler," *Chicago Daily News*, February 3, 1920, 21.

23. "Felsch Spills Beans; Helps Comiskey," *Chicago Tribune*, February 13, 1924, 27.

24. Tim Hornbaker, *Turning the Black Sox White: The Misunderstood Legacy of Charles A. Comiskey* (New York: Sports Publishing, 2019), 289.

25. William F. Lamb, email to author, April 24, 2020.

26. Joe Le Blanc, "Perry and Baker to White Sox in Big Deal," *Collyer's Eye*, February 7, 1920, 1.

27. "Felsch to Yankees for Pipp Is Trade Sought by Huggins," *Chicago Tribune*, February 14, 1920, 13.

28. James Crusinberry, "One Pitcher of Value Sought by White Sox Boss," *Chicago Tribune*, February 16, 1920, 13.

29. David L. Fleitz, *Shoeless: The Life and Times of Joe Jackson* (Jefferson, NC: McFarland & Company, 2001), 204–5; "Jackson Enters Holdout Ranks," *Chicago Herald and Examiner*, February 13, 1920, 11.

30. Frank G. Menke, "Joe Jackson Has Chance to Be Cleared in Scandal Case," *Nashville Banner*, April 23, 1923, 8; William F. Lamb, *Black Sox in the Courtroom: The Grand Jury, Criminal Trial and Civil Litigation* (Jefferson, NC: McFarland & Co., 2013), 174.

31. James Crusinberry, "White Sox Hear Another Threat by Chick Gandil," *Chicago Tribune*, February 23, 1920, 14.

32. I. E. Sanborn, "Gandil Visitor at Cubs' Camp; Refuses to Sign," *Chicago Tribune*, March 5, 1920.

33. Forrest B. Myers, "Comiskey and Gandil May Confer Today," *Chicago Daily News*, March 9, 1920, 9.

34. I. E. Sanborn, "Chesty Bruins Already Clamor for Real Game," *Chicago Tribune*, March 6, 1920, 13.

35. Risberg detective reports.

36. Ibid.

37. Ibid.

Chapter 5   Waco

1. W. S. Farnsworth, "Big Baseball Scandal Due to Break; Zim, Chase and Lee Magee Are Involved," *Chicago Herald and Examiner*, February 27, 1920, 14.

2. "Magee to Ask Courts About His Release," *Brooklyn Standard Union*, March 7, 1920, 20.

3. James J. Corbett, "'Blacklist' An Injustice to Ball Players," *San Francisco Examiner*, March 7, 1920, 14.

4. "Young Negro Burned Today," *Corsicana (Texas) Semi-Weekly Light*, May 16, 1916, 1; James M. SoRelle, "Jesse Washington Lynching," Texas State Historical Association, accessed April 30, 2020, https://tshaonline.org/handbook/online/articles/jcj01.

5. "Punished a Horror Horribly," *New York Times*, May 17, 1916, 10.

6. Cameron McWhirter, *Red Summer: The Summer of 1919 and the Awakening of Black America* (New York: Henry Holt and Company, 2011), 127–48.

7. Tim Odzer, "Rube Foster," Society for American Baseball Research, accessed May 1, 2020, https://sabr.org/bioproj/person/fcf322f7; Matt Kelly, "The Negro National League Is Founded," National Baseball Hall of Fame, accessed May 1, 2020, https://baseballhall.org/discover-more/stories/inside-pitch/negro-national-league-is-founded.

8. "In the Wake of the News," *Chicago Tribune*, March 7, 1920, 17; Forrest B. Myers, "Comiskey and Gandil May Confer To-Day," *Chicago Daily News*, March 9, 1920, 19.

9. "More Coin or Trade, Is Weaver's Demand," *Chicago Tribune*, March 16, 1920, 15.

10. Harry Neily, "Sox in Bad Way; Infield Still Holdouts," *Chicago Evening American*, March 18, 1920, 7.

11. Harry Neily, "Teeth Fixed for Grind," *Chicago Evening American*, March 17, 1920, 7.

12. Warren Corbett, email to author, March 22, 2020; Steve Boren, email to author, March 22, 2020.

13. "New Rules Fail to Rob Cicotte of Slab Craft," *Chicago Tribune*, March 19, 1920, 9; Larry Woltz, "Felsch Is Fanned by Cicotte, Who Says He's Ready," *Chicago Herald and Examiner*, March 19, 1920, 11.

14. Harry Neily, "Sox Spin Yarns to Scribes at Waco," *Chicago Evening American*, March 23, 1920, 5.

15. Larry Woltz, "Sox to Meet Dallas Today," *Chicago Herald and Examiner*, March 20, 1920, 11.

16. Harry Neily, "John Collins Still Tutor to Sox Rookies," *Chicago Evening American*, March 30, 1920, 5.

17. Harry Neily, "Gleason's Eyes on Two Young Pitchers," *Chicago Evening American*, March 24, 1920, 5.

18. Larry Woltz, "Weaver Jumps Sox After Row Over '20 Salary," *Chicago Herald and Examiner*, March 23, 1920, 11.

19. Larry Woltz, "Tabor, College Boy, Shows Sox Real Flinging," *Chicago Herald and Examiner*, March 24, 1920, 11; "Sox Trim Local Nine at Waco; Williams Hurt," *Chicago Tribune*, March 24, 1920, 12.

20. "Magee Says He'll Publish Charges," *New York Times*, March 24 1920, 10.

21. "Lee Magee Makes Formal Charge Against Gaming," *Atlanta Constitution*, March 28, 1920, 2; "'Magee's Charges Empty,' Heydler," *Chicago Herald and Examiner*, March 30, 1920, 7.

22. "Comiskey Issues Warning to His Balky Athletes," *Chicago Tribune*, March 27, 1920, 13.

23. "In the Wake of the News," *Chicago Tribune*, March 30, 1920, 13.

24. Harry Neily, "Gleason Stuck with Extra Infielders," *Chicago Evening American*, March 31, 1920, 5; Harry Neily, "Sox Pitching Staff Team's Best Bet," *Chicago Evening American*, April 1, 1920, 5.

25. Forrest B. Myers, "White Sox Regulars Play at Fort Worth," *Chicago Daily News*, March 27, 1920, 15.

26. Larry Woltz, "Sox Sure They Will Cop Again," *Chicago Herald and Examiner*, April 4, 1920, 7.

27. "Misfortune Dogs Yanks' Footsteps," *New York Times*, March 26, 1920, 14; "Yankees to Close Jacksonville Stay," *New York Times*, April 3, 1920, 18.

28. Larry Woltz, "Gleason Talks: Sox Play Ball," *Chicago Herald and Examiner*, April 3, 1920, 7.

29. "'Hit the Gong,' Says Gleason, 'Sox Are Ready,'" *Chicago Evening Post*, April 5, 1920, 12.

30. "Sox Flee Downpour After 4 ½ Innings at Memphis," *Chicago Tribune*, April 9, 1920, 9; Larry Woltz, "White Sox Are Beaten in Last Exhibition Fray," *Chicago Herald and Examiner*, April 12, 1920, 7.

31. Harry Neily, "Lefty Leibold Proves Size Isn't It," *Chicago Evening American*, April 10, 1920, 5.

32. "Redskin Hurler Victim for Sox, Who Win, 10-5," *Chicago Tribune*, April 7, 1920, 9; Larry Woltz, "White Sox Starting Year with Heads Up," *Chicago Herald and Examiner*, April 11, 1920, section 2, 1.

33. Harry Neily, "Sox in Shape for Opener Here Wednesday," *Chicago Evening American*, April 12, 1920, 5.

34. Neily, "Sox in Shape for Opener"; "In the Wake of the News," *Chicago Tribune*, April 11, 1920, 17; Forrest B. Myers, "Sox Home in Shape; Ready to Open Play," *Chicago Daily News*, April 12, 1920, 19.

35. Larry Woltz, "Ty and Tigers Open with Sox Here This P.M.," *Chicago Herald and Examiner*, April 14, 1920, 7.

Chapter 6   A Good Start

1. James Crusinberry, "Sox Victors in Eleven Rounds of Thrills, 3-2," *Chicago Tribune*, April 15, 1920, 9.

2. Ibid.

3. Swede Risberg detective reports, Chicago White Sox and 1919 World Series baseball scandal collection, Chicago History Museum, series 1, box 1, FF1.

4. Ibid.

5. "Cubs Sued by Magee for Season's Salary; Also Series Coin," *Chicago Tribune*, April 15, 1920, 8.

6. James Crusinberry, "Cicotte Pitches Sox to Easy Win Over Tigers, 4–0," *Chicago Tribune*, April 18, 1920, 17.

7. I. E. Sanborn, "Browns' Local Debut Delayed Because of Too Much Rainfall," *Chicago Tribune*, April 19, 1920, 19.

8. Fred Turbyville, "Sleuths to Spy on Gamblers in Major League," *Chicago Evening Post*, April 18, 1920, 13.

9. Al Spink, "Early Jinx Has Resigned Job of Pestering Sox," *Chicago Evening Post*, April 18, 1920, 5.

10. I. E. Sanborn, "Sox Game Called in Third with Another Victory All but Won," *Chicago Tribune*, April 21, 1920, 15.

11. I. E. Sanborn, "Brown Blunders Make Going Easy for Sox, 7 to 4," *Chicago Tribune*, April 22, 1920, 15.

12. Irving Vaughan, "Faber on Mound as Sox 'Gloom' Tiger Fans, 8–2," *Chicago Tribune*, April 23, 1920, 14.

13. "Notes of the Game," *Detroit Times*, April 26, 1920, 6.

14. "Races in Major Leagues Showing Some Surprises," *Detroit Times*, April 26, 1920, 6; Malcolm MacLean, "Dick Jemison Picks the Sox in Flag Race," *Chicago Evening Post*, April 27, 1920, 10.

15. MacLean, "Dick Jemison Picks the Sox in Flag Race."

16. Eliot Asinof, *Bleeding between the Lines* (New York: Holt Rinehart and Winston, 1979), 117; Bill Veeck with Ed Linn, *The Hustler's Handbook* (New York: G. P. Putnam's Sons, 1965), 284; Lawrence S. Ritter, *The Glory of Their Times* (Prince Frederick, MD: Highbridge Audio, 1998), disk 3.

17. Bruce S. Allardice, "Playing Rotten, It Ain't That Hard to Do," *Baseball Research Journal*, Spring 2016, 64, https://sabr.org/journal/article/playing-rotten-it-aint-that-hard-to-do-how-the-black-sox-threw-the-1920-pennant/.

18. Asinof, *Eight Men Out: The Black Sox and the 1919 World Series* (New York: Holt, Rineholt and Winston, 1963), 145.

19. "Brings New Sox Evidence," *Chicago Evening American*, October 1, 1920, 1–2.

20. Asinof, *Eight Men Out*, 145.

21. Irving Vaughan, "Sox Lose First Game of Season to Speakers, 3–2," *Chicago Tribune*, April 28, 1920, 15.

22. Harry Neily, "Pale Hose Lost First Game of Season," *Chicago Evening American*, April 29, 1920, 5.

23. Forrest B. Myers, "Indians Defeat Sox in Ninth Inning 3–2," *Chicago Daily News*, April 27, 1920, 19.

24. Larry Woltz, "Sox Lose First of Season to Indians in Ninth," *Chicago Herald and Examiner*, April 28, 1920, 7.

25. Henry P. Edwards, "Tribe Puts Over Deciding Marker in Ninth Session," *Cleveland Plain Dealer*, April 28, 1920, 6.

26. Bruce Allardice, email to author, February 23, 2020.

27. Harry Neily, "Watch the Sox, Rivals Warned by Cleveland," *Chicago Evening American*, April 28, 1920, 5.

28. James Crusinberry, "A Newsman's Biggest Story," *Sports Illustrated*, September 17, 1956, 70; Neily, "Watch the Sox, Rivals Warned by Cleveland."

29. Risberg detective reports.

30. Malcolm MacLean, "On the Sport Trail," *Chicago Evening Post*, May 1, 1920, 8; Larry Woltz, "White Sox Rout Browns 8 to 5; Jackson Shines," *Chicago Herald and Examiner*, May 2, 1920, 11.

31. "Sox Notes," *Chicago Tribune*, May 3, 1920, 19.

32. "ABCs Score Double Win Before Big Crowd," *Indianapolis News*, May 3, 1920, 18; Dave Wyatt, "ABC's Triumph in First Home Games," *Chicago Defender*, May 8, 1920, 9; Robert C. Cottrell, *Blackball, the Black Sox and the Babe: Baseball's Crucial 1920 Season* (Jefferson, NC: McFarland & Company, 2002), 150–51.

33. Harry Neily, "Boners Cost Sox Four Games," *Chicago Evening American*, May 7, 1920, 5.

34. Ibid.

35. Irving Vaughan, "Risberg Spiked as Careless Sox Drop 4–3 Clash," *Chicago Tribune*, May 10, 1920, 19.

36. Harry Neily, "Poor Fielding Costly to Sox," *Chicago Evening American*, May 10, 1920, 5.

37. "Sox Notes," *Chicago Tribune*, May 7, 1920, 15.

38. Oscar Reichow, "Why Do Honest Ball Players Stand for Crooks in Ranks?" *Sporting News*, May 6, 1920, 1.

39. William J. Slattery, "Seals Drop Pitchers Seaton and Smith in Baseball Scandal," *San Francisco Examiner*, May 8, 1920, 14.

40. "Coast League President Opens Drive on Gambling Hyenas; Will Bar Them from All Parks," *Los Angeles Times*, May 10, 1920, 6; "League Votes $20,000 for War on Gambling," *San Francisco Examiner*, May 11, 1920, 13.

41. "Pays $100,000 for Honor of Sport," *Salt Lake Telegram*, May 14, 1920, 5.

Chapter 7   The Absent Brother

1. Hunter's Secret Service summary report, May 11, 1920, Chicago White Sox and 1919 World Series baseball scandal collection, Chicago History Museum, series 1, box 1, FF1.

2. Ibid.

3. Gene Carney, "Comiskey's Detectives," *Baseball Research Journal*, Fall 2009, 116, https://sabr.org/journal/article/comiskeys-detectives/.

4. Babe Ruth, "Give Sox Brown Derby, Says Ruth," *Chicago Tribune*, May 12, 1920, 15.

5. W. J. Macbeth, "Ruth Gets Another Homer; Williams' String Broken," *New York Tribune*, May 13, 1920, 14; Larry Woltz, "20 Hits, 2 Homers, As Yankee Bats Buy Sox, 14 to 8," *Chicago Herald and Examiner*, May 13, 1920, 7.

6. Irving Vaughan, "Sox Quit Rainbound Gotham for Boston; Cicotte Left Behind," *Chicago Tribune*, May 15, 1920, 13; Larry Woltz, "Sox Idle, Play Red Sox Today," *Chicago Herald and Examiner*, May 15, 1920, 9.

7. Harry Neily, "Lively Hitting May Feature Season," *Chicago Evening American*, May 14, 1920, 5.

8. Irving Vaughan, "Faber Breaks Losing Streak of Sox, 2–1," and "Sox Notes," *Chicago Tribune*, May 16, 1920, 17.

9. Grantland Rice, "The Sportlight," *New York Tribune*, May 16, 1920, 18.

10. Larry Woltz, "Sox and Boston to Scrap Today," *Chicago Herald and Examiner*, May 17, 1920, 8.

11. Irving Vaughan, "Sox Bobbles Cost Game to Boston, 2–1," *Chicago Tribune*, May 18, 1920, 13.

12. Vaughan, "Sox Bobbles Cost Game"; James C. O'Leary, "Stellar Fielding in Ninth Balks Chicago," *Boston Globe*, May 18, 1920, 7; Larry Woltz, "Boston Trims White Sox, 2–1, on Close Play," *Chicago Herald and Examiner*, May 18, 1920, 9.

13. Asinof, *Bleeding between the Lines*, 117.

14. "Dishonest Playing by Lee Magee Is Alleged by President of Chicago Club," *Cincinnati Enquirer*, May 21, 1920, 9.

15. "Magee Seeks Details," *Washington* (DC) *Evening Star*, May 27, 1920, 26; "Lee Magee Gains Point," *Baltimore Sun*, May 30, 1920, 13.

16. "Majors Set Sleuths on Gamblers' Trail in Every Ball Park," *Chicago Tribune*, May 21, 1920, 13.

17. Bill Lamb, "Charles A. Stoneham," Society for American Baseball Research, accessed May 18, 2020, https://sabr.org/node/42320.

18. Denman Thompson, "Joe Jackson This Year May Win Cobb's Title," *Washington Evening Star*, May 20, 1920, 26.

19. J. V. Fitz Gerald, "White Sox Rout Johnson to Gain a 13–5 Victory," *Washington Post*, May 21, 1920, 12.

20. Irving Vaughan, "Sox Notes," *Chicago Tribune*, May 30, 1920, 15.

21. James Henle, "'Betting Ring' Shows Peril of Ball Gambling," *Chicago Evening Post*, May 25, 1920, 5.

22. Harry Neily, "Hoodoo Still Pursues Sox Pitcher," *Chicago Evening American*, May 26, 1920, 16; Irving Vaughan, "Macks Act Like Real Ball Club; Trim Sox, 10 to 2," *Chicago Tribune*, May 27, 1920, 13.

23. Gary Webster (quoting *Cleveland News*), *Tris Speaker and the 1920 Indians: Tragedy to Glory* (Jefferson, NC: McFarland & Company, 2012), 46.

24. Larry Woltz, "Sox Drop into Second Division," *Chicago Herald and Examiner*, May 31, 1920, 8.

25. Irving Vaughan, "Sox Notes," *Chicago Tribune*, June 1, 1920, 23.

26. Harry Neily, "Sox Game Is Off," *Chicago Evening American*, June 1, 1920, 16; Irving Vaughan, "Slipping Sox Idle: Rain Prevents Tilt With St. Louis Team," *Chicago Tribune*, June 2, 1920, 15.

27. Irving Vaughan, "Sox Put on 11th Frame Thriller, Beat Tigers, 7-6," *Chicago Tribune*, June 7, 1920, 19.

28. Harry Neily, "Collins Mighty Handy Veteran to Sox," *Chicago Evening American*, June 8, 1920, 7.

Chapter 8 Trials and Triumphs

1. "'Treason' Hint," *Cincinnati Post*, June 7, 1920, 1.

2. Ibid.

3. Ibid.

4. Lee Allen, *The National League Story: The Official History* (New York: Hill & Wang, 1961), 161.

5. "Witness Says Magee Bet," *Cincinnati Enquirer*, June 8, 1920, 14.

6. "Heydler Says Magee Confessed Betting," *Cincinnati Post*, June 8, 1920, 1.

7. "Betting on Games Admitted," *Cincinnati Enquirer*, June 9, 1920, 12.

8. "Evidence All In," *Cincinnati Post*, June 9, 1920, 1.

9. "Magee Loses in Court," *Cincinnati Enquirer*, June 10, 1920, 9.

10. Tom Swope, "Magee and Chase Now Barred by National," *Cincinnati Post*, June 10, 1920, 14.

11. "Evidence All In."

12. Allen, *National League Story*, 163.

13. "Baseball's Housecleaning," *Cincinnati Post*, June 10, 1920, 4.

14. Sean Deveney, *The Original Curse: Did the Cubs Throw the 1918 World Series to Babe Ruth's Red Sox and Incite the Black Sox Scandal?* (New York: McGraw-Hill, 2010), 124.

15. Harry Neily, "Wilkinson Jinx Again Costly to Sox," *Chicago Evening American*, June 10, 1920, 7.

16. Irving Vaughan, "Lefty Williams Helps Red Sox Beat Sox, 3-2," *Chicago Tribune*, June 10, 1920, 17; Charles Dryden, "Two Passes by Williams Give Boston Another," *Chicago Herald and Examiner*, June 10, 1920, 9; "Hooper's Triple Big Biff in Downing Chisox, 3 to 2," *Boston Herald*, June 10, 1920, 17.

17. Jim Nasium, "White Sox Ragged, Merely Await K.O.," *Philadelphia Inquirer*, October 7, 1919, 14.

18. "Cincinnati Again Beats White Sox," *New York Times*, October 7, 1919, 1; Henry P. Edwards, "Those Were the Days," *Cleveland Plain Dealer*, January 14, 1948, 17.

19. Irving Vaughan, "White Sox Notes," *Chicago Tribune*, June 10, 1920, 17.

20. David George Surdam and Michael J. Haupert, *The Age of Ruth and Landis: The Economics of Baseball during the Roaring Twenties* (Lincoln and London: University of Nebraska Press, 2018), 81; 284.

21. "'Babe' Is a Home Body, Says Mrs. Ruth," *Chicago Evening Post*, June 9, 1920, 8.

22. Irving Vaughan, "Sox and Big Wind Hold Ruth to One Homer; Score 7–2," *Chicago Tribune*, June 18, 1920, 15.

23. Harry Neily, "Sox Drive Home Seven Runs in Fourth," *Chicago Evening American*, July 26, 1920, 1.

24. James Crusinberry, "Sox Slough Off Messy Game to Indians, 4 to 1," *Chicago Tribune*, June 28, 1920, 19; Ed Reticker, "Bagby's Hurling Too Good for Sox," *Chicago Herald and Examiner*, July 28, 1920, 19.

25. Harry Neily, "Pennant Hopes Soar in Sox Camp," *Chicago Evening American*, June 28, 1920, 9.

26. J. Ashley-Stevens, "World's Series Scandal Re-Opened," *Collyer's Eye*, July 3, 1920, 1.

27. James Crusinberry, "Browns Crushed by Avalanche of Sox Swats, 11–3, *Chicago Tribune*, July 4, 1920, 13.

28. James Crusinberry, "Sox Notes," *Chicago Tribune*, July 4, 1920, 13.

29. James Crusinberry, "Expert Defense Aids Cicotte to Beat Browns, 6–3," *Chicago Tribune*, July 5, 1920, 19.

30. James Crusinberry, "Sox Notes," *Chicago Tribune*, July 5, 1920, 19.

31. James Crusinberry, "Felsch's Homer Clinches Hectic Game, 5–4," *Chicago Tribune*, July 7, 1920, 15.

32. James Crusinberry, "Sox Intrenched for Dash to First Place on Swing Over East," *Chicago Tribune*, July 8, 1920, 15.

Chapter 9 Abe Tells

1. Robert Creamer, *Babe: The Legend Comes to Life* (New York: Simon and Schuster, 1974), 230–31.

2. W. O. McGeehan, "Home Run King Steers Car into Ditch to Avoid Crash," *New York Tribune*, July 8, 1920, 8; "Ruth is Unhurt in Auto Wreck," *Chicago Herald and Examiner*, July 8, 1920, 9; "Ruth's Leg Bruised, but Not Badly Enough to Keep Him Out of Game," *New York Evening World*, July 8, 1920, 19; Creamer, *Babe*, 231.

3. Harvey T. Woodruff, "In the Wake of the News," *Chicago Tribune*, July 9, 1920, 15.

4. James Crusinberry, "Sox Notes," *Chicago Tribune*, July 9, 1920, 15.

5. James Crusinberry, "Weaver, Hit by Ball, Tries to Smile in a Run for White Sox," *Chicago Tribune*, July 12, 1920, 15.

6. James Crusinberry, "Sox Grab Four Run Lead, But Griffs Pick Up Six and Win in 8th," *Chicago Tribune*, July 15, 1920, 13.

7. Fred A. Haynor, "White Sox Score 4 Runs in 3 Innings," *Chicago Daily News*, July 14, 1920, 19; Jack Nye, "Rice's Home Run and Courtney's Hurling Help Griffs Beat Sox," *Washington Herald*, July 15, 1920, 10.

8. Eliot Asinof, *Bleeding between the Lines* (New York: Hold, Rinehart and Winston, 1979), 116–17.

9. James Crusinberry, "Sox Beat Griffs Twice on Ninth Inning Rallies," *Chicago Tribune*, July 17, 1920, 7.

10. Harold Johnson, "Sox Drive for Pennant Now Begins," *Chicago Evening American*, July 17, 1920, 5.

11. Charles Somerville, "'Twas a Strange Game at the Polo Grounds, But, Oh, That Finish!" *New York Evening World*, July 16, 1920, 10.

12. "Ruth's 29th Wins Overtime Battle," *New York Times*, July 16, 1920, 20.

13. Malcolm MacLean, "On the Sport Trail," *Chicago Evening Post*, July 15, 1920, 4.

14. James Crusinberry, "Yankees Trounce Gleasons, 20–5, as 37,000 Jeer," *Chicago Tribune*, July 18, 1920, 15.

15. James Crusinberry, "A Newsman's Biggest Story," *Sports Illustrated*, September 17, 1956, 70.

16. Babe Ruth, "White Sox Not in Race Avers Ruth," *Atlanta Constitution*, July 19, 1920, 8.

17. "Babe Sets Record, Then Adds Another," *New York Times*, July 20, 1920, 14.

18. James Crusinberry, "Sox Notes," *Chicago Tribune*, July 21, 1920, 15.

19. Malcolm MacLean, "On the Sport Trail," *Chicago Evening Post*, July 22, 1920, 6.

20. "Erratic Defense of Sox Lets Indians Cop by 7–2 Count" and "Sox Notes," *Chicago Tribune*, July 26, 1920, 11; Henry P. Edwards, "Indians Hit Williams Hard and Defeat Chicago White Sox, 7 to 2," *Cleveland Plain Dealer*, July 26, 1920, 12.

21. "Erratic Defense of Sox Lets Indians Cop"; "Reds Play Indians in Exhibition Tilt Today," *Cleveland Plain Dealer*, July 26, 1920, 12.

22. Larry Woltz, "Eddie Collins Is Beaned, But Sox Trim Tigers," *Chicago Evening Examiner*, July 27, 1920, 8.

23. "Keefe Holds Sox and Macks Win," *Philadelphia Inquirer*, August 1, 1920, 17; I. E. Sanborn, "E. Collins Loses Ball and 5 to 1 Game in Sun," *Chicago Tribune*, August 1, 1920, 15.

Chapter 10   Scandal, Tragedy—and First Place

1. Malcolm MacLean, "Coming of Ruth Stirs Sox Fans to Real Frenzy," *Chicago Evening Post*, July 29, 1920. 7.

2. I. E. Sanborn, "Cicotte Blanks Ruth and Yanks; 40,000 Present," *Chicago Tribune*, August 2, 1920, 15.

3. I. E. Sanborn, "Pitcher Cicotte vs. Slugger Babe Ruth in 4 Times at Bat," *Chicago Tribune*, August 2, 1920, 15.

4. "Eddie Cicotte Tells How He Keeps Ruth from Poling Homers," *Chicago Tribune*, August 4, 1920, 13.

5. Babe Ruth, "Ruth Lauds Kerr for at Least Giving Him a Chance to Hit," *Chicago Tribune*, August 5, 1920, 11.

6. James Crusinberry, "Pace Too Fast for Cubs and Phillies Run Over Them, 4–1," *Chicago Tribune*, August 5, 1920, 11.

7. I. E. Sanborn, "Sox React from Ruth Strain and Boston Wins, 4–2," *Chicago Tribune*, August 6, 1920, 11.

8. "Harper's Gilt-Edged Pitching Brings 4 to 2 Triumph to Red Sox," *Boston Herald*, August 8, 1920, 14; Eliot Asinof, *Bleeding Between the Lines* (New York: Hold, Rinehart and Winston, 1979), 93–94.

9. Larry Woltz, "Sox Only Two Games From Top, Trip Griffs, 2–1," *Chicago Herald and Examiner*, August 12, 1920, 9.

10. Larry R. Gerlach, "The Bad News Bees: Salt Lake City and the 1919 Pacific Coast League Scandal," in *Base Ball: A Journal of the Early Game, Vol. 6*, ed. William Lamb (Jefferson, NC: McFarland & Co., Spring 2012), 44–45; "Babe Borton Is Released," *Los Angeles Times*, August 11, 1920, 27.

11. Al Joy, "Rod Murphy Names Nate Raymond as Baseball Briber," *San Francisco Examiner*, August 12, 1920, 15.

12. Gerlach, "The Bad News Bees," 47.

13. William Slattery, "Harl Maggert Unfolds Tale to Coast League President," *San Francisco Examiner*, August 13, 1920, 12F.

14. "Expel Crooks, Says Wrigley," *Los Angeles Times*, August 13, 1920, 25.

15. Mike Sowell, *The Pitch That Killed: Carl Mays, Ray Chapman and the Pennant Race of 1920* (New York: Macmillan, 1989), 20.

16. Ibid., 22.

17. Ibid., 61.

18. Ibid., 197.

19. "Mays May Not Pitch Again, Says Johnson," *New York Times*, August 21, 1920, 11.

20. Jim Nasium, "Mackmen Lose Two, One by Forfeit," *Philadelphia Inquirer*, August 21, 1920, 6.

21. I. E. Sanborn, "Sox Notes," *Chicago Tribune*, August 22, 1920, 15.

22. Ernie Harwell, "'What a Team!' Says Nemo Leibold, Recalling Black Sox Crew of 1919," *Sporting News*, December 27, 1961, 27; Donald Honig, *The Man in the Dugout: Fifteen Big League Managers Speak Their Minds* (Lincoln and London: University of Nebraska Press, 1977), 216.

23. Harold Johnson, "Gotham Scribes Change Tune, Laud Sox," *Chicago Evening American*, August 25, 1920, 10; Oscar C. Reichow, "White Sox Welcome Rest," *Chicago Daily News*, August 25, 1920, 21; Larry Woltz, "Sox Play Final Gotham Series," *Chicago Herald and Examiner*, August 26, 1920, 7; I. E. Sanborn, "Sox, As Leaders, Await 'Crucial' Yankee Series," *Chicago Tribune*, August 26, 1920; 11.

Chapter 11   The Suspicious Slump

1. Malcolm MacLean, "On the Sport Trail," *Chicago Evening Post*, August 20, 1920, 4.

2. Hal Erickson, *The Baseball Filmography: 1915–2001 Second Edition* (Jefferson, NC: McFarland & Company, 2002), 230.

3. Donald Honig, *The Man in the Dugout: Fifteen Big League Managers Speak Their Minds* (Lincoln and London: University of Nebraska Press, 1977), 216.

4. I. E. Sanborn, "Sox Drive Mays Off Mound, But Yanks Win in Twelfth, 6–5," *Chicago Tribune*, August 28, 1920, 9.

5. I. E. Sanborn, "Ruth-Less Yanks Mop Up Sox, 3–0," *Chicago Tribune*, August 29, 1920, 17.

6. I. E. Sanborn, "Jones of Red Hose Blanks Sox, 4–0: Williams is Bumped," *Chicago Tribune*, August 31, 1920, 13; James C. O'Leary, "White Sox Helpless Against Sam Jones," *Boston Globe*, August 31, 1920, 7; Harold Johnson, "Jones Defeats Sox Again; Score 4–0," *Chicago Evening American*, August 30, 1920, 8.

7. James C. O'Leary, "Cicotte Hammered Merrily by Red Sox," *Boston Globe*, September 1, 1920, 7; Ed Cunningham, "White Sox Again Yield to Prowess of Hub Hose," *Boston Herald*, September 1, 1920, 8; I. E. Sanborn, "Mud Field Glues Sox to Loser's End of 7–3 Game," *Chicago Tribune*, September 1, 1920, 19.

8. Oscar C. Reichow, "Sox Drop Another One to Boston, 7–3," *Chicago Daily News*, August 31, 1920, 17; Sanborn, "Mud Field Glues Sox to Loser's End of 7–3 Game."

9. James C. O'Leary, "Recall Defeat Handed Cicotte on Last Trip," *Boston Globe*, October 1, 1920, 9.

10. Malcolm MacLean, "White Sox Fans Will Give 'Gala Day' for a Regular Fellow," *Chicago Evening Post*, September 1, 1920, 12.

11. Harold Johnson, "Sox Play in East; Start Home," *Chicago Evening American*, September 1, 1920, 16.

12. Gerry Hern, "The Tipoff on the Black Sox," *Baseball Digest*, June 1949, 10.

13. Rick Huhn, *Eddie Collins: A Baseball Biography* (Jefferson, NC: McFarland & Company, 2008), 172.

14. I. E. Sanborn, "Sox Back, Glum but Grim, for Final Flag Dash," *Chicago Tribune*, September 3, 1920, 15.

15. Larry Woltz, "Sox Home for Browns Series Starting Today," *Chicago Herald and Examiner*, September 3, 1920, 7.

16. Oscar C. Reichow, "Sox Lose and Drop Back to Third Place," *Chicago Daily News*, September 3, 1920, 21; I. E. Sanborn, "Browns Win, 2–1, and Crowd Sox into Third Place," *Chicago Tribune*, September 4, 1920, 11.

17. "Heavy Wagering on Cub Game Causes Outbreak of Gambling Charges," *Chicago Evening Post*, September 4, 1920, 12.

18. "Start Quiz to Save Baseball from Gamblers," *Chicago Tribune*, September 5, 1920, 1.

19. I. E. Sanborn, "Sox Notes," *Chicago Tribune*, September 5, 1920, 14.

20. Ibid.

21. I. E. Sanborn, "Sox Let Browns Down, 4 to 1, and Move Up a Peg," *Chicago Tribune*, September 6, 1920, 15.

22. Malcolm MacLean, "Scope Out Gambling, Judge Tells Grand Jury," *Chicago Evening Post*, September 7, 1920, 1.

23. Eugene C. Murdock, *Ban Johnson: Czar of Baseball* (Westport, CT: Greenwood Press, 1982), 190.

24. Eddie Cicotte, "Any One of Three American Loop Teams Can Win Flag by Stepping Out Right Now, Declares Cicotte," syndicated in the *Pittsburgh Press*, September 7, 1920, 8.

25. I. E. Sanborn, "Asleep on Feet, Sox Dropped by Tigers, 5 to 0," *Chicago Tribune*, September 8, 1920, 24.

26. "Detroit's Huge Bets on 'Fixed' Cub Game Now Shrink to $3,000," *Chicago Tribune*, September 9, 1920, 19.

27. Letter from John Heydler to Ban Johnson, Black Sox Scandal (American League Records) 1914–1969, National Baseball Hall of Fame Library, Cooperstown, New York, Johnson HOF Files, box 1, folder 2, September 10, 1920.

28. "Ruth Injury Story a Gamblers' Canard," *New York Times*, September 10, 1920, 17.

29. I. E. Sanborn, "Five Runs Behind in Eighth, Sox Battle to 6–5 Triumph," *Chicago Tribune*, September 10, 1920, 15.

30. Joe LeBlanc, "Ouster of 'Wrecking Crew' Demanded of White Sox," *Collyer's Eye*, September 11, 1920, 5.

31. Oscar C. Reichow, "Gleason Begins to Prod His White Sox," *Sporting News*, September 12, 1920, 1; "Cicotte Begins Morning Drill to Regain Form," *Chicago Tribune*, September 11, 1920, 13.

32. Oscar C. Reichow, "First Place within Reach of the Sox," *Chicago Daily News*, September 11, 1920, 13; "Red Waves Over White 9 to 7 in Final Hose Encounter of Season," *Boston Herald*, September 12, 1920, 14; Larry Woltz, "Red Sox Rout Whitehose, 9–7, in Wild Game," *Chicago Herald and Examiner*, September 12, 1902, section 2, 1; "Red Sox Victors on John Collins' Day," *Boston Globe*, September 12, 1920, 15.

33. Joe Vila, "Baseball Menaced by the Gamblers," syndicated in *Philadelphia Inquirer*, September 11, 1920, 17.

Chapter 12   The Grand Jury

1. "Griffs Jolt Chicago's Pennant Chances," *Washington Post*, September 13, 1920, 10.

2. Joe Vila, "Baseball Menaced by the Gamblers," syndicated in *Philadelphia Inquirer*, September 11, 1920, 17; "Calls Upon Scribe to Tell His Tale," *Washington Times*, September 14, 1920, 16; "Gotham Scribe Too Busy to Bring Scandal Evidence," *Chicago Tribune*, September 17, 1920, 15.

3. "Gamblers Busy; Five Nabbed at White Sox Park," *Chicago Tribune*, September 14, 1920.

4. I. E. Sanborn, "Gift Tallies of Sox Hand Cinch to Griffs, 7–0," *Chicago Tribune*, September 15, 1920, 19.

5. Bill Felber, *Under Pallor, Under Shadow: The 1920 American League Pennant Race That Rattled and Rebuilt Baseball* (Lincoln and London: University of Nebraska Press, 2011), 189.

6. Gary Webster, *Tris Speaker and the 1920 Indians: Tragedy to Glory* (Jefferson, NC: McFarland & Company, 2012), 141–42.

7. Frank O. Klein, "Sox Reveal 'Inside' of Big Scandal?" *Collyer's Eye*, September 18, 1920, 1.

8. Larry Woltz, "Sox Grab First 'Croocial' From Yanks, 8 to 5," *Chicago Herald and Examiner*, September 17, 1920, 5.

9. David Fleitz, *Shoeless: The Life and Times of Joe Jackson* (Jefferson, NC: McFarland & Company, 2001), 300.

10. Larry Woltz, "Cicotte Holds Back Enemy as Mates Slug," *Chicago Herald and Examiner*, September 19, 1920, 9.

11. "Rumler to Sue for $50,000; League Will Be Defendant," *Salt Lake Tribune*, September 17, 1920, 12.

12. "Wild Heaves and Such," *Salt Lake Tribune*, September 18, 1920, 10.

13. "Wanted: a Brakeman. Apply Salt Lake Baseball Club," *Salt Lake Tribune*, September 21, 1920, 10.

14. "Is Anything Wrong with Sox? Fan Seeks Answer to Rumors," *Chicago Tribune*, September 19, 1920, 17.

15. James Crusinberry, "A Newsman's Biggest Story," *Sports Illustrated*, September 17, 1956, 69.

16. "Call Baseball Chieftains to 'Scandal' Quiz," *Chicago Tribune*, September 21, 1920, 1.

17. Robert C. Cottrell, *Blackball, the Black Sox and the Babe: Baseball's Crucial 1920 Season* (Jefferson, NC: McFarland & Company, 2002), 149.

18. Tim Odzer, "Rube Foster," Society for American Baseball Research, accessed June 13, 2020, https://sabr.org/bioproj/person/fcf322f7.

19. "Rommel Blows in 6th and Sox Win," *Philadelphia Inquirer*, September 20, 1920, 14.

20. I. E. Sanborn, "Cicotte Strikes Stride," *Chicago Tribune*, September 22, 1920, 15.

21. Larry Woltz, "Sox Must Take First Two from Indians to Lead," *Chicago Herald and Examiner*, September 23, 1920, 8.

22. William Lamb, *Black Sox in the Courtroom*, 37–38; "Sox President is First Witness of Day," *Chicago Daily News*, September 22, 1920; 1.

23. Lamb, *Black Sox in the Courtroom*, 39.

24. James Crusinberry, "Bare 'Fixed' World Series," *Chicago Tribune*, September 23, 1920, 1; Harold Seymour and Dorothy Seymour Mills, *Baseball: The Golden Age* (New York: Oxford University Press, 1971), 300.

25. Lamb, *Black Sox in the Courtroom*, 39–40.

26. "Plan Probe of Cohan-Tennes Losses on Sox," *Chicago Tribune*, September 24, 1920, 1.

27. Lawrence S. Ritter, *The Glory of Their Times* (Prince Frederick, MD: Highbridge Audio, 1998), disk 3.

28. "Plan Probe of Cohan-Tennes Losses on Sox"; "Charges Anger Sox Players," *Chicago Daily News*, September 24, 1920, 3.

29. "Game Today Is Last of League Season Here," *Cleveland Plain Dealer*, September 25, 1920, 18.

30. Henry P. Edwards, "Mails Proves Hero, Hurling Brilliantly," *Cleveland Plain Dealer*, September 25, 1920, 18; "Game Today Is Last of League Season Here."

31. "State's Attorney Defied, Hoynes Questions Validity of White Sox Indictments," *Denver Post*, September 30, 1920, 2.

32. Game Today Is Last of League Season Here."

33. "Proof of Baseball Bribery Found, Says Grand Jury Foreman," *Chicago Daily News*, September 24, 1920, 1; Lamb, *Black Sox in the Courtroom*, 42.

34. "Proof of Baseball Bribery Found, Says Grand Jury Foreman."

35. Charles A. Comiskey, "Comiskey Assails Johnson in Bribe Case," *Chicago Herald and Examiner*, September 25, 1920, 2.

36. "Grand Jury Hears World Series Plot," *New York Times*, September 25, 1920, 7; "Inside Story of Plot to Buy World's Series," *Chicago Tribune*, September 25, 1920, 1.

37. Henry P. Edwards, "Chicago Closes in on Tribe in 5 to 1 Battle," *Cleveland Plain Dealer*, September 26, 1920, 25.

38. Oscar C. Reichow, "World Series Fixed in August, Weeghman Says; 7 Sox 'In Bad,'" *Chicago Daily News*, September 25, 1920, 1.

39. Ibid.

40. "Crookedness Winked at by Club, Is Claim," *Chicago Herald and Examiner*, September 26, 1920, 1.

41. "First Evidence of Money Paid to Sox Bared," and James Crusinberry, "Sox Suspected by Comiskey During Series," *Chicago Tribune*, September 27, 1920, 1.

42. Crusinberry, "Sox Suspected by Comiskey During Series."

43. Larry Woltz, "Sox Suspects Skin Tigers by 8-1 Count," *Chicago Herald and Examiner*, September 27, 1920, 9.

Chapter 13 Busted

1. "Ex-Boxer Bares Plot of How World Series Was Framed by 'Ring,'" syndicated in *Washington Times*, September 28, 1920, 1.

2. Edward Cicotte grand jury testimony synopsis, Chicago White Sox and 1919 World Series baseball scandal collection, Chicago History Museum, series 1, box 1, FF2; William Lamb, *Black Sox in the Courtroom: The Grand Jury, Criminal Trial and Civil Litigation* (Jefferson, NC: McFarland & Co., 2013), 50–51.

3. "Eight of White Sox Indicted," *Chicago Daily News*, September 28, 1920, 1.

4. Ibid.

5. "Didn't Play Best, Jackson Told Chicagoan, Charge," *Milwaukee Journal*, February 4, 1924. 1; Lamb, *Black Sox in the Courtroom*, 178, 182.

6. All Jackson testimony quoted in the paragraphs that follow from Joe Jackson grand jury testimony, September 28, 1920, Chicago White Sox and 1919 World Series baseball scandal collection, Chicago History Museum, box 1, FF2.

7. Shoeless Joe Jackson as told to Furman Bisher, "This Is the Truth!" *Sport*, October 1949, 14.

8. William Lamb, email to author, June 15, 2020.

9. "Weaver, Felsch Deny They Took Part in 'Frame'" and "'Bunk,' Attel Says; 'I'll Blow Lid Sky High!'" *Chicago Tribune*, September 29, 1920, 2.

10. "Honest Sox Say They Had Plenty Suspicions," *Minneapolis Star*, September 29, 1920, 5.

11. "New York Offers All, Even Its Great Ruth, to Assist Comiskey" and "Boston Offers Aid," *Chicago Tribune*, September 29, 1920, 2.

12. Associated Press, "Eight White Sox Are Indicted; Cicotte and Jackson Confess Gamblers Paid Them $15,000," syndicated in *New York Tribune*, September 29, 1920, 1; "'It Ain't True, Is It, Joe?' Youngster Asks," *Minneapolis Star*, September 29, 1920, 5.

13. "Two Sox Confess; Eight Indicted; Inquiry Goes On," *Chicago Tribune*, September 29, 1920, 1.

14. All Williams testimony quoted in the paragraphs that follow from Claude Williams grand jury testimony, September 29, 1920, Chicago White Sox and 1919 World Series baseball scandal collection, Chicago History Museum, box 1, FF2.

15. Hugh S. Fullerton, "Expert for Evening World Tells How Championship Ball Games Were Thrown," *New York Evening World*, September 29, 1920, 1.

16. Bill Veeck with Ed Linn, *The Hustler's Handbook* (New York: G. P. Putnam's Sons, 1965), 261; Peter Williams, ed., *The Joe Williams Baseball Reader* (Chapel Hill, NC: Algonquin Books, 1989), 44.

17. "Hoyne Halts Baseball Probe," *New York Daily News*, October 1, 1920, 26.

18. "Indict Two Gamblers in Baseball Plot" and "McGraw Tells of Dumping Players," *New York Times*, September 30, 1920, 1.

19. "Halts Sox Inquiry; Hoyne Doubts Jury Power," *Chicago Tribune*, September 30, 1920, 1; Lamb, *Black Sox in the Courtroom*, 67–68, 76.

20. Harry Reutlinger, "'I Got Mine—$5,000,'—Felsch," *Chicago Evening American*, September 30, 1920, 1.

21. "Chicago Gandil, in Hospital, Calls Charges 'Bunk,'" *Chicago Tribune*, September 30, 1920, 2.

22. I. E. Sanborn, "Loyal Sox Idle; Match Close to Disgraced Suits," *Chicago Tribune*, September 30, 1920, 15.

23. "Believe Pennant Has Been Thrown," *Cleveland Plain Dealer*, September 30, 1920, 5.

24. "Umpires Say Sox 'Threw' 1920 Pennant," *Washington Times*, September 30, 1920, 1.

25. "John Heydler Puts Blame on Gleason," *Philadelphia Inquirer*, September 28, 1920, 14.

26. Alexander F. Jones, "'Benedict Arnolds' of Baseball Slink from View of Oldtimers, Who Can't Believe Disclosures," syndicated in the *Pittsburgh Daily Post*, September 30, 1920, 8.

27. Grantland Rice, "The Sportlight," *New York Tribune*, September 30, 1920, 12.

28. "New and Stronger Evidence Against Players Expected," *Washington Evening Star*, October 1, 1920, 1.

29. "Hoyne Claims 6 1920 Games Were Thrown," *Chicago Herald and Examiner*, October 2, 1920, 1

30. "4 White Sox Begin Fight on Fixing Charge," *Chicago Evening Post*, October 2, 1920, 1; "Four Ousted Sox to Fight for Jobs," *Chicago Evening American*, October 2, 1920, 1.

31. "Four Ousted Sox to Fight for Jobs."

32. "'Sport' Sullivan to Name Scandal's 'Master Mind," *Boston Globe*, October 2, 1920, 1; "Rothstein Quits as King of Gamblers," *New York Herald*, October 2, 1920, 2.

33. "Riddle White Sox, Loyal, Confident, Play Browns Today," *Chicago Tribune*, October 1, 1920, 19.

Chapter 14   A Bitter Month

1. Jonathan Yardley, *Ring: A Biography of Ring Lardner* (New York: Atheneum, 1984), 5.

2. Ring Lardner, "Lardner Dopes World Series," syndicated in *Chicago Herald and Examiner*, October 3, 1920, 15.

3. "White Sox Players Accuse Teammates," *New York Times*, October 4, 1920, 8.

4. James Crusinberry, "Comiskey Gives $1,500 Each to His Honest Sox," *Chicago Tribune*, October 5, 1920, 19.

5. John B. Sheridan, "Back of Home Plate," *Sporting News*, October 7, 1920, 4.

6. "Fix These Faces in Your Memory," *Sporting News*, October 7, 1920, 2.

7. "Men Higher Up Involved in Scandal, Players Hint," *Boston Globe*, October 6, 1920, 11.

8. William Lamb, *Black Sox in the Courtroom* (Jefferson, NC: McFarland & Co., 2013), 70–71; "National Leaguers Facing Indictment," *Boston Globe*, October 6, 1920, 1.

9. "Marquard's Days with Robins Ended," *New York Times*, October 13, 1920, 21.

10. "Lardner Quits in 7th Inning," syndicated in *Chicago Herald and Examiner*, October 11, 1920, 10.

11. Oscar C. Reichow, "Chicago Fans Grieve Most for Weaver and Still Hope for Him," *Sporting News*, October 14, 1920, 2.

12. Ibid.

13. "Prize Offered for Best Plan to Place National Game Above Suspicion," *Chicago Evening Post*, October 13, 1920, 12.

14. "Chase Prime Mover in 'Framing' 1919 Series," *Boston Globe*, October 23, 1920, 6.

15. "Abe Attell Tells How Big Series Games Were Fixed," *San Francisco Chronicle*, October 30, 1920, 22.

16. Harry G. Redmon grand jury testimony, October 26, 1920, and Carl Zork deposition, October 27, 1920, Chicago White Sox and 1919 World Series baseball scandal collection, Chicago History Museum, Box 1, FF2.

17. "Sox Club Denies Redmond Story of Series Proof," *Chicago Herald and Examiner*, October 28, 1920, 9.

18. Harold Seymour and Dorothy Seymour Mills, *Baseball: The Golden Age* (New York: Oxford University Press, 1971), 309.

19. "Rothstein Is Cleared of World Series 'Fixing,'" *New York Herald*, October 27, 1920, 12; David Pietrusza, *Rothstein: The Life, Times, and Murder of the Criminal Genius Who Fixed the 1919 World Series* (New York: Basic Books, 2011), 184.

20. "Six Indicted in Ball Pool Quiz: Police Blamed," *Chicago Tribune*, November 7, 1920, 6.

21. Frank O. Klein, "Collins Charges 1920 Games 'Fixed,'" *Collyer's Eye*, October 30, 1920, 1.

22. Ibid.

23. Ibid.

24. "High Coast Baseball Bribe Plot Revealed," *Los Angeles Evening Express*, October 15, 1920, 1; "Maggert in Support of Borton Charges," *Los Angeles Evening Express*, October 20, 1920, 1.

25. Hugh S. Fullerton, "Baseball on Trial," *New Republic*, October 20, 1920, https://newrepublic.com/article/63733/baseball-trial.

26. Ibid.

27. Ibid.

28. Ibid.

Chapter 15 Here Comes the Judge

1. Harold Seymour and Dorothy Seymour Mills, *Baseball: The Golden Age* (New York: Oxford University Press, 1971), 312.

2. David Pietrusza, *Judge and Jury: The Life and Times of Kenesaw Mountain Landis* (South Bend, IN: Diamond Communications, 1998), 163.

3. "Owners to Discuss Baseball Changes," *New York Times*, October 18, 1920, 22.

4. Malcolm MacLean, "New Baseball Deal May Wreck American League and Bounce Ban Johnson," *Chicago Evening Post*, October 19, 1920, 4; Larry Woltz, "11 Big League Clubs Discuss Lasker's Plan," *Chicago Herald and Examiner*, October 19, 1920, 12.

5. "Says Lasker Plan Is Not Feasible," *New York Times*, October 30, 1920, 17.

6. Bill Veeck with Ed Linn, *The Hustler's Handbook* (New York: G. P. Putnam's Sons, 1965), 282.

7. Harry Neily, "Minors Agree to Five-Man Comish," *Chicago Evening American*, November 6, 1920, 7.

8. "League Baseball Ripped Wide Open," *Boston Globe*, November 9, 1920, 1; Cobb Pans New 12-Club League," *Chicago Herald and Examiner*, November 10, 1920, 10.

9. James C. O'Leary, "Break Staggering Blow to Baseball," *Boston Globe*, November 9, 1920, 7.

10. "Cobb Pans New 12-Club League"; "War in Baseball," *New York Times*, November 10, 1920, 12.

11. "Johnson Declares War to a Finish," *San Francisco Examiner*, November 10, 1920. 15.

12. Seymour and Mills, *Baseball*, 319.

13. "Baseball Peace Declared; Landis Named Dictator," *New York Times*, November 13, 1920, 1.

14. Pietrusza, *Judge and Jury*, 171.

15. Larry Woltz, "General Baseball Public Indorses Judge Landis," *Chicago Herald and Examiner*, November 14, 1920, 15; J. G. Taylor Spink, *Judge Landis and 25 Years of Baseball* (New York: Thomas Y. Crowell Company, 1947), 76.

16. "Landis Discusses Baseball Reform," *New York Times*, November 29, 1920, 21.

17. "Baseball Peace Declared; Landis Named Dictator."

18. "Huston Launches Attack on Johnson," *New York Times*, December 21, 1920, 20.

19. Ibid.

20. "Frazee Launches Attack on Johnson," *New York Times*, December 23, 1920, 17; James C. O'Leary, "Row Wide Open Again in American League," *Boston Globe*, December 23, 1920, 5.

21. Harry Neily, "Fans Back Ban in Stand in B. B. Row," *Chicago Evening American*, December 29, 1920, 4.

22. "Frazee Launches Attack on Johnson."

23. Damon Runyon, "Oh, See the Dove of Peace!" *Chicago Herald and Examiner*, December 23, 1920, 8.

24. "Grand Jury Indicts Trio of Coast Ball Players," *Los Angeles Times*, December 11, 1920, 13.

25. Larry R. Gerlach, "The Bad News Bees: Salt Lake City and the 1919 Pacific Coast League Scandal," in *Base Ball: A Journal of the Early Game, Vol. 6*, ed. William Lamb (Jefferson, NC: McFarland & Co., Spring 2012), 48, 60–61.

26. "Court Dismisses Charges Against Accused Players," *Salt Lake Tribune*, December 25, 1920, 6.

27. "M'Carthy Backs His Own Proposition," *Salt Lake Tribune*, December 25, 1920, 6.

28. Gerlach, "The Bad News Bees," 65–66.

29. "Three Sox Players Give $10,000 Bonds," *Chicago Tribune*, November 6, 1912, 12; "Indicted Ball Player in L.A. Denies Charge," *Los Angeles Evening Express*, November 12, 1920, 1.

30. James L. Kilgallen, "'Buck' Weaver Tending Soda Fountain; Expects to Return to the White Sox," *Brooklyn Daily Eagle*, November 24, 1920, 18.

31. Ibid.

32. "Sam Hall's Xmas Fund," *Chicago Herald and Examiner*, November 30, 1920, 8.

33. "Never Confessed, Jackson Now Says," *Boston Globe*, November 24, 1920, 5.

34. "Chase Won't Come Here From Coast Unless Extradited," *Chicago Tribune*, November 18, 1920, 18.

35. "Cicotte to Aid State; Escapes 'Fixing' Penalty," *Chicago Tribune*, November 17, 1920, 18.

36. William Lamb, email to author, April 24, 2020.

37. James L. Kilgallen, "No Trial Soon in Scandal," syndicated in *Atlanta Constitution*, November 28, 1920, 10.

38. "Row Over Hoyne Copy of Records in Ball Scandal," *Chicago Tribune*, December 8, 1920, 15; Lamb, *Black Sox in the Courtroom* (Jefferson, NC: McFarland & Co., 2013), 83.

39. Lamb, *Black Sox in the Courtroom*, 83–84.

40. Paul H. Shannon, "Collins Shows Crooks Fooled Fellow Players," *Boston Post*, November 27, 1920, 1.

41. Ibid.

42. Ibid.

43. Ibid.

44. Joe Vila, "Gleason Says Indicted Men Must Not Play for Any Team," syndicated in *Philadelphia Inquirer*, December 20, 1920, 14.

Epilogue: Trials, Tribulations, and Thoughts

1. William Lamb, *Black Sox in the Courtroom* (Jefferson, NC: McFarland & Co., 2013), 141.

2. William F. Lamb, "The Black Sox Scandal," in *Scandal on the South Side*, ed. Jacob Pomrenke (Phoenix, AZ: Society for American Baseball Research, 2015), 307.

3. "Crooks Scared Out of Baseball, Says M'Donald," *Chicago Tribune*, August 4, 1921, 21.

4. James T. Farrell, *My Baseball Diary* (Carbondale and Edwardsville: Southern Illinois University Press, 1998), 186.

5. Dwight Chapin, "Gandil Continues to Claim His Innocence," *Los Angeles Times*, August 14, 1969, 11.

6. Tim Hornbaker, *Turning the Black Sox White: The Misunderstood Legacy of Charles A. Comiskey* (New York: Sports Publishing, 2019), v.

7. Larry Moffi, *The Conscience of the Game: Baseball's Commissioners from Landis to Selig* (Lincoln: University of Nebraska Press, 2006), 42.

8. Merl F. Kleinknecht, "The Negro Leagues: A Brief History," in *The Negro Leagues Book: A Monumental Work from the Negro Leagues Committee of the Society for American Baseball Research*, eds. Dick Clark and Larry Lester (Cleveland: Society for American Baseball Research, 1994), 18.

9. "Didn't Play Best, Jackson Told Chicagoan, Charge," *Milwaukee Journal*, February 4, 1924, 1.

10. Ray Robinson, "No Glory in Winning What Others Lost," *New York Times*, October 7, 1984, section 5, 2.

11. William Lamb, email to author, April 24, 2020; Oscar C. Reichow, "Chicago Fans Grieve Most for Weaver and Still Hope for Him," *Sporting News*, October 14, 1920, 2.

12. David Fleitz, *Shoeless: The Life and Times of Joe Jackson* (Jefferson, NC: McFarland & Company, 2001), 280.

13. David Pietrusza, *Judge and Jury: The Life and Times of Judge Kenesaw Mountain Landis* (South Bend, IN: Diamond Communications, 1998), 194.

BIBLIOGRAPHY

Books

Alexander, Charles C. *John McGraw*. New York: Viking, 1988.

———. *Our Game: An American Baseball History*. New York: MFJ Books, 1991.

Allen, Lee. *The American League Story*. New York: Hill & Wang, 1962.

———. *The Cincinnati Reds: An Informal History*. New York: G. P. Putnam's Sons, 1948.

———. *The National League Story: The Official History*. New York: Hill & Wang, 1961.

Asinof, Eliot. *1919: America's Loss of Innocence*. New York: Donald I. Fine, 1990.

———. *Bleeding between the Lines*. New York: Hold, Rinehart and Winston, 1979.

———. *Eight Men Out: The Black Sox and the 1919 World Series*. New York: Holt, Rineholt and Winston, 1963.

Axelson, G. W. *"Commy": The Life Story of Charles A. Comiskey*. Chicago: The Riley & Lee Co., 1919.

Carney, Gene. *Burying the Black Sox: How Baseball's Cover-Up of the 1919 World Series Almost Succeeded*. Dulles, VA: Potomac Books, 2006.

Clark, Dick, and Larry Lester, eds. *The Negro Leagues Book: A Monumental Work from the Negro Leagues Committee of the Society for American Baseball Research*. Cleveland: Society for American Baseball Research, 1994.

Cook, William A. *The 1919 World Series: What Really Happened?* Jefferson, NC: McFarland & Company, 2001.

———. *Bibb Falk: The Man Who Replaced Shoeless Joe*. Jefferson, NC: McFarland & Company, 2015.

Cooper, Brian E. *Ray Schalk: A Baseball Biography*. Jefferson, NC: McFarland & Company, 2009.

———. *Red Faber: A Biography of the Hall of Fame Spitball Pitcher: A Baseball Biography*. Jefferson, NC: McFarland & Company, 2007.

Cottrell, Robert C. *Blackball, the Black Sox and the Babe: Baseball's Crucial 1920 Season.* Jefferson, NC: McFarland & Company, 2002.

Creamer, Robert. *Babe: The Legend Comes to Life.* New York: Simon and Schuster, 1974.

Dellinger, Susan. *Red Legs and Black Sox: Edd Roush and the Untold Story of the 1919 World Series.* Cincinnati: Emmis Books, 2006.

Deveney, Sean. *The Original Curse: Did the Cubs Throw the 1918 World Series to Babe Ruth's Red Sox and Incite the Black Sox Scandal?* New York: McGraw-Hill, 2010.

Dewey, Donald, and Nicholas Acocella. *The Black Prince of Baseball: Hal Chase and the Mythology of the Game.* Lincoln and London: University of Nebraska Press, 2004.

Einstein, Charles, ed. *The Third Fireside Book of Baseball.* New York: Simon and Schuster, 1968

Erickson, Hal. *The Baseball Filmography: 1915–2001.* 2nd ed. Jefferson, NC: McFarland & Company, 2002.

Farrell, James T. *My Baseball Diary.* Carbondale and Edwardsville: Southern Illinois University Press, 1998.

Felber, Bill. *Under Pallor, Under Shadow: The 1920 American League Pennant Race That Rattled and Rebuilt Baseball.* Lincoln and London: University of Nebraska Press, 2011.

Fleitz, David L. *Shoeless: The Life and Times of Joe Jackson.* Jefferson, NC: McFarland & Company, 2001.

Foster, John B., ed. *Spalding's Official Base Ball Guide 1920.* New York: American Sports Publishing Company, 1920.

Fountain, Charles. *The Betrayal: The 1919 World Series and the Birth of Baseball.* New York: Oxford University Press, 2016.

Frommer, Harvey. *Shoeless Joe and Ragtime Baseball.* Dallas, TX: Taylor Publishing, 1992.

Ginsburg, Daniel E. *The Fix Is In: A History of Baseball Gambling and Game Fixing Scandals.* Jefferson, NC: McFarland & Company, 1995.

Gropman, Donald. *Say It Ain't So, Joe!: The True Story of Shoeless Joe Jackson.* New York: Citadel Press, 1992.

Honig, Donald. *Baseball America: The Heroes of the Game and the Times of Their Glory.* New York: Macmillan, 1985.

———. *The Man in the Dugout: Fifteen Big League Managers Speak Their Minds.* Lincoln and London: University of Nebraska Press, 1977.

Hornbaker, Tim. *Fall from Grace: The Truth and Tragedy of "Shoeless Joe" Jackson.* New York: Sports Publishing, 2018.

———. *Turning the Black Sox White: The Misunderstood Legacy of Charles A. Comiskey.* New York: Sports Publishing, 2019.

Huhn, Rick. *Eddie Collins: A Baseball Biography.* Jefferson, NC: McFarland & Company, 2008.

Jones, David, ed. *Deadball Stars of the American League*. Dulles, VA: Potomac Books, Inc., 2006.

Kahanowitz, Ian S. *Baseball Gods in Scandal: Ty Cobb, Tris Speaker and the Dutch Leonard Affair*. South Orange, NJ: Summer Game Books, 2019.

Kohout, Martin Donell. *Hal Chase: The Defiant Life and Turbulent Times of Baseball's Biggest Crook*. Jefferson, NC: McFarland & Company, 2001.

Lamb, William, ed. *Base Ball: A Journal of the Early Game, Vol. 6*. Jefferson, NC: McFarland & Co., Spring 2012.

———. *Black Sox in the Courtroom: The Grand Jury, Criminal Trial and Civil Litigation*. Jefferson, NC: McFarland & Co., 2013.

Leavy, Jane. *The Big Fella: Babe Ruth and the World He Created*. New York: Harper, 2018.

Lieb, Fred. *Baseball As I Have Known It: From Honus Wagner to Johnny Bench, A Remarkable Eye-Catching Account of Sixty-Six Glorious Seasons by Baseball's Preeminent Historian*. New York: Coward, McCann & Geoghegan, 1977.

Luhrs, Victor. *The Great Baseball Mystery: The 1919 World Series*. South Brunswick, NJ: A. S. Barnes & Co., 1966.

Lynch, Michael T., Jr. *Harry Frazee, Ban Johnson and the Feud That Nearly Destroyed the American League*. Jefferson, NC: McFarland & Company, 2008.

———. *It Ain't So: A Might-Have-Been History of the White Sox in 1919 and Beyond*. Jefferson, NC: McFarland & Company, 2009.

McWhirter, Cameron. *Red Summer: The Summer of 1919 and the Awakening of Black America*. New York: Henry Holt and Company, 2011.

Moffi, Larry. *The Conscience of the Game: Baseball's Commissioners from Landis to Selig*. Lincoln: University of Nebraska Press, 2006.

Muchlinski, Alan. *After the Black Sox: The Swede Risberg Story*. Bloomington, IN: AuthorHouse, 2005.

Murdock, Eugene. *Ban Johnson: Czar of Baseball*. Westport, CT and London: Greenwood Press, 1982.

———. *Baseball between the Wars: Memories of the Game by the Men Who Played It*. Westport, CT and London: Meckler Publishing, 1992.

———. *Baseball Players and Their Games: Oral Histories of the Game 1920–1940*. Westport, CT and London: Meckler Publishing, 1991.

Nathan, Daniel A. *Saying It's So: A Cultural History of the Black Sox*. Urbana and Chicago: University of Illinois Press, 2003.

Pemrenke, Jacob, ed. *Scandal on the South Side: The 1919 Chicago White Sox*. (Phoenix, AZ: Society for American Baseball Research, 2015.

Pietrusza, David. *Judge and Jury: The Life and Times of Judge Kenesaw Mountain Landis*. South Bend, IN: Diamond Communications, 1998.

———. *Rothstein: The Life, Times and Murder of the Criminal Genius Who Fixed the 1919 World Series*. New York: Basic Books, 2011.

Povich, Shirley. *All Those Mornings . . . At the Post: The 20th Century in Sports from Famed Washington Post Columnist Shirley Povich*. New York: PublicAffairs, 2005.

Rathkamp, Thomas. *Happy Felsch: Banished Black Sox Center Fielder*. Jefferson, NC: McFarland & Company, Inc., 2016.

Richter, Francis C., ed. *Reach American League Base Ball Guide*. Philadelphia: A. J. Reach Company, 1921 and 1922 editions.

Ritter, Lawrence S. *The Glory of Their Times: The Story of the Early Days of Baseball Told By the Men Who Played It*. New York: Quill, 1984.

———. *The Glory of Their Times: The Story of the Early Days of Baseball Told by the Men Who Played It* (audio version). Prince Frederick, MD: Highbridge Audio, 1998.

Seymour, Harold, and Dorothy Seymour Mills. *Baseball: The Golden Age*. New York: Oxford University Press, 1971.

Smith, Leverett T. *The American Dream and the National Game*. Bowling Green, OH: Bowling Green University Popular Press, 1975.

Sowell, Mike. *The Pitch That Killed: Carl Mays, Ray Chapman and the Pennant Race of 1920*. New York: Macmillan, 1989.

Spink, J. G. Taylor. *Judge Landis and 25 Years of Baseball*. New York: Thomas Y. Crowell Company, 1947.

Stein, Irving M. *The Ginger Kid: The Buck Weaver Story*. Metairie, LA: Elysian Fields Press, 1992.

Surdam, David George, and Michael J. Haupert. *The Age of Ruth and Landis: The Economics of Baseball during the Roaring Twenties*. Lincoln and London: University of Nebraska Press, 2018.

Veeck, Bill, with Ed Linn. *The Hustler's Handbook*. New York: G. P. Putnam's Sons, 1965.

Webster, Gary. *Tris Speaker and the 1920 Indians: Tragedy to Glory*. Jefferson, NC: McFarland & Company, 2012.

Williams, Peter, ed. *The Joe Williams Baseball Reader: The Glorious Game, from Ty Cobb and Babe Ruth to the Amazin' Mets*. Chapel Hill, NC: Algonquin Books, 1989.

Wood, Gerald. *Smoky Joe Wood: The Biography of a Baseball Legend*. Lincoln and London: University of Nebraska Press, 2013.

Yardley, Jonathan. *Ring: A Biography of Ring Lardner*. New York: Atheneum, 1984.

Newspapers and Magazines

The following newspapers and magazines were referenced extensively for the 1917–1921 period.

Atlanta Constitution
Baltimore Sun
Baseball Digest
Baseball Magazine
Boston Globe
Boston Herald

Boston Post
Chicago Daily News
Chicago Evening American
Chicago Evening Post
Chicago Herald and Examiner
Chicago Tribune
Cincinnati Enquirer
Cincinnati Post
Cleveland Plain Dealer
Collyer's Eye
Denver Post
Detroit Free Press
Detroit Times
Los Angeles Evening Express
Los Angeles Times
New York Daily News
New York Evening World
New York Herald
New York Times
New York Tribune
Philadelphia Inquirer
Pittsburgh Daily Post
Pittsburgh Press
Sacramento Bee
St. Louis Post-Dispatch
St. Louis Star-Times
Salt Lake Telegram
Salt Lake Tribune
San Francisco Chronicle
San Francisco Examiner
Sporting News
Sports Illustrated
Washington Evening Star
Washington Post
Washington Times

Websites

Baseball Reference: baseball-reference.com
Retrosheet: Retrosheet.org
Seamheads.com
Society for American Baseball Research: SABR.org

INDEX

ABOUT THE AUTHOR

A member of the Society for American Baseball Research since 1979, **Don Zminda** retired in 2016 after two-plus decades with STATS LLC, where he served first as director of publications and then director of research for STATS-supported sports broadcasts that included the World Series, the Super Bowl, and the NCAA Final Four. Don has also written or edited over a dozen sports books, including *The Legendary Harry Caray: Baseball's Greatest Salesman* (a finalist for the 2019 Casey Award), and the SABR publication *Go-Go to Glory: The 1959 Chicago White Sox*. A Chicago native, he lives in Los Angeles with his wife, Sharon.